Exchange Rates and Open Economy Macroeconomics

Edited by Ronald MacDonald and Mark P. Taylor

Basil Blackwell

Copyright © Basil Blackwell 1989

First published 1989

Basil Blackwell Ltd
108 Cowley Road, Oxford, OX4 1JF, UK

Basil Blackwell Inc.
3 Cambridge Center
Cambridge, MA 02142, USA

British Library Cataloguing in Publication Data
Exchange rates and open economy macroeconomics
   1. Open economies. Foreign exchange. Rates.
   Macroeconomic aspects
   I. MacDonald, Ronald   II. Taylor, Mark P.
   1958–
   332.4′56′
   ISBN 0–631–16238–0

Library of Congress Cataloging in Publication Data
Exchange rates and open economy macroeconomics.
   1. Foreign exchange problem.   2. Macro-
economics.   I. MacDonald, Ronald.   II. Taylor,
Mark P., 1958–
HG3821.E874   1989   332.4′56   88–7730
ISBN 0–631–16238–0

Typeset in 10 on 12pt
by Colset Private Limited, Singapore
Printed in Great Britain by Camelot Press, Southampton.

Exchange Rates and Open Economy Macroeconomics

Contents

List of Figures

List of Tables

List of Contributors

Michael J. Artis	University of Manchester and Centre for Economic Policy Research, London
David G. Barr	Bank of England
Robin Bladen Hovell	University of Manchester
Laurence S. Copeland	University of Manchester Institute of Science and Technology
David Currie	London Business School and Centre for Economic Policy Research, London
Christopher Green	Cardiff Business School
Stephen Hall	Bank of England
Andrew J. Hughes Hallett	University of Newcastle upon Tyne and Centre for Economic Policy Research, London
Edmond Levy	Midland Montagu, London
Ronald MacDonald	University of Aberdeen
Patrick Minford	University of Liverpool and Centre for Economic Policy Research, London
Vito Antonio Muscatelli	University of Glasgow
A. Robert Nobay	University of Liverpool and University of California, Los Angeles
Emmanuel Pikoulakis	University of Hull
Andrew Stevenson	University of Glasgow
Mark P. Taylor	City University Business School, London, Bank of England and Centre for Economic Policy Research, London
Thomas S. Torrance	University of Aberdeen
Merih Uctum	University of Laval, Quebec
David Vines	University of Glasgow and Centre for Economic Policy Research, London
Michael R. Wickens	University of Florida and University of Southampton

Abbreviations

AD   aggregate demand
ADF   augmented Dickey–Fuller test
AIC   Akaike information criterion
AMEX   American Express Bank
AR   autoregression model
ARMA   autoregressive moving average representations
AS   aggregate supply
DCE   domestic credit expansion
DR   Dickey–Fuller test
DW   Durbin–Watson statistic
ECM   error correction model
EEC   European Economic Community
EMH   efficient market hypothesis
EMS   European Monetary System
ERM   exchange rate mechanism
ETAS   Economic Trends Annual Supplement
FFP   external balance schedules
FIML   full information maximum likelihood
FLPM   flex-price monetary model
FT   *Financial Times*
GNP   gross national product
IFS   International Financial Statistics
iid   independently and identically distributed errors
IMF   International Monetary Fund
LDCs   less developed countries

MA   moving average
MAE   mean absolute error
ME   mean error
MEI   main economic indicators
MMS   Money Market Services
MR   Meese and Rogoff
NRCCs   non-reserve currency countries
OECD   Organization for Economic Co-operation and Development
OLS   ordinary least squares
PBM   portfolio balance model
PPP   purchasing power parity
RCC   reserve currency country
REPBM   rational expectations PBM
RID   real interest differential
RMSE   root mean square error
ROECD   rest of OECD
ROW   rest of world
RXR   real exchange rate
3SLS   three stage least squares
SPM   sticky-price monetary model
UIP   uncovered interest parity
UK   United Kingdom
USA   United States of America
VAR   vector autoregression
VARMA   VAR moving average
XXP   aggregate demand schedule
ZSURE   Zellner's seemingly unrelated regression estimator

Editors' Introduction

Ronald MacDonald and Mark P. Taylor

The major Organization for Economic Co-operation and Development (OECD) countries have now experienced over 15 years with floating exchange rates. Very few people can claim to have foreseen the amount of turbulence in foreign exchange markets that this period was to bring. Although the very early, flexible-price monetary models of the exchange rate, which assume continuous purchasing power parity, were quickly replaced by a sticky-price version which allows temporary movements in the real exchange rate, or 'overshooting', the degree of volatility in real exchange rates over the period still provides a major puzzle. Moreover, other puzzles such as the failure of exchange rate models to outperform simple random walks in forecast tests, the very weak mean-reverting tendencies of deviations from purchasing power parity, and the empirical failure of the efficient markets hypothesis for many foreign exchange markets are all phenomena that have yet to be satisfactorily explained. Major international developments during the floating rate period, such as two oil shocks and the rise in the level of international capital mobility, have coincided with major developments in economic theory – such as the rational expectations revolution – and in econometric methodology, so that exchange rate and open-economy economics has become a remarkably dynamic area of the discipline. Institutional developments such as the recent moves towards greater international policy co-ordination amongst the major OECD countries, the use of exchange rate targeting and the success of the European Monetary System have provided further scope for researchers.

Given this state of affairs, we judged the fifteenth anniversary of floating rates to be an appropriate occasion for taking stock of the literature and for presenting some state of the art research on exchange rates and open-economy macroeconomics.

The book is split into four parts: the first three are concerned with exchange rate economics and the fourth is on open-economy macroeconomics more generally.

Part I contains a single chapter by the editors which seeks to provide a comprehensive survey of the main strands in the exchange rate economics literature, namely the reduced form exchange rate determination literature – both theoretical and empirical – and the evidence on the efficiency of the market for forward foreign exchange. We also look at issues such as the impact of news on foreign exchange markets and exchange market bubbles.

Exchange rate determination is the focus of part II. The Buiter–Miller (1982) macro-model is used by David Barr in chapter 2 to derive a real exchange rate 'semi-reduced form' equation. The model is estimated using UK data for the period 1973–82 and results supportive of the model are reported. The relative success of Barr's reduced form model is interesting since, as is shown in chapter 1, most exchange rate reduced forms estimated for the recent floating experience have been singularly unsuccessful. David Currie and Stephen Hall, in chapter 3, derive and estimate (using monthly UK data) a model of the UK effective exchange rate based on a stock-flow view of capital movements. Interestingly, their estimated model indicates that there is a moderate long-run trade-off between larger external deficits and higher domestic interest rates. Chapter 4 is a theoretical contribution by Merih Uctum and Michael Wickens which seeks to extend the portfolio balance approach to the determination of the exchange rate by modelling bank loans and deposits, physical capital and equity, in addition to money and bonds. Such an extension is useful in shedding light on the joint behaviour of exchange rates and stock market prices, such as those occurring at the time of the international stock market crash in October 1987. A similar portfolio balance model is used by Anton Muscatelli, Andrew Stevenson and David Vines in chapter 5 to show that the form that the interest parity equation takes in a small open-economy macro-model is crucially dependent on the nature of risk faced by economic agents and that this has important implications for exchange dynamics and the econometric modelling of exchange rates. The final chapter of the exchange rate modelling section, by Emmanuel Pikoulakis, provides a practitioner's guide to the analysis of rational expectations models containing two or more predetermined variables and one forward-looking variable – the exchange rate. Pikoulakis demonstrates how the qualitative nature of complex simulation exercises can be encapsulated in simple diagrammatic analysis.

In Part III the efficiency of foreign exchange markets is considered. This part commences with a useful stocktaking paper by Ed Levy and Bob Nobay (chapter 7) on tests of the speculative efficiency hypothesis (the joint hypothesis that agents are rational and risk neutral). More specifically, the chapter focuses on the relative power of regression-based tests of efficiency and those which rely on variance bounds analysis, the use of time-series methodology to test the restrictions implied by the efficiency hypothesis, and the appropriate stationarity-inducing transformations to use in efficiency tests. The chapter also contains an interesting implementation of the news approach to modelling the exchange rate. Chapter 8, by Laurence Copeland, investigates the impact of new information on the British pound and German mark bilateral exchange rates against the US dollar, over the period January 1977 to January 1984. The main novelty of this chapter lies in the use of a vector autoregressive methodology to estimate the 'news' and forecasting equations jointly; this procedure overcomes certain problems associated with the traditional two-step methodology. In chapter 9, Ronnie MacDonald and Tom Torrance utilize survey data on exchange rate expectations to test the uncovered interest parity relation. Previous tests of this parity condition have been tests of a joint hypothesis; the use of survey data, however, allows single hypothesis tests to be conducted. Interestingly, evidence suggesting that the uncovered interest parity condition fails because of both risk aversion and irrationality is reported.

The final part of the book contains more policy-related contributions in the area of open-economy macroeconomics. The first two chapters utilize the classic Mundell–Fleming (MF) model. Robin Bladen Hovell and Chris Green's paper (chapter 10) is a useful expositional piece which has the central aim of providing a unified treatment of the MF model and its subsequent extensions. In addition, the chapter has some distinctive features of its own, such as a useful geometric technique which allows analysis of simultaneous variations in output and prices under different monetary regimes. In chapter 11 Patrick Minford considers one of the key predictions of the MF model, namely that a flexible exchange rate would insulate a country from foreign shocks. This prediction is considered using two models which are regarded as descendents of the MF model – the New Classical Liverpool macroeconomic model and the New Keynesian Taylor macroeconomic model. It is demonstrated that the existence of rational expectations in these models vitiates the MF insulation prediction. Chapter 12, by Michael Artis and Mark Taylor, looks at some issues concerning the long-run credibility of the European Monetary System. Although the European Monetary System has attained certain short-run objectives, such as the reduction of exchange rate and interest rate volatility, Artis and Taylor argue that there has still been a tendency for currencies to become misaligned within the system and that it has not been successful in bringing about perfect substitutability of member countries' financial assets. This may be worrying since it is easy to imagine that the stock of credibility which the European Monetary System has earned will be dissipated as sophisticated and forward-looking capital markets begin to focus on the longer-run stability properties of the system. A contribution to the recent policy co-ordination literature is presented in the final chapter, by Andrew Hughes Hallett. He compares co-operative and non-co-operative policies for the USA and the rest of the OECD, in the context of seven major macroeconomic models, when there is uncertainty about the 'true' model. The chapter presents a number of new results, some which answer questions raised in the literature and others which relate to the possibility of using fixed policy rules or simple exchange rate targets as a way of reducing the risks which policy-makers face.

This volume demonstrates very clearly the broad range and high quality of research which leading international macroeconomists are producing in response to the challenges in this area. If the book is able to communicate something of their enthusiasm and understanding of the subject to the reader, then it will have been a success.

Part I
Assessing the Literature

1 Economic Analysis of Foreign Exchange Markets: An Expository Survey

Ronald MacDonald and Mark P. Taylor

1.1 INTRODUCTION

The period since the advent of generalized floating exchange rates in 1973 has generated a wealth of data on exchange rates and on the factors which supposedly determine them, giving econometricians and applied economists an unprecedented opportunity to test a number of propositions relating to foreign exchange markets. Indeed, a huge theoretical and empirical literature on exchange rate economics has emerged over the last 15 years and it seems an appropriate juncture at which to conduct a stocktaking exercise of the salient findings in this literature. That is the purpose of this chapter. More particularly, we are concerned to survey three strands of the literature on exchange rate economics. The first strand is concerned with theories of exchange rate determination as they have evolved during the period. This theoretical literature is not, of course, independent of the applied literature as economists have continually sought to explain and improve upon the poor performance of theoretical exchange rate models confronted with real-world data. The second strand is concerned with this empirical aspect of relating exchange rates to data on their determinants or fundamentals. The third develops a body of theory from the finance literature to determine whether foreign exchange market participants are efficient processors of information. However, the third strand in the literature is also not unrelated to the other two, since researchers testing for the effect of fundamentals on exchange rates often invoke certain efficiency conditions and those testing for efficiency often use the fundamentals suggested by theory in their tests.

The first two strands referred to above, each concerned with relating exchange rates to fundamentals, are considered in some detail in sections 1.2 and 1.3. In particular, in section 1.2 we examine the two main views of exchange rate determination that have evolved since the early 1970s: the monetary approach to the exchange rate (in both its flex-price and sticky-price guises) and the portfolio balance approach to the exchange rate. In section 1.3 we present some reduced form econometric estimates of the models outlined in section 1.2. The application of the efficient markets hypothesis (EMH) to the forward market for foreign exchange is examined in some detail in section 1.4. As we shall see, the main finding to emerge from such tests is that the EMH is often rejected by the data (where the hypothesis being rejected is normally taken to be the joint hypothesis that agents are risk neutral *and* rational). A large amount of literature has emerged, considered in sections 1.4.6 and 1.4.7, which seeks to rationalize such rejections. In section 1.5 a literature which attempts to model the impact of new information on exchange rates is discussed (this literature may be seen as a synthesis of developments in the fundamentals literature and the efficiency literature). In the concluding section we summarize the salient findings of the empirical literature and indicate how the future research strategy is likely to develop.

1.2 THEORIES OF EXCHANGE RATE DETERMINATION

As the study of the allocation of scarce resources to human wants, all branches of economics are fundamentally concerned with supply and demand. It has been argued that the theory of exchange rate determination is no exception: the exchange rate is simply the price of foreign currency which clears the foreign exchange market. Theories of exchange rate determination therefore differ only in their different specifications of the supply and demand for foreign exchange. The insight of the classic Mundell–Fleming model of exchange rate determination (Mundell, 1968; Fleming, 1962) was that net excess demand for foreign exchange is just the overall balance of payments (current plus capital account). Under a free float, this must be equal to zero in equilibrium. Combining this equilibrium condition with standard equilibrium conditions for the goods market (the IS curve) and the money market (the LM curve) it is then possible to solve for the exchange rate (and the other endogenous variables, normally real output and the interest rate) and to determine the comparative static effects of fiscal and monetary policy. The integration of asset markets and capital mobility into open-economy macroeconomics was a major innovation of the Mundell–Fleming model, but it contains a fundamental flaw: it is cast almost entirely in flow terms. In particular, current account imbalances can be offset by flows across the capital account; eventually, however, a stock equilibrium in the holding of net foreign assets must obtain and the current and capital accounts must balance independently. In papers dating from the 1950s (see for example Johnson, 1958), Harry Johnson had stressed the distinction between stock and flow equilibria in the open-economy context, and this was to become a hallmark of the monetary approach to balance of payments analysis (see for example Frenkel and Johnson, 1976) and, subsequently, the monetary approach to the exchange rate (see for example Frenkel and Johnson, 1978). Indeed, since an exchange rate, by definition, is the price of one country's money in terms of that of another, it is perhaps natural to analyse the determinants of that price in terms of the outstanding stocks of and demand for the two monies.

The monetary approach to the exchange rate is given further treatment below. However, we might indicate one or two shortcomings in the monetary approach at this point. The monetary approach to the balance of payments grew out of work at the International Monetary Fund (IMF) and the University of Chicago primarily in the late 1950s and 1960s (see for example Polak, 1957) and was probably the dominant view of balance of payments determination at the inception of floating exchange rates in the early 1970s. Since, under a free float, the overall balance of payments (net excess demand for foreign exchange) must sum to zero, the natural tendency was to take the monetary model and solve for the exchange rate, holding the balance of payments fixed (at zero); this is essentially what the monetary approach to the exchange rate involves. However, in moving from a theory of balance of payments determination to one of exchange rate determination, a fundamental issue was overlooked: the flexibility of prices. The more extreme versions of the monetary approach to the balance of payments assume continuous purchasing power parity (PPP). Over a typical period of six months to a year or more, during which a country might attempt to deal with a balance of payments disequilibrium, prices may be assumed to be reasonably flexible. The same cannot be said, however, for the much shorter periods of time during which changes in the exchange rate may cause concern. It is clear that monetarist advocates of floating rates (see for example Friedman, 1953) assumed that PPP would hold more or less continuously under a free float, and a PPP condition is often used much as an identity in the derivation of empirical monetary approach exchange rate equations (see below). If we have learnt anything at all from the recent experience with floating, however, it is that there can be manifest short-term deviations from PPP, if only because the wide gyrations in exchange rates have not been matched by movements in relative prices. This observation gave rise to a second generation of monetary exchange rate models associated primarily with Dornbusch (1976) and (in the UK) Buiter and Miller (1981).

These 'sticky-price' monetary (SPM) models allow for substantial overshooting of the nominal and real (price-adjusted) exchange rate above their long-run equilibrium (PPP) levels. The mechanism by which this is achieved is relatively straightforward, as the following simple example demonstrates. Say the economy is initially in equilibrium and the exchange rate is at its PPP level. The government then engineers a reduction in the money supply. In the long run, the domestic price level will fall equiproportionately. Assuming long-run PPP, the equilibrium level of the exchange rate will therefore be higher. The interesting overshooting result arises, however, because prices are less than perfectly flexible in the short run. Given that the nominal money supply has been reduced and prices adjust sluggishly, the *real* money supply must have fallen. Domestic interest rates therefore rise to clear the money market. This attracts an inflow of foreign capital and the exchange rate accordingly appreciates. Foreign investors will continue investing in domestic securities (and therefore stemming further rises in interest rates while contributing to further upward pressure on the nominal exchange rate) as long as the known capital gain (i.e. domestic–foreign interest differential) is less than the expected foreign exchange loss (the expected rate of exchange rate depreciation over the relevant period) and will stop investing when these are equal, i.e. when uncovered interest parity (UIP) holds. Since the expected rate of depreciation must therefore be non-zero, the exchange rate must overshoot its long-run level. As prices adjust in the medium to long run, real liquidity rises, interest rates fall and the exchange rate declines steadily to its equilibrium level. The model can also be used to explain overshooting in response to other shocks such as a natural resource discovery.

The SPM model is clearly an advance over the simple (continous PPP) monetary model in that it more closely explains the observed facts. It is fundamentally monetary, however, in that attention is focused on equilibrium conditions in the money market. Monetary models of the open economy are able to do this by assuming perfect substitutability of domestic and foreign non-money assets. These can then be aggregated into a single extra market ('bonds') and excluded from explicit analysis by application of Walras's law. This perfect substitutability assumption is relaxed in the portfolio balance model (PBM) of exchange rate determination. In addition, the PBM is stock-flow consistent in that it allows for current account imbalances to have a feedback effect on wealth and hence on long-run equilibrium.

In its simplest form, the PBM divides net financial wealth W, into three components – holdings B of domestic bonds, holdings SF of foreign bonds in domestic currency (where S is the domestic price of foreign currency) and money M, each of which is a function of domestic and foreign interest rates (r and r^* respectively):

$$B = B(\overset{+}{r}, \overset{-}{r^*})W$$

$$SF = F(\overset{-}{r}, \overset{+}{r^*})W$$

$$M = M(\overset{-}{r}, \overset{-}{r^*})W$$

$$W \equiv M + B + SF$$

(note that entering wealth as a homogeneous scale variable means that analysis can be conducted entirely in nominal terms).

This provides a simple framework for analysing the effect of, for example, monetary and fiscal policy on the exchange rate. Thus, a contractionary monetary policy reduces nominal financial wealth and thereby reduces the demand for both domestic and foreign bonds. As foreign bonds are sold, the exchange rate appreciates. The effects of fiscal policy (operating through changes in B) on the exchange rate are more ambiguous, depending on the degree of substitution between domestic and foreign bonds (see below for further details). In addition, the model has sophisticated dynamics incorporating interaction between the current account and asset holding and is capable of explaining exchange rate overshooting with or without price level stickiness.

The PBM is sometimes used to illustrate the recent behaviour of the dollar, at least before the end of 1985. President Reagan's loose fiscal policy, combined with the reluctance of the then Chairman of the Federal Reserve, Paul Volcker, to monetize the debt, pushed the dollar up and led to a transfer of wealth via a persistent current account deficit.

We now consider each of the aforementioned exchange rate models in a little more detail.

1.2.1 The flex-price monetary model

The flex-price monetary (FLPM) model takes as its starting point the proposition that the exchange rate is, in fact, the relative price of two monies. It therefore seeks to analyse movements in the exchange rate in terms of the relative supply of and demand for the currencies concerned.

The FLPM model relies on the PPP condition and stable demand-for-money functions. The (logarithm of the) demand for money may be assumed to depend on (the logarithm of) real income y, the (logarithm of the) price level p and the level of the interest rate r. We assume a similar foreign demand-for-money function (foreign variables are denoted by an asterisk). Monetary equilibria in the domestic and foreign country respectively are given by

$$m^s = p + \phi y - \lambda r \qquad (1.1)$$

$$m^{s*} = p^* + \phi^* y^* - \lambda^* r^* \qquad (1.2)$$

In the FLPM model, the domestic interest rate, at least in the long run, is exogenous because of the implicit assumptions of perfect capital mobility – domestic interest rates are determined on world markets.

Equilibrium in the traded goods market (i.e. the current account) ensues when there are no further profitable incentives for trade flows to occur, i.e.

when prices in a common currency are equalized and PPP holds. Again using lower-case letters to denote logarithms, the PPP condition is

$$s = p - p^* \tag{1.3}$$

The foreign price, p^*, is exogenous to the domestic economy, being determined by the foreign money supply. The domestic money supply determines the domestic price level and hence the exchange rate is determined by relative money supplies. Algebraically, substituting (1.1) and (1.2) into (1.3) gives

$$s = (m^s - m^{s*}) - \phi y + \phi^* y^* + \lambda r - \lambda^* r^* \tag{1.4}$$

From (1.4), we can see that an increase in the domestic money supply, relative to the foreign money stock, will lead to an exchange rate depreciation. This seems intuitive enough. On the other hand, an increase in domestic output *appreciates* the exchange rate – exactly the converse of what the Mundell–Fleming approach would predict (in the latter approach, higher real income worsens the trade balance, as imports rise, and requires a *depreciation* to return to equilibrium). Similarly, a rise in domestic interest rates *depreciates* the exchange rate (in the Mundell–Fleming model, this would lead to capital inflows and hence an *appreciation*). In order to resolve these apparent paradoxes, one has to remember the fundamental role of relative money demand in the FLPM model. A relative rise in domestic real income creates an excess demand for the domestic money stock. As agents try to increase their (real) money balances, they reduce expenditure and prices fall until money market equilibrium is achieved. As prices fall, PPP ensures an exchange rate appreciation. An exactly converse analysis explains the response of the exchange rate to the interest rate – an increase in interest rates *reduces* the demand for money and so leads to an exchange rate depreciation.

In the latter half of the 1970s, the FLPM model ceased to be an accurate description of the behaviour of exchange rates for a number of small open economies (this will be discussed in more detail in section 1.3). For example, in the UK over the period 1979–81 the sterling nominal effective exchange rate (i.e. the rate against a basket of currencies) appreciated substantially even though the UK money supply grew rapidly relative to growth in the 'world' money supply. However, more startling, the real exchange rate (i.e. the price competitiveness or the terms of trade) appreciated by about 40 per cent over this period and this was followed by an equally sharp fall over the 1981–4 period. Large and volatile swings in the real exchange rate may lead to large swings in net trade with consequent multiplier effects on domestic output and employment. In the FLPM model, output is determined exogenously and unless the model is extended it is incapable of explaining changes in real output. SPM models provide an explanation of exchange rate overshooting together with short-run changes in real output, as for example occurred in the very severe recession of 1979–82 in the UK. The seminal paper in this context is by Dornbusch (1976).

1.2.2 The sticky-price monetary model

The intuition underlying the overshooting result in the SPM model is relatively straightforward. Imagine the effects of a cut in the nominal UK money supply. Since prices are sticky in the short run, this implies an initial fall in the real money supply and a consequent rise in interest rates in order to clear the money market (this may also impact on real output – see below). The rise in domestic interest rates then leads to a capital inflow and an appreciation of the nominal (and, given sticky prices, the real) exchange rate. Foreign investors are aware that they are artificially forcing up the exchange rate and that they may therefore suffer a foreign exchange loss when the proceeds of their investment are reconverted into their local currency. However, as long as the expected foreign exchange loss (expected rate of depreciation) is less than the known capital market gain (i.e. the interest differential), risk-neutral investors continue to buy sterling assets. A short-run equilibrium is achieved when the expected rate of depreciation is just equal to the interest differential (UIP holds). Since the expected rate of depreciation must then be non-zero for a non-zero interest differential, the exchange rate must have overshot its long-run equilibrium (PPP) level. In the medium run, however, domestic prices begin to fall in response to the fall in money supply. This alleviates pressure in the money market and domestic interest rates begin to decline. The exchange rate then depreciates slowly in order to converge on the long-run PPP level. This model therefore explains the paradox that countries with relatively high interest rates tend to have currencies whose exchange rate is expected to depreciate. The *initial* rise in interest rates leads to a step appreciation of the exchange rate after which a slow depreciation is expected in order to satisfy UIP. We now consider the Dornbusch (1976) model in more detail.

Since the model is set up in (log-) linear form, we can apply the 'certainty equivalence principle', i.e. that solving the model assuming perfect foresight yields the same solution as assuming rational expectations (see for example Begg, 1982, p. 52). Thus, in continuous time, the *actual* rate of depreciation $\dot{s}$ must be equal to the interest differential, according to UIP. The full set of equations for our simplified Dornbusch model is

$$\dot{s} = r - r^* \tag{1.5}$$

$$m - p = \phi\bar{y} - \lambda r \tag{1.6}$$

$$\dot{p} = \pi[\alpha + \delta(s-p) - \sigma r - \bar{y}] \tag{1.7}$$

For simplicity, we assume that output is fixed at $\bar{y}$. Equation (1.5) is the UIP condition. Equation (1.6) is the condition for money market equilibrium (the LM curve). Equation (1.7) is a Phillips curve, which relates the rate of change of prices to the excess of demand over output supply. Demand is assumed to be a function of an autonomous component α, the real exchange rate (holding foreign prices constant and normalized so that $p^* = 0$) $s - p$, and interest rates.

In long-run equilibrium, the rate of depreciation will be zero (and hence $r = r^*$ by (1.5), and the price level settles down to its long-run value $\bar{p}$. Hence, the long-run money market equilibrium condition is

$$m - \bar{p} = \phi\bar{y} - \lambda r^* \tag{1.8}$$

Subtracting (1.6) from (1.8) yields

$$p - \bar{p} = \lambda(r - r^*) \tag{1.9}$$

or, using (1.5) and (1.9),

$$\dot{s} = (1/\lambda)(p - \bar{p}) \tag{1.10}$$

On the goods market side, solving (1.6) for the domestic rate of interest and substituting into (1.7) yields

$$\dot{p} = \pi[\alpha + \delta(s - p) + (\sigma/\lambda)(m - p) - (1 + \sigma\phi/\lambda)\bar{y}] \tag{1.11}$$

or, in long-run non-inflationary equilibrium,

$$0 = \pi[\alpha + \delta(\bar{s} - \bar{p}) + (\sigma/\lambda)(m - p) - (1 + \sigma\phi/\lambda)\bar{y}] \tag{1.12}$$

Subtracting (1.12) from (1.11)

$$\dot{p} = \pi\delta(s - \bar{s}) - \pi(\delta + \sigma/\lambda)(p - \bar{p}) \tag{1.13}$$

Equations (1.10) and (1.13) can be expressed in matrix form as

$$\begin{bmatrix} \dot{s} \\ \dot{p} \end{bmatrix} = \begin{bmatrix} 0 & 1/\lambda \\ \pi\delta & -\pi(\delta + \sigma/\lambda) \end{bmatrix} \begin{bmatrix} s - \bar{s} \\ p - \bar{p} \end{bmatrix} \tag{1.14}$$

For the system to have a unique convergent saddlepath, the necessary and sufficient condition is that the coefficient matrix in (1.14) has a negative determinant (so that the characteristic equation has one positive and one negative root) (see for example Blanchard and Khan, 1980), and this is easily seen to be the case:

$$-\pi\delta/\lambda < 0$$

The qualitative solution to (1.14) is given in figure 1.1, where the $\dot{s} = 0$ and $\dot{p} = 0$ loci are obtained from (1.10) and (1.13). Given the arrows of motion, the qualitative shape of the saddlepath is easily inferred (see for example Begg, 1982; Cuthbertson and Taylor, 1987; MacDonald, 1988).

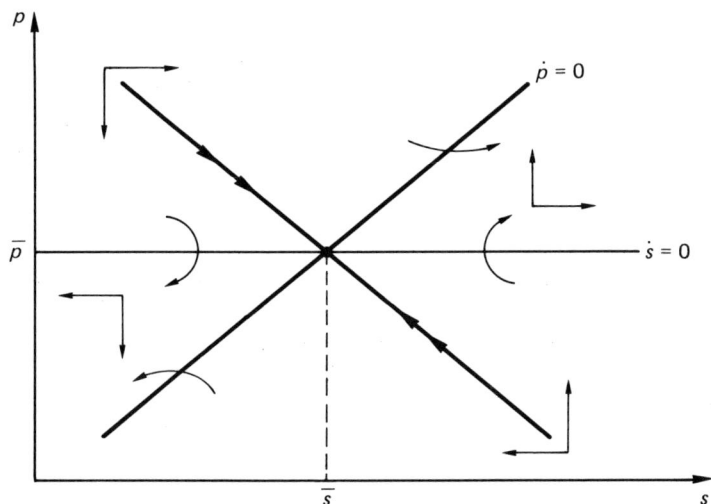

Figure 1.1   The saddlepath equilibrium for the sticky-price monetary model

Now, assuming that agents will be unwilling to participate in an unstable economy (see for example Shiller, 1978; Begg, 1982, ch. 3) the economy will always be located on the saddlepath and, given the stickiness of prices, this means that the exchange rate has to jump in response to shocks which cause a shift in the saddlepath and then to converge slowly to the equilibrium along the new saddlepath.

If $-\theta$ is the stable (negative) root of the system, then we know that the equation of motion for s must satisfy

$$\dot{s} = -\theta(s - \bar{s}) \tag{1.15}$$

Substituting (1.15) into (1.10) gives

$$s = \bar{s} - (1/\lambda\theta)(p - \bar{p})$$

and this is, in fact, the equation describing the saddlepath.

Take the example of an increase in the money supply m. From (1.8) this implies a rise in the long-run price level $\bar{p}$ (given exogenous $\bar{y}$ and r^*) and hence, from (1.12), a rise in $\bar{s}$ (long-run depreciation). Thus, the saddlepath shifts up and to the right (figure 1.2) given the initial stickiness of prices, and the exchange rate initially jumps from A to B and then slowly converges to the new equilibrium C. The distance $s_{os} - \bar{s}_2$ then measures the amount of exchange rate overshooting.

The model can also be extended to allow for short-run effects on output. Buiter and Miller (1981) extend the model to allow for a non-zero rate of core

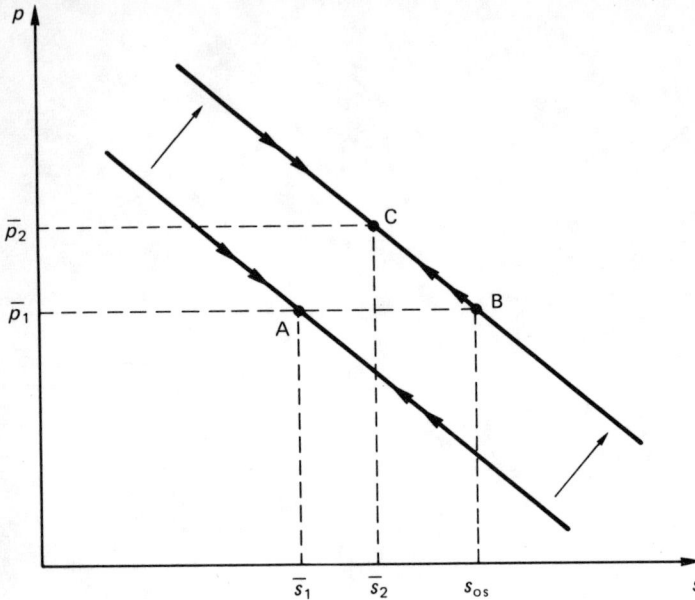

Figure 1.2   Exchange rate overshooting in the sticky-price monetary model

inflation (i.e. $\dot{p} \neq 0$ even when net excess aggregate demand is zero) and analyse the impact of a natural resource discovery (e.g. oil or gas) on the exchange rate. Since the higher income resulting from the resource discovery leads to a higher demand for non-oil output, with long-run output fixed, the long-run exchange rate must appreciate in order to worsen the terms of trade and reduce long-run demand (the so-called 'Dutch disease' – Forsyth and Kay, 1980).

1.2.3 The portfolio balance model

The FLPM and SPM models which have been the subject matter of the preceding sections make at least two important simplifying assumptions: domestic and foreign assets are perfect substitutes (so that no distinction need be made between them)[1] and the wealth effects of a current account surplus or deficit are negligible. The PBM of exchange rates explores the consequences of explicitly relaxing these assumptions (see for example Branson, 1977; Dornbusch and Fischer, 1980; Isard, 1980).

In common with the FLPM and SPM models, the level of the exchange rate in the PBM is determined, at least in the short run, by supply and demand in the markets for financial assets. The exchange rate, however, is a principal determinant of the current account of the balance of payments.

Now, a surplus (deficit) on the current account represents a rise (fall) in net domestic holdings of foreign assets which in turn affects the level of wealth, which in turn affects the level of asset demand, which again affects the exchange rate. Thus, the PBM is an inherently dynamic model of exchange rate adjustment which includes in its terms of reference asset markets, the current account, the price level and the rate of asset accumulation. Moreover, we can distinguish between short-run equilibrium (supply and demand equated in asset markets) and the dynamic adjustment to long-run equilibrium (a static level of wealth and no tendency of the system to move over time). We begin by analysing the short-run determination of the exchange rate.

Short-run exchange rate determination in the portfolio balance model

In the short run (on a day to day basis), the exchange rate is determined purely by the interaction of supply and demand in asset markets. During this period, the level of financial wealth (and the individual components of that level) can be treated as fixed. For simplicity, we shall treat the net financial wealth of the private sector as composed of three assets: money (M), domestically issued bonds (B) and foreign bonds denominated in foreign currency (F). B is essentially government debt held by the domestic private sector and F is the level of net claims on foreigners held by the private sector. Since, under a free float, a current account surplus on the balance of payments must be exactly matched by a capital account deficit (i.e. capital outflow and hence an increase in net foreign indebtedness to the domestic economy), the current account must give the rate of accumulation of F over time.

With foreign and domestic interest rates given by r and r^* as before, we can write our definition of wealth and simple domestic demand functions for its components as follows:

$$W \equiv M + B + SF \tag{1.16}$$

$$M = M(r, r^*)W \qquad M_r < 0, M_{r^*} < 0 \tag{1.17}$$

$$B = B(r, r^*)W \qquad B_r > 0, B_{r^*} < 0 \tag{1.18}$$

$$SF = F(r, r^*)W \qquad F_r < 0, F_{r^*} > 0 \tag{1.19}$$

Relation (1.16) is an identity defining wealth. The major noteworthy characteristics of equations (1.17)–(1.19) are that, as is standard in the PBM, the scale variable is the level of wealth W and the demand functions are homogeneous in wealth; this allows them to be written in nominal terms (assuming homogeneity in prices and real wealth, prices cancel out) (see Tobin, 1969). For the moment, we shall assume that expectations are static – in particular, that the expected rate of depreciation is zero. We need not, therefore, include exchange rate expectations in the asset demand functions. This assumption is

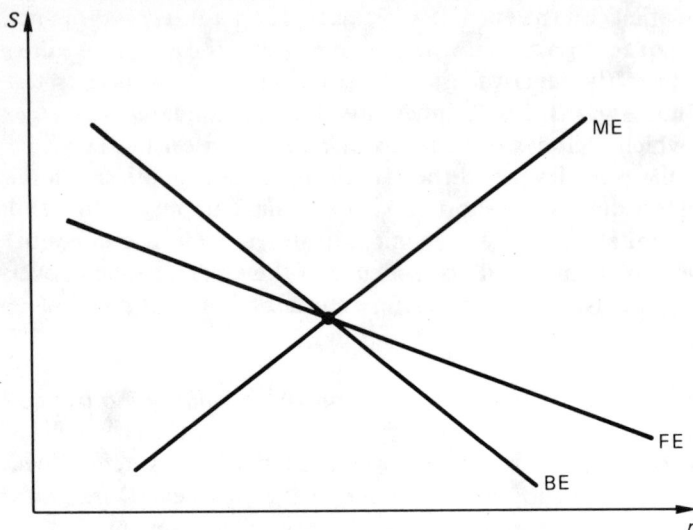

Figure 1.3   Short-run equilibrium in the portfolio balance model

relaxed below when we consider the model under the assumption of rational expectations. Note that we are no longer working in log-linear terms – thus S is the *level* and not the logarithm of the exchange rate.

Figure 1.3 shows the short-run determination of the exchange rate diagrammatically in (S, r) space. Line BE gives the locus of points in (S, r) space at which, *ceteris paribus*, the supply and demand for domestic assets are equated. Similarly, line FE gives the equilibrium locus along which the domestic demand for foreign assets is equal to the (short-run) fixed supply, and ME describes the money market equilibrium locus.

A depreciation of the exchange rate (a rise in S) raises the domestic currency value F of foreign assets, and hence increases wealth W. This raises the demand for both M and B. In order to maintain equilibrium in the money market, interest rates must rise – thus the ME schedule is upward sloping in (S, r) space. Similarly, in order to maintain domestic bond market equilibrium, the domestic interest rate must fall – the BE schedule is downward sloping.

As the domestic interest rate r rises, the domestic demand for foreign bonds falls as agents substitute domestic for foreign bonds in their portfolios. As foreign assets are sold, the foreign currency proceeds are converted into domestic currency, thus bidding up the exchange rate (S falls) – hence FE is downward sloping in (S, r) space. Since it seems reasonable to suppose that a given change in r will have a greater effect on domestic than on foreign bond demand, the FE schedule is less steep than the BE schedule.

The intersection of the ME, BE and FE schedules gives the short-run equilibrium levels of the interest rate and the exchange rate. In fact, because of the 'adding-up' constraint (1.16) we know that equilibrium in any two markets implies equilibrium in the third (Walras's law), so our analysis of the PBM can be conducted using any two of the three schedules.

Before we proceed to analyse the short-run comparative statics of the model, however, it is as well to inquire as to its stability properties, i.e. does the equilibrium point in figure 1.3 represent a stable equilibrium? Consider any point to the right of the BE schedule. At such a point, we know that the domestic interest rate is too high, for the given level of S, for there to be domestic bond market equilibrium, i.e. there must be excess demand for the (short-run) fixed level of domestic assets. This excess demand will tend to depress r towards the BE line. A converse argument applies to any point to the left of the BE schedule, so we can draw in the horizontal arrows of motion as in figure 1.4.

Now consider any point above the FE schedule. At such a point, the level of S is too high, given r, for the domestic level of demand for foreign assets to be equal to the (short-run) fixed supply. This means that the domestic currency value SF of foreign asset holdings is too high. Thus, agents will attempt to sell foreign assets and convert the proceeds into domestic currency, causing the exchange rate to appreciate (S falls). Thus, at any point above FE, the vertical arrows of motion must point towards the FE schedule

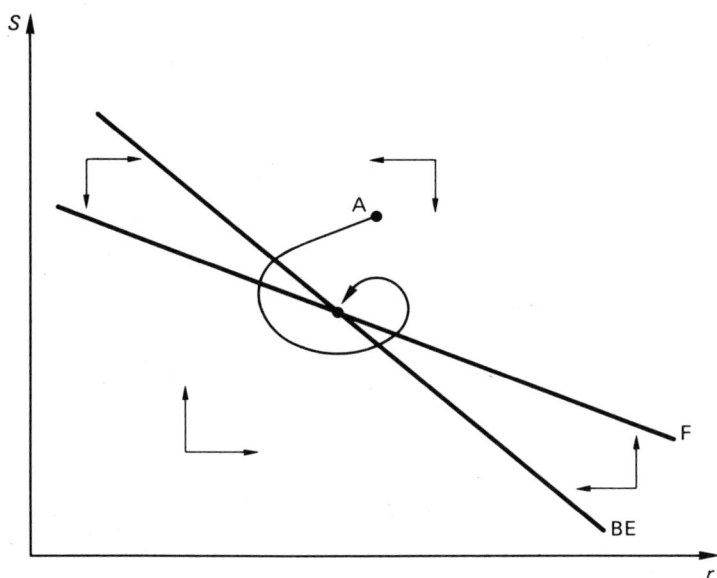

Figure 1.4   Global stability of short-run equilibrium

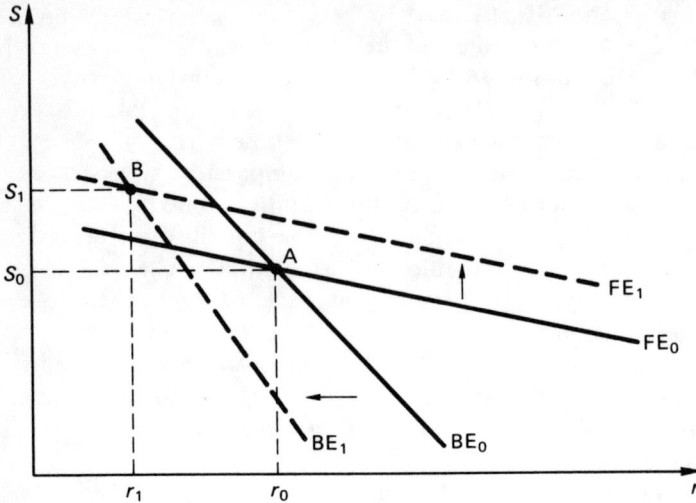

Figure 1.5   Increase in M

and, by a converse argument, at any point below FE, the vertical arrows of motion must point upwards, as in figure 1.4.

Combining these observations, we can see from figure 1.4 that starting from any point away from the intersection of the BE and FE schedules, such as point A, the economy will tend to move towards the equilibrium – the system is globally stable.

We now consider the short-run comparative-static effects of changes in the various components of net domestic wealth.

Increase in M   Since in practice, and as we shall presently discuss, the authorities can (in this model) only bring about an increase in the amount M of money held by redeeming public debt (i.e. reducing bonds B), in general, changes, ΔM, in M, will be equal and opposite to changes, ΔB, in B; i.e. $\Delta M + \Delta B = 0$. For the moment, however, we can think of a pure 'helicopter drop' of money.

As money holdings rise, agents attempt to rebalance their portfolios by buying both foreign bonds, F, and domestic bonds, B. This will tend to depreciate the exchange rate (S rises), as agents buy foreign currency with which to purchase F, and depress the domestic interest rate, as domestic bond prices rise. Diagrammatically, this results in a shift to the left of the BE schedule and an upward shift of the FE schedule, as in figure 1.5. The new short-run equilibrium must therefore be at a point such as B (figure 1.5) which is above and to the left of the initial equilibrium A, i.e. a pure increase in M leads to a reduction in the domestic interest rate and a depreciation of the exchange rate.

Increase in B   If we ignore the effects of an open-market sale of domestic bonds on the level of the money supply, the effect of an increase in B is illustrated in figure 1.6 and 1.7: in order to induce domestic wealth holders to hold more domestic bonds, r rises (bonds prices fall) for a given level of S, i.e. the BE schedule shifts to the right.

For a given level of r, the increase in wealth brought about by the rise in B leads to an increase in the demand for foreign assets – the concomitant purchase of foreign currency will tend to depreciate the exchange rate (S rises), i.e. FE shifts upwards. If there is only a relatively small upward shift in FE, as in figure 1.6, the new equilibrium will be below and to the right of the initial equilibrium – interest rates are higher and the exchange rate has appreciated (S is lower). This would be the case if domestic and foreign assets were fairly close substitutes in domestic portfolios. The increase in wealth due to the rise in B tends to raise the demand for foreign assets, but this is more than offset by a substitution effect towards domestic bond holding because of the rise in r. The net effect is a sale of domestically held foreign assets (and hence

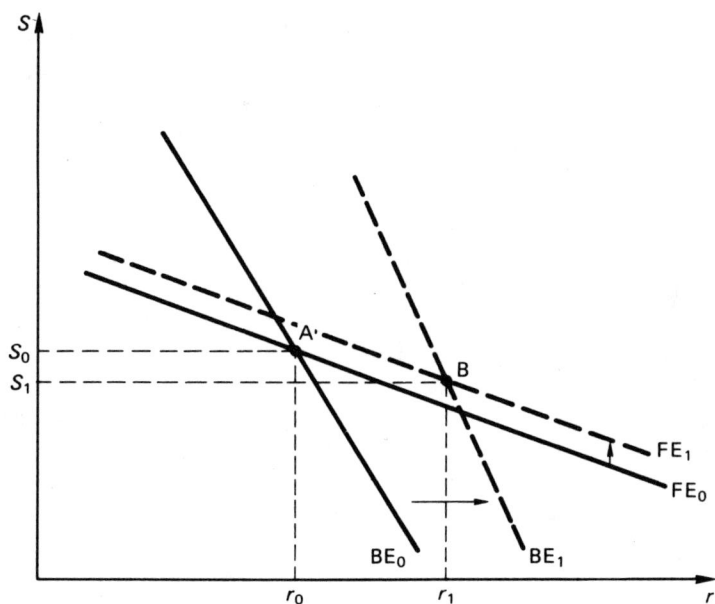

Figure 1.6   Increase in B, where domestic and foreign assets are close substitutes

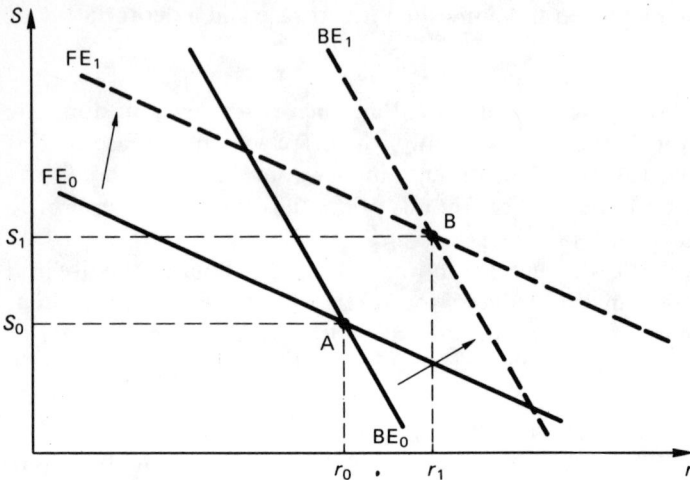

Figure 1.7   Increase in B, where domestic and foreign assets are not close substitutes

foreign currency) and the exchange rate appreciates (figure 1.6). If, on the other hand, domestic and foreign assets were not viewed as closely substitutable by domestic wealth holders, the wealth effect would dominate the substitution effect, the demand for foreign assets (and hence foreign currency) would rise and the exchange rate would depreciate (figure 1.7).

Thus, an increase in B will unambiguously raise the domestic interest rate, but the net effect on the exchange rate is ambiguous.

Increase in F   An increase in domestic holdings of net foreign assets, brought about by a current account surplus, will lead to an excess supply of domestically held foreign assets and thus foreign currency. As the exchange rate appreciates (i.e. S falls), the domestic currency value SF of foreign asset holdings rises. Clearly, S will continue to fall until the new value of foreign asset holdings ($S_1 F_1$ say) is just equal to the initial value $S_0 F_0$, the initial level of wealth is restored and the domestic bond and money markets are unaffected. Thus, a rise in F leads to a fall in S (exchange rate appreciation) with r unchanged. Diagrammatically, this can be represented by a vertical downward movement of the short-run equilibrium, as in figure 1.8.

The impact of monetary policy in the PBM   Having established the basic short-run comparative statics of the PBM, we are now in a position to examine the impact effects of monetary policy. As we noted above, the authorities can in general only affect the money supply through open-market

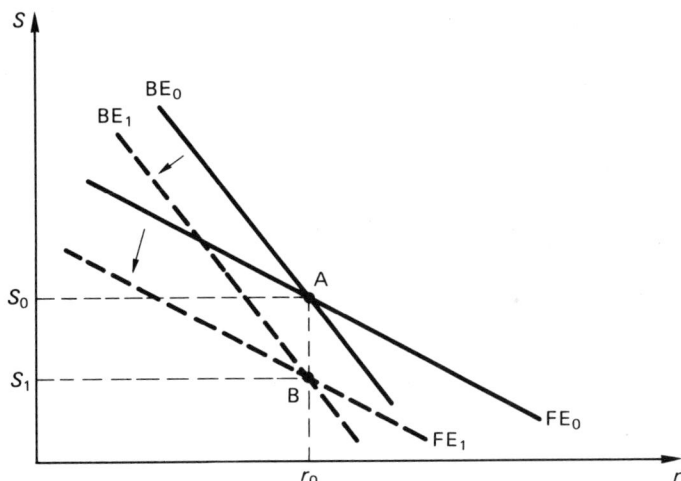

Figure 1.8 Increase in F

operations. They can either effect a net repurchase of government debt from the private sector ($\Delta B + \Delta M = 0$), or they can purchase foreign assets ($\Delta M + S\Delta F = 0$) (or some combination or the two).

Consider first a net purchase of B by the authorities. Since this directly affects the money and domestic bond markets, it will be convenient to use the BE and ME schedules for our analysis. The increase in private sector money holding can only be brought about by reducing the opportunity cost of money holding, i.e. r must fall for a given level of S (equivalently, the authorities drive up domestic bond prices and hence depress r in their attempts to repurchase government bonds). Thus the ME schedule must shift to the left (figure 1.9). Similarly, in order to induce wealth holders to part willingly with domestic assets, the rate of return r must fall for given S – the BE schedule also shifts to the left (figure 1.9). Now although the FE schedule is not drawn in figure 1.9, we know that the new short-run equilibrium must lie on FE. Thus, since FE is negatively sloped and less steep than BE, we know that the new short-run equilibrium B must be above and to the left of the initial equilibrium A – the interest rate falls and the exchange rate depreciates (point B).

Now consider the impact of open-market operations in foreign assets ($\Delta M + S\Delta F = 0$). There will again be a tendency for r to fall because of the excess supply of money (the ME schedule shifts to the left). The government purchase of foreign assets (and hence foreign currency) will tend to depreciate the exchange rate (the FE schedule shifts upward). Since the new equilibrium must lie on the BE schedule (unchanged) the new equilibrium B

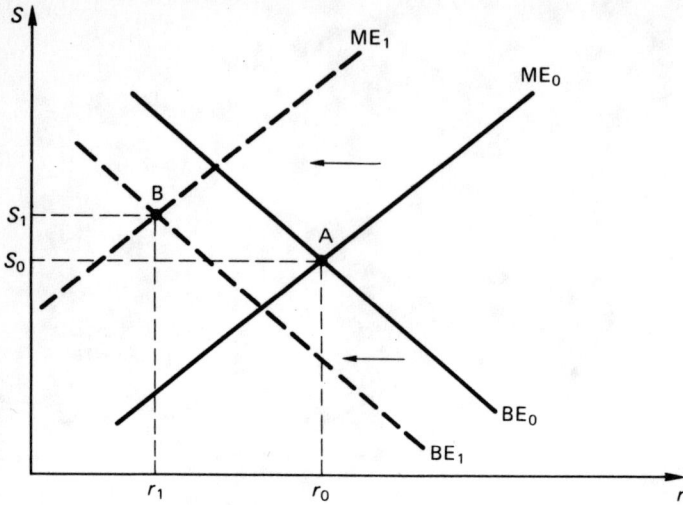

Figure 1.9   Increase in $M(\Delta M + \Delta B = 0)$

must again be above and to the left of the initial equilibrium A (figure 1.10). The exchange rate has depreciated and the domestic interest rate is lower.

   Thus, the qualitative effects of open-market operations are the same whether the government buys domestic or foreign assets. The quantitative effects, however, are different. In figure 1.9 the new equilibrium must lie on

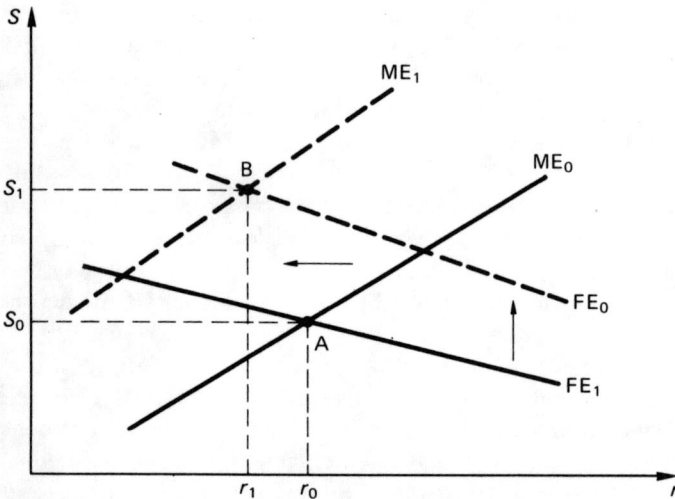

Figure 1.10   Increase in $M(\Delta M + \Delta B \neq 0)$

the unchanged FE schedule, whilst in figure 1.10 the new equilibrium must lie on the unchanged BE schedule. Since the FE schedule is less steep than the BE schedule, the change $S_1 - S_0$ in the exchange rate must be smaller in figure 1.9 than in figure 1.10, whilst the change in the interest rate must be larger. This is quite intuitive – open-market purchases of domestic assets affect r directly while open-market purchases of foreign assets affect S directly. Thus, the real impact of monetary policy on the tradables-producing sector (through S) and the sector producing interest-sensitive durable goods will depend upon the mix of open-market operations.

We can now summarize all the impact effects of changes in the components of wealth and monetary policy on the exchange rate and the domestic interest rate as in table 1.1 before going on to examine dynamic adjustment to long-run equilibrium in the PBM.

Table 1.1 Impact effects in the portfolio balance model

Effect on	Changes in stocks			Open-market operations	
	ΔF	ΔM	ΔB	$\Delta B + \Delta M = 0$	$\Delta M + S\Delta F = 0$
S	–	+	?	+	+
r	0	–	+	–	–

Dynamic adjustment in the portfolio balance model

So far we have not analysed the effect of monetary policy on the exchange rate through changes in the price level, nor have we looked at the dynamic stock-flow interaction of changes in the exchange rate, the current account and the level of wealth. An increase in the money supply would be expected to lead eventually to a rise in domestic prices, but a change in prices will affect net exports and hence will have implications for the current account of the balance of payments. This in turn affects the level of wealth which, in the adjustment to long-run equilibrium, feeds back into asset market and hence exchange rate behaviour.

Holding the (exogenous) foreign price level constant, the current account balance (in foreign currency) can be written as

$$CA = N(S/P) + r^*F \tag{1.20}$$

In equation (1.20), $N(.)$ represents the trade balance – this will improve as S rises[2] and/or P falls (competitiveness improves for a given level of foreign prices). The term r^*F represents net interest income from domestic holdings F of foreign assets. If the economy has traditionally been a net capital exporter, so that r^*F is positive, then a balance on the current account requires a trade deficit. Since a non-zero current account implies changes in F and hence in wealth, a trade deficit may be required in long-run equilibrium.

Now consider an increase in the money supply brought about by an open-market purchase of domestic bonds by the authorities. As we saw above, the impact effect of this will be to cause an immediate depreciation of the exchange rate. This is not the end of the story, however. Suppose the economy was initially in equilibrium with a trade balance of zero and net foreign asset holdings of zero (and hence a current account balance of zero). This is depicted in figure 1.11 at the point corresponding to time t_0. Figure 1.11 is drawn so that the initial values (at time t_0) of the price level and the exchange rate are normalized to unity, $P_0 = S_0 = 1$. The impact effect is a jump in the exchange rate S_0 to S_1 (AC). Moreover, assuming that the

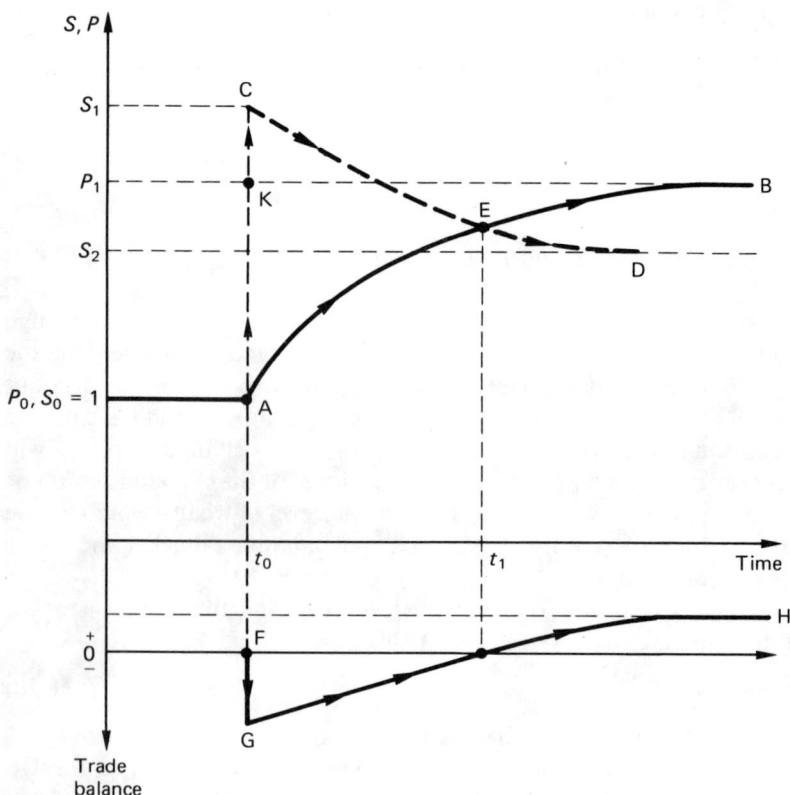

Figure 1.11   Dynamic adjustment in the portfolio balance model: increase in $M(\Delta M + \Delta B = 0)$

Marshall–Lerner condition holds, the improvement in competitiveness will improve the trade balance from zero to a positive amount (FG).[3] This means that the current account goes into surplus and domestic residents begin to acquire net foreign assets (F accumulates). As we discussed above, an increase in F will tend to appreciate the exchange rate from C along CD, and the trade balance will thus begin to worsen along GH. Meanwhile, the increase in the money supply will have begun to increase prices along the path AB towards the new long-run equilibrium price level P_1. This adds to the deterioration of competitiveness and hence the trade balance. At point E (time t_1) the exchange rate and the price level are equal in value and hence their ratio is unity ($S/P = 1$); but this is the same as the initial ratio at time t_0. Hence, the trade balance at time t must be back to its original level, i.e. zero. However, this is no longer enough to restore long-run equilibrium. Domestic wealth holders have now acquired a positive level of net foreign asset holdings and will be receiving a stream of investment income r^*F. In order for the current account balance to be zero, therefore, the trade balance must actually go into deficit. This requires a further appreciation of the exchange rate (fall in S) to its long-run equilibrium level S_2, by which time the price level has reached its long-run equilibrium level P_1 and the current account just balances ($-N(S_2/P_1) = r^*F$) so there is no further net accumulation of foreign assets.

Note that the PBM gives an alternative derivation of the overshooting result described in section 1.2.2 – the exchange rate S jumps immediately above its long-run level and then falls slowly. Moreover, overshooting in the PBM does not rely solely on price level stickiness as in the Dornbusch over-shooting model. Say, for example, that the price level adjusted immediately to P_1, following the increase in the money supply, along AK in figure 1.11. As long as the new short-run equilibrium exchange rate S_1 exceeds P_1, competitiveness will have increased, the trade balance will have gone into surplus and a slow appreciation to the long-run exchange rate level will ensue as above.

Rational expectations in the portfolio balance model

We now extend our analysis of the PBM to consider rational expectations (following Branson, 1983). In the analysis so far, the exchange rate jumps immediately in order to clear the asset markets and then adjusts slowly in response to induced current account imbalances. In the rational expectations version of the PBM, the essential difference is that expectations of *future* current account imbalance impact immediately on the exchange rate as the market looks ahead. Comparing the two versions of the models we shall find that the *long-run* effects of various shocks remain the same, whilst the *impact* effects become magnified.

The rational expectations PBM (REPBM) is as follows:

$$W = M + B + SF \tag{1.21}$$

$$M = M(r, r^* + \hat{S})W \tag{1.22}$$

$$B = B(r, r^* + \hat{S})W \tag{1.23}$$

$$SF = F(r, r^* + \hat{S})W \tag{1.24}$$

$$\dot{F} = N(S/P, Z) + r^*F \tag{1.25}$$

In fact, relations (1.21)–(1.24) (which correspond to relations (1.16)–(1.19)) implicitly assume that the certainty equivalence principle applies, so that the foreign rate of return is augmented by the actual rather than the expected proportional rate of depreciation of the exchange rate ($\hat{S} = \dot{S}/S = \dot{s}$). Relation (1.25) corresponds to (1.20), where we have made explicit that the current account surplus represents the rate of accumulation of foreign assets and we have included a real shift variable Z in the trade balance function ($N_z > 0$).

We shall solve the model qualitatively by sketching the phase diagram and the stable manifold in (F, S) space. Equation (1.25) already gives a dynamic equation for F. A corresponding equation for S can be derived as follows. Divide (1.22) and (1.24) by W and differentiate totally, holding the foreign yield constant:

$$\begin{bmatrix} d(SF/W) \\ d(M/W) \end{bmatrix} = \begin{bmatrix} F_r & F_s \\ M_r & M_s \end{bmatrix} \begin{bmatrix} dr \\ dS \end{bmatrix}$$

which implies that

$$\begin{bmatrix} dr \\ dS \end{bmatrix} = (F_r M_s - M_r F_s)^{-1} \begin{bmatrix} M_s & -F_s \\ -M_r & F_r \end{bmatrix} \begin{bmatrix} d(SF/W) \\ d(M/W) \end{bmatrix}$$

so that dS is given by

$$dS = (F_r M_s - M_r F_s)^{-1}[-M_r d(SF/W) + F_r d(M/W)] \tag{1.26}$$

The coefficients of SF/W and M/W in (1.26) can be interpreted as the partial derivatives of an adjustment function for $\hat{S}$

$$\hat{S} = \phi[(SF/W), (M/W)], \phi_1 > 0 \quad \phi_2 < 0 \tag{1.27}$$

where the signs of the derivatives of (1.27) are inferred from (1.26).

Now consider setting $\hat{S} = 0$ (and hence $\dot{S} = 0$) in (1.27). Since S and F enter ϕ multiplicatively (in SF and in W), changes in S and F which keep the product SF constant will keep $\hat{S}$ constant. In particular, therefore, the locus of points for which $\hat{S} = 0$ and hence $\dot{S} = 0$ must be a rectangular hyperbola

$$SF = \lambda \tag{1.28}$$

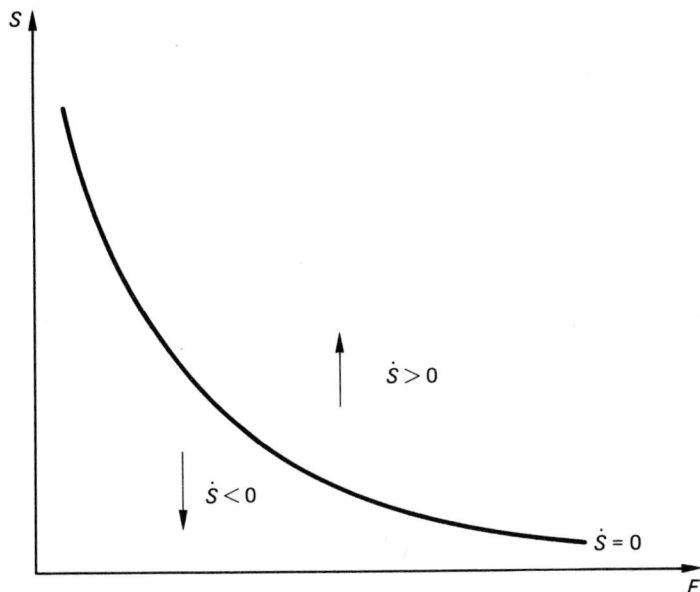

Figure 1.12   The $\dot{S} = 0$ locus

where λ is a constant. This is sketched in figure 1.12. From (1.27) we can see that an increase in S or F from a point on the $\dot{S} = 0$ locus will lead to rising (i.e. depreciation) S: $\dot{S} > 0$.

From (1.25) we can infer that the $\dot{F} = 0$ locus must be downward sloping in (F, S) space and that increases in S or F will lead to rising F: $\dot{F} > 0$; this is sketched in figure 1.13.

From figure 1.12 and 1.13 we can see that a saddlepath equilibrium will only exist if, as in figure 1.14, the $\dot{F} = 0$ locus is less steep than the $\dot{S} = 0$ locus in the neighbourhood of the intersection. From (1.28) we have

$$\frac{\mathrm{d}S}{\mathrm{d}F}\bigg|_{\dot{S}=0} = -\frac{S}{F}$$

while from (1.25) we have

$$\frac{\mathrm{d}S}{\mathrm{d}F}\bigg|_{\dot{F}=0} = -\frac{r^*}{N_s}$$

Hence, for a saddlepath equilibrium we require

$$\frac{-S}{F} < \frac{-r^*}{N_s}$$

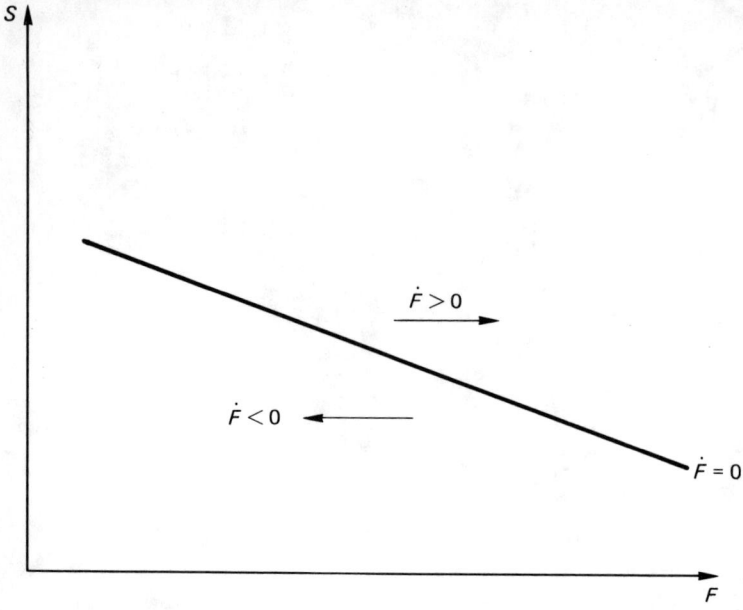

Figure 1.13   The $\dot{F} = 0$ locus

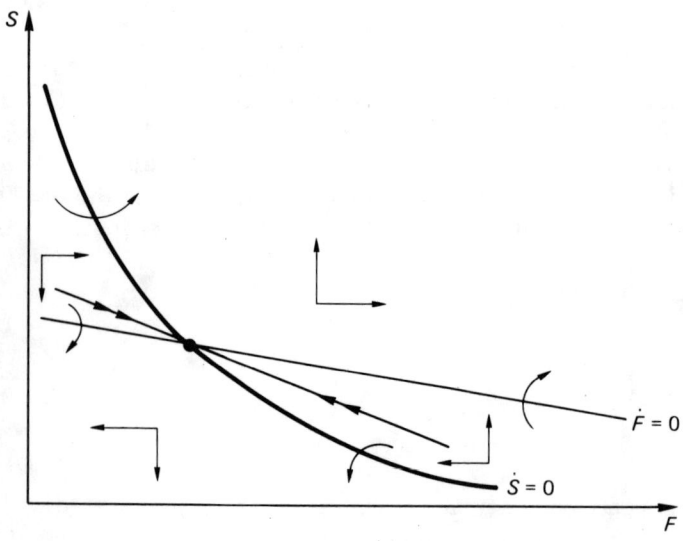

Figure 1.14   The saddlepath equilibrium for the rational expectations portfolio balance model

At equilibrium $\dot{F} = 0$ and hence, from (1.25), $N = -r^*F$, so that the equilibrium condition reduces to

$$SN_s/N > 1$$

which is, of course, the familiar Marshall–Lerner condition for foreign exchange market stability.

Now consider a positive real shock to the current account. From (1.25), this means that the new $\dot{F} = 0$ locus must have lower values of S and F for higher Z. Thus, in figure 1.15 the $\dot{F} = 0$ locus shifts down. From initial equilibrium at A, the exchange rate therefore jumps in a steep appreciation to point B and then appreciates slowly along the stable manifold, with S appreciating further and F accumulating until the new long-run equilibrium at point C is reached.

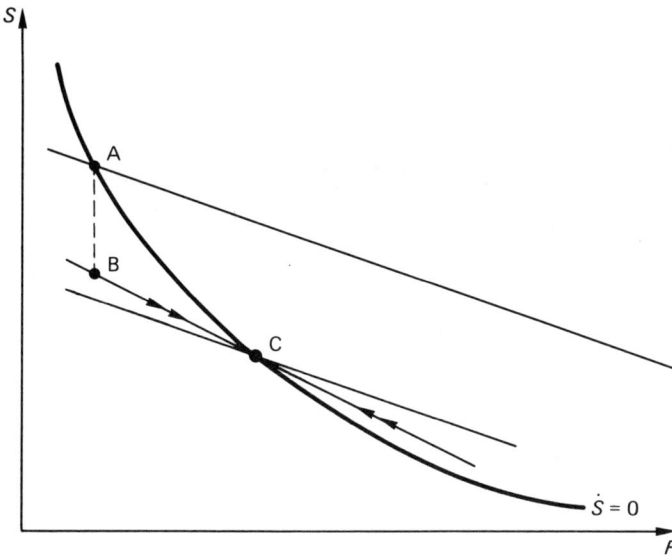

Figure 1.15   A positive current account disturbance in the rational expectations portfolio balance model

1.2.4 Conclusion for theoretical exchange rate models

Monetary models of exchange rate determination were a clear advance over more traditional, Mundell–Fleming models, in that they took explicit account of stock equilibria in international asset markets rather than concentrating on the simpler flow equilibrium conditions as the earlier analyses had done. Early FLPM exchange rate models, however, soon began to disagree seriously with the observed facts during the turbulent 1970s. In particular, early FLPM models assumed continuous PPP whilst large and sustained deviations from PPP were often manifestly clear. This defect was remedied by the second generation monetary models – the SPM over-shooting exchange rate models. In SPM models, differencs in the speed of adjustment of goods and asset prices cause the exchange rate to act as a jump variable which can consistently overshoot long-run equilibrium levels in response to real and financial shocks.

Both these kinds of monetary model make a number of implicit assumptions, however. In particular, they assume that domestic and foreign assets are essentially perfectly substitutable in investors' portfolios and that the wealth effects of a current account surplus or deficit are negligible. These assumptions are relaxed in the PBM of exchange rate determination.

Although the PBM (or rather REPBM) is clearly the most general of the exchange rate theories we have examined, the question concerning which theory best fits the observed facts is clearly an empirical matter. We now turn to a consideration of the empirical evidence on exchange rate determination.

1.3 MONETARY VERSUS PORTFOLIO MODELS OF THE EXCHANGE RATE: WHICH DOES THE EVIDENCE FROM THE RECENT FLOAT SUPPORT?

In section 1.2 we surveyed the various modern approaches to exchange rate determination. At the heart of this literature is the asset approach to the exchange rate, which posits that in the short run – on a day to day basis – the exchange rate is determined by the interaction of asset supplies and asset demands. The choice of assets to be included in an asset market model depends crucially on a modeller's belief about the existence of risk in foreign exchange markets. Thus, proponents of the monetary approach to the exchange rate (see *inter alia* Dornbusch, 1976; Frenkel, 1976; Mussa, 1976; Bilson, 1978a; Frankel, 1979a) argue that speculators in the foreign exchange market are risk neutral and regard non-money assets denominated in different currencies as perfect substitutes: this assumption, combined with the assumption of perfect capital mobility (which we take to mean the instantaneous adjustment of portfolios), implies that UIP holds and that the exchange rate is determined by relative money supplies. However, proponents of the portfolio balance approach argue that risk aversion on the part of speculators implies that non-money assets are imperfect substitutes: the exchange rate is determined by the interaction of moncy and bond market equilibria. In fact, unless a risk premium was assumed to enter the simple UIP condition, domestic and foreign interest rates could not enter separately into the asset demand functions of the PBM (relations (17)–(19)) or the REPBM (relations (1.22)–(1.24)).

Whether the monetary approach or PBM is correct is clearly of consider-able importance. For example, if the monetary approach is a better approximation to reality then this implies that only non-sterilized foreign exchange intervention is effective, thereby limiting the role of monetary policy (sterilized intervention can only have an effect in this model to the extent that it alters agents' perceptions of future monetary policy (see Genberg, 1981)). If the PBM is correct, then both sterilized and non-sterilized intervention can be efficacious, thus giving the policy-maker an extra tool with which to conduct macroeconomic policy.

In this section we conduct a stocktaking exercise to determine which of the two competing asset models is supported by the evidence from the recent floating experience. To do this, we survey various strands of the empirical exchange rate literature. In particular, we start, in section 1.3.1, by outlining some of the relationships which underpin the asset approach. In section 1.3.2 we present a survey of the theory and evidence relating to various formula-tions of the monetary approach to the exchange rate. In section 1.3.3 we discuss the more general portfolio balance approach and in section 1.3.4 consider a synthesis of the monetary and portfolio balance approaches. In section 1.3.5 we examine the evidence on the predictive performance of the various exchange rate models which have been put forward. The discussion is summed up in section 1.3.6.

1.3.1 Some modelling relationships

At the outset it is useful to gather together some relationships which we shall refer to repeatedly throughout our survey. Equations (1.30) and (1.31) denote home and foreign log-linear (Cagan style) money demand functions:

$$m_t^d = p_t + \phi y_t - \lambda r_t \tag{1.30}$$

$$m_t^{d*} = p_t^* + \phi^* y_t^* - \lambda^* r_t^* \tag{1.31}$$

Assuming money market equilibrium then yields the equilibrium conditions given in equations (1.1) and (1.2).

The relationship between the home and foreign interest rates is assumed to be governed by a risk-adjusted interest parity relationship such as (1.22):

$$r_t = r_t^* + \Delta s_{t+1}^e + \rho_t \tag{1.32}$$

where Δs_{t+1}^e denotes the expected change in the exchange rate, s is the natural logarithm of the home currency price of a unit of foreign exchange and ρ_t denotes a risk premium.[4] Further, if covered interest parity holds, i.e.

$$r_t - r_t^* = \text{fp}_t \tag{1.33}$$

(fp_t is the forward premium $f_t - s_t$ where f_t is the log of the forward exchange rate), we may usefully write the risk premium ρ_t as

$$\Delta s_{t+1}^e - \text{f}\text{p}_t = \rho_t \qquad (1.34)$$

The risk premium is that part of the expected rate of depreciation not allowed for in the forward premium.

Finally, we can define the (logarithm of the) real exchange rate, q_t, as the deviation from PPP:

$$q_t = s_t - p_t + p_t^* \qquad (1.35)$$

1.3.2 The monetary approach – three formulations

We now consider three approaches to the exchange rate reduced form which we believe are representative of the monetary view. In particular, we consider a reduced form which purports to capture the FLPM approach, a reduced form derived from the Dornbusch (1976) SPM model and finally a reduced form due to Frankel (1979a), called the real interest differential (RID) model, which purports to discriminate between the FLPM and SPM models. For the purposes of exposition it will also prove useful to split empirical evidence about the monetary reduced forms into three subsections.

We consider what we term the 'first tests' of the FLPM and RID models. Such tests, conducted, by and large, for the German mark–US dollar and UK pound–US dollar exchange rates, run from 1972 to 1978 and are largely supportive of the monetary approach. The second period tests of the FLPM and RID models, for the period from 1978 onwards are then considered and are seen to question the validity of the approach. Finally tests of the SPM model for the whole of the floating period are examined.

The flex-price monetary formulation

In section 1.2.2 we derived an equation representative of the FLPM model, equation (1.4). Assuming that the domestic and foreign money demand coefficients are equal ($\phi = \phi^*$, $\lambda = \lambda^*$), (1.4) reduces to

$$s_t = (m - m^*)_t - \phi(y - y^*)_t + \lambda(r - r^*)_t \qquad (1.36)$$

A further assumption underlying the FLPM model is that the risk premium ρ_t in (1.32) is identically zero and therefore UIP holds continuously. Thus we may substitute Δs_{t+1}^e for $(r - r^*)_t$ in (1.36) to get

$$s_t = (m - m^*)_t - \phi(y - y^*)_t + \lambda \Delta s_{t+1}^e \qquad (1.37)$$

Thus, the expected change in the exchange rate and the interest differential, which reflects inflationary expectations through (1.35), are interchangeable in this model. Some researchers relax the constraint that the income and interest rate elasticities are equal and thus specify an equation of the form (1.4) or, as a sort of hybrid,

$$s_t = (m - m^*)_t - \phi y_t + \phi^* y_t^* + \lambda \Delta s_{t+1}^e \tag{1.38}$$

Note also that (1.38) can be expressed as

$$s_t = (1 + \lambda)^{-1}(m - m^*)_t - \phi(1 + \lambda)^{-1} y_t + \phi^*(1 + \lambda)^{-1} y_t^* + \\ \lambda(1 + \lambda)^{-1} s_{t+1}^e \tag{1.39}$$

By interating forward, it is easy to show that (1.39) can be expressed in the form

$$s_t = (1 + \lambda)^{-1} \sum_{i=0}^{\infty} \left(\frac{\lambda}{1 + \lambda}\right)^i [(m - m^*)_{t+i}^e - \phi y_{t+i}^e + \phi^* y_{t+i}^{*e}] \tag{1.40}$$

where it is understood that expectations are conditioned on information at time t. Equation (1.40) makes clear that the monetary model, with rational expectations, involves solving for the entire expected future path of the 'forcing variables', i.e. relative money and income. Thus, for example, expected relative money supply growth is discounted into the current spot rate in a manner analogous to that in which expected future dividend payments are discounted into current share prices.

One immediate problem facing empirical researchers in attempting to implement equation (1.36) for the recent floating experience is that PPP has manifestly not held continuously (see for example Frenkel, 1981; Taylor, 1986, 1988d) and thus the assumption necessary to derive (1.36) (i.e. $q \equiv 0$) does not hold. Monetarists such as Mussa (1976) counter this by arguing that since the exchange rate is the relative price of national monies, and is thus determined in asset markets, a researcher should go directly from the relative money market equilibrium relations to equation (1.36) or (1.37).

However, even though (1.36) may be derived without imposing PPP directly, the interpretation placed on the interest differential in such equations may still be questionable. For example, and as we shall see below, proponents of (1.36) usually use short-term interest rates to capture inflationary expectations. But is this realistic in periods when PPP does not hold and inflationary expectations are only moderate? It seems likely to reflect real monetary changes, as in the SPM model, rather than inflationary expectations. Thus, it would be useful if equation (1.36) could be modified to allow for the separate effects of money supply changes on real interest differentials and also on inflationary expectations. Frankel (1979a) has in fact developed a monetary approach reduced form which relaxes the assumption that PPP holds continuously and splits the interest rate effect of a monetary change into real and inflationary components. We consider the Frankel (1979a) formulation below, but first we turn to an examination of empirical models of the SPM formulation.

The sticky price monetary formulation

An alternative monetary approach reduced form may be derived using the structural equations from the Dornbusch (1976) SPM model which we discussed in section 1.2. As our starting point, we take the relative monetary equilibrium equation derived from (1.1) and (1.2) with the assumption of identical foreign and domestic money demand coefficients:

$$(m - m^*)_t = (p - p^*)_t + \phi(y - y^*)_t - \lambda(r - r^*)_t \qquad (1.41)$$

Since PPP does not hold continuously in the SPM model, we need an additional equation to describe the evolution of the price level. We follow Driskell (1981) in assuming that relative prices evolve according to

$$(p - p^*)_{t+1} = (p - p^*)_t + \pi[d - (y - y^*)]_t \qquad (1.42)$$

where d denotes relative aggregate demand which may be modelled as

$$d_t = \beta_1(s - p + p^*)_t + \beta_2(y - y^*)_t - \beta_3(r - r^*)_t \qquad (1.43)$$

Thus relative aggregate demand depends upon a competitiveness term, relative income and the relative interest rate. By combining (1.41)–(1.43) the relative price equation (1.44) can be obtained:

$$(p - p^*)_t = b_1(y - y^*)_{t+1} + b_2(p - p^*)_{t-1} + b_3(m - m^*)_{t-1} + b_4 s_{t-1} \quad (1.44)$$

Following Driskell (1981), we assume that exchange rate expectations are regressive and that the long-run exchange rate is proportional to relative money supply:

$$\Delta s_{t+1}^e = \theta[(m - m^*)_t - s_t] \qquad (1.45)$$

Using (1.41)–(1.45) plus the UIP condition, the following reduced form can be derived:

$$s_t = \pi_0 + \pi_1 s_{t-1} + \pi_2 m_t' + \pi_3 m_{t-1}' + \pi_4 p_{t-1}' + \pi_5 y_t' + \pi_6 y_{t-1}' \qquad (1.46)$$

where $\Sigma_{i=1}^4 \pi_i = 1$, $\pi_1 < 0$, $\pi_2 > 1$, $\pi_3 < 0$, $\pi_4 < 0$, $\pi_5 < 0$, $\pi_6 < 0$ and $x' = x - x^*$ with $x = m, p, y$.

The first constraint indicates that PPP must hold in the long run in this model. Note particularly the sign of π_2 which suggests that an increase in the money supply leads to a more than proportionate impact rise in the exchange rate: overshooting. An interesting feature of the above derivation is that by substituting for relative interest rates we arrive at a reduced form exchange rate equation purged of the effects of a relative interest rate term on the exchange rate.

A further interesting feature of the reduced form equation (1.46) is that it may be derived by using the imperfect capital flow function (i.e. retaining the assumption of risk neutrality, agents' portfolios take time to adjust) so that net capital inflows are modelled as

$$C = \beta(r_t - r_t^* - \Delta s_{t+1}^e); \quad 0 \leqslant \beta \leqslant \infty$$

instead of UIP. Although the reduced form is identical regardless of whether the perfect or imperfect capital mobility route is used, the interpretation placed on the reduced form coefficients differs. Thus, although the PPP constraint holds in the imperfect capital mobility derivation of the SPM model, other constraints are ambiguous (see Driskell, 1981, for a proof), i.e. $\Sigma_{i=1}^4 \pi_i = 1$, $\pi_1 < 1$, $\pi_2 > 0$, $\pi_3 < 0$, $\pi_4 > 0$, $\pi_5 < 0$ and $\pi_6 < 0$.

Note particularly that the coefficient on the relative money supply term need not be greater than unity. Thus, tests of (1.46) allow discrimination between the perfect and imperfect capital mobility versions of the SPM model.

The real interest differential formulation

Frankel (1979a) argues that a shortcoming of the Dornbusch (1976) formulation of the SPM monetary model is that it does not allow a role for differences in secular rates of inflation. His model is therefore an attempt to allow for this defect and the upshot is an exchange rate equation which includes the RID as an explanatory variable – the RID variant of the monetary model.

In section 1.2.2 we showed that the rationally expected rate of depreciation in the Dornbusch model is proportional to the deviation from the long-run rate (equation (1.15)). Frankel modifies this to allow for secular rates of inflation:

$$\Delta s_{t+1}^e = -\theta(s_t - \bar{s}_t) + \pi_t^e - \pi_t^{*e} \tag{1.47}$$

where π_r^e represents the current rate of expected long-run inflation. Combining this with the UIP condition (1.32) (with ρ_t set to zero) we have

$$s_t - \bar{s}_t = \theta^{-1}[(r - \pi^e)_t - (r^* - \pi^{*e})_t] \tag{1.48}$$

Although π_t^e and π_t^{*e} refer to *long-run* inflation expectations, (1.48) can be viewed as relating the exchange rate to RIDs. Given UIP and (long-run) PPP, the long-run interest differential must be equal to the long-run expected inflation differential,

$$\bar{r}_t - \bar{r}_t^* = \pi_t^e - \pi_t^{*e}$$

so that (1.48) can be alternatively expressed as

$$s_t - \bar{s}_t = -\theta^{-1}[(\bar{r}_t - r_t) - (\bar{r}_t^* - r_t^*)]^- \tag{1.49}$$

The exchange rate appreciates above its long-run level whenever the relative nominal interest differential does.

Now, using (1.36) and (1.49) and denoting long-run values by a bar, as before, we have

$$\bar{s}_t = (\bar{m} - \bar{m}^*)_t - \phi(\bar{y}_t - \bar{y}_t^*) + \lambda(\pi_t^e - \pi_t^{*e}) \tag{1.50}$$

Substituting (1.50) into (1.48) and assuming, for simplicity, that the current equilibrium money supplies and income levels are given by their current actual levels (which amounts to assuming that they follow random walks), we derive the RID formulation:

$$s_t = (m - m^*)_t - \phi(y - y^*)_t - \theta^{-1}(r - r^*)_t + (\theta^{-1} + \lambda)(\pi^e - \pi^{*e})_t$$

or

$$s_t = \alpha_1(m - m^*)_t + \alpha_2(y - y^*)_t + \alpha_3(r - r^*)_t + \alpha_4(\pi^e - \pi^{*e})_t \tag{1.51}$$

Note that (1.51) is similar to the FLPM formulation (1.36) with the addition of the long-run expected inflation differential, so that a test of the significance from zero of α_4 should, in principle, allow discrimination. Since the RID formulation however involves only *long-run* PPP in its derivation, it can be viewed as a variant of the SPM model. The discriminating factor might then depend on whether the relative inflation expectations term should appear, as here, or not, as in the SPM formulation. However, under the FLPM formulation, the nominal interest differential coefficient is expected to be positive, whilst under both the RID and SPM formulation it should be negative. The various alternative hypotheses concerning these coefficients are summarized in table 1.2.

Table 1.2 Alternative hypotheses for equation (1.51)

Model	α_3	α_4
FLPM	0	+
SPM	−	0
RID	−	+

Econometric issues

Having derived equations (1.36), (1.46) and (1.51) it is tempting to view them as ideal candidates for estimation. There are important econometric issues, however, that should be considered before any attempt is made to estimate equations such as these. For illustrative purposes only equation (1.36), rewritten here with a white noise error term, is considered in the following discussion:

$$s_t = \alpha_0(m - m^*)_t + \alpha_1(y - y^*)_t + \alpha_2(r - r^*)_t + \epsilon_t \qquad (1.52)$$

First, a researcher estimating equation (1.52) for the recent floating exchange rate period faces a potential simultaneity problem – is this truly a reduced form equation? For example, it is now clear that the recent float has been one in which monetary authorities have intervened, at times substantially, in foreign exchange markets (see for example Artus, 1976; Mussa, 1981). Hence the domestic money supply term in (1.52) may be correlated with the error term (as will the foreign money supply if the foreign monetary authorities intervene). This can be seen from the following simple example. If m represents the money supply of the consolidated monetary sector, the familiar money supply identity will hold:

$$m_t = d_t + v_t$$

where d is the (logarithm of the) domestic component and v the (logarithm of the) foreign reserve component of the money stock (we are assuming for pedagogic purposes that $\ln(D + V) \sim \ln D + \ln V$). If the monetary authorities have some notional target for the exchange rate $\tilde{s}$, which may be in terms of PPP or simply last period's exchange rate, and they intervene when the current exchange rate rises above or falls below this target according to the simple rule

$$v_t = v_{t-1} + a(\tilde{s} - s)_t + u_t, \quad a > 0$$

then to the extent that the effect of v on m is not sterilized it is clear that foreign exchange intervention imparts a classical simultaneous equation bias into ordinary least squares (OLS) estimates of (1.52), resulting in biased and inconsistent estimates of α_0, i.e. the OLS estimates $\hat{\alpha}_0$ will overestimate the true α_0. Simultaneous equation bias will also be present in OLS estimates of equation (1.52) if interest rates are used to support the exchange rate, e.g.

$$r_t = \lambda(s_t - s_{t-1}) + u_t, \quad \lambda > 0 \qquad (1.53)$$

In this case the coefficient on the interest rate differential will be biased upwards. Furthermore, note that if (1.53) is the authorities' interest rate reaction function then we should not be surprised if a positive correlation between the interest differential and s is obtained (but note that this association is not reflecting inflationary expectations as predicted by the FLPM). Aside from the interest rate reaction function specified in (1.53) the relative interest rate term in (1.52) is likely to be endogenous because of the interest parity relationship and the rationality of expectations. Thus, in estimating (1.52) the interest rate terms should perhaps be eliminated, using the forward substitution method of rational expectations as in equation (1.40).

The above discussion indicates that in implementing asset approach exchange rate equations in periods with foreign exchange intervention, researchers should carefully specify the reaction function for interest rates and money and use this information in estimating an equation such as (1.52) (e.g. by two-stage least squares). A simpler method of accounting for the simultaneity of s and $m - m^*$ has been proposed by a number of researchers (see for example Frankel, 1979a) and involves constraining the coefficient on $m - m^*$ to unity and estimating equation (1.54):

$$s_t - (m - m^*)_t = \alpha_1(y - y^*)_t + \alpha_2(r - r^*)_t + \epsilon_t \qquad (1.54)$$

Thus the variables on the right-hand side of (1.54) reflect money demand influences which will lead to exchange rate movements under flexible rates or changes in the money supply under fixed rates as in the monetary approach to the balance of payments (see Frenkel and Johnson, 1976).

Constraining the coefficient of $m - m^*$ to unity makes sense for another reason. During the recent float there have been large errors in money demand equations which, because of the close correlation with the money stock, would bias the coefficient on $m - m^*$ downwards. Constraining $m - m^*$ to have a coefficient of unity means that such errors are forced into the dependent variable and thus cannot bias the coefficient estimates for the independent variables.

A final point worth making in this section concerns the expected values of the coefficients in estimated versions of equations such as (1.36) and (1.46). Most researchers (often implicitly) expect coefficients on income and the rate of interest to have values close to those found in estimates of closed-economy money demand equations. Thus Bilson (1978b), for example posits α_1 is to lie between 0.5 and 1.5 and α_2 to lie between 0 and 3 in equation (1.52).

The first tests of the flex-price monetary and real interest differential reduced forms

One of the first tests of equation (1.37) was conducted by Frenkel (1976) for the German mark–US dollar exchange rate over the period 1920–3. Since this period corresponds to the German hyperinflation, Frenkel argues that domestic monetary impulses will overwhelmingly dominate equation (1.37), and thus domestic income and foreign magnitudes can be dropped and attention can be focused simply on the effects of German money and the expected inflation exchange rate change on the exchange rate. Frenkel's version of equation (1.37) is therefore

$$s_t = \alpha_0 + \alpha_1 m_t^G + \alpha_2 \Delta s_t^e + \epsilon_t \qquad (1.55)$$

where all variables are in natural logarithms and a G superscript denotes a German variable. The estimated version of (1.55) is

$$s_t = 5.135 + 0.975\, m_t^G + 0.571\, \Delta s_t^e \qquad (1.56)$$
$$\quad\ \ (7.02)\quad (19.50)\qquad\ (8.10)$$

$$R^2 = 0.99 \qquad \text{DW} = 1.91$$

where t ratios are in parentheses, R^2 is the coefficient of determination and DW is the Durbin–Watson statistic. Since the elasticity of the exchange rate with respect to the money supply does not differ significantly from unity and the elasticity of the expected change in the exchange rate is positive, as predicted by the theory, this result clearly offers support for the FLPM model. But what happens when we consider periods in which monetary impulses do not dominate as in the hyperinflation model?

A number of researchers have estimated FLPM equations for the more recent experience with floating exchange rates. For example, Bilson (1978a) tests equation (1.38) for the German mark–UK pound exchange rate (with the forward premium fp substituted for Δs^e) over the period January 1972 to April 1976, and his OLS results are reported as column A in table 1.3. Although all the coefficients are correctly signed in this equation, only one coefficient differs significantly from zero. The insignificance of the coefficients combined with the high value of R^2 lead Bilson to conclude that multicollinearity is also a problem, and the presence of autocorrelation is suggestive of model mis-specification. To account for the latter, Bilson incorporates a familiar partial adjustment scheme for the exchange rate and a first-order autoregressive process for the error term into equation (1.38) and obtains

$$s_t = \alpha_0 + \alpha_1 m_t + \alpha_2 m_t^* + \alpha_3 y_t + \alpha_4 y_t^* + \alpha_5 \text{fp}_t + \alpha_6 s_{t-1}$$
$$+ \rho u_{t-1} + u_t \qquad\qquad (1.57)$$

Bilson's estimated version of (1.57) is reported as column B in table 1.3. This equation appears to fit the data better than (1.38) does as it has a higher R^2, lower standard error (SER) and higher DW; but again only one coefficient differs significantly from zero. The second stage of Bilson's attempt to improve equation (1.38) is to account for the evident multicollinearity using the Theil–Goldberger mixed estimation procedure. Using coefficient estimates from closed-economy money demand equations as his priors for the procedure, Bilson derives an equilibrium exchange rate equation (column C in table 1.3) which is clearly supportive of the FLPM model. In a further paper, Bilson (1978b) extends equation (1.38) by including a time trend to capture the "secular decline in the demand for pounds relative to the DM" for the longer period 1970–7. Again, utilizing the Theil–Goldberger procedure, results in accord with the monetary approach are reported. (The use of proxies to capture money demand shifts is relatively popular in monetary approach reduced forms and will be considered again below.)

Hodrick's (1978) tests of equation (1.38) for the US dollar–German mark and UK pound–US dollar over the period July 1972 to June 1975 are highly supportive of the FLPM model. For example, the dollar–mark equation, reported as column D in table 1.3, has the home and foreign money supply terms close to plus and minus unity (the hypothesis that they *are* equal to plus and minus unity cannot be rejected at the 5 per cent significance level); the

Table 1.3 The first-period tests of the flex-price monetary and real interest differential reduced forms

Variable	A	B	C	D	E	F	G
	OLS	Bilson (1978) Mark–pound January 1972–April 1976 OLS	Theil-Goldberger mixed estimation	Hodrick (1978) Dollar–mark April 1973–September 1975 OLS	Putnam and Woodbury (1979) Mark–dollar 1972–7 Hildreth–Lu	Dornbusch (1979) Pound–dollar March 1974–May 1978 AR 1	AR 1
m_t	0.417 (0.94)	0.358 (0.94)	1.001	1.520 (2.98)	—	—	—
m_t^*	−0.915 (4.32)	−0.586 (2.86)	−1.008	−1.390 (2.48)	—	—	—
$(m-m^*)_t$	—	—	—	—	0.630 (9.50)	1	1
y_t	−0.208 (0.72)	−0.408 (1.58)	−1.018	−2.230 (2.16)	—	—	—
y_t^*	−0.171 (0.56)	−0.014 (0.06)	0.999	0.070 (0.18)	—	—	—
$(y-y^*)_t$	—	—	—	—	−0.770 (6.10)	−0.410 (2.50)	−0.230 (1.35)

	(1)	(2)	(3)	(4)	(5)	(6)	(7)
r_t	—	—	—	2.530 (2.16)	—	—	—
r_t^*	—	—	—	1.930 (2.88)	—	—	—
$(r-r^*)_t$	—	—	—	—	0.140 (7.60)	0.870 (0.54)	−1.050 (0.70)
$(r_L-r_L^*)_t$	—	—	—	—	—	—	10.270 (3.93)
$f\rho$	0.002 (0.59)	0.003 (1.39)	0.023 (1.46)	—	—	—	—
s_{t-1}	—	0.423 (2.95)	—	—	—	—	—
$s-m+m^*$	—	—	—	—	—	—	0.67 (6.09)
Constant	4.454 (4.78)	3.097 (2.21)	−0.014	7.850 (3.03)	—	1.130 (11.30)	0.46 (2.30)
R^2	0.92	0.96	0	0.66	0.88	N.A.	N.A.
Durbin–Watson	0.51	1.89	—	1.61	1.75	1.28	1.94
SER	0.047	0.031	—	0.37	—	0.021	0.018
$\hat\rho$	—	—	—	—	0.53	0.97	0.53

Where: SER, standard error of regression, R^2, co-efficient of determination, $\hat\rho$, estimated first order autocorrelation co-efficient. t ratios in parentheses.

income coefficients are both correctly signed, but only the US term is significant (although its magnitude is too great); the interest rate coefficients are both significant, but the German interest rate has the wrong sign. Notice that in the studies by Bilson (1978a, b) and Hodrick (1978) no account is taken of the potential simultaneous equation bias that may exist in monetary approach reduced forms.

In estimating equation (1.38) Bilson found it necessary to use a sophisticated econometric technique to account for the multicollinearity. An alternative, and much simpler, method that researchers have used to overcome this problem is to introduce relative money supplies, incomes and interest rates in a constrained fashion and estimate equation (1.36). Putnam and Woodbury (1979) estimate equation (1.36) for the UK pound–US dollar exchange rate over the period 1972–4 and their estimated result is reported as column E in table 1.3 (because OLS estimates of (1.36) revealed autocorrelation, the equation was estimated using the Hildreth–Lu technique). Notice that all the coefficients in column E are significantly different from zero at the 5 per cent significance level and all are correctly signed in terms of the monetary approach; however, the money supply term is significantly different from unity. Putnam and Woodbury fail to allow for any potential simultaneity between the right-hand side variables and the exchange rate in equation (1.36). Dornbusch (1979), in his study of the mark–dollar exchange rate (March 1974 to May 1978), proposed accounting for any simultaneity between $m - m^*$ and s by estimating equation (1.54). An equation representative of Dornbusch's results is reported as column F in table 1.3 and, although both the income and interest rate terms are correctly signed, only the former is significant. Furthermore, judging by the Durbin–Watson statistic the equation suffers from acute first-order autocorrelation even after the equation is initially estimated with a first-order autoregressive process specified for the error term. This may be a consequence of the lack of dynamics in the model. For instance, most single country money demand studies do not assume that money market equilibrium is continuously maintained and indeed find evidence of strongly significant partial adjustment terms (see for example Coghlan, 1978, for the UK and Goldfeld, 1976, for the USA). In an attempt to improve the performance of the monetary approach equation, Dornbusch assumes that the dependent variable $s - m + m^*$ follows a simple partial adjustment scheme and improves the specification of the money demand function by introducing a long-term interest rate as an additional opportunity cost variable (it is important to note that such specification changes will not be legitimate in models where regressive expectations are also assumed to be rational – see Minford and Peel, 1983, for a discussion). The resulting equation is

$$s_t = (m - m^*)_t + \alpha_0(s - m + m^*)_{t-1} + \alpha_1(y - y^*)_t + \alpha_2(r - r^*)_t + \alpha_3(r_L - r_L^*)_t \qquad (1.58)$$

where r_L is the long-term bond interest yield.

The estimates of this equation are reported as G in table 1.3. This specification of the FLPM reduced form is claimed by Dornbusch to be a substantial improvement over the simple monetary approach specification. In particular, the lagged adjustment term is significant, the long interest rate differential is statistically significant and the SER is lower than that for F; however, in other ways the equation is somewhat disappointing (e.g. the relative income and short interest rate terms are both insignificant).

The long interest rate term in equation (1.58) was included as an empirical expedient: its introduction was hoped to improve the empirical fit of equation (1.36). However, an interpretation may be placed on the long interest rate differential which is consistent with Frankel's RID equation. Thus Frankel (1979a) in his implementation of equation (1.51) for the mark–dollar exchange rate over the period July 1974 to February 1978 uses a long bond interest differential as an instrument for the expected inflation term, on the assumption that long-term real rates of interest are equalized. His estimated equation is

$$s_t = \begin{array}{c} 1.39 \\ (0.12) \end{array} + \begin{array}{c} 0.97 \\ (0.21) \end{array} (m - m^*) - \begin{array}{c} 0.52 \\ (0.22) \end{array} (y - y^*)_t - \begin{array}{c} 5.40 \\ (2.04) \end{array} (r - r^*)_t$$
$$+ \begin{array}{c} 29.40 \\ (3.33) \end{array} (\pi^e - \pi^{*e})_t \qquad (1.59)$$

$$R^2 = 0.91 \quad \hat{\rho} = 0.46$$

where estimated standard errors are given in parentheses. Comparing the coefficient signs in equation (1.59) with the hypothesized signs of the RID equation (1.51), we see that all variables are correctly signed and statistically significant. Frankel argues that since the coefficients on the interest rate and expected inflation terms are both significant the extreme FLPM and SPM models are both rejected in favour of his RID model (see table 1.2). Using the coefficient on the interest differential from equation (1.59), an estimate of θ in (1.47) may be obtained as $1/5.4$ (which equals 0.1854) so that 81.5 per cent of any deviation from PPP remains after one quarter and 44.1 per cent (i.e. $(0.815)^4$) is expected to obtain after one year.

The estimated values in equation (1.59) allow a calculation of how much the mark–dollar exchange rate would have to depreciate for a once-and-for-all increase in the US money supply of 1 per cent. The calculated fall in the RID (i.e. the SPM effect) gives a current exchange rate overshoot of 1.23 per cent. If, however, the monetary expansion signals to investors a new higher target for monetary growth, the initial overshooting will be greater. Frankel estimates that if agents' expected inflation rate is raised by 1 per cent per annum, this will lead to a short-run exchange rate overshoot of 1.58 per cent. Thus, neglect of the expected inflation effect biases our estimate of any short-run exchange rate overshooting downwards.

This completes our review of the early tests of the monetary approach to the exchange rate. On balance, the results seem to lend support to the monetary approach in both its FLPM and RID versions. However, for two reasons the results should be treated with caution. First, few researchers consider the simultaneity issue and the attention of those that do is focused only on the relative money supply term with no consideration of short-term interest rates. Second, all the researchers for the 1970s report autocorrelated residuals from their estimates of the monetary approach equation. Indeed Dornbusch (1979) reports autocorrelated residuals after correcting for first-order autocorrelation. This suggests that the monetary model is mis-specified: either variables which are important determinants of the exchange rate have been excluded or the dynamics of the equation, in terms of the lag structure, are inadequate. We shall return to these issues after discussing tests of the monetary approach equation for the second half of the floating period.

The second period tests of the flex-price monetary and interest differential reduced forms

Although the monetary approach appears to be reasonably well supported for the period up to 1978, the picture alters dramatically once the sample period is extended beyond 1978. For example, in table 1.4 we report estimates of the RID model by Dornbusch (1980), Haynes and Stone (1981), Backus (1984) and Frankel (1984), which cast serious doubt on its ability to track the exchange rate in-sample: few coefficients are correctly signed (many are wrongly signed), the equations have poor explanatory power in terms of the coefficient of determination, and autocorrelation is a problem. One particularly disturbing feature of columns A, C and D (the mark–dollar) is that the sign on the relative money supply term is negative for the period suggesting that an increase in the home relative money supply leads to an exchange rate *appreciation*! The latter phenomenon, of the price of the mark rising as its supply is increased, has been labelled by Frankel (1982a) the 'mystery of the multiplying marks' (we shall return to this below).

How can one explain this poor performance of the monetary approach equations for the second half of the floating sample? Rasulo and Wilford (1980) and Haynes and Stone (1981) have suggested that the root of the problem may be traced to the constraints imposed on relative monies, incomes and interest rates. The imposition of such constraints may be justified on the grounds that, if multicollinearity is present, constraining the variables will increase the efficiency of the coefficient estimates. However, Haynes and Stone (1981) show that the subtractive constraints used in monetary approach equations are particularly dangerous because they can lead to biased estimates and also (in contrast with additive constraints) to sign reversals, i.e. this could explain the 'perverse' sign on the relative money supply terms reported in table 1.4. Indeed, when Haynes and Stone estimate an unconstrained version of the RID model the sign on the relative money term is as predicted by the theory – see column E. However, notice that in Haynes and Stone's estimated equation we have a textbook example of multicollinearity: high R^2 combined with few statistically significant variables.

An alternative explanation for the poor performance of the monetary model in the second period has been given by Frankel (1982a): he attempts to explain the mystery of the multiplying marks by introducing wealth into the money demand equations. The justification for this inclusion is that Germany was running a current account surplus in the late 1970s which was redistributing wealth from US residents to German residents, thus increasing the demand for marks and reducing the demand for dollars, independently of the other arguments in the money demand functions. By including home and foreign wealth (defined as the sum of government debt and cumulated current account surpluses) in equation (1.51) and by not constraining the income, wealth and inflation terms to have equal and opposite signs, Frankel (1982a) reports a monetary approach equation in which all variables, apart from the income terms, are correctly signed and most are statistically significant; the explanatory power of the equation is also good.

A further explanation for the failure of the monetary approach equations may lie in the relative instability of the money demand functions underlying reduced forms such as (1.51). Thus, a number of single-country money demand studies strongly indicate that there have been shifts in velocity for the measure of money utilized by the above researchers (see Artis and Lewis, 1981, for a discussion). Frankel (1984) incorporates shifts in money demand functions into equation (1.51) by introducing a relative velocity shift term $v - v^*$, which is modelled by a distributed lag of $(p + y - m)$ – $(p^* + y^* - m^*)$. Including the $v - v^*$ term in equation (1.51) (along with a term capturing the real exchange rate – the inclusion of such a term in an asset reduced form will be considered below) for five currencies leads to most of the monetary variable coefficients becoming statistically significant and of the correct signs. However, significant first-order serial correlation remains a problem in all the reported equations.

Driskell and Sheffrin (1981) argue that the poor performance of the monetary model can be traced to the failure to account for the simultaneity bias introduced by having the expected change in the exchange rate (implicitly) on the right-hand side of monetary equations. However, taking account of this in a rational expectations framework, Driskell and Sheffrin (1981) find no support for the RID monetary model and suggest that the reason for its failure may lie in an assumption underlying all the monetary models – that assets are perfect substitutes. Relaxing this assumption implies

Table 1.4 The second-period tests of the flex-price monetary and real interest differential reduced forms

Variable	Dornbusch (1980) Dollar–mark February 1973–1979 AR 1 A	OLS B	Frankel (1984) Mark–dollar February 1974–July 1981 AR 1 C	Haynes and Stone (1981) Mark–dollar July 1974–April 1980 AR 1 D	AR 1 E	Backus (1984) Canadian dollar–US dollar 1971 1st quarter–1980 4th quarter OLS F
m_t	—	—	—	—	0.24 (0.84)	—
m_t^*	—	—	—	—	−1.84 (3.95)	—
$(m - m^*)_t$	−0.03 (0.07)	1	−0.05 (0.15)	−0.57 (1.89)	—	1.097 (3.64)
y_t	—	—	—	—	0.20 (0.77)	—
y_t^*	—	—	—	—	0.56 (2.20)	—
$(y - y^*)_t$	−1.05 (0.97)	0.16 (0.17)	0.07 (0.32)	0.02 (0.08)	—	−0.453 (0.82)

r_t	—	—	—	—	0.02 (0.01)	—
r_t^*	—	—	—	—	-2.50 (1.29)	—
$(r - r^*)_t$	0.01 (1.90)	-0.01 (1.36)	-0.61 (2.26)	0.22 (0.13)	—	-0.000 (0.03)
$\Delta p^e - \Delta p^{e*}$	0.04 (2.07)	0.01 (0.67)	1.34 (1.63)	13.33 (3.57)	—	-0.106 (3.00)
Δp^e	—	—	—	—	2.62 (0.67)	—
Δp^{e*}	—	—	—	—	3.53 (0.75)	—
$(s - m + m^*)_{t-1}$	—	0.83 (8.26)	—	—	—	—
Constant	5.76 (2.81)	0.23 (0.12)	0.80 (3.80)	-4.08 (23.40)	1.86 (1.65)	—
$\bar{R}^2$	0.33	0.88	—	0.38	0.85	0.43
Durbin–Watson	1.83	1.85	0.33	—	—	0.60
SER	0.05	1.85	0.95	—	—	—
$\hat{\rho}$	0.88	—	—	0.77	0.59	—

t ratios in parentheses.

that an additional variable such as a risk premium needs to be included in the monetary model. This line of argument supports our earlier contention that the persistent autocorrelation reported in monetary models is suggestive of model mis-specification. In section 1.3.4 we investigate attempts to improve on the basic monetary models by introducing a broader menu of variables, but first we look at the empirical implementation of the SPM and portfolio balance approaches.

Tests of the sticky price monetary reduced form equation

We now turn to some empirical estimates of the SPM reduced form. Driskell (1981) presents an estimate of equation (1.46) for the Swiss franc–US dollar rate for the period 1973–7 (quarterly data):

$$s_t = 2.22 + 0.43s_{t-1} + 2.37(m - m^*)_t - 2.45(m - m^*)_{t-1} +$$
$$ (2.82) \quad (3.65) \qquad (5.73) \qquad\qquad (5.60)$$

$$0.93(p - p^*)_{t-1} \qquad\qquad\qquad (1.60)$$
$$(2.23)$$

$$R^2 = 0.99 \qquad \text{Durbin's } h = 0.21 \qquad \hat{\rho} = 0.35$$
$$\phantom{R^2 = 0.99 \qquad \text{Durbin's } h = 0.21 \qquad} (1.37)$$

where, because of the unavailability of a quarterly income series, the *y* terms have been dropped and the presence of first-order autocorrelation necessitated estimation using the Cochrane–Orchutt procedure. Note that $\Sigma\pi$ equals 1.28 and is insignificantly different from unity at the 5 per cent level, thus supporting PPP as a long-run phenomenon. Interestingly, although the coefficient on m'_t is greater than unity, which is clearly supportive of the perfect capital mobility version of the SPM model, the coefficients on s_{t-1} and p'_{t-1} are both positive, which is supportive of the imperfect capital mobility version of the SPM model. Driskell does not use a structural equation estimator to account for potential simultaneity between *s* and *m'* on the grounds that the Swiss franc's float was relatively clean for this period (because of currency substitution the Swiss authorities adopted a managed float in the period after 1977 – see Vaubel, 1980).

Other tests of the SPM reduced form have been conducted by Wallace (1979), Hacche and Townend (1981) and Backus (1984). Wallace estimates using OLS and unconstrained version of equation (1.46) for the Canadian dollar–US dollar for the period 1951 second quarter to 1961 second quarter. Results supportive of the SPM model are presented and, interestingly, it is shown that the coefficient on the domestic money supply is significantly less than unity which is supportive of the imperfect capital mobility version of the model. Backus (1984) tests equation (1.46) for the same exchange rate as Wallace for the recent Canadian floating experience (1971 quarter first to

1980 fourth quarter) and in support of the earlier results finds no evidence of overshooting ($\Sigma\pi = 0.16$). However, Backus's OLS results differ from those of Wallace in that he finds few statistically significant coefficients. Estimates of a more dynamic version of equation (1.46) by Hacche and Townend (1981) for the UK pound effective exchange rate, May 1972 to February 1980, are suggestive of exchange rate overshooting, but in other respects the estimated equation is unsatisfactory: many coefficients are insignificant and wrongly signed and the equation does not exhibit sensible long-run properties. Clearly, the problems associated with the models discussed in the previous section are equally valid here, and this may explain the mixed empirical support for equation (1.46). A version of the SPM model due to Buiter and Miller (1981) has been empirically implemented by Barr (this volume) and Smith and Wickens (1987, 1988). Barr (this volume) reports results favourable to the Buiter–Miller model. Favourable empirical estimates of the Buiter–Miller model are also presented by Smith and Wickens (1987, 1988) who estimate the model structurally for sterling's effective exchange rate (period 1973–81). In simulating the model, Smith and Wickens (1987) find that the exchange rate overshoots by 21 per cent in response to a 5 per cent change in the level of the money supply.

1.3.3 The portfolio balance approach

As we discussed in section 1.2, the distinctive features of the PBM are that domestic and foreign bonds are assumed to be imperfect substitutes and wealth enters asset demand equations as a scale variable. Thus the asset sector of a simple portfolio model for the home country (similar relationships are assumed to hold for the foreign country) may be described as

$$m_t - p_t = \alpha_0 y_t + \alpha_1 r_t + \alpha_2 r_t^* + \alpha_3 w_t$$
$$\alpha_0, \alpha_3 > 0; \; \alpha_1, \alpha_2 < 0 \qquad (1.61)$$

$$b_t - p_t = \beta_0 y_t + \beta_1 r_t + \beta_2 r_t^* + \beta_3 w_t$$
$$\beta_0, \beta_1, \beta_3 > 0; \; \beta_2 < 0 \qquad (1.62)$$

$$f_t + s_t - p_t = \pi_0 y_t + \pi_1 r_t + \pi_2 r_t^* + \pi_3 w_t$$
$$\pi_0, \pi_2, \pi_3 > 0; \; \pi_1 < 0 \qquad (1.63)$$

where b denotes domestic (non-traded) bonds, f denotes foreign (traded) bonds, w denotes real wealth, money and bond demands have been set equal to their respective supplies and home and foreign interest rates are linked via the interest parity relationship. The main implication of equations (1.61)–(1.63) is that the exchange rate is determined not just by money market conditions, as in the monetary model, but also by conditions in bond markets.

Compared with the monetary approach to the exchange rate, relatively little empirical work has been conducted on the PBM, mainly because of the limited availability of good disaggregated data on non-monetary assets. Broadly, two types of empirical test of the PBM have been conducted by researchers. The first concentrates on solving the short-run portfolio model as a reduced form (assuming that expectations are static) in order to determine its explanatory power (this is the approach adopted by, for example, Branson et al., 1977). The second, indirect type of test involves solving the PBM for the risk premium in the UIP equation (1.32) in order to determine whether bonds denominated in different currencies are perfect substitutes.[5] The latter type of test is considered in section 1.4 and also by MacDonald and Taylor (1988a).

The reduced form exchange rate equation derived from the above system may be written as (see Branson et al., 1977) (the assumed short-run nature of the relationship allows y and p to be assumed exogenous and constant)

$$s_t = g(m_t, m^*_t, b_t, b^*_t, f_t, f^*_t) \tag{1.64}$$

Branson et al. (1977) estimate a log-linear version of equation (1.64) for the German mark–US dollar exchange rate, August 1971 to December 1976. The actual form of the equation estimated is

$$s_t = \alpha_0 + \alpha_1 m_t + \alpha_2 m^*_t + \alpha_3 f_t + \alpha_4 f^*_t + \epsilon_t \tag{1.65}$$

where the money supplies are defined as M1 and the foreign assets are proxied by cumulated current accounts. To move from (1.64) to (1.65), Branson et al. drop the b and b^* terms because of the ambiguous effect that they have on the exchange rate. However, as Bisignano and Hoover (1983) point out, this rather arbitrary exclusion will generally result in biased regression coefficients. Although the OLS estimates of equation (1.65) are deemed supportive of the PBM, once account is taken of acute first-order autocorrelation only one coefficient, that on the US money supply, is statistically significant. By specifying a simple reaction function, which purports to capture the simultaneity of the German money supply, Branson et al. re-estimate equation (1.65) using two-stage least squares and report more satisfactory estimates of the portfolio model; however, autocorrelation remains a problem (the estimate of ρ is 0.87 which suggests that unexplained shocks have persistent effects on the exchange rate and hence that this version of the PBM does not fully explain the mark–dollar exchange rate). Branson et al. (1979) estimate equation (1.65) for the longer period, August 1971 to December 1978, for the mark–dollar, but the results are shown not to differ significantly from the earlier ones; again persistent autocorrelation is a problem. In a further paper, Branson and Halttunen (1979) estimate equation (1.65) for five currencies (the Japanese yen, the French franc, the

Italian lira, the Swiss franc and the UK pound) against the German mark for a variety of samples over the 1970s. Although Branson and Halttunen report equations which seem supportive of the PBM, in terms of statistically significant and correct coefficients, a note of caution must be sounded since the residuals in their OLS equations are all highly autocorrelated.

One problem with the Branson et al. implementation of the PBM lies in its use of cumulated current accounts for the stock of foreign assets. Such an approximation will, of course, include third-country items which are not strictly relevant to the determination of the bilateral exchange rate in question. Bisignano and Hoover (1983) pick up this point and argue that the PBM approach should be implemented using only bilateral data for foreign assets and also that, to be consistent, b and b^* should be included in the PBM reduced form (see above). Incorporating such modifications in their estimates of equation (1.65) for the Canadian dollar–US dollar, over the period March 1973 to December 1978, Bisignano and Hoover (1983) report moderately successful econometric results; in particular, they show that it is wrong to neglect domestic non-monetary asset stocks in exchange rate reduced forms.

1.3.4 The portfolio balance and monetary reduced forms: a synthesis

In an attempt to improve on the estimates of the reduced form monetary approach and portfolio balance equations, and in particular to overcome the model mis-specification suggested by the typically high value of the first-order autocorrelation coefficient in such equations, a number of researchers have attempted to combine features of both the monetary and portfolio approaches into a reduced form exchange rate equation. Thus, if risk is important the monetary approach reduced form will be mis-specified to the extent that it ignores the imperfect substitutability of non-money assets. The portfolio balance reduced form is also likely to be mis-specified because of its failure to incorporate expectations into the model (i.e. the reduced form equations in section 1.3.3 were derived by invoking static expectations rather than the more general formulation of the REPBM considered in section 1.2). However, since the PBM stresses that in long-run equilibrium the real exchange rate will be determined so as to balance the current account, we would expect, with rational expectations, that agents would revise their estimates of the expected real exchange rate as new information about the future path of the current account reaches the market: the spot exchange rate in a portfolio balance reduced form should include news about the current account as an explanatory variable. We now turn to some empirical attempts to synthesize the portfolio and monetary approaches, with emphasis being placed on the modelling of the risk premium and news about the current account.

Two developments of our basic monetary approach framework are required to derive a hybrid portfolio–monetary approach equation. First, we divide the equilibrium nominal exchange rate into relative price and real components:

$$\bar{s}_t = \bar{p}_t - \bar{p}_t^* + \bar{q}_t \tag{1.66}$$

where $\bar{q}_t$ is the equilibrium real exchange rate. Following Hooper and Morton (1982) we assume that the expected change in the equilibrium real exchange rate is zero and $\bar{q}$ moves over time in response to unexpected developments, or news, about the current account, c. Thus

$$\bar{q}_t - \bar{q}_{t-1} = \alpha(c_t - E_{t-1}c_t) \qquad \alpha < 0 \tag{1.67}$$

and on integrating this expression over time we obtain

$$\bar{q}_t = \bar{q}_0 + \alpha \sum_{i=0}^{n} (c_{t-i} - E_{t-1-i}c_{t-i}) \tag{1.68}$$

i.e. the equilibrium exchange rate in period t is a function of an initial condition $\bar{q}_0$ and the cumulative sum of past (non-transitory) unexpected current account shocks. The second relationship utilized in the derivation of a hybrid monetary–portfolio model is a UIP equation

$$r_t - r_t^* - \Delta s_{t+1}^e = \rho \tag{1.69}$$

which is familiar from our discussion in section 1.3.1 but where we now assume that the risk premium is constant.

By substituting the regressive expectations equation (1.47) into (1.69), we obtain

$$s_t - \bar{s}_t = \theta^{-1}[(r - \pi^e)_t - (r^* - \pi^{*e}_t] + \theta^{-1}\rho \tag{1.70}$$

and by substituting (1.50), (1.66) and (1.68) into (1.70) we obtain the following hybrid model:

$$s = m' + \beta_1 y' + \beta_2 \pi^{e'} - \beta_3(r' - \pi^{e'}) + \beta_4\rho$$

$$+ \sum_{i=0}^{n} [c_{t-i} - E_{t-1-i}c_{t-1}] + \bar{q}_0 \tag{1.71}$$

Versions of (1.71) have been estimated by a number of researchers (Isard, 1980; Hooper and Morton, 1982; Frankel, 1983, 1984; Hacche and Townend, 1983). In Hooper and Morton's implementation of equation (1.71) the risk premium is assumed to be a function of the cumulated current account surplus net of the cumulation of foreign exchange market intervention. With this modification, the equation is estimated for the dollar effective exchange rate 1973 second quarter to 1978 fourth quarter using an instrumental variables estimator; representative coefficients are reported in table 1.5 in column A. Notice that all the monetary approach variables in column A enter with the correct sign and two are statistically significant but that of the portfolio balance variables only the current account news term is statistically significant (and correctly signed); the risk premium is insignificant (and wrongly signed). An interesting feature of the equation is the absence of first-order autocorrelation (the researchers unfortunately do not report diagnostics for higher-order autocorrelation) and thus on this criterion we appear to have a better specified reduced form exchange rate equation than either the simple monetary or portfolio balance reduced form equation. Another interesting feature of the Hooper and Morton reduced form is that it can be used to show that about 80 per cent of the dollar's decline in 1977–8 can be explained by the current account revision term and only 20 per cent by the monetary approach variables (see the discussion above regarding the breakdown of the monetary model for the mark–dollar rate post-1977).

Using Hooper and Morton's specification, Hacche and Townend (1983) implement equation (1.71), with the addition of the price of oil, for the sterling effective exchange rate over the period June 1972 to December 1981. A representative result reported as column B in table 1.5 is clearly disappointing: few coefficients are significant and, of those that are, the risk premium is wrongly signed and the oil price term rightly signed. In contrast with Hooper and Morton's estimates, column B exhibits severe first-order autocorrelation. Two factors may explain the poor performance of Hacche and Townend's implementation of equation (1.71). One is the use of monthly data which is widely regarded as being extremely noisy, resulting in a low signal to noise ratio. Also, in contrast with Hooper and Morton, Hacche and Townend do not use a simultaneous equation estimator and thus their results are likely to be biased and inconsistent.

In Frankel's (1984) implementation of the portfolio–monetary hybrid reduced form model, the current account news term is not considered and the risk premium is derived as the solution to the PBM (see chapter 5). The Frankel version of equation (1.71) is estimated for five currencies against the dollar for the period 1974–81 (monthly data, with the exact beginning and end points being currency specific). Two of Frankel's equations, for the German mark–US dollar and the UK pound–US dollar, are reported as columns C and D in table 1.5. Interestingly, although all the monetary coefficients are insignificant and some are wrongly signed, the risk premium terms, in contrast with the estimates in the previous section, are significant and correctly signed in four of the six terms. The failure of the monetary variables to enter with significant coefficients may perhaps be traced, as in the Hacche and Townend estimates, to the use of monthly data and the failure to account for simultaneity.

Table 1.5 The hybrid monetary-portfolio model

Variable	Hopper and Morton (1982) Dollar effective 1973 1st quarter– 1978 4th quarter Instrumental A	Hacche and Townsend (1983) Sterling effective November 1977– December 1981 ALS B	Frankel German mark– US dollar February 1974– July 1981 ALS C	Frankel UK pound– US dollar February 1974– June 1981 ALS D
$m - m^*$	0.770 (2.56)	0.032 (0.84)	0.150 (1.50)	−0.030 (0.6)
$y - y^*$	−1.840 (2.72)	−0.114 (1.01)	0.060 (1.20)	0.030 (0.75)
$\pi^e - \pi^{e*}$	2.410 (0.98)	−0.005 (1.66)	−0.240 (1.00)	0.000 (0)
$(i - \pi^e) - (i^* - \pi^{e*})$	−0.150 (0.27)	−0.009 (1.80)	0.050 (1.00)	0.030 (0.60)
$c - Ec$	−1.690 (3.90)	0.033 (0.47)	—	—

	(1)	(2)	(3)	(4)
ρ	0.970 (0.82)	-0.095 (4.32)	—	—
Oil price	—	0.139 (5.79)	—	—
B/W	—	—	-0.060 (0.14)	-3.440 (10.75)
W_a/W	—	—	-2.210 (6.90)	2.260 (5.14)
W_{US}/W	—	—	1.130 (7.06)	1.670 (11.93)
Constant	4.550 (131.90)	3.733 (28.72)	-0.050 (0.22)	-2.070 (8.63)
R^2	0.78	0.97	—	—
Durbin-Watson	1.87	—	—	—
SER	—	0.014	0.008	0.007
$\hat{\rho}$	—	0.778 (6.59)	0.98 (-)	1.00 (-)

1.3.5 The out-of-sample forecasting performance of some asset approach reduced forms

Hitherto, we have considered only the in-sample properties of the asset approach reduced forms. A stronger test of the model's validity would be to determine how well they perform out-of-sample compared with an alternative, such as the naive random walk model. Meese and Rogoff (hereafter MR) (1983) have conducted such a study for the dollar–pound, dollar–mark, dollar–yen and trade-weighted dollar exchange rates using data running from March 1973 to June 1981. The reduced form asset equations tested by MR in their study are the FLPM model (equation (1.36)), the RID model (equation (1.51)) and the portfolio–monetary synthesis equation (1.71). The out-of-sample performance of these equations is compared with the forecasting performance of the random walk model, the forward exchange rate, a univariate autoregression of the spot rate and a vector autoregression formed using lagged values of the explanatory variables of equation (1.51) plus cumulated home and foreign trade balances. MR compute their forecasts in the following way. First, the equations are estimated using data from the beginning of the sample to November 1976 and four forecasts are made for one, three, six and twelve months ahead. The data for December 1976 are then added to the original data set, the equations are re-estimated and a further set of forecasts is made for the four time horizons. This 'rolling regression' process is then continually repeated. The statistics used to gauge the out-of-sample properties of the models are the mean error (ME), the mean absolute error (MAE) and the root mean square error (RMSE). A sample of MR's RMSE results (for the six-month forecast and excluding the forward rate, univariate and vector autoregression forecasts) are reported in table 1.6 where the reduced forms derived from structural models have been estimated using the Fair (1970) procedure.

The devastating conclusion that emerges from table 1.6 is that none of the asset reduced forms considered outperform the simple random walk model. This result is all the more striking when it is remembered that the reduced form forecasts have been computed using actual values of the various assets etc. To try to improve on the poor performance of the asset reduced forms, MR alternatively attempt to estimate the models in first differences, allow home and foreign magnitudes to enter unconstrained, include price levels as additional explanatory variables, use different definitions of the money supply and replace long-term interest rates with other proxies for inflationary expectations. But all to no avail: the modified reduced form equations still fail to outperform the simple random walk model.

In a further paper, MR (1984) consider possible explanations of why the reduced form asset models fail to beat the random walk model out of sample.

Table 1.6 Root mean square forecast errors for selected exchange rate equations

Exchange rate	Forecast horizon	Random walk	FLPM	RID	Monetary–portfolio synthesis
Dollar–mark	6 months	8.71	9.64	12.03	9.95
Dollar–yen	6 months	11.58	13.38	13.94	11.94
Dollar–pound	6 months	6.45	8.90	8.88	9.08
Trade-weighted dollar	6 months	6.09	7.07	6.49	7.11

Source: Meese and Rogoff, 1983

In particular, MR (1984) show – using the vector autoregressive methodology – that the instruments used in simultaneous estimates of asset reduced forms may not be truly exogenous and thus that the estimated parameters may be extremely imprecise. To overcome this problem MR impose coefficient constraints, culled from the empirical literature on money demand equations, on the asset reduced forms and re-estimate the RMSEs for the same period as MR (1983). Interestingly, MR find that although the coefficient-constrained asset reduced forms still fail to outperform the random walk model for most horizons up to a year, they find that in forecasting beyond a year (which was not possible because of degrees of freedom problems with the unconstrained estimates in MR 1983) the asset reduced forms do outperform the random walk model in terms of RMSE. As Salemi (1984) points out, this tends to suggest that the exchange rate acts like a pure asset price in the short term (i.e. approximately a random walk – see for example Samuelson, 1965) but that in the longer term its equilibrium is systematically related to other economic variables.

Finn (1986) estimates the rational expectations form of the FLPM model, equation (1.40) (with allowance for partial adjustment in money demand), using vector autoregressions to model expected future income and money, and performs an out-of-sample forecasting test similar to that of MR (Woo, 1985, conducts a similar exercise). Surprisingly, for forecast horizons of one, six and twelve months, the model performs well in the sense of having RMSEs and MAEs close to those of a random walk model. Finn attributes this to explicit, and therefore more accurate, allowance for the dynamics of the forcing variables. However, despite the improvement in forecasting performance, even the rational expectations formulation of the FLPM model fails to *outperform* a simple random walk model. We outline below some other possible explanations for the poor out-of-sample forecasting performance of the exchange rate. But one problem with MR's tests of the out-of-sample forecasting performance of asset approach reduced forms is that they use monthly data. As we discussed earlier, monthly data is inherently noisy and perhaps it is unfair to expect the asset approach to perform particularly well on such data.

1.3.6 Empirical exchange rate models: summing up

In this section the econometric evidence on models of exchange rate determination has been considered in some detail. The broad conclusion that emerges is that the asset approach seems to work well for some time periods, such as the interwar period, and, to some extent, for the first part of the recent floating experience (i.e. 1973–8), but not so well for the second part of the recent float (see earlier).

The failure of simple asset approach equations to perform satisfactorily for the latter period may be due to mis-specification. Such mis-specification may be of an econometric nature in so far as the dynamic properties of the asset equations, in relation to the Hendry et al. (1984) methodology, have been very poorly specified (the persistent indication of first-order auto-correlation is supportive of this view). Simple asset reduced forms may also be mis-specified from an economic point of view. Thus the 'breakdown' in the performance of the monetary model could be a consequence of the omission of important variables such as the current account, wealth and risk factors. However, when such additions are added to the simple asset models little improvement in equation performance is reported. One useful way of ensuring that the exchange rate models are correctly specified (in terms of the correct variables to include, the exogeneity assumptions made and the dynamic specifications) is to estimate the models structurally, and this seems to be a useful avenue for future research (see Kearney and MacDonald, 1985, and Smith and Wickens, 1988, for recent examples).

A more general explanation for the failure of researchers to implement asset approach reduced forms successfully may be traced to the innumerable instabilities impinging on the international monetary system during the 1970s and 1980s. We referred earlier to the general instability of money demand equations in this period, but other instabilities, less amenable to incorporation in an econometric model, were also particularly important. Thus, factors such as the debt problems of the less developed countries (LDCs), the oil crisis and the shifting institutional arrangements of the international monetary system have all played a role in imparting instability to the world economic order of the last 15 years.

Perhaps the most devastating conclusion of this section is the finding that all the asset approach reduced forms fail to beat a naive random walk model in an out-of-sample forecasting context. The explanatory power of the random walk model is to some extent supportive of the view that the exchange rate is an asset price and behaves in an analogous fashion to other asset prices. More generally, if the exchange rate is an asset price then the EMH suggests that the tests reported in this chapter are somewhat misplaced. Thus, instead of regressing the actual exchange rate on actual asset stocks etc., the researcher perhaps should be regressing the unanticipated exchange rate on unanticipated movements, or news, in asset markets. Perhaps an empirical investigation utilizing such measures would offer more support to the asset approach (the extant evidence on the news approach is reported in section 1.5).

1.4 THE EFFICIENT MARKETS HYPOTHESIS

The previous sections have surveyed the theory and evidence on asset market approaches to exchange rate determination. One particular aspect of asset prices is that they are usually regarded as being determined in efficient markets and it seems natural to ask whether the foreign exchange market behaves in a manner consistent with the EMH. More specifically, are forward exchange rates optimal predictors of future exchange rates? Is the market using all relevant information in forming its expectations of future spot rates? Are unexpected changes in the exchange rate random? Does the exchange rate follow a random walk (indeed does market efficiency necessarily imply random exchange rate changes)? These are the issues considered in this section.

1.4.1 The efficient markets hypothesis and the forward market for foreign exchange

Following Fama (1970), an efficient market can be defined as a market which 'fully reflects' all relevant information instantly. Thus it should not be possible for a market operator to earn abnormal profits. The macro-economic importance of efficient asset markets derives from the fact that they can be shown to be conducive to an optimal allocation of resources (Fama, 1970, 1976). As Levich (1979) has emphasized, in order to implement the hypothesis empirically and to make sense of the term 'fully reflect', some view of equilibrium expected returns or equilibrium prices is required. Using equilibrium expected returns, for example, the excess market return on asset i is given by

$$z_{it} = x_{it} - E(\bar{x}_{it}|I_{t-1})$$

where x_{it} is the one-period percentage return, I_{t-1} is the information set, a bar denotes an equilibrium value and z_{it} represents the excess market return. If the market for asset i is efficient then the sequence z_{it} should be orthogonal to the information set ($E(z_{it}|I_{t-1}) = 0$) and serially uncorrelated. This example

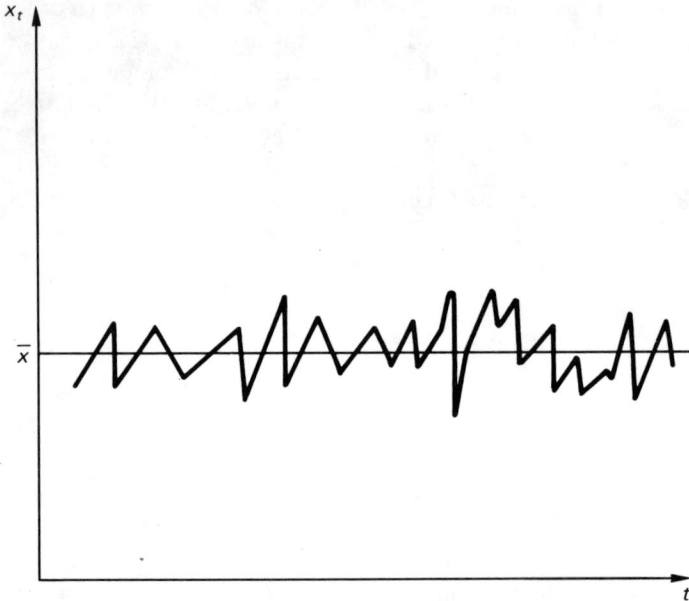

Figure 1.16   Asset returns with a constant equilibrium

makes clear that the EMH is a *joint hypothesis* because it assumes that agents in forming their expectations in period $t - 1$ are rational, in the sense that they do not make systematic forecasting errors, and that they know the market equilibrium process. This clearly raises an important issue for the testing of the EMH. Thus, a researcher who rejects the EMH for some asset cannot discern whether the rejection is due to the irrationality of market participants or to his mis-specification of the equilibrium expected returns. Levich (1979) has usefully demonstrated this issue with two examples which counter the view that market efficiency necessarily implies that prices should follow a random walk. In figure 1.16 actual market returns x_t are assumed to vibrate randomly around the constant equilibrium expected return $\bar{x}$.

In Figure 1.17 actual returns again fluctuate randomly around the expected equilibrium return $\bar{x}_t$, but in this case the equilibrium return is assumed to be non-constant. In figure 1.16 prices follow a random walk with drift (equal to $\bar{x}$). In figure 1.17 prices do not follow a random walk since prices and returns are serially correlated around their mean values. Thus, even if asset prices do not follow a random walk, the market may still be efficient: randomness in price movements is neither a necessary nor a sufficient condition for market efficiency. This is a point which a number of researchers of the efficiency of foreign exchange markets have failed to appreciate (see for example Caves and Feige, 1980).

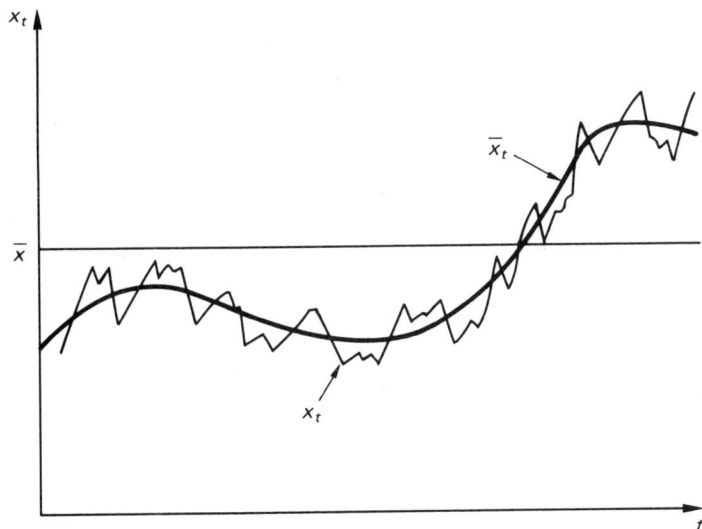

Figure 1.17   Asset returns with a time-varying equilibrium

Grossman and Stiglitz (1980) have pointed to a conundrum underlying our definition of efficiency. For example, if asset prices *do* fully and instantly reflect all available information, then presumably there will be no incentive for individuals to collect and process information since this will already have been reflected in market prices. How can market prices simultaneously reflect all relevant information *and* give agents potential profits to induce arbitrage? This paradox is in fact more apparent than real, since data are collected for discrete periods and all that is necessary for market efficiency is that arbitrage has occurred within the period, i.e. there may be very short-run arbitrage opportunities available. This assumption allows us to analyse the effects of information on asset prices without modelling the actual arbitrage process.

Efficiency can be more precisely defined with reference to the information set available to market operators (i.e. I_{t-1} in our examples above). For example, and again following Fama (1970), a market is described as *weakly efficient* when it is not possible for a trader to make abnormal returns using only the past history of prices or returns. If, on increasing the information set to include all publicly available information (e.g. information on money supplies, interest rates and income), it is still not possible for a market participant to make abnormal profits, then the market is said to be *semi-strong form efficient*. *Strong form efficiency* holds when it is impossible for a trader to make abnormal profits using a trading rule based on either public or private information. For the purposes of our discussion in this chapter, only the weak and semi-strong form efficiency definitions will have relevance. Strong form efficiency may have implications for the presence of insider trading.

As Minford and Peel (1983) point out, semi-strong form efficiency conforms most closely with the concept of rational expectations since agents are assumed to know the model generating equilibrium prices and use publicly available information in determining the expectations of the asset price. However, weak form efficiency may also be equivalent to rational expectations if agents' information set is restricted to the past history of prices because of, say, the costs of obtaining and processing the information set underlying the true economic model (see Feige and Pierce, 1976).

The above discussion concerning efficient markets has general applicability to a whole range of asset prices. We now consider the application of the hypothesis to the forward market for foreign exchange. First, it is assumed that agents, at time $t-1$, set the one-period forward exchange rate, for maturity in period t, equal to the expected future spot rate for period t:

$$s_t^e = f_{t-1} \tag{1.72}$$

In a world where speculators are risk neutral and there are no impediments to arbitrage, such as transaction costs or liquidity constraints, speculation will ensure that (1.72) holds continuously (thus, (1.72) captures our market equilibrium relationship). The second leg of the joint hypothesis of efficiency is that speculators are rational and thus

$$s_t = s_t^e + u_t \tag{1.73}$$

where s_t^e is equal to $E(s_t|I_{t-1})$, $E(.|.)$ is the conditional mathematical expectational operator, I_{t-1} is the information set at time $t-1$ on which expectations are conditioned and u_t is a white noise error term orthogonal to I_{t-1}. By using (1.73) we obtain the market efficiency condition under the stated assumptions

$$s_t = f_{t-1} + u_t \tag{1.74}$$

which simply states that the spot rate in period t should be equal to the corresponding forward rate plus a random forecasting error $E(u_t|I_{t-1}) = 0$.

The sensitivity of market efficiency with respect to the assumed joint hypothesis may be demonstrated in the following way. Suppose that agents are rational, so that equation (1.73) continues to hold, but that they are risk averse and therefore in order to be persuaded to hold forward foreign exchange have to receive a risk premium to compensate for the uncertainty regarding the expected future spot rate. This may be written as

$$f_{t-1} = s_t^e + \rho_{t-1} \tag{1.75}$$

For example, we might assume that the risk premium ρ_{t-1} may be modelled as

$$\rho_{t-1} = \alpha + \epsilon_{t-1} \tag{1.76}$$

where α is the mean of the risk premium and the term ϵ_{t-1} is a (possibly serially correlated) stochastic term that allows for the possibility that the risk premium may vary randomly over time (see for example Frenkel, 1981). Using (1.75) instead of (1.72) we obtain

$$s_t = -\alpha + f_{t-1} + u_t - \epsilon_{t-1}$$

where, as Frenkel (1981) notes, the forward exchange rate is a 'noisy' predictor of the future exchange rate. Thus, one might econometrically estimate an equation of the form

$$s_t = a_0 + a_1 f_{t-1} + \phi_t \tag{1.77}$$

If speculators are risk neutral, market efficiency implies that $a_0 = 0$, $a_1 = 1$ (the joint hypothesis of unbiasedness) and the forecast error ϕ_t should be serially uncorrelated and orthogonal to the information set (i.e. $E(\phi_t | I_{t-1}) = 0$). If such conditions hold then the forward exchange rate is regarded as an efficient predictor of the future spot rate. If, however, speculators are risk averse we would expect a_0 to be significantly different from zero, the error term to be correlated with f_{t-1} resulting in biased and inconsistent estimates of a_1, and the error term to be non-white. Hence, if we estimate equation (1.77) by OLS, believing that equation (1.72) holds, and find that a_0 is statistically significant and a_1 is statistically different from unity, we may be wrong to conclude that market participants are irrational since our results may simply reflect the existence of a risk premium as defined by (1.76). In order to allow market efficiency to encompass a risk premium, Bilson (1981) classifies equation (1.74) as the speculative efficiency hypothesis. However, in common with most other researchers we shall define (1.74) as (forward) market efficiency.

If the foreign exchange market is efficient then, as has been suggested, f_{t-1} should contain all the relevant information for forecasting the future spot rate s_t. Thus on adding information to (1.77), available to agents when they are forming their expectations, we should obtain statistically insignificant coefficient estimates for the additional variables. More specifically, since the forward rate at time $t-1$ summarizes all relevant information available to the market, it should contain all relevant information contained in the forward rates f_{t-2}, f_{t-3} and so on, and thus add further lagged values should not improve the equation's explanatory power. For example, in estimating equation (1.78)

$$s_t = a_0 + a_1 f_{t-1} + a_2 f_{t-2} + u_t \tag{1.78}$$

market efficiency, in the absence of a risk premium, implies that $a_0 = 0$, $a_1 = 1$, $a_2 = 0$ and that the error term is white and orthogonal to I_{t-1}. The effects of lagged information, which should have already been incorporated in the period $t - 1$ forward rate, may be tested in an alternative way. By sub-tracting f_{t-1} from s_t we obtain the current period forecasting error $s_t - f_{t-1}$ and if the market is efficient this forecasting error should be uncorrelated with past forecasting errors, i.e.[6]

$$s_t - f_{t-1} = a_0 + a_i \sum_{i=0}^{n} (s_{t-i} - f_{t-1-i}) + u_t \tag{1.79}$$

where market efficiency implies that the constant and all other coefficients should equal zero and u_t should be white noise.

The above tests of the EMH may be classified as weak tests since the information set used includes only the past history of exchange rates. Hansen and Hodrick (1980) classify the incorporation of lagged forecasting errors from *other* exchange markets as a semi-strong form test of market efficiency. Thus, in a regression of the forecasting error from market k,

$$s_t^k - f_{t-1}^k = a_k + \sum_{i=0}^{n} \sum_{j=1}^{m} a_{ij}(s_{t-i}^j - f_{t-1-i}^j) + \epsilon_t^k \tag{1.80}$$

On its own lagged forecasting error and the lagged forecasting error from m other markets, semi-strong form efficiency implies that the intercept and a_{ij} terms should be statistically insignificant. A semi-strong form test may also be captured by the equation

$$s_t - f_{t-1} = a_0 + \mathbf{a}_1' X_{t-1} + u_t \tag{1.81}$$

where X represents an $n \times 1$ vector of publicly available information, such as money supplies, and it is expected that a_0 and the vector $\mathbf{a}_1$ equal zero.

Although equation (1.77) proved the most popular way of testing the efficiency of the forward exchange market for the early part of the recent float, more recent research has tested this relationship in rates of change. This follows from the findings of a number of researchers (see for example Hansen and Hodrick, 1980; Meese and Singleton, 1982; Meese and Rogoff, 1984; MacDonald and Taylor, 1987a, b) that the stochastic processes generating s_t and f_{t-1} may be non-stationary and in fact contain a unit root. Thus, on subtracting s_{t-1} from s_t and f_{t-1} in (1.77), we obtain

$$s_t - s_{t-1} = a_0 + a_1(f_{t-1} - s_{t-1}) + u_t \tag{1.82}$$

where, again, it is expected that $a_0 = 0$, $a_1 = 1$ and u_t is a white noise process orthogonal to the information set on which agents form their expectations.

Tests of equation (1.82) are a means of determining how good a predictor the forward premium is of the actual realized change in the exchange rate (see for example Bilson, 1981; Fama, 1984; Taylor, 1988a).

As we shall see below, all researchers who test equation (1.82) find that the joint efficiency hypothesis is rejected by the data. Most researchers have attributed such rejection either to the existence of a time-varying risk premium or to the irrationality of expectations. Consider each of these views, starting with the rationality of expectations. If speculators' expectations are rational then the expected prediction error in an equation such as

$$s_t^e - s_t = b_0 + b_1 \Delta s_t^e + \epsilon_t \qquad (1.83)$$

should be zero which implies $b_0 = b_1 = 0$. Since the left-hand side of (1.83) may alternatively be expressed as $\Delta s_t^e - \Delta s_t$, we obtain

$$\Delta s_t = - b_0 + (1 - b_1)\Delta s_t^e - \epsilon_t \qquad (1.84)$$

and by assuming risk neutrality, i.e. $f_{t-1} = s_t^e$, we have (1.82) where $a_0 = - b_0$, $a_1 = 1 - b_1$ and $u_t = - \epsilon_t$. Hence if we estimate (1.82) and find $a_1 < 1$ this implies that $b_1 > 0$ and speculators could improve on their speculative strategy by reducing the size of their forecast of exchange rate changes Bilson (1981) labels the case of $b_1 > 0$ as 'excessive speculation' and the case of $b_1 < 0$ as 'insufficient speculation'.

Alternatively, a failure to find $a_0 = 0$, $a_1 = 1$ in (1.82) may be attributable, as in our earlier discussion, to the existence of a risk premium, written here as that part of the expected change not already discounted into the forward premium:

$$\rho_{t-1} = (f_{t-1} - s_{t-1}) - (s_t^e - s_{t-1}) \qquad (1.85)$$

As in tests of equation (1.77), the crucial issue in analysing systematic prediction errors in equation (1.82) is whether they are due to the failure of agents' expectations to be optimal or to the separation of the forward rate from speculators' expected rate because of a risk premium or other factors.

Fama (1984) also considers a related regression relationship – the projection of $f_{t-1} - s_t$ onto $f_{t-1} - s_{t-1}$:

$$f_{t-1} - s_t = g_0 + g_1(f_{t-1} - s_{t-1}) + \epsilon_t \qquad (1.86)$$

The regression coefficients in (1.82) and (1.86) are defined as

$$a_1 = \frac{\text{cov}(f_{t-1} - s_{t-1}, s_t - s_{t-1})}{\text{var}(f_{t-1} - s_{t-1})} \qquad (1.87)$$

$$g_1 = \frac{\text{cov}(f_{t-1} - s_t, f_{t-1} - s_{t-1})}{\text{var}(f_{t-1} - s_{t-1})} \qquad (1.88)$$

Under the assumption of rationality and using (1.85), equation (1.87) and (1.88) can be expressed in the alternative forms

$$a_1 = \frac{\text{var}(s_t^e - s_{t-1}) + \text{cov}(\rho_{t-1}, s_t^e - s_{t-1})}{\text{var}(\rho_{t-1}) + \text{var}(s_t^e - s_{t-1}) + 2\,\text{cov}(\rho_{t-1}, s_t^e - s_{t-1})} \qquad (1.89)$$

$$g_1 = \frac{\text{var}(\rho_{t-1}) + \text{cov}(\rho_{t-1}, s_t^e - s_{t-1})}{\text{var}(\rho_{t-1}) + \text{var}(s_t^e - s_{t-1}) + 2\,\text{cov}(\rho_{t-1}, s_t^e - s_{t-1})} \qquad (1.90)$$

From (1.89) we can infer that, even under the maintained hypothesis of rational expectations, the slope coefficient in (1.82) will differ from unity whenever the risk premium ρ_{t-1} is time varying. In the special case where $\text{cov}(\rho_{t-1}, s_t^e - s_{t-1}) = 0$, the regression coefficients g_1 and a_1 split the variance of the forward premium $f_{t-1} - s_{t-1}$ into two parts – the proportion due to variation in the risk premium and the proportion due to variation in the expected depreciation. In general, however, this will not be the case.

Notice that in the above discussion we have been using the logarithm of the spot and forward rates rather than actual values. The usefulness of logarithmic transformations in efficiency tests has been demonstrated by Siegel (1972). Thus if we were to conduct our efficiency test of, say, equation (1.77), using the levels of the spot and forward exchange rates we would obtain two different answers depending on whether we used, as the definition for our exchange rates, the home currency value of a unit of foreign exchange or the foreign currency value of a unit of home currency. This follows because the expectation of a variable and of its inverse are *not* equivalent in levels (i.e. the mathematical expectation of S_t is not the same as the mathematical expectation of $1/S_t$). 'Siegel's paradox' is simply an application of a well-known statistical theorem known as Jensen's inequality. This problem does not apply to the variables in logarithms, however, since $E(-s_t|I_{t-1}) = -E(s_t|I_{t-1})$.[7]

Before considering some of the empirical evidence on the relationships considered in this section we must deal with another methodological problem – the overlapping contracts issue. For example, if in testing equation (1.77) we use a forward exchange rate with a one-month contract and weekly data we would expect a priori the error term ϕ_t to be serially correlated. This follows because when more than one observation is recorded during the period to maturity the error term will not be independent of past forecast errors but will instead follow a moving average process (of order $n-1$ for an n-period forward contract). Under rational expectations and risk neutrality, an n-period forward rate should be an optimal predictor of the n-period ahead spot rate:

$$s_{t+n} = f_t^n + u_{t+n} \qquad (1.91)$$

u_{t+n} is the unforecastable error due to unforeseen events, or news, occurring between period $t+1$ and $t+n$:

$$u_{t+n} = \Phi(\text{News}_{t+1}, \text{News}_{t+2}, \ldots, \text{News}_{t+n}) \qquad (1.92)$$

where $\Phi(.)$ is intended to convey the notion 'is a function of'. Similarly, we have

$$u_{t+n-1} = \Phi(\text{News}_t, \text{News}_{t+1}, \ldots, \text{News}_{t+n-1}) \qquad (1.93)$$

Since from (1.92) and (1.93) we can see that the forecasting errors at $t + n$ and $t + n - 1$ will share a number of news items in common, they will clearly be correlated. Moreover, it is easy to see that any $n - 1$ successive forecasting errors will share at least one news item and hence may be correlated. This is consistent with assuming that the forecasting errors follow a moving average process of order $n - 1$ at most.[8]

Point estimates of the regression parameters raise no serious problems since the OLS estimator remains unbiased and consistent (although no longer most efficient) in the presence of serially correlated errors. A problem does arise, however, in estimating the covariance matrix of the estimates, which is of course necessary for inference. Moreover, it can be shown that standard generalized least squares estimators will in general be inappropriate

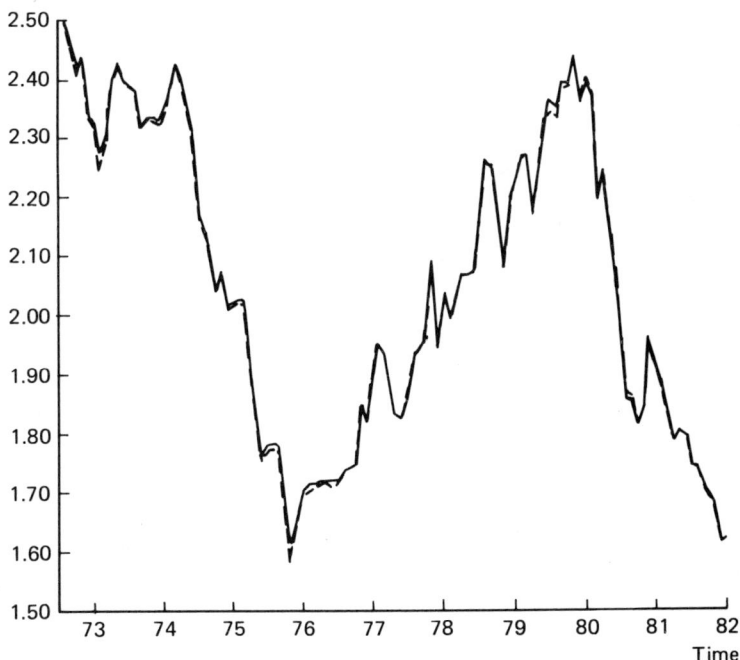

Figure 1.18 The contemporaneous spot (--) and forward (——) rates, the dollar–pound

in rational expectations models because of the distortion of certain orthogonality conditions (Flood and Garber, 1980a; Hansen and Hodrick, 1980; Hakkio, 1981a). However, Hansen (1982) has developed a consistent covariance matrix estimator which can be used in conjunction with OLS and this procedure is adopted, for example, by Hansen and Hodrick (1980).

1.4.2 Some empirical regularities of spot and forward exchange rates

Prior to presenting some econometric evidence which seeks to test the concept of forward market efficiency outlined in the previous section, we discuss some empirical regularities on the behaviour of spot and forward exchange rates which will prove useful. Firstly the relationship between *contemporaneous* spot and forward rates is considered, secondly the power of the forward rate as a predictor of the future spot rate is examined graphically and thirdly the unanticipated nature of exchange rate changes is examined.

In the preceding discussion, the concept that the forward exchange rate is

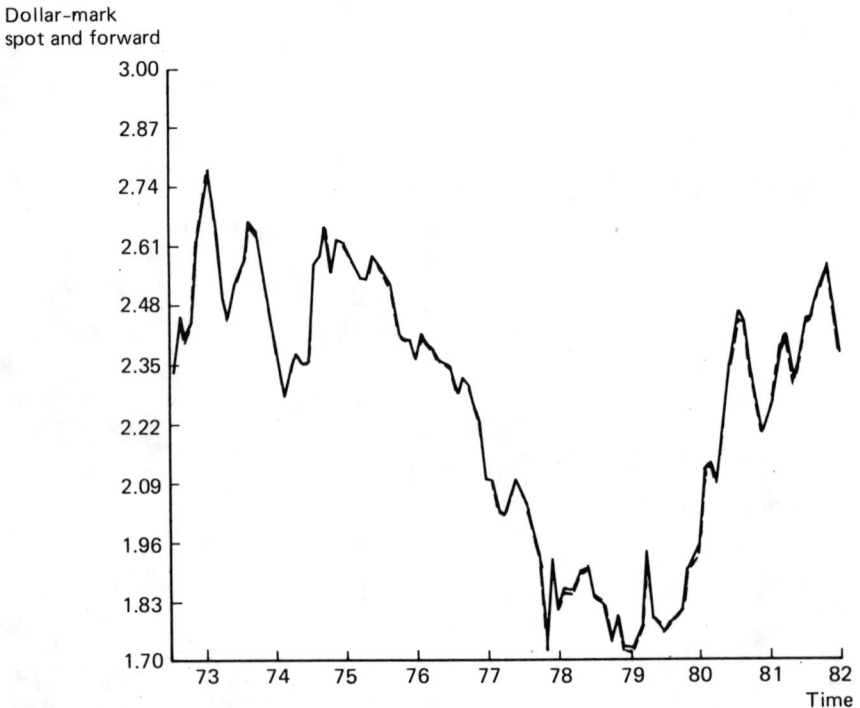

Figure 1.19 The contemporaneous spot (--) and forward (——) rates, the dollar–German mark

closely related to the markets' expected future spot rate has been considered in various contexts. In figures 1.18 and 1.19 the relationship between the contemporaneous spot and forward exchange rates is illustrated for the UK pound–US dollar and the German mark–US dollar exchange rates. Notice that, as expected, the spot rate and the forward rate were closely tied together, the correlation coefficient for the mark–dollar and pound–dollar being 0.99.

But how good a predictor of the future spot rate is the forward rate? In figures 1.20 and 1.21, by simply lagging the forward exchange rate one period, it is demonstrated that the predictive powers of the mark–dollar and pound–dollar forward rates are not very impressive: in both cases the forward rates are very poor predictors of the future spot exchange rate. This does not necessarily imply, however, that agents have been inefficient processors of information during this period. Rather, this may imply that there has been a great deal of new information which has led to a divergence of the actual spot rate from the expected value set last period. This unanticipated

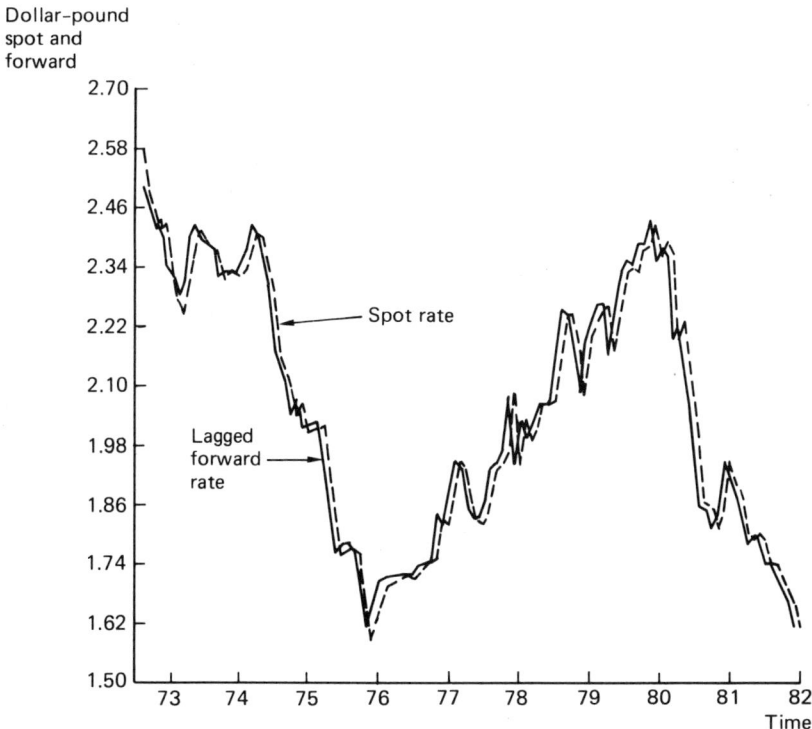

Figure 1.20 The forward rate as a predictor of the spot rate, the dollar–pound

Dollar–mark
spot and
forward

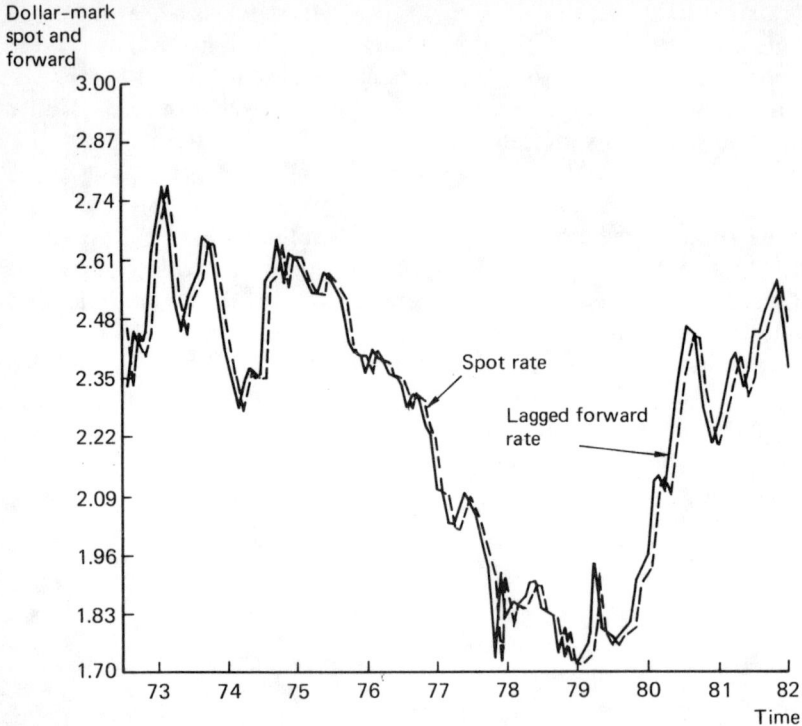

Figure 1.21 The forward rate as a predictor of the spot rate, the dollar–German mark

nature of exchange rates may be illustrated further by considering the *change* in the exchange rate against the predicted change in the exchange rate given by the forward *premium*. This relationship is plotted in figures 1.22 and 1.23 for the two exchange markets considered hitherto and it is clear that most of the changes in exchange rates are wholly unanticipated. This unanticipated nature of exchange rates is discussed further in the following sections.

1.4.3 Some weak tests: the forward rate as an unbiased predictor of future spot rates

Analysis of forecasting errors

Perhaps the simplest type of test of efficiency of the forward foreign exchange market is to compute the forecasting error $s_t - f_{t-1}$ and examine whether the mean error differs significantly from zero and whether it is serially correlated. Such a test, as Frankel (1979b) notes, amounts to

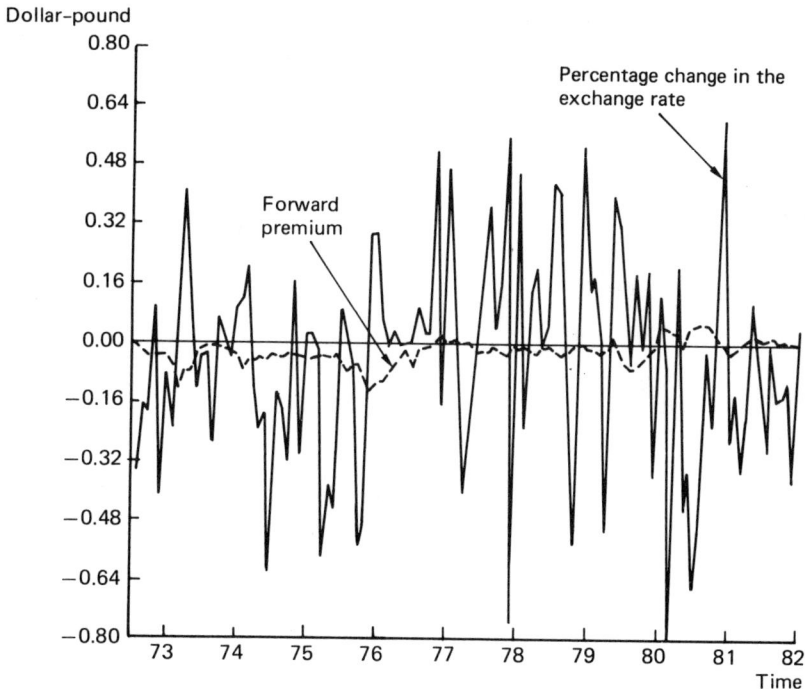

Figure 1.22   The forward premium and the percentage change in the exchange rate, the dollar–pound

including only a constant term in the information set. Early analyses of the forecast errors were conducted by Aliber (1974), Giddy and Dufey (1975), Kolhagen (1975), Levich (1979) and Frankel (1979b). Levich (1979) summarizes such evidence as follows. First, the mean error tends to be small and statistically insignificant for the majority of currencies studied. Second, forecasting errors in independent time periods tend to be serially uncor-related, thus precluding agents from using past forecasting errors to obtain better future forecasts. Thus on the basis of this, admittedly very weak, test the forward exchange market would appear to be efficient. Does this con-clusion alter when we consider somewhat stronger tests?

Regression-based efficiency tests

The majority of tests of the unbiasedness of the forward exchange rate have concentrated on econometrically estimating equation (1.77) or its equivalent representation (1.82). Such equations have been tested by a large number of researchers for a variety of different currencies and time periods. It has

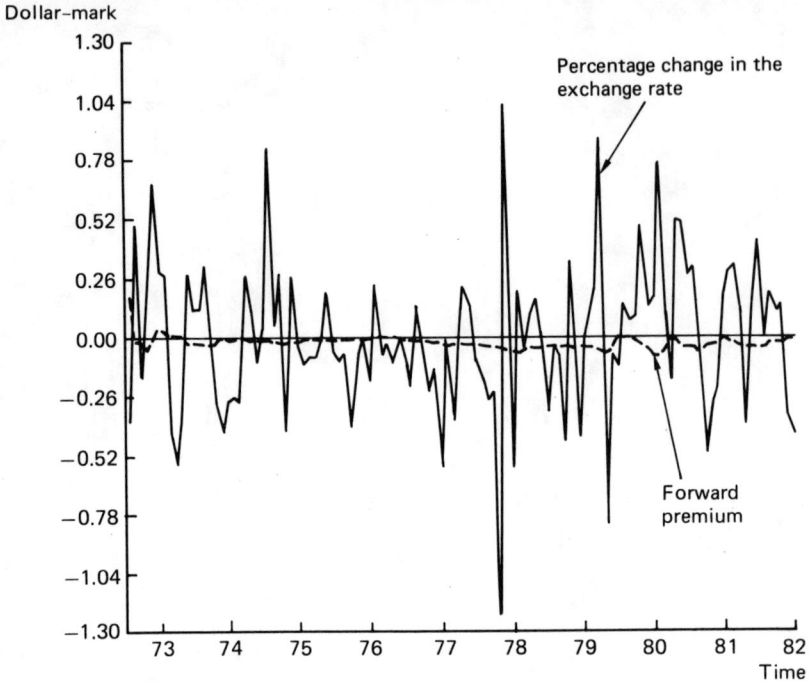

Figure 1.23   The forward premium and the percentage change in the exchange rate, the dollar–German mark

already been indicated that, if the forward market for foreign exchange is efficient, we expect a_0 to be statistically insignificant, a_1 to differ insignificantly from unity and the error term to be serially uncorrelated. In tables 1.7 and 1.8 a selection of evidence from the interwar experience with floating and the more recent floating experience is presented. The evidence from the interwar period is broadly supportive of the EMH. Thus the four exchange markets studied by Frenkel (1980) all pass the test of unbiasedness: the computed F statistic, which tests the joint hypothesis that $a_0 = 0$ and $a_1 = 1$, cannot be rejected at the 5 per cent significance level. Furthermore, the Durbin–Watson statistics do not indicate the presence of first-order autocorrelation.

Frenkel (1980) finds that in estimating equation (1.78) the overall fit of equation (1.82), in terms of the $\bar{R}^2$, is not improved upon and, equivalently, that the coefficient of f_{t-2} is insignificant as required by the EMH. In order to determine whether f_{t-1} is independent of the error term (as we showed above, a non-constant risk premium may result in the correlation of f_{t-1} with the error term leading to biased OLS estimates of a_1), Frenkel (1980) uses a

Table 1.7 The forward rate as an unbiased predictor of the future spot exchange rate: some evidence from the interwar floating experience

$$s_t = a_0 + a_1 f_{t-1} + u_t$$

Investigator	Exchange rate	Time period	a_0	a_1	Durbin–Watson	$\bar{R}^2$	$F_{(2,50)}$	m	Estimation technique
Frenkel (1980)	Franc–pound	February 1921–May 1925	0.169 (0.179)	0.962 (0.042)	1.92	0.91	0.88	0.09	OLS
	Dollar–pound	February 1921–May 1925	0.057 (0.056)	0.964 (0.038)	1.54	0.93	0.63	0.02	OLS
	Franc–dollar	February 1921–May 1925	0.203 (0.149)	0.928 (0.054)	1.95	0.85	1.05	0.52	OLS
	Mark–pound	February 1921–August 1923	−0.454 (0.254)	1.094 (0.029)	1.89	0.98	—	0.38	OLS
MacDonald (1983b)	Franc–pound	February 1921–May 1925	0.156 (0.109)	0.965 (0.026)	—	—	1.41	—	ZSURE
	Dollar–pound	February 1921–May 1925	0.037 (0.044)	0.976 (0.03)	—	—	0.59	—	ZSURE
	Franc–dollar	February 1921–May 1925	0.114 (0.072)	0.960 (0.026)	—	—	1.33	—	ZSURE

Standard errors are in parentheses.

Table 1.8 Weak form error orthogonality tests

$$s_t - f_{t-1}^t = a_0 + a_i \sum_{i=0}^{n} (s_t - f_{t-1})_{t-1-i}$$

(a) Interwar floating experience

Investigator	Exchange rate	Time period	a_0	a_1	a_2	a_3	X_3^2	F	R^2
Hansen and Hodrick (1980)	Mark–pound	21 January 1922–1 September 1923	0.343 (0.137)	0.419 (0.26)	−0.220 (0.271)	—	15.196	—	0.051
	Franc–pound	21 January 1922–31 July 1976	0.019 (0.009)	0.233 (0.122)	0.232 (0.122)	—	9.402	—	0.022
	Dollar–pound	21 January 1922–25 April 1926	0.002 (0.002)	0.141 (0.099)	−0.016 (0.095)	—	3.252	—	0.020
MacDonald (1983b)	Franc–pound	February 1921–May 1925	0.020 (0.011)	−0.077 (0.148)	−0.267 (0.142)	−0.200 (0.148)	—	1.75	0.21
	Dollar–pound	February 1921–May 1925	0.0012 (0.003)	0.101 (0.168)	0.337 (0.158)	−0.125 (0.166)	—	1.76	0.26
	Franc–dollar	February 1921–May 1925	0.013 (0.011)	−0.074 (0.148)	−0.194 (0.147)	−0.214 (0.122)	—	1.25	0.12

(b) Recent floating experience

Investigator	Exchange rate	Time period	a_0	a_1	a_2	X_3	F	R^2
Hansen and Hodrick (1980)	Pound–dollar	9 October 1973–16 January 1979	0.001 (0.011)	0.385 (0.317)	−0.423 (0.313)	1.860	—	0.015
	Franc–dollar	9 October 1973–16 January 1979	0.007 (0.011)	0.269 (0.220)	−0.072 (0.218)	2.609	—	0.043
	Mark–dollar	9 October 1973–16 January 1979	0.008 (0.011)	0.662 (0.269)	−0.910 (0.272)	11.966	—	0.135
Frankel (1979b)	Pound–dollar	5 July 1974–April 1978	−0.001 (0.003)	0.326 (0.141)	—		3.24	
	Franc–dollar	5 July 1974–April 1978	0.002 (0.003)	0.327 (0.138)	—		4.06	
	Mark–dollar	5 July 1974–April 1978	0.004 (0.003)	0.136 (0.148)	—		2.42	

Standard errors are in parentheses.

Table 1.9 The forward exchange rate as an unbiased predictor of the future spot exchange rate for the recent floating experience

Investigator	Currency	Time period	a_0	a_1	DW	R^2	F	m	Estimation technique
Levich (1979)	UK pound	March 1973–May 1978	0.017 (0.103)	0.980 (0.105)	1.51	0.81	87.6	—	OLS
	French franc	March 1973–May 1978	0.004 (0.004)	0.864 (0.171)	1.79	0.59	25.5	—	OLS
	German mark	March 1973–May 1978	0.001 (0.001)	0.997 (0.009)	1.40	0.99	204.69	—	OLS
Frankel (1979b)	UK pound	January 1974–December 1977	0.015 (0.015)	0.980 (0.020)	—	—	—	—	IV
	French franc	January 1974–December 1977	-0.237 (0.090)	0.843 (0.059)	—	—	—	—	IV
	German mark	January 1974–December 1977	-0.109 (0.052)	0.876 (0.057)	—	—	—	—	IV
Frenkel (1981)	UK pound	June 1973–July 1979	0.030 (0.018)	0.961 (0.025)	1.74	0.95	1.86[a]	2.01	IV
	French franc	June 1973–July 1979	-0.235 (0.080)	0.844 (0.053)	2.24	0.78	4.83[a]	2.26	IV
	German mark	June 1973–July 1979	-0.021 (0.027)	0.978 (0.032)	2.10	0.93	0.51[a]	0.91	IV

					DW	R^2	F	m	
Baillie et al. (1983b)	UK pound	June 1973–April 1980	0.033 (0.016)	0.956 (0.22)	1.33	0.99	2.12	—	OLS
	French franc	June 1973–April 1980	−0.174 (0.060)	0.884 (0.039)	1.85	0.99	4.57	—	OLS
	German mark	June 1973–April 1980	−0.024 (0.019)	0.968 (0.024)	1.98	0.99	0.97	—	OLS
Edwards (1983)	UK pound	June 1973–September 1979	−0.033 (0.018)	0.957 (0.025)	1.70	0.95	3.52[a]	—	ZSURE
	French franc	June 1973–September 1979	−0.568 (0.179)	0.816 (0.058)	2.14[a]	0.74[a]	7.67[a]	—	ZSURE
	German mark	June 1973–September 1979	0.026 (0.027)	0.967 (0.032)	2.11[a]	0.93[a]	0.76[a]	—	ZSURE
MacDonald (1983b)	UK pound	1972 1st quarter–1979 4th quarter	0.048 (0.03)	0.943 (0.04)	1.56[a]	0.88[a]	1.25[a]	—	ZSURE
	French franc	1972 1st quarter–1979 4th quarter	0.284 (0.11)	0.808 (0.07)	1.77[a]	0.54[a]	3.75[a]	—	ZSURE
	German mark	1972 1st quarter–1979 4th quarter	0.101 (0.10)	0.871 (0.03)	2.04[a]	0.88[a]	6.95[a]	—	ZSURE

DW, the Durbin–Watson statistic; R^2, the adjusted coefficient of determination; F, an F statistic which tests the joint hypothesis of unbiasedness; m, the Hausman specification test; standard errors are in parentheses.
[a] The test statistics have been derived from OLS estimates.

specification test devised by Hausman (1978). This compares the OLS estimator, which is inconsistent under the alternative hypothesis (non-independence), with an instrumental variables estimator, which is consistent under both the null and alternative hypotheses. The Hausman statistic is distributed as χ^2 with two degrees of freedom (the number of over-identifying instruments) under the null hypothesis. The Hausman statistics, reported in table 1.7 (m) are insignificant at standard test sizes and thus indicate that using the forward rate as a proxy for expectations does not introduce significant errors in variables bias into the estimates: OLS appears to be an appropriate estimator. Frenkel (1980) also reports estimates of equation (1.82) and again cannot reject the null hypothesis that $a_0 = 0$ and $a_1 = 1$. Interestingly, the forward premium explains only a small fraction of the actual variation of the spot rate, suggesting that the bulk of exchange rate changes in this period are due to the arrival of new information (we shall return to this point below).

Although the forward exchange rate may not be correlated with the error term for the interwar period, the error term *across* the equations reported in table 1.7 may be correlated (because of contemporaneous news items), which means that OLS estimates of equation (1.77) may not be the most efficient estimates available. The potential correlation of error terms across equations follows from the fact that all four currencies are related either directly, because they involve the pound, or indirectly, as a result of arbitrage. Thus a shock emanating from the UK will affect all four currencies simultaneously. An estimator which accounts for this potential correlation across equations is Zellner's seemingly unrelated regression estimator (ZSURE) (see Edwards, 1983, and MacDonald, 1983a, for further discussion). MacDonald (1983b) has estimated equation (1.77) for the franc–pound, dollar–pound and franc–dollar over the period February 1921 to May 1925 using the ZSURE techique and the results, reported in table 1.7, reinforce those of Frenkel (1980).

In table 1.9 a selection of results from estimating equation (1.77) for the recent floating experience are reported. Both Frankel (1979b) and Frenkel (1981) use instrumental variables to estimate (1.77) although the Hausman statistics reported by Frenkel indicate that f_{t-1} is not correlated with the error term. For the period studied and the data frequency used by Frenkel, the joint hypothesis cannot be rejected and, furthermore, no indication of serial correlation is found. Also, when equation (1.78) is tested none of the f_{t-2} terms is statistically significant, which is supportive of the error ortho-gonality property. Frankel (1979b), however, rejects the joint hypothesis for the French franc and German mark (and for two other currencies: the Italian lira and Dutch guilder). The OLS results of Levich (1979) are supportive of the efficiency propositions. Edwards (1983) reports OLS estimates of (1.77) which are unfavourable to the hypothesis of market efficiency for the franc–dollar exchange rate (the individual hypotheses $a_0 = 0$ and $a_1 = 1$ and the joint hypothesis $a_0 = 0$ *and* $a_1 = 1$ are rejected) but which are favourable for the pound–dollar and mark–dollar. These conclusions do not change when Edwards uses ZSURE – see table 1.9 (the lira–dollar rate failed the market efficiency test when OLS was used, but passed the test when ZSURE was used). MacDonald's (1983a) ZSURE estimates indicate a rejection of the individual hypothesis $a_0 = 0$ and $a_1 = 1$.

We have already mentioned, in passing, that there is some evidence to suggest that spot and forward rates may be characterized as non-stationary series, indeed that their time-series representations may contain a unit root (Meese and Singleton, 1982; Corbae and Ouliaris, 1986; Goodhart and Taylor, 1987; Taylor, 1988d). If this is the case, then econometric evidence based on estimates of equation (1.77) may be brought into doubt, since valid large-sample inference generally requires at least stationarity and ergodicity

Table 1.10 The forward premium as a predictor of the rate of depreciation

Investigator	Currency	Time period	a_0	a_1	Estimation technique
Bilson (1981)	UK pound	July 1974–January 1980	1.928 (5.21)	0.628 (0.99)	OLS
	Canadian dollar	July 1974–January 1980	−4.010 (2.05)	−0.804 (0.92)	OLS
	Japanese yen	July 1974–January 1980	3.917 (4.03)	−0.665 (0.86)	OLS
	Swiss franc	July 1974–January 1980	1.32 (8.52)	−0.184 (1.38)	OLS
Longworth (1981)	Canadian dollar	July 1970–December 1978	0.0013 (0.0012)	0.0521 (0.6916)	OLS
	Canadian dollar	January 1971–December 1978	0.0017 (0.0012)	−0.0937 (0.6916)	OLS
Fama (1984)	UK pound	August 1973–December 1982	−0.52 (0.26)	−0.69 (0.51)	ZSURE
	Canadian dollar	August 1973–December 1982	−0.26 (0.11)	−1.04 (0.59)	ZSURE
	Japanese yen	August 1973–December 1982	0.12 (0.28)	−0.28 (0.35)	ZSURE
	Swiss franc	August 1973–December 1982	0.81 (0.42)	−1.15 (0.50)	ZSURE
Taylor (1988a)	UK pound	March 1976–July 1986	−0.0024 (0.0032)	0.0148 (0.1232)	ZSURE
	Japanese yen	March 1976 July 1986	0.0126 (0.0041)	−0.7496 (0.2885)	ZSURE
	Swiss franc	March 1976–July 1986	0.0062 (0.0061)	−0.1778 (0.3115)	ZSURE

of the variables in a regression relationship. One might therefore wish to examine a stationarity-inducing transformation of (1.77), and this is one reason why the formulation (1.82), the regression of the rate of depreciation onto the lagged forward premium, is of interest. This is the approach taken by, for example, Bilson (1981), Cumby and Obstfeld (1981), Longworth (1981), Fama (1984), Huang (1984) and Taylor (1988a). Table 1.10 reports a selection of estimates of equation (1.82) which have been reported in the literature. The results of such tests of the EMH are generally rather mixed. For example, the hypothesis that the slope coefficient differs insignificantly from unity cannot, in general, be rejected on the basis of the single-equation estimates of Bilson (1981) or Longworth (1981). However, when the more efficient ZSURE method is employed, as it is by Fama (1984) and Taylor (1988a) this hypothesis is easily rejected. Moreover, perhaps the most striking point to notice is that the estimate of the slope coefficient is negative in ten out of 13 cases (and indeed is often closer to *minus* unity than *plus* unity). In terms of equations (1.83) and (1.84) this implies that $b_1 > 1$, indicating the presence of 'excess speculation' in Bilson's (1981) terminology. In order to explain this finding, Bilson (1981) develops a trading rule strategy which could have been exploited by speculators and demonstrates that pursuing this strategy would have resulted in substantial profits for market operators – itself a rejection of the (simple, risk-neutral) EMH. This finding is also supported by Hodrick and Srivastava (1984) using a longer sample period. Recall, however, our discussion of Fama's (1984) interpretation of this regression coefficient:

$$a_1 = \frac{\text{var}(s_t^e - s_{t-1}) + \text{cov}(\rho_{t-1} s_t^e - s_{t-1})}{\text{var}(\rho_{t-1}) + \text{var}(s_t^e - s_{t-1}) + 2\,\text{cov}(\rho_{t-1} s_t^e - s_{t-1})} \qquad (1.89)$$

This equation is derived under the maintained hypothesis of rational expectations but relaxes the assumption of risk neutrality – recall that ρ_{t-1} is a time-varying risk premium as defined in (1.85). If the population regression coefficient a_1 is negative, as the estimates reported in table 1.10 imply, then it is easy to infer from (1.89) that there must be negative covariation between the risk premium and the expected rate of depreciation. Fama (1984) notes that 'A good story for negative covariation between [the risk premium] and [the expected depreciation] is difficult to tell'. Intuitively, the greater the expected depreciation of the dollar, the greater the expected return that one should require for bidding a dollar-denominated security (all exchange rates are defined as dollars per unit of currency). Hodrick and Srivastava (1986) provide a solution to this paradox. They point out that the risk premium in this empirical work (as defined in (1.85)) is the expected profit from an open forward *purchase* of dollars, and so this is in fact denominated in foreign currency (the maturing long dollar position is eventually sold in the spot market). The expected (dollar-denominated) profit from an open forward *sale* of dollars is $-\rho_{t-1}$, and the results in table 1.10 suggest that this will be *positively* correlated with the expected rate of dollar depreciation.

As noted above, Fama (1984) also considers the regression relationship

$$f_{t-1} - s_t = g_0 + g_1(f_{t-1} - s_{t-1}) + \epsilon_t \tag{1.86}$$

and an interpretation of the regression coefficient g_1 was given in (1.90). Subtracting (1.89) from (1.90)

$$g_1 - a_1 = \frac{\text{var}(\rho_{t-1}) - \text{var}(s_t^e - s_{t-1})}{\text{var}(f_{t-1} - s_{t-1})} \tag{1.94}$$

Thus, the difference between the regression slope coefficients in (1.86) and (1.82) will be determined by the relative variances of the risk premium and the expected rate of depreciation. Fama (1984) calculates this difference for nine major dollar exchange rates and finds a range for (1.94) from 1.58 (Japanese yen) to 4.16 (Belgian franc). Moreover, in six out of nine cases the estimate of $g_1 - a_1$ is more than two estimated standard errors away from zero, and in all cases it is more than one and a half estimated standard errors away from zero. Fama thus confidently concludes that the variance in the risk premium is reliably greater than the variance in the expected depreciation. As we saw in section 1.2, virtually all work on exchange rate determination which incorporates expectations terms has concentrated on the expected rate of depreciation. As Hodrick and Srivastava (1986) note, future work might usefully concentrate on the implications of risk-averse behaviour in foreign exchange markets. Further discussion of foreign exchange risk premia is given below in section 1.3.6.

Weak form error orthogonality tests

In this subsection some evidence pertaining to equation (1.79) is presented: the weak form error orthogonality equation (i.e. we include only lagged forecasting errors in the information set assumed available to agents). Equation (1.79) has been tested by *inter alia* Geweke and Feige (1978), Frankel (1979b), Hansen and Hodrick (1980) and MacDonald (1983b). For example, Hansen and Hodrick (1980), by setting $n = 1$, estimate equation (1.79) with weekly data and one-month forward rates (i.e. they use overlapping data) for three currencies for the interwar floating experience. The results, reported in table 1.8, tend to cast doubt on the EMH for two exchange markets: in the case of the mark–dollar rate the constant term is statistically significant; for the franc–dollar the constant and two lagged forecasting errors are statistically significant. The null hypothesis of market efficiency cannot be rejected for the dollar–pound. MacDonald (1983b), using a one-month forward rate and non-overlapping data for the interwar period finds in favour of the null hypothesis (the disparity between Hansen and Hodrick's and MacDonald's results is perhaps attributable to the higher quality data used by the former researchers). A rejection of the null hypothesis emerges from analyses of the recent floating experience. Thus Hansen and Hodrick (1980) estimate equation (1.79) using weekly data and three-month forward rates for seven currencies and find that for three currencies – the Swiss franc, the Italian lire and the German mark (all against the dollar) – the ortho-gonality property is violated. Frankel (1980), who includes a single lagged value of the forecasting error in his study of six currencies, for the period January 1973–8, also finds statistically significant lagged forecasting errors for the German mark–US dollar, UK pound–US dollar and Italian lira–US dollar. Geweke and Feige (1978), who also set $n = 1$ in equation (1.79), reject weak form efficiency only for one currency (the Canadian dollar–US dollar) out of seven currencies tested for the period 1972 third quarter to 1977 first quarter.

1.4.4 Some semi-strong form tests

The definition of semi-strong form efficiency given earlier refers to tests of the error orthogonality property which utilize more information than simply the past history of forecasting errors. Hansen and Hodrick (1980) define a semi-strong form test of market efficiency as a test of equation (1.80), i.e. does the inclusion in the information set of lagged forecasting errors from *other* exchange markets in the help to explain the current forecasting error? For the recent floating experience, Hansen and Hodrick find that lagged forecasting errors do have significant explanatory power in the cases of the Canadian dollar–US dollar, the German mark–US dollar and the Swiss franc–US dollar exchange markets and therefore that the (simple) EMH must be rejected for these markets. Geweke and Feige (1978) find that the hypothesis that the coefficients are equal to zero can only be rejected for the Canadian dollar from a selection of seven currencies; however, estimating equation (1.80) for the seven currencies jointly, using ZSURE, results in the hypothesis that all the coefficients are insignificant being rejected at the 1 per cent level (Geweke and Feige classify this as a test of 'multimarket efficiency').

1.4.5 The bivariate autoregression approach

To many researchers, one particularly appealing feature of the rational expectations hypothesis is that it normally implies certain cross-equation, often non-linear, restrictions on a model's parameters. Indeed, Hansen and Sargent (1982) have termed this the 'hallmark' of dynamic rational expecta-tions models.

Using an approach originally suggested by Sargent (1979), a number of researchers notably Hakkio (1981a, b), test the EMH as a set of non-linear cross-equation restrictions on the parameters of a vector autoregression of spot and forward rates.

This methodology can perhaps be illustrated best by means of a simple example. Suppose the current rate of depreciation and the forward premium together form a jointly covariance stationary process. Then a statistical theorem, known as Wold's decomposition (see for example Hannan, 1970; Sargent, 1979) implies the existence of a unique, infinite-order moving average representation. In finite samples, this can generally be approximated by a finite-order vector autoregression. Suppose, for the purposes of exposition, that the vector autoregression is first order:

$$\Delta s_t = \alpha \Delta s_{t-1} + \beta(f_{t-1} - s_{t-1}) + \epsilon_t \tag{1.95}$$

$$f_t - s_t = \gamma \Delta s_{t-1} + \delta(f_{t-1} - s_{t-1}) + \eta_t \tag{1.96}$$

Advancing (1.95) by one period

$$\Delta s_{t+1} = \alpha \Delta s_t + \beta(f_t - s_t) + \epsilon_{t+1} \tag{1.97}$$

Using (1.95) and (1.96) in (1.97)

$$\Delta s_{t+1} = \alpha[\alpha \Delta s_{t-1} + \beta(f_{t-1} - s_{t-1}) + \epsilon_t]$$
$$+ \beta[\gamma \Delta s_{t-1} + \delta(f_{t-1} - s_{t-1}) + \eta_t] + \epsilon_{t+1}$$

or

$$\Delta s_{t+1} = (\alpha^2 + \beta\gamma)\Delta s_{t-1} + \beta(\alpha + \delta)(f_{t-1} - s_{t-1})$$
$$+ \alpha\epsilon_t + \beta\eta_t + \epsilon_{t+1} \tag{1.98}$$

Now consider an information set consisting only of lagged values of the rate of depreciation and the forward premium:

$$\Lambda_{t-1} = \{\Delta s_{t-1}, \Delta s_{t-2}, \ldots, f_{t-1} - s_{t-1}, f_{t-2} - s_{t-2}, \ldots\}$$

The expected values of current and future ϵ and η, conditional on this information set, must clearly be zero since by definition they are the innovations in the vector autoregression. Thus, from (1.96) and (1.97) we have

$$E(f_t - s_t|\Lambda_{t-1}) = \gamma \Delta s_{t-1} + \delta(f_{t-1} - s_{t-1}) \tag{1.99}$$

$$E(\Delta s_{t+1}|\Lambda_{t-1}) = (\alpha^2 + \beta\gamma)\Delta s_{t-1} + \beta(\alpha + \delta)(f_{t-1} - s_{t-1}) \tag{1.100}$$

Now the simple market efficiency condition (1.74) states that the spot rate should only differ from the lagged forward rate by a rational expectations forecasting error. Since the expected value of the forecasting error, given the available information set, is zero, this is equivalent to saying that the expected difference between the rate of depreciation and the lagged forward premium, conditional on the available information set, must be zero:

$$E[\Delta s_{t+1} - (f_t - s_t)|I_t] = 0 \tag{1.101}$$

where I_t is the 'full' information set at time t. The law of iterated mathematical expectations states that

$$E[E(x|\Omega_i)|\Omega_j] = E(x|\Omega_j) \text{ for } \Omega_j \subseteq \Omega_i$$

Thus, taking expectations of (1.101) with respect to Λ_{t-1} implies that (1.99) and (1.100) must be identically equal (since clearly $\Lambda_{t-1} \subseteq \Omega_t$). Thus, equating coefficients in (1.99) and (1.100) yields the non-linear cross-equation restrictions implied by the EMH:

$$\alpha^2 + \beta\gamma - \gamma = 0 \tag{1.102}$$

$$\beta(\alpha + \delta) - \delta = 0 \tag{1.103}$$

Intuitively, these restrictions are necessary if the predicted rate of depreciation from the model (as given by the chain rule of forecasting) is to be equal to the process determining the forward premium, as given by the model.

These non-linear restrictions can then be tested by standard asymptotic tests such as Wald or likelihood ratio tests. In practice, one might choose a higher-order vector autoregression on statistical grounds, so that the EMH restrictions may be even more complex than those derived above, but the principle remains the same. Another potential complication involves the use of overlapping data – again the principle is the same, and no special estimation techniques are required.

It should be clear from the above discussion that this procedure is really nothing more than a test of the error orthogonality condition (see (1.99)–(1.100)). Since orthogonality is effectively tested with respect to lagged spot and forward rates, it is in fact a weak form test. Its advantages over the simpler regression-based tests discussed above are as follows. Firstly, no special problems arise due to overlapping data and serially correlated disturbances. Secondly, the information set upon which the tests are conditioned is made explicit. Thirdly, since this approach exploits the time series properties of the data, the tests should be more efficient – they should have greater power to reject a false null hypothesis in any particular application.

Hakkio (1981a) uses this methodology to test the EMH restrictions on a vector autoregression of the rate of depreciation and the change in the forward rate using weekly data and one-month forward rates for the period April 1973 to May 1977 for five currencies against the US dollar – Dutch guilder, German mark, Canadian dollar, Swiss franc and UK sterling – and generally rejects the EMH for all currencies. Hakkio estimates the vector autoregressions both with and without the restrictions imposed and computes likelihood ratio statistics. Because of the complexities involved in estimating the restricted model, Hakkio arbitrarily sets the lag length in his vector autoregressions to four periods. Although he finds no evidence of serial correlation in the estimated residuals, it is conceivable that arbitrary truncation may have biased the test statistics. Baillie et al. (1983b) suggest that Wald statistics should be used in this context and thus only estimate unconstrained vector autoregressions, where spot and forward rates enter as first differences. Levy and Nobay (1986) demonstrate that the EMH restrictions · cannot be imposed on a vector autoregression in first differences, however, so that the results of Baillie et al. are in fact invalid. Levy and Nobay then extend the above methodology to develop a test of the EMH based on vector autoregression moving average processes for the rate of depreciation and the forward premium. Again using weekly data and one-month forward rates for five currencies against the US dollar – UK sterling, German mark, Swiss franc, French franc and Canadian dollar – for the period January 1976 to December 1981, the EMH is easily rejected in all cases.

The unconstrained bivariate autoregression methodology has also been utilized to test the efficiency of the forward market for foreign exchange for the interwar period. MacDonald and Taylor (1987a) implement the approach for the 1920s floating period (using appropriate stationarity-inducing transformations – the change in the exchange rate and the forward premium). It is demonstrated, *inter alia*, that the joint market efficiency hypothesis is resoundingly rejected for the forward maturities and currencies studied.[9]

The bivariate autoregression methodology can also be implemented to test the efficient markets view of the term structure of forward foreign exchange premia. Thus the EMH has implications not just for the relationship between single maturity spot and forward rates, but also for the relationship between spot and forward rates of different maturities. This may be seen in the following way.

Consider a representative agent who wants to buy foreign exchange now for delivery n periods ahead. He may engage in an n-period forward contract and pay a forward premium r_t, say, or he can buy and 'roll over' a succession of one-period contracts, $r_t, r_{t+1}, \ldots, r_{t+n-1}$, say. Assuming that the agent is rational and risk neutral (and that there are zero transactions costs in forward markets) then it follows, by arguments parallel to those used in the literature concerning the rational expectations model to the term structure of interest rates (e.g. Sargent, 1979), that

$$r_t^n = \frac{1}{n} (r_t^1 + E_t r_{t+1}^1 + \ldots + E_t r_{t+n-1}^1) \qquad (1.104)$$

The forward premium with maturity n is simply an average of the expected one-period premia over the holding period (note that $E_t(.)$ is the mathematical conditional expectation operator, given information at time t).

Hakkio (1981b) tests equation (1.104) using the BVAR methodology for the one- and six-month forward premia of the German mark–US dollar and Canadian dollar–US dollar exchange rates over the period 30 March 1975 to 30 December 1976 (weekly data). The BVAR systems are estimated both with and without the restrictions imposed and both likelihood ratio and Wald statistics are computed. Both statistics indicate rejection of the null for Canada but not for Germany. However, these results should be interpreted with some caution since Hakkio arbitrarily restricts the lag length to four: it would perhaps have been more appropriate to use some selection criteria, such as the Akaike information criterion (AIC). MacDonald and Taylor (1988b) test equation (1.104) for the early 1920s experience with floating for one- and three-month forward premia for the dollar–sterling, the franc–sterling and the franc–dollar exchange rates. The AIC is used to select the optimal bivariate autoregression lag length, and the restrictions are tested using Wald statistics. Two data sets were utilized by MacDonald and Taylor, one where the shortest forward premium exactly matched the observation interval and the other where the observation interval was weekly.[10] For both data sets a resounding rejection of the null was reported for all currencies, although the rejection was stronger when the overlapping data were used.

1.4.6 Rationalizing inefficiency findings: the 'peso problem', bubbles and risk premia

Many economists who would demur at the rational expectations hypothesis in general would accept it as a reasonable approximation to the behaviour of participants in asset markets – such agents are, after all, highly motivated, highly professional individuals with easy access to potentially vast information sets. Thus, perhaps motivated largely by a desire to salvage something of the rational expectations hypothesis in the light of the available, largely non-supportive evidence on foreign exchange market efficiency, researchers have pointed to a number of other possible explanations, beyond the failure of rational expectations, for the rejection of efficiency.

The 'peso problem'

Krasker (1980) pointed out that, where there is a small probability of a large change in the underlying determinants of the exchange rate (the 'market fundamentals'), standard econometric tests of forward exchange market efficiency may be invalid – this is the so-called 'peso problem'.[11] This sort of argument may be illustrated as follows.

Consider the rational expectations 'forward solution' to the FLPM model given in equation (1.40), which we write here as

$$s_t = \sum_{i=0}^{\infty} \theta^i \, E_t \, \nu_{t+i} \tag{1.105}$$

where

$$0 < \theta = \lambda(1 + \lambda)^{-1} < 1$$

and

$$\nu_t = (1 + \lambda)^{-1} \left[(m - m^*)_t - \phi y_t + \phi^* y_t^* \right]$$

Now suppose that the driving processes ν_t are relatively stable but that there is a non-zero probability of a discrete change – for example a shift to a new monetary regime. A simple model for the fundamentals ν_t might then be

$$\nu_t = \nu_t^* + u_t \tag{1.106}$$

$$\nu_t^* = \nu_{t-1}^* + g\omega_t \tag{1.107}$$

$$\omega_t = \begin{cases} \omega_{t-1}, & \text{with probability } \pi \\ 0, & \text{with probability } 1 - \pi \end{cases}$$

$$\omega_0 = 1$$
$$\nu_0 = \bar{\nu}$$

where u_t is a white noise disturbance. Thus, (1.106) describes the fundamentals as having a systematic part ν_t^* and a non-systematic part u_t. In turn, (1.107) and the probability model for ω_t imply that there is a probability of $1 - \pi$ of a discrete reduction of g in the rate of change of the systematic fundamentals. Advancing (1.107) by i periods and taking conditional expectations

$$E_t \nu_{t+i}^* = E_t \nu_{t+i-1}^* + g\omega_{t+i}$$

which, after continued substitution for the first term on the right-hand side, becomes

$$E_t \nu_{t+i}^* = \nu_t^* + g\pi(1 - \pi^i)(1 - \pi)^{-1} \tag{1.108}$$

when $\omega_t = 1$, and

$$E_t \nu_{t+i}^* = \nu_t^* \tag{1.109}$$

when $\omega_t = 0$. Thus, the fundamentals model (1.105) may be written

$$s_t = \begin{cases} (1 - \theta)^{-1}\nu_t^* + g\pi\theta(1 - \theta)^{-1}(1 - \theta\pi) + u_t, & \text{if } \omega_t = 1 \\ (1 - \theta)^{-1}\nu_t^* + u_t & \text{if } \omega_t = 0 \end{cases}$$

Now consider the one-step-ahead rational expectations forecasting error

$$s_{t+1} - E_t s_{t+1} = (1 - \theta)^{-1}(\nu_{t+1}^* - E_t \nu_{t+1}^*) + u_{t+1} \tag{1.110}$$

If the regime shift has already occurred, then $\omega_t = 0$. Hence, using (1.109), (1.110) becomes

$$s_{t+1} - E_t s_{t+1} = u_{t+1} \qquad (1.111)$$

Thus, once the regime shift has occurred, the rational expectations forecasting error is white noise – in particular it is distributed symmetrically with zero mean. Now consider the case where the regime shift has not yet occurred, so that $\omega_t = 1$. Using (1.108), (1.110) becomes

$$s_{t+1} - E_t s_{t+1} = (1 - \theta)^{-1}(v^*_{t+1} - v^*_t + g\pi) + u_{t+1}$$

Using (1.107) we have

$$s_{t+1} - E_t s_{t+1} = (1 - \theta)^{-1}g(\omega_{t+1} - \pi) + u_{t+1} \qquad (1.112)$$

Now the rational expectations forecasting error described in (1.112) will clearly have a zero conditional mean; however, it does have a non-zero conditional median under certain circumstances. To see this, compute the conditional probability that the forecasting error is greater than or equal to zero; if this is not equal to 0.5 the distribution must be non-symmetric and the median must differ from the mean. Now

$$\begin{aligned}
\Pr(s_{t+1} - E_t s_{t+1} \geqslant 0) &= \tfrac{1}{2}\{\Pr[(1-\theta)^{-1}g(\omega_{t+1} - \pi) \geqslant 0] + \Pr(u_{t+1} \geqslant 0)\} \\
&= \tfrac{1}{2}[\Pr(\omega_{t+1} - \pi \geqslant 0) + \tfrac{1}{2}] \\
&= \tfrac{1}{2}(\pi + \tfrac{1}{2}), \text{ (given } \omega_t = 1).
\end{aligned}$$

Hence

$$\Pr(s_{t+1} - E_t s_{t+1} \geqslant 0) = \tfrac{1}{2} \Leftrightarrow \Pi = \tfrac{1}{2} + \tfrac{1}{4} = \tfrac{1}{2}$$

Thus, as long as the probability of a regime shift differs from 50 per cent, the distribution of the forecasting error will be non-symmetric, i.e. skewed. This type of situation might arise where agents believe that there is a small probability of a regime shift in any *given* period, but a high probability that the shift will eventually occur (i.e. $\pi > 0.5$) – for example a devaluation, or a European Monetary System (EMS) realignment.

The significance of this analysis is due to the fact that, under the null hypothesis of efficient markets, the regression disturbances in equations such as (1.82) are in fact the rational expectations forecasting errors. If these are non-symmetrically distributed, then the econometric theory used to derive inferences about the regression parameters will generally be invalid – they may lead to erroneous conclusions.

The peso problem may be particularly worrying in certain circumstances – Krasker cites the example of the German hyperinflation of the 1920s where participants in the forward foreign exchange market may have perceived a small probability, in each period, that there would be a monetary stabilization which would end the hyperinflation. Another obvious example would be where there is clear tension within an adjustment peg regime such as the EMS, or in the run-up to a general election.

Foreign exchange market bubbles

The peso problem arises when agents perceive a non-zero probability of a shift in the market fundamentals. Rational bubbles may occur because, in general, there will be a number of feasible rational expectations equilibria other than the market fundamentals solution.

As an example, consider again the FLPM exchange rate model – this time equation (1.39), which we write here as

$$s_t = \theta s_{t+1}^e + v_t \tag{1.113}$$

where θ and v_t are as defined above.

One rational expectations solution to (1.113) is the market fundamentals solution described in (1.40) and (1.105). In order to distinguish this from other solutions, we shall denote the market fundamentals solution by a tilde, as in (1.114):

$$\tilde{s}_t = \sum_{i=0}^{\infty} \theta^i \, \mathrm{E}_t v_{t+i} \tag{1.114}$$

Now it is easy to show that (1.113) has multiple rational expectations solutions, each of which can be written in the form

$$s_t = \tilde{s}_t + b_t \tag{1.115}$$

where $\tilde{s}_t$ is as defined in (1.114) and the only stipulation concerning b_t is

$$b_t = \theta \, \mathrm{E}_t b_{t+1} \tag{1.116}$$

To see that (1.115) solves (1.113), note that from (1.115)

$$\mathrm{E}_t s_{t+1} = \mathrm{E}_t \tilde{s}_{t+1} + \mathrm{E}_t b_{t+1}$$

$$= \sum_{i=0}^{\infty} \theta^i \mathrm{E}_t v_{t+i+1} + \mathrm{E}_t b_{t+1}$$

or, using (1.116)

$$E_t s_{t+1} = \sum_{i=0}^{\infty} \theta^i E_t \nu_{t+i+1} + \theta^{-1} b_t$$

i.e.

$$\theta\, E_t s_{t+1} = \sum_{i=0}^{\infty} \theta^{i+1} E_t \nu_{t+i+1} + b_t$$

$$= \tilde{s}_t - \nu_t + b_t$$

which, rearranging and using (1.115), yields

$$s_t = \theta\, E_t s_{t+1} + \nu_t \tag{1.117}$$

Under rational expectations, (1.117) is identical with (1.113).

The term b_t in the general solution (1.115) is the 'bootstrap' or bubble variable – if agents believe it to be important, then it will be so.[12] Such a rational bubble might arise where the market exchange rate has been bid away from the fundamentals solution. Agents then have to weigh the probability of a continued deviation from fundamentals – a continuation of the bubble – against the probability of a return to the fundamentals – the bubble bursting. Because of the asymmetry in the probability distribution of the bubble term, an asymmetry may be imparted into the distribution of exchange rate innovations. As an example, consider the following probability model for b_t:[13]

$$b_t = \begin{cases} (\pi\theta)^{-1} b_{t-1} \text{ with probability } \pi \text{ (the bubble continues)} \\ 0 \text{ with probability } 1 - \pi \text{ (the bubble bursts)} \end{cases}$$

This model clearly satisfies (1.116). For simplicity, but without loss of generality, we assume that the market fundamentals follow a stationary first-order Markov process:

$$\nu_t = \phi\nu_{t-1} + u_t \qquad |\phi| < 1 \tag{1.118}$$

where u_t is a white noise disturbance. Relation (1.118) implies that the market fundamentals solution (1.114) can be written as

$$\tilde{s}_t = (1 - \phi\theta)^{-1}\nu_t + u_t \tag{1.119}$$

Now consider the rational expectations forecasting error. Using (1.115), (1.116) and (1.119), this can be written

$$s_{t+1} - E_t s_{t+1} = u_{t+1} + b_{t+1} - \theta^{-1} b_t \tag{1.120}$$

Hence

$$\Pr\{(s_{t+1} - E_t s_{t+1}) \geqslant 0\} = \tfrac{1}{2}[\Pr(u_{t+1} \geqslant 0) + \Pr\{(b_{t+1} - \theta^{-1} b_t) \geqslant 0\}]$$
$$= \tfrac{1}{2}(\tfrac{1}{2} + \pi)$$

Hence

$$\Pr\{(s_{t+1} - E_t s_{t+1}) \geqslant 0\} = \tfrac{1}{2} \Leftrightarrow \pi = \tfrac{1}{2}$$

Thus, if agents expect that the speculative bubble will ultimately burst but that there is only a small probability of its bursting in any one period (i.e. $\pi > 1/2$), then the rational expectations forecasting error will have zero conditional mean but will be distributed asymmetrically (will have non-zero median). As in the peso problem, this may invalidate standard econometric inference procedures in finite samples.

Note that although both the peso problem and rational bubbles generate similar results – a skew in the distribution of rational forecasting errors – they are distinct phenomena. In the case of the peso problem, the difficulty arises because of a non-zero probability of a shift *in* the fundamentals. In the case of rational bubbles, the problem is due to a drift *away from* the fundamentals.

The empirical evidence on bubbles is rather scant and researchers have generally not been able to distinguish between the presence of bubbles and other deviations from the maintained hypothesis.

One type of test which can be interpreted as a test for bubbles involves testing for 'excess volatility'. Consider, for example, the market funda-mentals solution for the FLPM model, equation (1.114):

$$\tilde{s}_t = \sum_{i=0}^{\infty} \theta^i \, E_t \nu_{t+i}$$

or

$$\tilde{s}_t = E_t s_t^* \qquad\qquad (1.121)$$

where

$$s_t^* = \sum_{i=0}^{\infty} \theta^i \nu_{t+i}$$

i.e. s_t^* is a 'discounted present value' of actual future fundamentals – the 'perfect foresight' or '*ex post* rational' exchange rate. The perfect foresight rate will differ from its expected value $\tilde{s}_t$ (see (1.121)) by a rational expectations forecasting error

$$s_t^* = \tilde{s}_t + u_t \qquad\qquad (1.122)$$

where

$$u_t = \sum_{i=0}^{\infty} \theta^i (\nu_{t+i} - E_t \nu_{t+i})$$

Because $\tilde{s}_t$ is the rational expectation and u_t the rational forecasting error, $\tilde{s}_t$ and u_t must be orthogonal. Hence, from (1.122) we have

$$\text{var}(s_t^*) = \text{var}(\tilde{s}_t) + \text{var}(u_t)$$

which implies

$$\text{var}(s_t^*) \geq \text{var}(\tilde{s}_t) \tag{1.123}$$

Thus, if the actual observed exchange rate is the market fundamentals solution, inequality (1.123) should hold.[14] If, on the other hand, the actual rate (s_t, say) is characterized by bubbles, then substituting (1.115) into (1.122) we have

$$s_t^* = s_t - b_t + u_t$$
$$\text{var}(s_t^*) = \text{var}(s_t) + \text{var}(b_t) + \text{var}(u_t) - 2\,\text{cov}(s_t, b_t) \tag{1.124}$$

Because there is no a priori reason to exclude the possibility that s_t and b_t are positively correlated, an inequality similar to (1.123) cannot be derived from (1.124). Thus, evidence of 'excess volatility' (inequalities such as (1.123) being significantly violated) is prima-facie evidence for the presence of bubbles.

Huang (1981) uses this approach to test for excess volatility in the dollar–mark, dollar–UK pound and UK pound–mark exchange rates over the period March 1973 to March 1979, assuming an FLPM model of fundamentals. His results are supportive of excess volatility. Wadhwani (1984) also reports evidence of excess volatility in the dollar–sterling rate over the period 1973 first quarter to 1982 third quarter, using an SPM model of fundamentals. These results do therefore tend to indicate the presence of foreign exchange market bubbles. However, there are a number of problems with variance bounds tests. First, they are conditional on an assumed model. Second, there may be other possible explanations for violation of the variance inequalities besides the presence of bubbles – for example some of the implicit stationarity assumptions may be false or there may be small-sample bias (see Leroy, 1984).

Meese (1986) applies a different type of test for bubbles, based on the Hausman (1978) specification test. This procedure can be illustrated as follows. First, rewrite the FLPM equation (1.114) with an error term:

$$s_t = \theta E_t s_{t+1} + v_t + u_t \tag{1.125}$$

This would result, for example, if the PPP relationship included an error term (i.e. $s_t = p_t - p_t^* + u_t$). Now (1.125) will hold regardless of whether the market is characterized by fundamentals or bubbles. Thus θ can be consistently estimated from (1.125) by applying McCallum's (1976) instrumental variable technique, i.e. the actual value of s_{t+1} is substituted for $E_t s_{t+1}$ and the resulting equation is estimated by instrumental variables. Moreover, this estimate will be consistent under both the null hypothesis (no bubbles) and the alternative hypothesis (bubbles). Now consider the market fundamentals solution to (1.125):

$$\tilde{s}_t = \sum_{i=0}^{\infty} \theta^i E_t \nu_{t+i} + u_t \tag{1.126}$$

If we assume that the fundamentals have a well-determined, stable ARMA representation, we can derive a closed form for (1.126). Assume, for expositional simplicity, that ν_t has a first-order autoregressive representation

$$\nu_t = \phi \nu_{t-1} + \epsilon_t \tag{1.127}$$

Then, from (1.127),

$$E_t \nu_{t+i} = \phi^i \nu_t$$

Hence, the closed-form version of (1.126) is

$$\tilde{s}_t = (1 - \phi\theta)^{-1} \nu_t + u_t \tag{1.128}$$

Under the assumption of no bubbles, (1.127) and (1.128) can be estimated jointly to yield an estimate of θ. This estimate will only be consistent, however, under the null hypothesis (no bubbles). To see this, note that if ν_t is exogenous with respect to $\tilde{s}_t$ then ϕ and θ are just identified in (1.127) and (1.128) and indirect least squares is the efficient estimation strategy. If we denote

$$(1 - \phi\theta)^{-1} = \gamma$$

then a consistent estimate of γ from OLS applied to (1.128) will yield a consistent estimate of θ by using the consistent estimate of ϕ obtained by OLS applied to (1.127) to solve for θ. The OLS estimate of γ is

$$\hat{\gamma} = \frac{\sum_{t=1}^{T} s_t \nu_t}{\sum_{t=1}^{T} \nu_t^2} \tag{1.129}$$

for $s_t = \tilde{s}_t$ (no bubbles) and where T is the sample size. If the market is characterized by bubbles, then the observed exchange rate s_t will differ from the market fundamentals rate $\tilde{s}_t$ by the bubble term b_t. Thus, (1.129) becomes

$$\hat{\gamma} = \frac{\sum_{t=1}^{T} (\tilde{s}_t + b_t)\nu_t}{\sum_{t=1}^{T} \nu_t^2}$$

Hence, using (1.128) and (1.127),

$$\underset{Tg \to \infty}{\text{plim}} \ \hat{\gamma} = \gamma + \underset{T \to \infty}{\text{plim}} \ \frac{1}{T} \ \frac{\sum_{t=1}^{T} b_t \nu_t}{(1 - \phi)^{-1}\sigma^2} \qquad (1.130)$$

where σ^2 is the variance of ϵ_t in (1.127). Since there is no a priori reason to believe that the bubble term is uncorrelated with the fundamentals, this estimation technique will generally yield an inconsistent estimate of γ and hence of θ under the alternative hypothesis (bubbles). Thus, Hausman's (1978) specification test can be used to test for a significant difference between the estimate of θ obtained by McCallum estimation applied to (1.125) and the estimate obtained by indirect least squares applied to (1.127) and (1.128).

Meese (1986) applies this methodology to test for bubbles in the dollar–yen, dollar–mark and dollar–sterling exchange rates using monthly data for the period October 1973 to November 1982, and in every case rejects the no-bubbles hypothesis. In common with the variance bounds tests, however, the specification test for bubbles is conditional on an assumed model. Meese uses a model which is in some ways similar to the FLPM formulation, except that the PPP deviation (u_t in (1.125)) is assumed to follow a random walk. Sustained short-run deviations from PPP can be interpreted as exchange rate overshooting, so that Meese's model is probably closer to the SPM formulation.

Evans (1986) tests for what he terms 'speculative bubbles' in the dollar–sterling rate over the period 1981–4 by testing for a non-zero median in excess returns, which he defines as the forward rate forecasting error $s_{t+1} - f_t$. Evans designs non-parametric tests for a non-zero median which are close in nature to runs tests, i.e. he tests for a significant deviation of the number of positive excess returns from the number which would be expected if the distribution of excess returns had zero median. In an analysis of monthly data, Evans decisively rejects the zero-median hypothesis for dollar–sterling excess returns. This result also goes through when Evans allows for a time-varying risk premium in a simple way.[15] Thus, conditional on rational expectations, Evans infers that this provides evidence of empirical speculative bubbles. Note, however, that Evans' definition of this phenomenon, i.e. a non-zero median in excess returns, encompasses both the peso problem and rational bubbles as defined above. Thus, Evans's results may indicate the presence of rational bubbles, the peso problem or non-rational expectations.

Risk premia in foreign exchange markets

Perhaps the major response to the mounting evidence which rejects the joint hypothesis of rational expectations and risk neutrality has been to absorb the hypothesis of rational expectations into the maintained hypothesis and to test for or model foreign exchange risk premia.

As we noted above, retaining the assumption of rational expectations but relaxing that of risk neutrality involves driving a wedge between the forward rate and the expected future spot rate equal to the risk premium (see equation (1.75)):

$$f_t = s_{t+1}^e + \rho_t \tag{1.131}$$

In section 1.4.1 we noted how a simple model of the risk premium (equal to a constant plus white noise) might be incorporated into tests for rational expectations in the foreign exchange market. Such an approach involves estimating a standard spot-forward regression by a structural equation estimator and allowing a non-zero intercept (see equation (1.77)). However, a more sophisticated model would allow the premium to be systematically time varying.

As we noted above, the risk premium can equivalently be viewed as the deviation from UIP (see equation (1.32)); thus

$$\rho_t = r_t - r_t^* - \Delta s_{t+1}^e \tag{1.132}$$

Frankel (1982b) attempts to assess the importance of foreign exchange risk premia by estimating portfolio balance asset demand functions across a number of currencies. If x_t denotes the vector of portfolio shares that an investor wishes to allocate to marks, pounds, yen, francs and Canadian dollars (and the residuals $1 - x'l$, where l is a unit vector, are the share allocated to US dollars), then under the assumption of mean–variance optimization in real wealth Frankel derives asset demands of the form

$$x_t = \alpha + (\theta\Omega)^{-1}R_t \tag{1.133}$$

where α is the vector of consumption shares allocated to German, British, Japanese, French and Canadian goods, θ is the Arrow–Pratt measure of relative risk aversion, Ω is the covariance matrix of depreciation

$$\Omega = E(\Delta\sigma_{t+1} - E\Delta\sigma_{t+1})(\Delta\sigma_{t+1} - E\Delta\sigma_{t+1})'$$

(where σ is a vector of spot dollar rates against the five currencies concerned) and R_t is a vector of the risk premia (as defined in (1.132)) for each of the currencies against the dollar:

$$R_t = \kappa_t - lr_t^* - \Delta\sigma_{t+1}^e$$

(where κ_t is a vector of the five interest rates).

Frankel estimates (1.133) by maximum likelihood methods using monthly data for the 1970s and is unable to reject the hypothesis of risk neutrality $\theta = 0$. He notes that 'while the power of the test may be low, imposing mean–variance optimisation has given us greater power than previous tests'.

In models advanced by, for example, Stockman (1978) and Frenkel and Razin (1982), the risk premium depends upon the concavity of the assumed utility function and the probability distribution of the exogenous processes. Given stability of this distribution, the premium will be constant. Frenkel (1976, 1980) finds some empirical support for a constant risk premium for some exchange rates but not for others whilst Stockman (1978) presents evidence that the premium may change in sign. As noted above, Fama (1984) finds quite strong support for the presence of time-varying premia, as does Taylor (1988a).

The theoretical case for time-varying foreign exchange risk premia has been made in papers by Grauer et al. (1976), Fama and Farber (1979), Lucas (1982) and Hodrick and Srivastava (1984). However, empirical work based on such models is hampered by the fact that, unlike in the Frankel (1982) mean–variance approach, tractable estimating equations are not generally forthcoming. Thus, empirical work on this topic generally tests models that are somewhat loosely related to the underlying theoretical model – see for example Hansen and Hodrick (1983), Hodrick and Srivastava (1984), Domowitz and Hakkio (1985), Wolff (1987) and Taylor (1988a).

Domowitz and Hakkio (1985) apply the ARCH-in-mean model of Engle et al. (1987) to derive an empirical model of the risk premium which they test using monthly data on a number of exchange rates for the period June 1973 to August 1987. Essentially, this involves assuming that the risk premium is a function of the conditional variance of exchange rate prediction errors and that this variance itself follows some sort of autoregressive process (see Engle, 1982). Domowitz and Hakkio conclude that 'While there is evidence against the unbiasedness hypothesis for a majority of the currencies, there is little support for the conditional variance of the exchange rate forecast error being an important sole determinant of the risk premium' (1985, p. 62).

Both Wolff (1987) and Taylor (1988a) use Kalman filtering techniques to model the risk premium as a latent variable. Wolff uses this methodology to identify and estimate premia as autoregressive processes, whilst Taylor models the premium as a latent variable depending upon domestic and foreign asset yield volatility. Thus, the type of model estimated by Taylor (1988a) is of the form

$$f_t - s_{t+1} = \rho_t + u_{t+1} \tag{1.134}$$

$$\rho_t = \phi\rho_{t-1} + \theta_1\pi_t^d + \theta_2\pi_t^f + \epsilon_t \tag{1.135}$$

where π_t^d and π_t^f are, respectively, summary measures of domestic and foreign asset yield volatility and ϵ_t is white noise. The simple intuition behind this formulation is that, other things equal, increased foreign asset yield volatility may tend to depress the forward relative demand for foreign currency and hence depress f_t, i.e. to reduce the risk premium ρ_t attached to holding domestic assets. Thus, θ_2 is expected to be negative and, by a converse argument, θ_1 is expected to be positive. Taylor estimates this model using monthly data for dollar–pound, dollar–Swiss franc and dollar–yen over the period March 1976 to July 1986. The dollar–pound results are as follows:

$$f_t - s_{t+1} = \hat{\rho}_t + \hat{u}_{t+1}$$

$$\hat{\rho}_t = 0.2841\hat{\rho}_{t-1} + 0.0818\pi_t^{\text{UK}} - 0.0177\pi_t^{\text{US}} + \hat{\epsilon}_t$$
$$\quad\ (0.1073) \qquad\ (0.0109) \qquad\ \ (0.0044)$$

$$Q(33) = 32.18$$

where figures in parentheses are asymptotic standard errors. The Ljung–Box statistic $Q(33)$ applied to the risk-adjusted forecasting errors indicates an absence of serial correlation, and the signs and significance of the estimated coefficients are also generally encouraging. Although Taylor's model is intuitively plausible and works well empirically, it is open to the criticism that it is essentially *ad hoc*. As noted above, however, this is a feature of much of the currently extant work on this topic.

The work discussed above largely represents attempts to *model* the risk premium. A slightly different approach involves testing equilibrium conditions involving *measures* of the risk premium. Korajczyk (1985), for example, notes that the risk premium, in equilibrium, should be equal to the *ex ante* RID and tests an equation of the form

$$s_{t+1} - f_t = \theta_0 + \theta_1 E_t(i_t^* - i_t) + \theta_2 Z_t + u_{t+1} \tag{1.136}$$

where i_t and i_t^* represent the domestic and foreign *real* interest rates (i.e. nominal rates at time t less inflation between times t and $t+1$) and Z_t is a vector of variables known at time t. The null hypothesis is then

$$H_0: \theta_0 = 0, \theta_1 = 1, \theta_2 = 0 \tag{1.137}$$

The rationale for (1.136) and (1.137) can be illustrated as follows. Consider the following equations:

covered interest parity	$s_t - f_t = r_t^* - r_t$	(1.138)
real exchange rate	$q_t = s_t - p_t + p_t^*$	(1.139)
domestic Fisher equation	$r_t = E_t i_t + E_t \Delta p_{t+1}$	(1.140)
foreign Fisher equation	$r_t^* = E_t i_t^* + E_t \Delta p_{t+1}^*$	(1.141)

Advancing (1.139) by one period, taking first differences and rearranging we have

$$s_{t+1} - s_t = q_{t+1} - q_t + \Delta p_{t+1} - \Delta p^*_{t+1}$$

Substituting for s_t from (1.138) and rearranging, we then have

$$s_{t+1} - f_t = q_{t+1} - q_t - (r_t - \Delta p_{t+1}) + (r^*_t - \Delta p^*_{t+1})$$

Using the Fisher equations (1.140) and (1.141) to substitute for r_t and r^*_t and taking expectations conditional on information at time t we then have

$$E_t s_{t+1} - f_t = E_t \Delta q_{t+1} + E_t(i^*_t - i_t) \tag{1.142}$$

Now there exists quite a lot of evidence to suggest that the real exchange rate follows, or is at least closely approximated by, a pure random walk (Roll, 1979; Adler and Lehmann, 1983; M.P. Taylor, 1986, 1988d), i.e. $E_t q_{t+1} = q_t$; using this and $s_{t+1} = E_t s_{t+1} + u_{t+1}$ in (1.142) then yields (1.136) and (1.137). Thus, however the risk premium is determined, it should be equal to the RID. This quite general measure will hold whether time variation is due to changes in risk or to changes in the price of risk. The models of Hansen and Hodrick (1983) and Hodrick and Srivastava (1984), for example, model premia variation as dependent upon variations in the expected excess return on a benchmark portfolio (the price of risk) whilst it may also be due to changes in conditional variances (which the Domowitz–Hakkio (1985) model is an attempt to capture).

Korajczyk estimates (1.136) for seven exchange rates against the dollar by a McCallum-type instrumental variables procedure, using monthly data for the period April 1974 to December 1980. He also uses a statistical technique (bootstrapping) to correct for small-sample bias in tests of (1.135). In general, Korajczyk is unable to reject the restrictions. These results therefore provide evidence which suggests the presence of time-varying risk premia, conditional on the assumption of rational expectations, which may be consistent with a number of asset pricing models.

Alternatively, it might be argued that Korajczyk's analysis is really only a roundabout way of testing the random walk property of real exchange rates (given rational expectations). If covered interest parity is treated as an identity (see for example Taylor, 1987a; MacDonald and Taylor, 1988a), the assumption of a random walk exchange rate is the only behavioural assumption in the analysis. Moreover, Korajczyk's findings here have been called into question by Levine (1987) who demonstrates (using a similar data base to that of Korajczyk) that when the forward premium is included in an estimate of (1.142), it consistently proves statistically significant, indicating that expected real interest rate differentials are not the only systematic component of forward forecasting errors (which they should be if the model is correctly specified).

1.4.7 The use of survey data to measure exchange rate expectations

One conclusion to emerge from our survey of the estimates of equations like (1.82) is that the joint null hypothesis is resoundingly rejected. As we have seen, the interpretation placed on such rejection depends crucially on a researcher's prejudices. Thus Bilson (1981), Longworth (1981) and Cumby and Obstfeld (1984) maintain that agents are risk neutral and therefore that rejection must be due to irrationality – speculation is excessive relative to the conditioning information set. On the other hand Fama (1984), Hodrick and Srivastava (1984) and Bilson (1985) adhere to the assumption that agents are rational and assert that the violation of the null is due to time-varying risk premia. Until recently, the jointness of the null meant it was impossible for other researchers to take anything more than an agnostic view. However, the recent availability of survey data on foreign exchange market participants' expectations of the exchange rate has allowed single-hypothesis tests of the joint hypothesis. That is, the availability of an independent source for s_t^e means that rational expectations do not have to be imposed to obtain (1.82). We may test therefore whether rejections of the null are due to irrationality or risk aversion. Thus, for example, on using (1.73), the a_1 coefficient in equation (1.82) may be expressed as

$$a_1 = \frac{\text{cov}[u_t, (f - s)_{t-1}] + \text{cov}[\Delta s_t^e, (f - s)_{t-1}]}{\text{var}[(f - s)_{t-1}]} \qquad (1.143)$$

On manipulating (1.143), a_1 can be written as equal to unity minus a term a_1^{RE} arising from any failure of rational expectations minus a further term a_1^{RP} arising from the presence of risk premia (see Frankel and Froot, 1986a, for a further discussion):

$$a_1 = 1 - a_1^{RE} - a_1^{RP}$$

where

$$a_1^{RE} = \frac{\text{cov}[u_t, (f - s)_{t-1}]}{\text{var}[(f - s)_{t-1}]}$$

and

$$a_1^{RP} = \frac{\text{var}(\rho_{t-1}) + \text{cov}(\Delta s_t^e, \rho_{t-1})}{\text{var}[(f - s)_{t-1}]}$$

Both a_1^{RE} and a_1^{RP} can be estimated with survey data and therefore it is in principle possible to discern whether rejection of the null is due to risk or irrationality. Thus a_1^{RE} may be estimated from a regression of the form

$$s_t^e - s_t = a_0 + a_1^{RE}(f - s)_{t-1} + v_t$$

and a_1^{RP} may be estimated from a regression of the form

$$s_t^e - s_{t-1} = b_0 + b_1(f - s)_{t-1} + u_t$$

as $1 - \hat{b}_1$. Recently, a number of researchers in the USA and UK have started to obtain estimates of a_1^{RP} and a_1^{RE}. Do their findings shed any light on the apparent failure of the joint null in estimates of (1.82)? Frankel and Froot (hereafter FF) (1986a, b, 1987) use a selection of survey data bases to discriminate between a_1^{RP} and a_1^{RE}. More specifically, FF (1987) utilize bi-annual American Express Bank (AMEX) survey data for the period 1976–84 (the forecasts are six months ahead) and survey data from the *Economist* financial report for three an six months ahead, from 1981–5 (these data are sampled six times a year): both the surveys are for five currencies against the dollar (the UK pound, French franc, German mark, Swiss franc and yen). The general conclusion to emerge in FF (1987) is that the failure of the joint hypothesis may be attributable to a statistically significant a_1^{RE} term:

> If the survey numbers are to be believed at all, the unconditional bias is present in actual investor expectations, and cannot be attributed to a risk premia. . . . If, however, the survey data are used as expectations, the alternative of a time-varying risk premium is eliminated, and we are left with a single, unambiguous alternative hypothesis: a failure of rational expectations in the form of excessive speculation.

Generally similar findings are reported in FF (1986a, b), where in addition to the AMEX and *Economist* survey data one- and three-month exchange rate forecasts from Money Market Services (MMS) (US) are utilized. Dominguez (1986) uses exclusively MMS (US) one-week, two-week, one-month and three-month forecast data for the US dollar against UK pound, the German mark, the Swiss franc and the Japanese yen for the period 1983–5 (the start and end points depend on the forecast horizon). It is demonstrated by Dominguez that the joint null fails because of the irrationality of exchange market participants: that is, a_1^{RE} is statistically significant at high levels of significance (indeed for some of the longer horizons, she finds both the magnitude and the direction of exchange rate change completely wrong!).

Two survey exercises have been conducted using UK data bases. Taylor (1988b) uses a survey data base constructed by Godwins (a firm of British management consultants) which consists of the expectations of chief investment managers of over 50 London investment houses on the sterling effective rate and the dollar–sterling rate. Taylor's findings contrast with those reported above in that he finds that the joint null hypothesis is violated because of a significant risk premium term.

MacDonald and Torrance (1988a) employ MMS (UK) data for expectations one week ahead (weekly data) and four weeks ahead (two-weekly data) for the German mark–US dollar over the period February 1985 to December 1986. MacDonald's and Torrance's results are supportive of FF, in that they argue that rejection of the null is attributable to the failure of the rational expectations leg of the joint hypothesis: speculation is deemed to be excessive for the exchange rate and data period studied.

On balance then, the above studies tend to indicate that the null hypothesis of efficiency is rejected as a result of the failure of the rational expectations component. This finding is supportive of the studies which have attempted to model the exchange risk premia: such studies have generally failed to unearth statistically significant risk premia. The absence of a risk premium has other important implications. It implies, for example, that the monetary view of the exchange rate is appropriate and as a consequence that the authorities cannot use sterilized foreign exchange market intervention. But the significant a_1^{RE} term reported in the above studies does not necessarily imply that agents are irrational processors of information, since the results could be explicable in terms of either rational speculative bubbles or the peso problem (the latter is the explanation used in MacDonald and Torrance, 1988a).

1.5 NEWS AND EXCHANGE RATES

One important implication of the rational expectations hypothesis is that it is unanticipated events or news that drive asset prices like the exchange rate. For example, although the strict EMH requires the forward exchange rate to be an unbiased forecast of the future spot rate, it does not predict that the forward rate will be a particularly good forecast (although it may be the best available) of the future spot rate in periods which contain a great deal of new information. Thus in section 1.4 the forecast error u_{t+n} in equation (1.91) was seen to be a function of new information arising between $t+1$ and $t+n$ (see (1.92)). If such news elements are small and insignificant then clearly the EMH predicts that s_{t+n} should be very close to f_t^n, but if a researcher is examining (1.91) for a period in which there has been a great deal of new information s_{t+n} could differ substantially from f_t^n. Without doubt the recent experience with floating exchange rates has been one in which there has been a great deal of new (i.e. unanticipated) information about economic factors, such as money supplies, current accounts and income, and also non-economic factors, such as political news. Recently, a number of researchers have attempted to implement the economic news approach empirically to modelling the exchange rate. Before discussing such news results, we consider the news approach in a little more detail.

Let the vector z include all variables relevant for the process of exchange rate determination, and thus our equation for the determination of the exchange rate is

$$s_t = \gamma z_t + v_t \tag{1.142}$$

where v_t is a white noise error. In forming their expectations agents use (1.142) and therefore

$$s_t^e = \gamma z_t^e \tag{1.145}$$

where $s_t^e = E(s_t | I_{t-1})$ etc. Thus on subtracting (1.145) from (1.144) we see that the current-period forecasting error is composed of a news term and a purely random term:

$$s_t - s_t^e = \gamma(z_t - z_t^e) + v_t \tag{1.146}$$

If we additionally assume that agents are risk neutral then we may rewrite (1.146) as

$$s_t - f_{t-1} = \gamma(z_t - z_t^e) + v_t \tag{1.147}$$

where the term in parentheses represents the news.

The derivation (1.144) to (1.147) highlights two factors which face a researcher in attempting to test the news approach empirically. First, some model of the process of exchange rate determination must be chosen. In terms of equation (1.144) a choice has to be made as to which variables should enter the z_t vector. Second, having decided on the appropriate model of exchange rate determination, the researcher must decide on an appropriate way to generate the expected values of the determining variables. As is demonstrated below, researchers have used essentially three methods to generate expected values: regression analysis, time-series analysis and the use of survey data. We order our discussion of the empirical results in terms of the method used to generate the news.

The first news study to use time-series analysis to generate the news was conducted by Frenkel (1981). Frenkel estimates a news equation of the form

$$s_t = a_0 + b_1 f_{t-1} + b_2(z_t - z_t^e) + w_t \tag{1.148}$$

where $z_t = (r - r^*)_t$ and w_t is white noise. Equation (1.148) is estimated for the US dollar–UK pound, US dollar–French franc and US dollar–German mark exchange rates, over the period June 1973 to June 1979, using an autoregression to generate the expected interest rate series.[16] In all Frenkel's estimated equations, b_2 is positive, but only in the case of one equation (for the US dollar–UK pound), reported here as equation (1.149), is b_2 statistically significant:

$$s_t = \underset{(0.02)}{0.031} + \underset{(0.02)}{0.959} f_{t-1} + \underset{(0.18)}{0.432} [(r - r^*)_t - (r - r^*)_t^e] \tag{1.149}$$

$$R^2 = 0.96 \qquad DW = 1.78 \qquad \text{(Estimation technique: instrumental}$$

variables, standard errors in
parentheses.)

The positive association between the exchange rate and the interest rate news
is asserted to be supportive of the FLPM model. An autoregressive approach
to generating the news is also favoured by Edwards (1982b) who estimates a
news representation of the FLPM model (i.e. the unanticipated exchange
rate is related to unanticipated money supplies, income and interest rates) for
the same currencies as Frenkel (and also the Italian lira–US dollar) over the
period June 1973 to September 1979: results which are reasonably supportive
of the FLPM news reduced forms in that the coefficients on some variables
are statistically significant and correctly signed are reported. Copeland
(1984a) also estimates a news representation of the FLPM model for the
pound sterling–US dollar rate (using autoregressive models to generate news)
and reports results, which, after accounting for potential simultaneity bias
are reasonably supportive of the approach. MacDonald (1985) uses autoregressive models to generate news for an FLPM reduced form from the
1920s experience with floating exchange rates: results which are generally
supportive of the news approach in that the equations exhibit a reasonable
explanatory power and the coefficients on the news variables are well
determined are reported.

Bomhoff and Korteweg (1983) also use a time-series methodology to
generate the news, but their approach is more sophisticated than those
discussed hitherto in that they allow the time-series parameters to be time
dependent. Using a multistate Kalman filter, news about relative money
supplies, income and the price of oil is generated for six currencies over the
period 1973–9 (quarterly data). Bomhoff and Korteweg summarize their
evidence in the following way:

> between 16 and 60 per cent of the variation of the unexpected rate of change of
> the various spot rates can be explained by the current and lagged effects of
> randomly arriving new information. . . . Furthermore, most 'news' terms
> appear to be correctly signed and significant at the 90 per cent level or better.
> Interestingly, 'news' affects the current exchange rate with long lags; in some
> instances there are lags of over one year before the domestic or foreign
> monetary impulses have their effect on spot rates.

Given that Mussa (1979) has suggested that a successful model of the
exchange rate should be able to explain at least 10 per cent of the quarter to
quarter exchange rate change, Bomhoff and Korteweg (1983) regard their
results as offering considerable support of the news model.

A number of researchers have implemented the news approach using more
information than simply the past history of the variable being forecast. In

particular, Branson (1983), Edwards (1983) and MacDonald (1983a,b) use either a vector autoregression or a version of Barro's (1978) methodology to generate the news.

A version of equation (1.147) has been estimated by MacDonald (1983a) for a selection of six currencies against the US dollar (the Canadian dollar, the Austrian schilling, the UK pound, the French franc, the German mark and the Swiss franc) over the period 1972 first quarter to 1979 fourth quarter using the ZSURE estimator. The variables entering the z vector are the growth of home and foreign money supplies and news about these variables is generated by regressing them on variables such as the inflation rate, income, interest rates, the current account surplus and the budget deficit (along the lines suggested by Barro, 1978) and retrieving the residuals. The reduced form exchange rate equation tested is

$$s_t - f_{t-1} = a + b_1 \sum_{i=0}^{4} u_{t+i} + b_2 \sum_{I=0}^{4} u_{t-1}^* \tag{1.150}$$

where u denotes the money growth surprise. Following the FLPM model, it is expected that domestic monetary news is positive and statistically significant and the foreign news term is significantly negative; it is further expected that the lagged news term should not have a significant role to play in determining the current forecasting error. MacDonald (1983b) implements the approach for three currencies from the interwar floating

Table 1.11 Monetary news and the exchange rate in two periods of floating exchange rates: $s_t - f_{t-1}^t = b_0 + b_1 u_t + b_2 u_t^*$

Exchange rate	Time period	b_0	b_1	b_2	Estimation technique
Pound–dollar[a]	1972 1st quarter–1979	0.047 (0.60)	−0.156 (1.06)	0.172 (0.14)	ZSURE
Franc–dollar[a]	1972 1st quarter–1979	−0.003 (0.38)	−0.291 (0.46)	−1.155 (1.02)	ZSURE
Mark–dollar[a]	1972 1st quarter–1979	−0.015 (1.85)	−2.017 (3.27)	3.173 (2.68)	ZSURE
Dollar–pound	February 1921–May 1925	−0.364 (2.57)	0.071 (2.45)	0.003 (1.11)	OLS
Franc–dollar	February 1921–May 1925	0.059 (1.15)	0.497 (1.06)	−3.854 (0.49)	OLS
Franc–pound	February 1921–May 1925	0.013 (1.17)	1.623 (1.60)	0.070 (0.09)	OLS

[a] The original reported results included lagged news items; t ratios are in parentheses.

Source: MacDonald (1983a,b)

period (monthly data, February 1921 to May 1925). A selection of the results from the two periods are reported in table 1.11.

Although a number of coefficients are significantly different from zero in table 1.11, notice that many are wrongly signed, suggesting that an unanticipated increase in home money results in an exchange rate appreciation. Another interesting feature of the studies by MacDonald was the finding that lagged news terms were statistically significant (in some cases lag $t - 4$ was significant). Although publication lags could explain some of the significant lagged news terms (perhaps at lag 1) the rest of the significant lagged news terms are perhaps harder to rationalize (see MacDonald, 1988, for a discussion). Interestingly, when MacDonald (1983b) used interest rate news in the interwar news equations more promising results, broadly supportive of the monetary approach, were reported.

In an attempt to implement the portfolio balance approach in a news context, Branson (1983) models news about money supplies, the current account and price levels as residuals from vector autoregressions (the unanticipated measure of the exchange rate is generated in a similar way). Branson's news approach is implemented by cross-correlating the exchange rate residual separately with each of the relevant news variables. For the exchange rates studied, the results are found to be supportive of the portfolio balance view since the current account and relative price terms generally have the correct sign; the money signs are somewhat more ambiguous due to the simultaneity of money that existed during the estimation period.

In a somewhat separate news literature from that outlined above, a number of researchers regress the *actual* exchange rate change on news about whether monetary authorities in the USA and UK have maintained their monetary targets (where the news is generated using survey data). This is illustrated by equation (1.151):

$$s_t^a - \hat{s}_t = a_0 + a_1(\dot{m}_t^a - \dot{m}_t^e) + w_t \qquad (1.151)$$

where $\dot{m}_t^a$ denotes the announcement of how much monetary growth has overshot its target, m^e denotes the expected monetary overshoot recorded immediately before the announcement, s_t^a denotes the log of the spot rate at the time of the announcement and $\hat{s}_t$ denotes the spot rate immediately before the announcement. The $\dot{m}_t^e$ term is taken to be the median value of a survey of money market operators conducted in both the USA and UK by MMS. Although, for obvious reasons, this literature cannot be thought of as a test of the EMH (the use of the actual exchange rate change precludes this) it is nevertheless useful in discriminating between market participants' beliefs about the future course of monetary policy (see Cornell, 1983, for a further discussion). For the USA, the evidence (see for example Cornell, 1983; Engel and Frankel, 1984) strongly supports the view that an overshoot of the monetary target is expected to be reversed by a future tightening of monetary policy (the so-called policy anticipation effect – see Urich and Wachtel, 1981): in terms of equation (1.151) the news term should have a negative coefficient since the expected future monetary contraction raises interest rates which in turn, following on from the SPM model, appreciate the exchange rate. The UK evidence also tends to indicate that a monetary over-shoot signals a future tightening of monetary policy (see MacDonald and Torrance, 1988b).[17]

The above results suggest that the news approach to the determination of the exchange rate is reasonably well supported by the data, and future research on this topic should usefully extend the range of news terms considered and the methods of generating the news. Nevertheless, a difficulty remains: as Davidson (1985) points out, the volatility of exchange rates appears to be greater than the volatility of the conventional news items. This finding is supported by the literature on variance bounds tests (section 1.4.6) which demonstrates that the volatility of the kinds of variables used in empirical news studies is much less than the volatility of exchange rates. How may this be explained? It is possible to supplement the news approach in a number of ways.

First of all it is quite possible that non-quantifiable news elements, such as political announcements and rumours, dominate the quantifiable elements which researchers use in their news models.

Second, as discussed in detail in section 1.4.6 high relative volatility of exchange rates may be due to the presence of rational bubbles.

A third rationalization for the greater volatility of exchange rates than the news is that market participants may be using a different economic model from that prescribed by international economists. It is relatively easy to demonstrate that the use of the wrong economic model can introduce greater exchange rate variability than the use of the 'correct' economic model (see Dornbusch, 1983a, for a further discussion). Even if agents possess the 'correct' economic model, they may be swayed by fashions as to which variables are 'newsworthy'. For example, in one period current account news may be fashionable, in the next it may be fiscal or monetary discipline. Frankel and Froot (1988), for example, have suggested that exchange rates may in fact be weighted averages of the market fundamentals and of the predictions of 'chartist' or 'technical' analysts, with the weights time varying.

1.6 CONCLUSION

In this chapter we have brought together and surveyed the theoretical and empirical literature on exchange rate economics. What are the main conclusions that may be drawn from this literature?

   The first conclusion to come from our study is that reduced form exchange rate models, which seek to relate the exchange rate to fundamentals, such as relative excess asset supplies, have been largely unsuccessful in explaining exchange rate behaviour during the recent float. In particular, such equations exhibit poor in-sample and out-of-sample explanatory power, have coefficients which often conflict with theoretical priors and exhibit numerous instabilities. But, as we pointed out in section 1.3.6, such findings are hardly surprising given the rather *ad hoc* way reduced form asset approach equations have been implemented. Thus, we argued that such equations have been subject to mis-specification, particularly with respect to their dynamic properties but also in terms of the actual variables included; also, it is doubtful whether such equations are in fact true reduced forms in that a number of explanatory variables (if not all the explanatory variables featured in such equations) have been simultaneously determined with the exchange rate. Perhaps, then, a useful way of ensuring that empirical exchange rate models are specified properly would be to estimate them structurally. This is an avenue of research which has recently proved relatively fruitful and would be a useful area for future work. It is likely, however, that, even if researchers are able to model exchange rates econometrically, they will have limited success in forecasting the future rate at least as long as the international monetary system is prone to such instabilities as have existed during the 1970s and 1980s.

   The second main conclusion to emerge from our study is that the joint hypothesis of market efficiency (i.e. risk neutrality and rationality) is strongly rejected by the data. Perhaps the most appealing explanation for this failure, and one which numerous researchers have adopted, is that, since the 1970s and 1980s have been periods of immense turbulence and uncertainty in financial markets, foreign exchange market operators have required a risk premium in return for holding open positions in foreign currencies. The research into whether risk premia have existed during the recent float has suggested that if they do exist (and this is debatable) they are of an extremely small magnitude. This finding clearly has important implications. It implies, for eample, that the appropriate asset model of the exchange rate is some version of the monetary model: in the absence of a risk premium UIP must hold exactly, and, as we demonstrated in section 1.2, non-monetary assets are irrelevant for the path of the exchange rate. This conclusion, in turn, has important policy implications since, if UIP holds continuously, sterilized, or pure, intervention will have no effect on the exchange rate,[18] thus limiting the number of policy instruments at the disposal of the Central Bank.

   Given the relative lack of success in explaining the failure of the EMH with risk aversion, researchers have started to focus attention on the expectations leg of the joint hypothesis by examining the so-called peso problem and rational and irrational bubbles.[19] It is our contention that the latter phenomenon offers a particularly exciting topic for future research. This is because most exchange rate modellers tend to overlook completely the way that foreign exchange markets actually operate. Thus, it is by now well known that many foreign exchange market operators, particularly those with a short horizon, are concerned not with fundamentals but simply with whether they can, say, buy a currency today and sell it in some future period at a profit – a simple trading rule strategy. The speculative bubble concept neatly formalizes this trading rule concept within the confines of a particular view of the fundamentals driving exchange rates. The fundamentals, in turn, are of more concern to exchange market operators who take a longer position, such as investment portfolio managers. The marriage of these two views of the exchange rate seems to offer a useful framework for the future modelling of exchange rates since it takes account of the actual behaviour of foreign exchange market operators rather than of how economists *think* they operate (for an interesting first application of this type of approach, see Frankel and Froot, 1988).

Notes

1   There are in fact a number of reasons (such as differential tax risk, liquidity considerations, political risk, default risk and exchange risk) which suggest that non-money assets issued in different countries are unlikely to be perfect substitutes. Here we concentrate on the role of exchange risk.
2   Assuming that the Marshall–Lerner conditions holds – see for example Cuthbertson and Taylor (1987), MacDonald (1988).
3   This abstracts from any short-run 'J-curve' effects.
4   See MacDonald and Taylor (1988) for a discussion of the empirical evidence on international parity relationships. Note that in this section we explicitly work in discrete rather than continuous time in order to ease the transition from the theoretical to the empirical model – data are usually available in discrete form.
5   Subject to a maintained hypothesis concerning expectations formation, e.g. rational expectations.
6   Meese and Singleton (1982) demonstrate that spot and forward rates tend to display non-stationary behaviour (contain unit roots). If market efficiency holds, however, spot and forward rates must be co-integrated (Engle and Granger, 1987), so that (1.79) is the correct form for econometric testing (see Levy and Nobay, this volume).
7   McCulloch (1975) however, has, shown that the operational aspects of the Siegel paradox may be very slight. Thus, '. . . these problems should concern only the pure theorist, since, as McCulloch has shown, the distortions caused by applying Jensen's inequality to an arbitrary choice of numeraire are so small as to be empirically insignificant' (Siegel, 1975).

8   It need not be the case, however, that the conditional autocorrelation coefficients – equivalently, the moving average coefficients – are constant over time; see Stockman (1978).

9   The currencies studied were the dollar–pound, dollar–franc, franc–pound and mark–dollar.

10 The use of overlapping data involves some modifications to equation (1.104) – see MacDonald and Taylor (1988b).

11 The term 'peso problem' was coined in deference to the phenomenon of a consistently non-zero forward premium for the Mexican peso–US dollar rate in the period preceding the devaluation of the peso in 1976, even though the spot rate was fixed.

12 Rational expectations solutions other than the market fundamentals solution have variously been called 'sunspot', 'bootstrap', 'rational bubble' and 'will o' the wisp' equilibria – see for example Taylor (1977), Flood and Garber (1980b), Blanchard (1981b), Blanchard and Watson (1982), Diba and Grossman (1983) and Minford and Peel (1983).

13 The example is essentially unchanged if in fact b_t takes a value κ_t with probability $1 - \pi$, rather than zero; as long as $E_{t-1} \kappa_t = 0$ (see Blanchard and Watson, 1982).

14 Researchers have generally used a slight variant of this inequality to account for potential non-stationarity of the variables – see for example Wadhwani (1987).

15 By subtracting out the interest differential at time $t + 1$ (as a proxy for the expected interest differential) – see Korajczyk (1985) and the next subsection.

16 Hartley (1983) also estimates equation (1.91) for the recent float. Instead of using a two-step methodology where the expected values are generated first and then plugged into (1.91), the forecasting equation and (1.91) are estimated jointly for increased efficiency. However, Hartley's results are disappointing since none of the estimated coefficients are statistically significant.

17 Dornbusch (1980) implements a news equation with biannual Organization for Economic Co-operation and Development (OECD) survey data.

18 It may have some, probably small, effect if it alters agents' expectations of future monetary growth. See Genberg (1981) for a further discussion.

19 Further evidence that it is the expectations leg of the joint hypothesis that is at fault is provided by the evidence using survey data (although see Taylor, 1988b).

Part II
Exchange Rate Modelling

2 Exchange Rate Dynamics: An Empirical Analysis

David G. Barr

2.1 INTRODUCTION

The exchange rate is determined in a market which is as close to the textbook ideal as we are likely to find. Although there is scope for research into the mechanism by which the rate is set in this market we may reasonably assume that it will lead to a situation in which supply and demand are equated. In this rather narrow sense the exchange rate is always at its equilibrium level. However, a more useful approach decomposes this equilibrium level of the exchange rate into two parts; a fundamental rate which is directly influenced by other macroeconomic variables and a component that derives from the volatile nature of foreign exchange markets and includes, for example, the effects of speculation.

The earliest attempts at producing an equation to determine the equilibrium rate were based on the assumption of perfect goods arbitrage, i.e. that the domestic price of any good should be the same as the foreign price converted into domestic currency. A slightly more sophisticated approach included two equations to determine the two national price levels and introduced to exchange rate analysis the wider issues of macroeconomic theory. A further advance was the introduction of interest-bearing assets and the assumption that these could be traded across national borders.

Each of these advances permitted more of the variation in exchange rates to be attributed to 'fundamental' factors rather than to the intrinsic volatility of the market. However, they resulted in a model that was static in the sense that after an equilibrium rate had been established the current rate was predicted to be equal to it or, at worst, to differ from it to a degree unrelated to the difference yesterday or tomorrow. The empirical finding of serial correlation in these differences (see Begg, 1982, for a useful summary) highlighted the practical deficiency of static exchange rate theory.

Although econometric methods can be employed to improve these static equations there is a need to explain at least part of the observed dynamic results in terms of economic theory. The most straightforward method is to recognize that, while the exchange rate may be free to jump to the equilibrium level in its own market, the demand for and supply of different currencies may depend upon prices and quantities determined in markets that do not respond as quickly to exogenous shocks. For example, if the real exchange rate is a function of the real money stock and prices adjust slowly to excess demand in the goods market, an increase in the nominal money stock now will cause an immediate change in the real exchange rate. As prices adjust, so the real money stock will decline and the exchange rate will move towards its new long-run equilibrium. Furthermore, as explained by Buiter and Miller (1981) it is possible for the initial exchange rate movement to exceed that required for long-run equilibrium, i.e. that the sluggish adjustment of prices might be the cause of (serially correlated) variations in rates in excess of those predicted by the earlier static models. This 'overshooting' of the exchange rate has been the subject of considerable analysis not only because of its theoretical interest but also because these large rate changes may have effects on output and employment and may themselves be a transmission variable for government policy.

A survey of the empirical results obtained using models of the type mentioned above is provided by Barr (1984) and the overshooting result has been analysed by Dornbusch (1976) and Buiter and Miller (1981) among others. Overshooting due to the sluggish adjustment of asset stocks rather than prices is discussed by Branson (1977b) and Barr (1983a).

The primary aim of this chapter is to find an exchange rate equation. As a guide during the search a particular macro-model (Buiter and Miller, 1981) is used to provide a set of fundamentals and a clear role for expectations. The secondary aim is to investigate the empirical basis for this model in its own right. A particular feature of the model and its major contribution to policy arguments is the implication that downward overshooting of competitiveness will occur when a credible announcement of reduced future monetary growth is made. The loss of UK competitiveness in the latter half of the 1970s coupled with an anti-inflation and tight money policy suggests that the model may have a lot to contribute to the policy debate.

The model may be resolved to the point where it becomes observationally equivalent to any other monetary model which includes lags of the explanatory variables. Although econometric methods exist to solve this problem (see Barr, 1983b) they are not feasible with the small sample used here. Instead the 'semi-reduced form' (Blanchard and Kahn, 1980) is estimated. No further restrictions are placed on the dynamic structures of the equations, with the result that the appearance of lagged variables may be due to lags in any of the structural equations of the model.

A particular advantage of the Blanchard–Kahn reduction of the model is that it retains the expected future exchange rate as a determinant of the current rate. Consequently, much of the exchange rate's behaviour that previously had to be accommodated in the unknown, or equation residual, is captured by proxy by the expectations variable. Thus the equations presented here are, in a sense, 'forward looking' and should outperform any of the more traditional 'backward-looking' equations discussed above.

The results obtained are mixed, as is usual in this area. With regard to the exchange rate equation in isolation, the search yielded a specification that performs well and appears to outperform the monetary and portfolio balance approaches (see Wadhwani, 1984) although the evidence is by no means conclusive. On the Buiter–Miller model the results are on the whole favourable and, while pointing the way to specific further research, suggest that the model has some empirical support.

2.2 THE MODEL

Buiter and Miller (1981) present a model in which the price of domestic output moves 'slowly' in response to excess goods demand while the overall price level including imported goods, the price of which depends in part on the exchange rate, is free to jump as the exchange rate jumps.

The discrete-time stochastic structural form of the model is as follows:

$$m_t - p_t = ky_t - \lambda r_t + \epsilon_{1t} \tag{2.1}$$

$$y_t = \delta(e_t - w_t + p_t^*) - \gamma(r_t - \hat{p}_{t+1} + p_t) + \psi z_t + \epsilon_{2t} \tag{2.2}$$

$$w_{t+1} - w_t = \phi(y_t - \bar{y}_t) + \pi_t + \epsilon_{3t+1} \tag{2.3}$$

$$p_t = \alpha w_t + (1 - \alpha)(e_t + p_t^*) + \epsilon_{4t} \tag{2.4}$$

$$r_t = r_t^* + \hat{e}_{t+1} - e_t + \epsilon_{5t} \tag{2.5}$$

where m_t is domestic nominal money stock, y_t is domestic real output, r_t is domestic nominal interest rate, w_t is domestic output price, e_t is the exchange rate in domestic units per foreign unit, p_t is the price index, p_t^* is world output price, r_t^* is world nominal interest rate, z_t is a vector of real exogenous variables, π_t is core inflation, ϵ_{it} represents errors with a normal independent distribution assumed and $\hat{X}_{t+1} = E(X_{t+1}|I_t)$ with $X = p, e$. All variables other than r_t, r_t^* are in logarithms and all coefficients are positive with the exception of ψ which is not defined as yet.

Equation (2.1) gives a simple LM relationship with real money balances equal to a function of real income and the nominal interest rate. Equation (2.2) is an IS equation to determine output demand (and supply) as a function of the level of competitiveness (or real exchange rate) $e_t - w_t + p_t^*$, the real interest rate $r_{Rt} = r_t - \hat{p}_{t+1} + p_t$ and a vector of exogenous variables to be discussed below. The domestic output price adjustment mechanism is summarized by equation (2.3) with prices responding to output y_t in excess of capacity $\bar{y}_t$ and the level of core inflation π_t. Buiter and Miller define core inflation as the current level to which inflation will settle in the long run. Current inflation of domestic prices then deviates from this level only by a log-linear function of excess output. While this is appealing theoretically since it permits long-run inflationary equilibrium, reference to the data series for monetary growth makes it untenable for empirical work. This problem is discussed more fully below. Domestic prices and imported goods prices are combined to produce 'the' price level in equation (2.4). Equation (2.5) has been the subject of a large amount of literature of its own (e.g. Frankel, 1979c; Cumby and Obstfeld, 1980; Hacche and Townend, 1981) and relates the return r_t available domestically to that anticipated from investment in foreign-currency-denominated assets made up of the foreign interest rate and the expected depreciation of the domestic currency. The strictest form of this assumption, commonly termed uncovered interest parity (UIP), has no error term. In the more general form permitted here ϵ_{st} may be taken to represent a risk premium or any other (white noise) deviation from UIP.

The functioning of the model is described fully by Buiter and Miller (1981, 1982a) and is not repeated here.

The model may be reduced to a suitable state space representation in the following way. Since we wish to have a stationary long run in the presence of non-zero core inflation, all nominal variables are scaled by a price level. In addition, the need to have one predetermined state variable requires that this scaling price should also be predetermined; hence the money stock and nominal exchange rate are normalized on the price of domestic output. We have therefore the additional identities

$$l_t \equiv m_t - w_t \tag{2.6}$$

$$c_t \equiv e_t - w_t + p_t^* \tag{2.7}$$

Further, let

$$\mu_t \equiv m_{t+1} - m_t \tag{2.8}$$

and assume that the expected growth of the money stock is related to the actual growth by

$$\mu_t \equiv \hat{\mu}_t + \epsilon_{mt+1} \tag{2.9}$$

From this we can obtain the following state space representation:

$$\begin{bmatrix} l_{t+1} \\ \hat{c}_{t+1} \end{bmatrix} = \frac{1}{|\bar{A}|} \begin{bmatrix} |\bar{A}| - \alpha\gamma\phi & \phi[\alpha\gamma(1-\alpha) - \lambda\delta] \\ -1 & |\bar{A}| + \delta(k - \lambda\phi) + (1-\alpha) \end{bmatrix} \begin{bmatrix} l_t \\ c_t \end{bmatrix}$$

$$+ \frac{1}{|\overline{A}|} \begin{bmatrix} \gamma\lambda\phi(1-\alpha) & |\overline{A}| & -(\lambda+\alpha\gamma k) & -\lambda\phi\psi & \phi(\lambda+\alpha\gamma k) \\ -[\lambda+\gamma(k-\lambda\phi)] & 0 & -\lambda & \psi(k-\lambda\phi) & \lambda\phi \end{bmatrix} \cdot$$

$$\begin{bmatrix} r_{Rt}^* \\ \mu_t \\ \pi_t \\ z_t \\ \bar{y}_t \end{bmatrix}$$

$$+ \frac{1}{|\overline{A}|} \begin{bmatrix} \alpha\gamma\phi & -\lambda\phi & -\gamma\lambda\phi & \gamma\lambda\phi(1-\alpha) & -|\overline{A}| \\ 1 & k-\lambda\phi & \gamma(k-\lambda\phi) & -[\lambda+\gamma(k-\lambda\phi)] & 0 \end{bmatrix} \begin{bmatrix} \epsilon_{1t} \\ \epsilon_{2t} \\ \epsilon_{4t} \\ \epsilon_{5t} \\ \epsilon_{3t+1} \end{bmatrix}$$

$$\text{(2.10)}$$

where

$$|\overline{A}| = \lambda + \alpha\gamma(k - \lambda\phi) \tag{2.11}$$

or

$$\begin{bmatrix} l_{t+1} \\ \hat{c}_{t+1} \end{bmatrix} = A \begin{bmatrix} l_t \\ c_t \end{bmatrix} + B \begin{bmatrix} r_{Rt}^* \\ \mu_t \\ \pi_t \\ z_t \\ \bar{y}_t \end{bmatrix} + D \begin{bmatrix} \epsilon_{1t} \\ \epsilon_{2t} \\ \epsilon_{4t} \\ \epsilon_{5t} \\ \epsilon_{3t+1} \end{bmatrix}$$

$$\text{(2.12)}$$

where A, B and D are as implied by (2.10).

This system will have a saddlepoint equilibrium if and only if the matrix A has one stable eigenvalue (modulus less than one) and one unstable eigenvalue. If this condition holds there is only one value of c_t at any time that will lead to the long-run solution.

The continuous-time equivalent of this discrete-time model has the transition matrix $(A - I)$. For this continuous version to have a saddlepoint equilibrium we require

$$|A - I| = -\frac{\delta\phi}{|\overline{A}|} < 0 \tag{2.13}$$

$$\Rightarrow \lambda + \alpha\gamma(k - \lambda\phi) > 0 \tag{2.14}$$

which is analogous to the condition given by Buiter and Miller (1981).

Unfortunately, the continuous saddlepoint condition does not relate to the discrete-time version in any useful fashion and $|A| > 0$ is neither necessary nor sufficient for a discrete-time saddlepath. This limits the extent to which the model restricts the signs on the semi-reduced form coefficients (see appendix B). The long-run solution to the model may be found by setting

$$
\begin{bmatrix} l_{t+1} \\ \hat{c}_{t+1} \end{bmatrix} = \begin{bmatrix} l_t \\ c_t \end{bmatrix} = \begin{bmatrix} \bar{l} \\ \bar{c} \end{bmatrix}
\tag{2.15}
$$

and

$$
\pi = \mu
\tag{2.16}
$$

Hence

$$
\begin{bmatrix} \bar{l} \\ \bar{c} \end{bmatrix} = -\frac{1}{\delta\phi} \begin{bmatrix} \phi[\delta\lambda - \gamma(1 - \alpha)] & \lambda\phi & \phi\psi(1 - \alpha) & -\phi(k\delta + 1 - \alpha) \\ -\gamma\phi & 0 & \phi\psi & -\phi \end{bmatrix} \begin{bmatrix} r_{Rt}^* \\ \mu \\ z \\ \bar{y} \end{bmatrix}
\tag{2.17}
$$

2.3 ECONOMETRIC METHODS

Rearranging equation (2.10) we obtain the following:

$$
l_t = a_{11}l_{t-1} + a_{12}c_{t-1} + b_{11}r_{Rt-1}^* + b_{12}\mu_t + b_{13}\pi_{t-1} + b_{14}z_{t-1} + b_{15}\bar{y}_{t-1} + \eta_{1t}
\tag{2.18}
$$

$$
c_t = a_{21}l_t + a_{22}\hat{c}_{t+1} + b_{21}r_{Rt}^* + b_{22}\mu_t + b_{23}\pi_t + b_{24}z_t + b_{25}\bar{y}_t + \eta_{2t}
\tag{2.19}
$$

The two error terms have the following form:

$$
\eta_{1t} = d_{11}\epsilon_{1t-1} + d_{12}\epsilon_{2t-1} + d_{14}\epsilon_{4t-1} + d_{15}\epsilon_{5t-1} + d_{13}\epsilon_{3t}
\tag{2.20}
$$

$$
\eta_{2t} = d_{21}\epsilon_{1t} + d_{22}\epsilon_{2t} + d_{24}\epsilon_{4t} + d_{25}\epsilon_{5t}
\tag{2.21}
$$

This raises a problem discussed by Barr (1983b, part II) in which one of the explanatory variables for l_t, c_{t-1}, is correlated with the error term. Consequently c_{t-1} must be instrumented in this equation. Suitable instruments include all the explanatory variables dated $t-2$ and earlier. Another problem occurs here in that, in setting up a general dynamic framework, all these possible instruments should be included, at least initially, as explanatory variables. Several methods for obtaining suitable instruments were tried and in no case did the first lag of c appear with a coefficient significantly different from zero. Since this was also true of all the other explanatory variables except l itself, we seem reasonably safe in omitting this lag from the equation and estimating consistently by ordinary least squares (OLS).

Equation (2.19) was estimated using the errors in variables method due to

Wickens (1982) and McCallum (1976) which entails substitution of c_{t+1} for $\hat{c}_{t+1}$ with the difference between the two being included in an augmented error term. The result is an errors in variables problem requiring that c_{t+1} be instrumented. Heuristically, this arises because the difference between c_{t+1} and $\hat{c}_{t+1}$ consists of all the unanticipated parts of the exogenous variables and all the structural errors dated $t + 1$. Consequently the augmented error has a forward moving-average structure in ϵ_1, ϵ_2, ϵ_4 and ϵ_5. While this does not result in inconsistent coefficient estimates (since the forward dependent variable is instrumented), it does mean that the standard errors reported by most estimation packages are inconsistent (see Hansen, 1982, for suggested methods of correcting for this). Further, the standard generalized least squares estimation procedures used in most instances of residual serial correlation cannot be used in rational expectations models because the implicit filtering of the data breaches certain orthogonality conditions (Flood and Garber, 1980a).

Each equation was estimated using as many lags as the data set, consisting of 37 (quarterly from 1973 to 1982) observations, would allow, i.e. four lags for (2.18) and three for (2.19). Seasonal dummies were also included. The number of explanatory variable lags was then reduced by a series of nested tests until a relatively parsimonious set was obtained. In the case of equation (2.19) the use of t statistics not corrected for serial correlation could lead to the erroneous omission of some variables. However, at no stage in the proceedings was there any indication of the serial correlation created by the Wickens substitution. This matter is discussed below but in the present context it is taken as support for hypothesis testing using the uncorrected t ratios.

Simultaneous estimation of (2.18) and (2.19) in normal circumstances would provide fully efficient estimates. However, in this model the intertemporal relationships in the error process cause considerable problems. In order to avoid these and still make the estimates more efficient we perform a weighted least-squares procedure which neglects all the cross-equation residual correlation. As a result, information concerning the error structure is lost, causing a loss of efficiency relative to consistent three-stage least squares. The gain is that we may impose the cross-equation restrictions without further consideration of the error structure and obtain coefficient estimates which will be more efficient than those obtained by separate estimation but which retain their consistency.

2.4 ESTIMATION RESULTS

A detailed listing of data sources and definitions is given in appendix A.

118   D.G. Barr

2.4.1 Single-equation estimates

Equations (2.18) and (2.19) are estimated with the following theoretical implications assumed (see appendix B for other model-consistent implications):

$$l_t = a_{11}l_{t-1} + a_{12}c_{t-1} + b_{11}r^*_{Rt-1} + b_{12}\mu_{t-1} + b_{13}\pi_{t-1} + b^1_{14}p^{OIL}_{t-1} + b^2_{14}y^*_{t-1} + b_{15}k_{t-1} + \eta_{1t} \tag{2.22}$$

$$c_t = a_{21}l_t + a_{22}c_{t+1} + b_{21}r^*_{Rt} + b_{22}\mu_t + b_{23}\pi_t + b^1_{24}p^{OIL}_t + b^2_{24}y^*_t + b_{25}k_{t-1} + \pi_{2t} \tag{2.23}$$

$a_{11} < 1$

$a_{12} \gtreqless 0$

$b_{11} > 0$

$b_{12} = 1$

$b_{13} < 0$

$b^1_{14} = -\lambda\phi|\overline{A}|^{-1}\psi^1 \qquad b^2_{14} = -\lambda\phi|\overline{A}|^{-1}\psi^2$

$b_{15} > 0$

Assuming that $B = |\overline{A}| + \delta(k - \lambda\phi) + (1 - \alpha) > 0$, then

$a_{21} > 0$

$a_{22} > 0$

$b_{21} \gtreqless 0$

$b_{22} = 0$

$b_{23} > 0$

$b^1_{24} = -\psi^1(k - \lambda\phi)B^{-1} \qquad b^2_{24} = -\psi^2(k - \lambda\theta)B^{-1}$

$b_{25} < 0$

This provides a fairly rigorous set of tests of the model provided that consistent estimates are obtained. The coefficients b_{14}, b_{24} are related in the following ways:

$$b^1_{14} = -\frac{\lambda\phi}{|\overline{A}|}\psi^1 \qquad b^1_{24} = \frac{k - \lambda\phi}{B}\psi^1 \tag{2.24}$$

$$b^2_{14} = -\frac{\lambda\phi}{|\overline{A}|}\psi^2 \qquad b^2_{24} = \frac{k - \lambda\phi}{B}\psi^2 \tag{2.25}$$

Since the sign of $k - \lambda\phi$ is unknown we cannot sign b^1_{24} or b^2_{24}. Assuming that increases in world income raise demand for domestic goods ($\psi^2 > 0$) then

$b^2_{14} < 0$

and if the real oil price has the same effect ($\psi^1 > 0$) then

$$b_{14}^1 < 0$$

although no importance is assigned to the assumption about ψ^1 since one could argue in favour of either sign. Note that b_{24} may be negative, given these assumptions, if and only if $k - \lambda\phi < 0$. Finally, all the coefficients in equation (2.23) assume $B > 0$ since this was the result obtained. A consistent set of coefficient hypotheses would of course exist for $B < 0$.

Real money balances equation

Table 2.1 gives the final estimated specification with the coefficient b_{12} on future monetary growth estimated freely in regression I. Since this coefficient estimate of 1.12 is only one-and-a-half standard deviations from unity we impose the unit coefficient implied above, regression II giving the results in this case.

Table 2.1 Final estimated specification with dependent variable l_t for the period 1973 first quarter to 1982 first quarter

	Regression I, OLS	Regression II, OLS
l_{t-1}	0.76	0.74
	(0.05)	(0.05)
c_{t-2}	0.05	0.06
	(0.01)	(0.01)
r_{Rt-3}^*	2.50	2.36
	(0.42)	(0.42)
π_{t-2}	-2.90	-3.23
	(0.6)	(0.58)
π_{t-4}	-1.65	-1.67
	(0.6)	(0.61)
y_{t-2}^*	-0.46	-0.47
	(0.09)	(0.09)
p_{t-2}^{OIL}	-0.05	-0.05
	(0.007)	(0.007)
k_{t-4}	0.64	0.64
	(0.12)	(0.11)
μ_{t-1}	1.12	1
	(0.08)	—
Durbin's h	0.59	0.64
Chow	2.65	2.17
F	588.4	476.4
SSR	0.0009	0.001
R^2	0.995	0.995

SSR, sum of squared residuals.
A constant and seasonal dummies were included. Standard errors are in parentheses.

The dynamic structure of the equation reflects the sluggishness of the domestic price level responses to changes in exogenous variables. The fact that core inflation appears lagged two and four times does not present a problem since we might expect some averaging process to occur and the third lag which was not significantly different from zero might be so as a result of collinearity problems in the data. Overall the equation seems well specified with good t statistics for I and II. Durbin's h gives no hint of first-order serial correlation. The Chow test for a structural break in the middle of the sample

Table 2.2 Final estimated specification with dependent variable c_t, instrumenting c_{t+1}, for the period 1973 first quarter to 1982 first quarter

	Regression III	Regression IV	Regression V	Regression VI
l_t	0.62	0.64	0.66	0.67
	(0.19)	(0.19)	(0.19)	(0.19)
c_{t+1}	0.81	0.81	0.69	0.73
	(0.08)	(0.08)	(0.15)	(0.13)
r_{Rt}^*	−4.95	−5.16	−6.41	−6.18
	(1.75)	(1.83)	(2.37)	(2.31)
π_t	—	2.10	—	2.74
	—	(2.76)	—	(2.86)
π_{t-1}	12.40	10.80	12.02	10.06
	(2.67)	(3.45)	(2.72)	(3.55)
π_{t-3}	6.44	6.92	7.45	7.73
	(2.85)	(2.98)	(3.08)	(3.14)
y_t^*	1.48	1.51	1.44	1.49
	(0.55)	(0.66)	(0.55)	(0.54)
k_{t-3}	−1.22	−1.23	−1.23	−1.24
	(0.62)	(0.63)	(0.63)	(0.62)
$z(1)$	1.08	0.8	0.94	1.18
$z(2)$	8.30	8.36	8.53	8.41
$z(3)$	1.72	1.63	0.83	1.25
SSR	0.0239	0.0234	0.0244	0.0226
see	0.0330	0.0306	0.0306	0.0301
R_c^2	0.812	0.824	0.620	0.641
Instruments	$\mu_{t-1}, \mu_{t-2}, c_{t-1}$	$\mu_{t-1}, \mu_{t-2}, c_{t-1}$	μ_{t-1}, μ_{t-2}	μ_{t-1}, μ_{t-2}

$z(1)$, test for first-order serial correlation (see Bean, 1981); $z(1) \sim \chi^2(1)$.
$z(2)$, test for a structural break; distributed χ^2 with degrees of freedom equal to the number of estimated coefficients.
$z(3)$, Sargan's (1958) test; distributed χ^2 (number of additional instruments).
SSR, sum of squared residuals; see standard error of the regression; R_c^2, R^2 from the regression of c_{t+1} on the instruments.
A constant and seasonal dummies were included. Standard errors are in parentheses.

is high but not significantly so. The high R^2 is due mainly to the fact that l_t is highly dependent upon l_{t-1} although with a coefficient significantly different from unity. The remaining explanatory variables appear to complete the determination of l_t very well.

All the coefficients are correctly signed with $a_{11} < 1$. Competitiveness appears with a well-defined although small and positive coefficient. The constructed *ex ante* real world interest rate appears with a strong t ratio and the real price of oil has a small but well-defined effect. This coefficient is negative implying that the real oil price has a positive effect on the demand for domestic output.

The variables in the inflation equation (2.5) are well represented and correctly signed with higher core inflation reducing the stock of real money balances in the long run and the real capital stock having the opposite effect.

These results suggest that on the basis of an estimation of equation (2.18) we cannot reject the Buiter–Miller model.

Competitiveness equation

Several versions of the final specification are given in tables 2.2 and 2.3. Since $b_{22} = 0$ is implied by the model, we impose this restriction and use $\{\mu_t\}$ as instruments. The number of potential instruments is infinite in this model since any lagged exogenous or endogenous variable may be used. In large samples there is an efficiency gain from increasing the number of instruments but this is not necessarily the case in small samples such as this. Hence regressions V and VI report the results of using only μ_{t-1} and μ_{t-2}. Regressions III and IV show the effects of adding the lagged endogenous variable c_{t-1} to this set. Table 2.3 presents regressions VII and VIII which instrument the long-term interest rate in the same way as in the equation for real money balances.

Overall the results are reasonably consistent with the theory although three possible exceptions are discussed below. The coefficient on l_t is positive as expected, as is that on the expected future real exchange rate $\hat{c}_{t+1}$. The capital stock enters with the predicted negative coefficient. The model does not suggest a sign for the coefficient b_{21} on the real world interest rate, i.e.

$$b_{21} = \frac{\lambda + \gamma(k - \lambda\gamma)}{B} \gtrless 0 \qquad (2.26)$$

although $b_{21} < 0 \Rightarrow k - \lambda\phi < 0$. Given $\hat{b}_{21} = -6$ we seem reasonably safe in assuming $k - \lambda\phi$ to be negative. This in turn implies that the real oil price and the level of world income should enter this equation with signs opposite to those obtained for regressions I–III. For world income this is indeed the case.

The coefficient estimates provide two less satisfactory results. Firstly, the oil price was not a significant variable at any stage of the estimation with the

Table 2.3 Final estimated specification with dependent variable c_t, instrumenting c_{t+1} and π_t, π_{t-1}, π_{t-3} proxies, for the period 1973 first quarter to 1982 first quarter

	Regression VII	Regression VIII
l_t	0.75	0.84
	(0.27)	(0.42)
c_{t+1}	0.75	0.72
	(0.10)	(0.16)
r^*_{Rt}	−5.08	−5.84
	(1.72)	(3.27)
π_t	—	5.62
	—	(20.26)
π_{t-1}	13.51	8.79
	(3.63)	(17.44)
π_{t-3}	10.22	13.38
	(6.55)	(13.36)
y_t^*	1.85	2.04
	(0.80)	(1.09)
k_{t-3}	−1.65	−1.83
	(0.91)	(1.17)
$z(1)$	1.13	1.78
$z(2)$	3.88	0.85
$z(3)$	1.77	1.49
SSR	0.0247	0.0267
se	0.0309	0.0327
R_c^2	0.874	0.874
Instruments	μ_{t-1}, μ_{t-2}, μ_{t-3}, μ_{t-4}, c_{t-1}	μ_{t-1}, μ_{t-2}, μ_{t-3}, μ_{t-4}, c_{t-1}

A constant and seasonal dummies were included.
See the notes to table 2.2.

highest t ratio being less than 0.5. As a result it was dropped from the regressions reported, without significant effects on the remaining estimates. This result is clearly not consistent with the model as described by equations (2.1)–(2.5). Possible explanations are that the oil price enters the structure in such a way that it would not be expected to appear in this equation. Note that any such structural alteration would not alter any of the coefficients attached to the other variables and that if this is the correct explanation then the non-appearance of the oil price does not constitute a point against the model as a whole. A more likely explanation is that the data and estimation method are not sensitive enough to pick up this variable – a systems estimator using more observations might succeed in doing so. This argument seems all the more plausible when one considers the small effect of the oil price on real money balances and that the instrumenting of c_{t+1} adds to the noise in the competitiveness equation.

The second problem is that the contemporaneous long-term interest rate does not have a particularly strong effect although it and its lags have the correct sign. The t ratios range from 0.96 in VI to 0.28 in VIII although all the t ratios suffer in the last equation. In a model of this type we would expect the contemporaneous core inflation rate to bring news even if it did not enter into the structural equation (2.3). Hence some response should be observed. Furthermore, changes in core inflation cause an unambiguous overshoot, i.e. the jump in c_t should exceed that in $\hat{c}_{t+1}$ so that with a coefficient of less than one on c_{t+1} we cannot claim that the impact of π_t has been absorbed by compensating changes in the expected future real exchange rate. (This is a possible explanation for the failure of the oil price to show up, however.) A plausible reason for this lies in problems with the data. The essense of core inflation is that it should be highly serially correlated for large parts of any sample period. This introduces a considerable problem of collinearity which may be behind the strong effects of μ_{t-1} and the weak effects of μ_t.

One might also expect a stronger effect on the lag if the *structure* includes only lagged values. The result of this is that π_t would simply constitute news while π_{t-1} would have a 'core' effect. The latter effect should be absorbed by l_t but here again the small sample size may be to blame. This seems to be a relatively trivial problem given that the core inflation coefficients are correctly signed and it is therefore not taken to be sufficient evidence to justify rejection of the model.

A third problem is that we find no evidence of serial correlation of the residuals despite the fact that the substitution of c_{t+1} for $\hat{c}_{t+1}$ should produce an MA(1) error. This is presumably because the induced serial correlation is swamped by the original error in this equation. As in the other cases it may be that the small sample size makes this a weak test. The absence of serial correlation means that the quoted standard errors are consistent. Transforming these using the Hansen (1982) method-of-moments correction would not make a significant difference to the results because the transformations use no more than the information that failed to indicate significant serial correlation in the tests reported.

Instrumenting the core inflation proxy does not lead to results that are qualitatively different from those in the first four regressions, although as one would expect the standard errors do increase relative to III and IV. Consequently these results are presented for consistency only and are not discussed further.

The overall impression gained from all eight regressions is that the model performs reasonably well. Eight independent qualitative restrictions on the coefficients are met where significant results are obtained.

2.4.2 Simultaneous equation estimates

In estimating the equations simultaneously we select results I and IV and reintroduce the oil price into the latter, i.e. the estimation starts from I and the following version of IV:

$$c_t = 0.66l_t + 0.82\hat{c}_{t+1} - 5.10r^*_{Rt} + 1.56\pi_t + 10.90\pi_{t-1}$$
$$ (0.20) \quad (0.09) \quad\quad (1.84) \quad\quad (3.28) \quad\quad (3.47)$$
$$+ 6.78\pi_{t-3} + 1.48y^*_t + 0.01p^{OIL}_t - 1.22k_{t-3}$$
$$ (3.03) \quad\quad (0.56) \quad\quad (0.03) \quad\quad (0.63) \quad\quad\quad (2.27)$$

A more rigorous approach would test within a general simultaneous framework. Restricting the imposition of the cross-equation restrictions to a

Table 2.4 Non-linear two-stage estimation, instruments c_{t+1}, for the period 1973 first quarter to 1982 first quarter

Regression IX, l_t		Regression X, c_t	
l_{t-1}	0.80	l_t	0.47
	(0.04)		(0.12)
c_{t-2}	0.06	c_{t+1}	0.84
	(0.02)		(0.03)
r^*_{Rt-3}	2.77	r^*_{Rt}	−4.52
	(0.42)		(1.30)
π_{t-2}	−3.60	π	−4.89
	(0.56)		(2.78)
π_{t-4}	−0.51	π_{t-1}	8.72
	(0.35)		(3.22)
y^*_{t-2}	−0.42	π_{t-3}	1.05
	(0.08)		(1.98)
p^{OIL}_{t-2}	−0.04	y^*_t	0.81
	(0.01)		(0.02)
k_{t-4}	0.56	p^{OIL}_t	0.08
	(0.10)		(0.02)
		k_{t-3}	−0.9
			(0.21)

λ	α	γ	k	ϕ	ψy^*	ψ^{OIL}	δ
10.50	0.43	4.67	2.44	0.18	0.40	0.40	0.05
(3.21)	(0.07)	(1.24)	(1.32)	(0.05)	(0.09)	(0.01)	(0.03)

$z(4) = 14.7 \sim \chi^2(6)$

$z(4)$ tests the validity of the cross-equation restrictions (see Gallant and Jorgenson, 1979).

particular dynamic specification loads the dice against the model to some degree.

Initially all the restrictions implied by the deterministic part of (2.10) are applied. The results are given in table 2.4. The coefficients are generally of the same order as those obtained from the separate regressions. Most of the deviations are in the competitiveness equation and the principal changes are to coefficients on real money balances and to current core inflation which changes sign but is still not significant. None of the implications of the model is contradicted, and the test for cross-equation restrictions does not reject the model at the 2 per cent level.

The estimated structural coefficients are also plausible apart from k and λ, i.e. the coefficients in the LM equation. In particular k has an 'implausible' sign and respecification of the LM equation is suggested.

2.5 CONCLUSION

In this chapter we set out to derive an equation to explain the behaviour of the real sterling exchange rate from 1973 to 1982. A particular feature of the equation was the inclusion of the expected future exchange rate in an attempt to capture the effects of 'non-fundamental' behaviour. The fundamentals were those suggested by the small macro-model of Buiter and Miller and a series of tests of this model formed an integral part of the search for the exchange rate equation *per se*.

The results were generally encouraging. The exchange rate equation performed well and the fundamentals made the contribution predicted by the model. The performance of the model as a whole, although acceptable in many respects, was less satisfactory and the results of simultaneous estimation of the real exchange rate and real money balances equations suggested further research on the structural LM equation.

An alternative line of investigation might be to apply the same model, on a bilateral basis (see Driskell, 1981), to the UK pound–US dollar rate in a sample period including the 'overvaluation' of the dollar and its subsequent adjustment. The presence of the expected future exchange rate in the estimated equations (to account for any speculative bubbles in the data) may allow the results to distinguish between 'bubble' and 'fundamental' causes of the overvaluation.

Appendix A

Data

The model is estimated under the 'small country' assumption with all foreign variables being exogenous and constructed as weighted indices of data from four countries: the USA, Germany, France and Japan. In all relevant cases quarterly averages are obtained or constructed since the end-of-period data on asset prices is likely to contain short-term variations which a model of this type cannot possibly explain.

Data Construction

Domestic capacity output is proxied by the capital stock. Quarterly data for this variable are not available and are constructed from annual stock and quarterly investment data with allowance for depreciation.[1]

Real final government expenditure was included as one of the exogenous variables in z_t but failed to appear significantly at any stage of the estimation process for either equation. This is rather surprising, though not crucial to the attempt to test the model.

The exchange rate is a geometric average of the rates for the dollar, Deutschemark, yen and franc, with the following weights:

USA, 0.392; Germany, 0.225; Japan, 0.218; France, 0.165. These are based on the International Monetary Fund multilateral exchange rate model (MERM) weights in use in 1982 and are used in the construction of all world variables. The four countries account for 62.8 per cent of total trade effects on this basis.

Two further exogenous variables are included; world income, constructed from the gross domestic products (GDPs) for each country (with the exception of France for which we use industrial production), and an index of real oil prices relevant to each country.

The real world interest rate appears as a construct rather than a structural variable and is explicitly an *ex ante* rate. This requires the inclusion of an expected future price change. The simplest way to obtain this is to regress world inflation on its own lags. This will give a reasonable approximation although an improved version would estimate a vector autoregressive moving average process to account for the dependence among the world variables. World inflation forecasts were based on the following equation:

$$\Delta p_{t+1}^* = \underset{(0.14)}{0.56\Delta p_t^*} + \underset{(0.17)}{0.26\Delta p_{t-1}^*} - \underset{(0.15)}{0.02\Delta p_{t-2}^*} - \underset{(0.13)}{0.13\Delta p_{t-3}^*}$$

$$+ \underset{(0.003)}{0.005} + \text{seasonals}$$

with residual autocorrelation tests[2] (standard errors in parenthesis)

$LM(4) = 1.50$, $LM(4) \sim \chi^2(4)$ 1962 quarter two to 1982 quarter four

$LM(1) = 0.94$, $LM(1) \sim \chi^2(1)$

The regressor[3] is then

$$r_{Rt}^* = r_t^* - \Delta \hat{p}_{t+1}^*$$

Sources

(a) Domestic money stock monthly M_1 (IFS): quarterly average constructed as quarter four $= \frac{1}{3}$ (Sept + Oct + Nov) since data refer to banking months.

(b) Domestic capital stock.

(c) Domestic long-term interest rate: 20-year government bond rate (ETAS) and (end of the month) quarterly averge (ETAS) $= \frac{1}{6}(M_{12} + 2M_1 + 2M_2 + M_3)$.

(d) Prices:

UK	$p(\text{UK}) = \dfrac{\text{GDP (current factor cost)}}{\text{GDP (1975 factor cost)}}$	ETAS
USA	implicit price deflator	MEI
Germany	implicit price deflator	MEI
Japan	implicit price deflator	MEI
France	hourly wage rates in manufacturing	MEI

(e) National income:

USA	GDP	MEI
Germany	GDP	MEI
Japan	GDP	MEI
France	industrial production	MEI

(f) Short-term interest rates:

UK	three-month Treasury Bills	ETAS
US	three-month Treasury Bills quarterly average	IFS
Germany	quarterly call money rate	IFS
Japan	quarterly call money rate	IFS
France	quarterly call money rate	IFS

Where possible these rates are from line IFS 60(b).

(g) Oil price (Bank of England): nominal US dollar price for Saudi marker crude oil to 1975 quater four. Thereafter a production-weighted average of OPEC effective prices:

$$p^{\text{OIL}} = \Sigma \frac{w_i e(i/\$)(\text{oil price})}{p_i}$$

where $e(i/\$)$ is the domestic currency per dollar exchange rate for each of the four countries ($e(\$/\$) = 1$).

ETAS   Economic Trends Annual Supplement
MEI   OECD Main Economic Indicators – Historical Data
IFS   IMF International Financial Statistics

For ETAS and MEI, updates were taken from the appropriate issues.

Appendix B

As noted in section 2.2 the saddlepoint condition does not restrict the model's coefficients uniquely. However, the relations between the semi-reduced form coefficients do permit four sets of model-consistent restrictions to be obtained, one of which is presented in section 2.4.1. All four are given below with the coefficients of z based on ψ^1, $\psi^2 > 0$.

1 $|A| > 0$ $B > 0$ (B is defined in section 2.4.1)

$a_{11} < 1$	$b_{11} > 0$	$b_{13} < 0$	$b_{15} > 0$
$a_{12} > 0$	$b_{12} = 1$	$b_{14} < 0$	
$a_{21} > 0$	$b_{21} > 0$	$b_{23} > 0$	$b_{25} < 0$
$a_{22} > 0$	$b_{22} = 0$	$b_{24} > 0$	

2 $|A| > 0$ $B < 0$

$a_{11} < 1$	$b_{11} > 0$	$b_{13} < 0$	$b_{15} > 0$
$a_{12} > 0$	$b_{12} = 1$	$b_{14} < 0$	
$a_{21} < 0$	$b_{21} > 0$	$b_{23} < 0$	$b_{25} > 0$
$a_{22} < 0$	$b_{22} = 0$	$b_{24} > 0$	

3 $|A| < 0$ $B > 0$

$a_{11} > 1$	$b_{11} < 0$	$b_{13} > 0$	$b_{15} < 0$
$a_{12} > 0$	$b_{12} = 1$	$b_{14} > 0$	
$a_{21} > 0$	$b_{21} > 0$	$b_{23} > 0$	$b_{25} < 0$
$a_{22} < 0$	$b_{22} = 0$	$b_{24} > 0$	

4 $|A| < 0$ $B < 0$

$a_{11} > 1$	$b_{11} < 0$	$b_{13} > 0$	$b_{15} < 0$
$a_{12} > 0$	$b_{12} = 1$	$b_{14} > 0$	
$a_{21} < 0$	$b_{21} > 0$	$b_{23} < 0$	$b_{25} > 0$
$a_{22} < 0$	$b_{22} = 0$	$b_{24} > 0$	

In each equation any one of the sign restrictions is sufficient to determine those that are consistent with the model. Hence we have five independent restrictions in equation (2.22). This will be sufficient to sign $|A|$. Hence we can use any one of a_{21}, a_{22}, b_{23} and b_{25} to sign B, leaving three independent sign tests. Set 1 is given in section 2.4.1 because intuitively it is the most likely result on the basis of $a_{11} < 1$ and $a_{22} > 0$.

Notes

1 I should like to thank Martyn Andrews for providing this series.
2 LM $= (T - M)R^2 : R^2$ is obtained from the regression of the residuals on the explanatory variables and residuals lagged 1 to 4 or 1 only, as appropriate. M is the number of explanatory variables, 8 in this case.
3 See Pagan (1984) for a discussion of the problems involved with the use of constructed regressors.

3 A Stock–Flow Model of the Determination of the UK Effective Exchange Rate

David Currie and Stephen Hall

3.1 INTRODUCTION

In this chapter there are two objectives. The first is to develop a model of the UK effective exchange rate which is based on a view of the determination of capital flows that combines both stock and flow elements. In this, we build on the earlier empirical work of Hall (1987). The second is to provide evidence on the nature of a longer-run external balance of payments equilibrium. More specifically, we wish to investigate the possible trade-off between larger external deficits in the long run and higher domestic interest rates. This is an issue of some importance in current policy debates, particularly when the longer-run viability of policy measures aimed at domestic expansion is considered.

Before proceeding, it is necessary to comment on the existing state of the literature on exchange rate modelling, particularly that concerned with the sterling exchange rate. This literature presents us with a picture of general failure. A broad prevailing view is that the best available model, from a forecasting point of view, is a simple random walk. Hacche and Townend (1981) concluded their paper surveying the competing empirical models by remarking that 'The predominant impression left by our results is one of failure. We have not succeeded in finding any empirical regularities in the data.' Similarly Frenkel (1982) in summarizing recent work on dollar exchange rates pointed out that 'The record of the 1970s shows that (i) the foreign exchange value of the dollar was highly volatile, (ii) by and large changes in exchange rates were unpredictable.' A similar conclusion was

The views expressed in this paper are solely the responsibility of the authors and do not necessarily reflect the views of the Centre for Economic Policy Research, the London Business School and the Bank of England.

reached by Mussa (1979), who summarized a number of studies: 'Over 90 per cent of month to month or quarter to quarter changes in exchange rates are attributable to unexpected exchange rate changes.'

This view is reflected in the large macro-models of the UK. In the London Business School model the exchange rate is determined so as to achieve equilibrium in the large monetary sector of the model. While attempts were made to estimate the sector, adverse results led the imposition of to a large proportion of the financial model. The exchange rate is therefore being generated by an at least partly imposed sector. The view taken by the Treasury is perhaps even more extreme: a recent paper outlining modelling plans 'takes as a starting assumption the view that further estimation work is unlikely to yield much, given the . . . lack of success in obtaining stable results by the many economists who have looked at the area. The role of empirical work is probably to check the consistency of any model, derived mainly on a priori grounds, with the data' (HM Treasury, 1985a).

We are inclined to a less pessimistic view. The current National Institute of Economic and Social Research model (model 8) contains an estimated model of the exchange rate, as did its two predecessors, models 6 and 7. The equations in the earlier models are of some interest because not only are they examples of estimated exchange rate equations which seem to be reasonably data coherent, but they have been tested in practical forecasting exercises for a number of years. The equation which first appeared in model 6 was re-estimated for model 7 and remained substantially unchanged. Hall et al. (1986) report a number of model exercises designed to show the ability of model 7 to produce sensible *ex ante* forecasts unaided by *ad hoc* intervention. In this chapter the ability of the estimated exchange rate equation, in conjunction with the rest of the model, to produce sensible mechanical forecasts is demonstrated. Saville and Gardiner (1986) used model 7 in an exercise analysing the performance of the British economy from 1968 to 1983; as part of this exercise they performed a model-tracking exercise over the period. They found that the model correctly forecast the large appreciation from 1978 to 1980 and the subsequent turning point and that it was within two points of the actual exchange rate at the end of the period.

Earlier work, reported by Hall (1987) and Currie and Hall (1986), estimated structural equations for the exchange rate, whereby the exchange rate is determined in a forward-looking manner by relative interest rates and trade effects.[1] The trade effects are incorporated in a way that allows for either a stock or a flow view of capital movements, or some combination of the two.

The theoretical literature on exchange rate determination has generally favoured a stock view of capital flows. Yet in a world where financial portfolios are growing, one would expect a change in relative yields to alter a country's share of world financial wealth and thereby to modify the steady state capital inflow at given interest differentials and exchange rate. In general, therefore, one could find considerable empirical support for a mixed stock and flow view of capital flows. Moreover, transaction and information costs may well lead institutions to modify their portfolio allocation, not through shifts of existing asset holdings but rather when making their placement of new funds. This will have the effect of enhancing the flow aspects of exchange rate determination and downplaying the stock aspects. For these reasons it seems preferable to allow the empirical evidence to discriminate between these two views and the evidence presented in Hall (1987) and Currie and Hall (1986) strongly favours the flow view. Accordingly, it is an exchange rate equation derived from a flow view of capital movements that is incorporated in model 8. Nonetheless, it should be noted that the data cannot reject the possibility that a stock view underlies the determination of capital flows in the longer run.

An equation with a stock determination would require rather larger real exchange rate changes in the long run in response to domestic expansionary policy measures and would therefore give a more pessimistic view of the inflationary consequences of domestic expansion. In view of the importance of this issue for policy purposes, it seems worthwhile to investigate more carefully the relative role of stock and flow elements in the determination of capital flows and hence in the determination of the exchange rate. This is the purpose of the remainder of this paper.

3.2 THE MODEL

As explained, the model which we deploy is designed to capture both stock and flow aspects of capital movements and their role in exchange rate determination. To this end, we postulate a relationship for the desired net flow of capital of the form

$$\Delta s_t^* = -a_1(r_t + e_{t+1,t}^e - e_t) - a_2 \Delta(r_t + e_{t+1,t}^e - e_t) \qquad (3.1)$$

where Δs_t^* is the desired net outflow of capital, e is the nominal exchange rate (measured as the foreign price of domestic currency, so that an increase represents an appreciation), r is the differential between domestic and foreign nominal short-term interest rates, and $e_{t+1,t}^e$ denotes the expectation, formed at time t, of the exchange rate at time $t+1$. The first term in (3.1) represents a dependence of the desired capital flow on the level of the exchange-rate-adjusted interest rate differential and therefore represents the flow aspects of the determination of capital movements, while the second term captures a dependence of the desired flow on the change in the exchange-rate-adjusted interest rate differential and therefore represents stock aspects.

Next we postulate an intertemporal objective function for investors of the form

$$\min{}_t E \sum_{i=0}^{\infty} h^i[(s_{t+i} - s^*_{t+i})^2 + a_3(s_{t+i} - s_{t+i-1})^2] \tag{3.2}$$

This penalizes deviations of the actual net stock s of capital from the desired level, given by cumulation of (3.1), and also penalizes changes in net stocks. The costs of adjustment may be rationalized in terms of transactions costs. Interpreted narrowly, such costs are likely to be quite low, but we may also wish to think of investors as having established patterns of behaviour or rules for allocating funds to assets of different currency denomination, adjustment of which involves costly monitoring and decision-making, possibly involving, at least for some investors, entry into new markets. Quadratic costs are assumed, for reasons of analytical tractability rather than realism. h represents a discount factor, and (3.2) penalizes the expected value of the discounted cost stream at period t.

From (3.2), the first-order condition (Euler equation) for a minimum is given by

$$s_t = c_1 s^*_t + h c_2 s^e_{t+1,t} + c_2 s_{t-1} \tag{3.3}$$

where $c_1 = [1 + a_3(1 + h)]^{-1}$ and $c_2 = a_3 c_1$. To close the model, we have the balance of payments identity $\Delta s_t = b_t$, where b is the current account surplus and we neglect revaluation effects. Then from (3.1) and (3.3) we have

$$b_t = -a_1 c_1 (r_t + e^e_{t+1,t} - e_t) - a_2 c_1 \Delta(r_t + e^e_{t+1,t} - e_t) \\ + h c_2 b^e_{t+1,t} + c_2 b_{t-1}$$

which may be rewritten as an equation for the current exchange rate as follows:

$$e_t = d_1 e^e_{t+1,t} + (1 - d_1)e_{t-1} + d_1 r_t - (1 - d_1)r_{t-1} \\ + d_2 c_1^{-1}(-c_2 b_{t-1} + b_t - c_2 h b^e_{t+1,t}) \\ + (1 - d_1)(e_t - e^e_{t,t-1}) \tag{3.4}$$

where

$$d_1 = \frac{a_1 + a_2}{a_1 + 2a_2} \qquad d_2 = \frac{1}{a_1 + 2a_2}$$

Note that $0.5 \leqslant d_1 \leqslant 1$. Equation (3.4) represents our equation to be estimated, treating the final term a white noise error term (on the assumption of rational expectations) and with the implied coefficient restrictions to be tested.

Equation (3.4) has significant similarities to that estimated by Hall (1987) and discussed further by Currie and Hall (1986). However, in the earlier work, the lagged exchange rate enters by virtue of the influence of foreign exchange market intervention by the authorities to smooth the path of the exchange rate. In this model, by contrast, we find a rationale for the inclusion of the lagged exchange rate even without intervention. The size of this effect depends on the relative influence of stock and flow aspects of the determination of capital flows. Thus as a_1/a_2 tends to zero, so that stock aspects dominate, $1 - d_1$ tends to 0.5, while as a_1/a_2 tends to infinity, so that flow aspects dominate, $1 - d_1$ tends to zero.

It is of interest to note that our model implies a long-run relationship between the exchange-rate-adjusted interest rate differential and the current account of the balance of payments. It does not imply a long-run relationship between the interest rate differential and the exchange rate of the kind investigated by Meese and Rogoff (1985) using co-integration methods. This is a point that we take up later when we consider the use of co-integration methods to determine the long-run relationship implied by this model.

3.3 ESTIMATION RESULTS

The model was estimated for the UK pound effective exchange rate using monthly data for the period 1973–84. The interest rate differential was taken to be the differential between UK and US three-month treasury bill rates.

The terms in the expected exchange rate and the expected current account were estimated by using the Wickens (1982) errors in variable technique. Equations are also specified for the interest rate differential and the current account in order to allow for possible endogeneity. These subsidiary equations are not the prime concern of this paper, so specific conceptual models are not developed for them. Instead fairly simple specifications which include the endogenous exchange rate, lagged terms in the dependent variables, inflation rates (for the interest rate differential equation) and UK net oil exports (for the current account equation) are used. The lagged dependent variables may be thought of as correcting a non-white noise error process induced by some missing explanatory variables.

The Wickens technique is an implementation of the rational expectations hypothesis which allows us to use actual lead data as a measure of expected future variables. The out-turns are then taken to be an estimate of expectations, where the data are subject to a white noise measurement error. The model is estimated by a systems estimation technique (in our case full information maximum likelihood (FIML)) where an equation is specified for each of the expectations terms. These equations will generally be an unrestricted reduced form of the model. Specifying these reduced form equations for expectations corrects for the bias produced by the measurement error and the Wickens estimates are shown to be consistent. As the

Table 3.1 Full information maximum likelihood estimates of the exchange rate model (data period March 1973 to June 1984, monthly) with dependent variable e_t

	Unrestricted	Restricted	
		$h = 1$	$h = 0$
Independent variables			
e_{t+1}	0.806 (22.8)	0.704	0.692
e_{t-1}	0.194 (5.5)	0.296	0.308
r_t	0.175 (0.4)	0.704	0.692
r_{t-1}	-0.334 (0.7)	-0.296	-0.308
b_{t+1}	-0.062 (1.2)	-0.080	0
b_t	0.223 (3.8)	0.185	0.065
b_{t-1}	-0.095 (1.3)	-0.080	-0.046
Coefficients of restricted model			
a_1		16.45 (3.0)	19.94 (1.3)
a_2		11.90 (3.6)	16.00 (1.4)
c_2		0.433 (4.2)	0.703 (1.5)
a_3		3.231	2.367
Log likelihood	2660.4	2658.4	2323.6
Durbin–Watson	1.65	1.99	

The model was estimated in a slightly different form from that given above and these parameters were derived from that form. The exact estimation form is given in the appendix.

expectations equations do not exploit the structure of the model, this technique will not generally by fully efficient.

The estimation results are reported in table 3.1. The unrestricted form of the equation (with none of the implied parameter restrictions imposed) is reported in the first column. The lead and lag of the exchange rate are both significant – the lead highly so – with coefficients that sum almost exactly to unity and with the larger coefficient on the lead. This is consistent with the view that the exchange rate is determined in a largely forward-looking manner and that it follows a process very close to a random walk. The current value of the balance of payments enters significantly, while the lead and lag are insignificant although of the expected sign. Moreover, the combined effect of the balance of payments terms is of the expected sign. By contrast, the combined effect of the interest rate differential terms is of the wrong sign, and the coefficients on these terms are insignificant.

Forms of the restricted equation are reported in the second and third columns of table 3.1. The discount factor could not be determined satisfactorily by the search procedure. Estimates are therefore presented for the two extremes of no discounting ($h = 1$) and complete discounting ($h = 0$). Of these two, the case of no discounting performs better as all coefficients are significant. For both restricted forms, the combined interest rate differential effects are of the expected sign, as are the combined balance of payments effects. The likelihood ratio test for the data-acceptability of the parameter restrictions is passed for both forms of the restricted equation, more easily for the no-discounting case (with the likelihood ratio test, LR = 2.6 for $h = 1$ and LR = 4.2 for $h = 0$, compared with a critical value of LR = 9.48).

In both cases, the parameter estimates imply that flow aspects of capital flow determination are quantitatively more important than stock aspects: thus $a_1/a_2 = 1.4$ for $h = 1$ and $a_1/a_2 = 1.2$ for $h = 0$. The estimates of a_3, the coefficient representing costs of adjustment, are large, perhaps surprisingly so, with $a_3 = 3.2$ for $h = 1$ and $a_3 = 2.4$ for $h = 0$. (The result that less discounting requires a higher estimated cost of adjustment is an intuitive one.)

It is of interest to consider the long-run relationship implicit in these estimated equations. Because of the perverse combined coefficient on interest rates, the unrestricted equation has a perverse long-run relationship between the interest rate differential and the current balance. For the restricted forms, letting the exchange-rate-adjusted interest rate differential ρ_t be $r_t + e^e_{t+1,t} - e_t$, we have

$$\frac{\partial b}{\partial \rho} = -a_1 = \begin{cases} -16.4 & h = 1 \\ -19.9 & h = 0 \end{cases}$$

Here ρ represents a monthly rate of return, measured as a proportion, while the current account is measured in units of £10b per month. Thus for $h = 1$ a sustained increae of £1b per month in the current account deficit is associated with a 0.006 rise in ρ, measured on a monthly basis, so that a £1b larger annual current account deficit is associated with a rise of 0.6 percentage points in ρ measured on an annual basis. For $h = 0$, the implied rise in ρ on an annual basis is slightly smaller at 0.5 percentage points. These point estimates suggest reasonable limits on the use of tighter monetary policy to finance permanent external deficits.

3.4 ERROR CORRECTION AND CO-INTEGRATION

As we have noted above, the long-run steady state of our model is characterized by a relationship between the exchange-rate-adjusted interest rate differential and the current account of the form

$$\rho_t = r_t + e^e_{t+1,t} - e_t = \gamma_0 - \gamma_1 b_t \tag{3.5}$$

(The parameter γ_1 is simply the inverse of the parameter a_1 in (3.1).) We may specify a rather *ad hoc* model of exchange rate behaviour by postulating an error correction mechanism of the form

$$\Delta\rho_t = -\alpha\Delta b_t + \beta(\gamma_0 - \gamma_1 b_{t-1} - \rho_{t-1}) \tag{3.6}$$

so that

$$r_t + e^e_{t+1,t} - e_t = -\alpha b_t + (\alpha - \beta\gamma_1)b_{t-1} + (1 - \beta)(r_{t-1} + e^e_{t,t-1} - e_{t-1}) + \beta\gamma_0$$

or

$$e_t = \frac{1}{2-\beta}e^e_{t+1,t} + \frac{1-\beta}{2-\beta}e_{t-1} + \frac{1}{2-\beta}r_t - \frac{1-\beta}{2-\beta}r_{t-1}$$
$$+ \frac{\alpha}{2-\beta}b_t - \frac{\alpha-\beta\gamma_1}{2-\beta}b_{t-1} + \frac{1-\beta}{2-\beta}(e_t - e^e_{t,t-1})$$
$$+ \frac{\beta\gamma_0}{2-\beta} \tag{3.7}$$

This has a rather similar form to (3.4) with $h = 0$, although the parameters bear a different interpretation. Equation (3.7) may be rewritten as

$$e_t = \frac{1}{2-\beta}(e^e_{t+1,t} + r_t + \gamma_1 b_{t-1}) + \frac{1-\beta}{2-\beta}(e_{t-1} + r_{t-1} - \gamma_1 b_{t-1})$$
$$+ \frac{\alpha}{2-\beta}\Delta b_t + \frac{1-\beta}{2-\beta}(e_t - e^e_{t,t-1}) + \frac{\beta\gamma_0}{2-\beta} \tag{3.8}$$

which makes clear the restrictions implicit in (3.7).

Equation (3.8) may be estimated in two alternative ways. We may use FIML to estimate (3.8) directly, along with auxiliary equations for expectations and current variables, as we did for equation (3.4). But if ρ and b are co-integrated, an alternative suggested by Engle and Granger (1987) is to estimate (3.5) to give an estimate of λ and then to estimate (3.8) with this estimate of λ taken as given. As Engle and Granger show, this procedure gives coefficient estimates which converge on the true parameter values as the sample size increases, and moreover 'these estimates converge even faster to the true value than Standard Econometric estimates'.

Meese and Rogoff (1985) have recently applied these methods to exchange rate equations. They examine the possibility that the exchange rate and interest rates are co-integrated. However, it is not obvious why a long-run relationship should hold between this pair of variables. Our model, in contrast, suggests that interest rates and the current account will be linked in the long run. We therefore examine whether this pair of variables is co-integrated.

3.5 CO-INTEGRATION AND THE TWO-STAGE PROCEDURE

The definition of co-integration given by Engle and Granger (1987) differs slightly in detail from that given by Granger and Weiss (1983), although its intuitive meaning is unchanged. A series X_t is said to be integrated of order d (denoted $X_t \sim I(d)$) if it is a series which has a stationary, invertible, non-deterministic autoregressive moving average representation after differencing d times. Co-integration is defined as follows: the components of the vector X_t are said to be co-integrated of order d, b (denoted $X_t \sim (d, b)$) if (a) all components of X_t are I(d) and (b) there exists a vector $\alpha \neq (0)$ so that $Z_t = \alpha' X_t \sim I(d - b)$, $b > 0$. The vector α is called the co-integrating vector. This definition represents a slight generalization of that of Granger and Weiss to the case where Z_t is not itself stationary.

The importance of this definition to the error correction model (ECM) is that if the levels part of the ECM is not made up of a co-integrated vector then this part of the error term will be non-stationary. Unless there is an exactly offsetting non-stationary coming from the difference terms in the equation the overall ECM term will also be non-stationary. In this case the resulting estimates will be meaningless.

The advantage of the Engle and Granger two-stage procedure is that the Z_t errors may be tested for stationarity and the co-integrating vector α can be imposed on the ECM estimated equation. So not only do we know that X_t is a properly co-integrating vector but we also know that the final equation is based on a consistent estimate of α.

3.6 EMPIRICAL RESULTS

Table 3.2 presents test statistics on the individual properties of the series for ρ and b. To test for the level of integration of these series, the Dickey–Fuller (DF) and the augmented Dickey–Fuller (ADF) tests were applied. These are both t tests and rely on rejecting the hypothesis that the series is a random walk in favour of stationarity: this requires a negative and significant test statistic. Table 3.2 reports the DF and ADF test results for the two series and their first differences. It is clear that the levels of both series are stationary processes. This diminishes the interest in the two-stage estimation results. If, nevertheless, we proceed, we obtain the following static relationship between ρ and b:

$$\rho_t = -0.003 - 0.030 b_t$$
$$\quad\quad (1.85) \quad (0.56)$$

$$R^2 = -0.005 \quad\quad DW = 1.14$$

Table 3.2 The time-series properties of interest rates and the current balance

Variable	Test	
	DF	ADF
ρ	—	-4.9
b	-5.8	—
$\Delta\rho$	—	-9.3
Δb	-18.6	—

(DW, Durbin–Watson statistic). It is evident that this provides no significant evidence on the possible long-term link between ρ and b. However, it is pertinent to note that the estimated coefficient on b is of a similar order of magnitude to the estimates of $a_1{}^{-1}$ presented above ($a_1{}^{-1} = 0.061$ for $h = 1$; $a_1{}^{-1} = 0.050$ for $h = 0$).

In view of these insignificant results, we abandoned the two-stage procedure and estimated equation (3.8) directly as before using FIML with auxiliary equations for expectations and current variables. The results of this are reported in table 3.3. The unrestricted form and the results of the two-stage estimation are also reported for purposes of comparison.

Table 3.3 Estimates of the error correction mechanism with dependent variable e_t

	Unrestricted	Restricted	
		Single stage	Two stage
Independent variables			
e_{t+1}	0.809 (23.1)	0.779	0.743
e_{t-1}	0.191 (5.5)	0.221	0.257
r_t	0.900 (0.7)	0.779	0.743
r_{t-1}	-1.350 (1.0)	-0.221	-0.257
b_t	0.160 (2.9)	0.055	0.043
b_{t-1}	-0.093 (1.4)	0.028	-0.029
Coefficients of restricted model			
γ_0		0.0037 (12.1)	0.0023 (1.3)
γ_1		0.150 (2.1)	0.030 (0.6)
α		0.071 (0.9)	0.058 (0.9)
β		0.717 (12.8)	0.655 (11.0)
Log likelihood	2477.5	2477.0	2476.3
Durbin–Watson	1.640	1.673	1.732

The results of the single-stage restricted estimation are satisfactory. The estimated parameters are all of the expected sign and the significant with the exception of the inessential parameter α. The parameter β which reflects the adjustment speed is large, particularly for monthly data. Moreover, the parameter γ_1, which reflects the long-run relationship between ρ and b, is well determined, in contrast with the two-stage estimation. The point estimate of γ_1 is larger by a factor of two or more than that implied by our earlier estimates (though not significantly so). This estimate implies a rather less favourable trade-off between external deficits and interest rates: thus a sustained £1b increase in the annual current deficit is associated with a 0.015 rise in the long run in ρ, measured on an annual basis, or by 1.5 percentage points.

3.7 CONCLUSION

In this chapter there were two aims. The first was to develop a model of the UK effective exchange rate that combined both flow and stock aspects of the determination of capital flows. The second was to investigate the long-run trade-off between external deficits and higher domestic interest rates. Building on the previous work of Hall (1987) who developed a forward-looking model of the UK exchange rate, we have been able to develop a model combining both stock and flow elements that performs satisfactorily on monthly data. The resulting estimates suggested a moderate long-run trade-off between larger external deficits and higher domestic interest rates. An error correction mechanism was also investigated, and this provided estimates of this long-run trade-off that were more disadvantageous.

Appendix

The Estimation Procedure Used in Table 3.1

It is not possible to estimate all the parameters in equation (3.4) because they are not all identified. The identification of parameters in non-linear models is a difficult area in applied work as there are no general theorems or rules which can be used for non-linear systems. The problem with equation (3.4) can be seen if we rewrite it in the following way:

$$
\begin{aligned}
e_t = {} & \frac{a_1 + a_2}{a_1 + 2a_2}(e_{t+1}^e + r_t) + \frac{a_2}{a_1 + 2a_2}(e_{t-1} - r_t) \\
& + \frac{b_t - c_2(hb_{t+1}^e + b_{t-1})}{c_1(a_1 + 2a_2)}
\end{aligned}
\tag{A.1}
$$

Now it is possible to re-parameterize this system exactly using one less parameter. Let

$$B_1 = c_1 a_1$$
$$B_2 = c_1 a_2$$

We can rewrite equation (A.1) as

$$e_t = \frac{B_1 + B_2}{B_1 + 2B_2} (e^e_{t+1} + r_t) + \frac{B_2}{B_1 + 2B_2} (e_{t-1} - r_{t-1})$$
$$+ \frac{b_t - c_2(hb^e_{t+1} + b_{t-1})}{B_1 + 2B_2} \tag{A.2}$$

Therefore it is not possible to determine c_1, a_1 and a_2 simultaneously as λc_1, a_1/λ and a_2/λ will give an identical log-likelihood function for any value of λ.

To estimate the model we have estimated the three parameters B_1, B_2 and c_2 and then used the restriction $c_1 = 1 - c_2(1 + h)$ (equation (3.3)) to derive c_1 and calculate the structural parameters a_1 and a_2.

Notes

1   The variable chosen was net trade in goods and services, rather than the current account. This was because some transfer items in the current account are imputed and do not correspond to actual flows, and considerations of reliability provide grounds for their exclusion. Moreover, the modelling of the trade sector is more reliable and robust than that of interest, profits and dividends, and transfers, so the use of trade terms may well be preferable from the perspective of overall model properties. In fact, the estimated equation has similar properties if the trade terms are replaced by the current account, and the overall simulation properties of the model are not greatly affected.

4 Exchange Rate Determination, the Stock Market and Investment Finance

Merih Uctum and Michael R. Wickens

4.1 INTRODUCTION

As the world's capital markets become better integrated and impediments to the international flow of capital are removed, the asset market approach to the determination of exchange rates seems increasingly appropriate. One of the main problems is how to represent asset markets in exchange rate models. A compromise has to be reached between analytical tractability and the need to take account of the complexities of a realistic model in which, for example, institutional arrangements are adequately reflected. Increasingly the assumption of perfect asset substitutability is being replaced by imperfect substitutability and a portfolio approach. But the assets represented in the portfolio are amorphous domestic and foreign securities with no provenance. A survey of portfolio models is provided by Branson and Henderson (1985).

In practice most international financial transactions are between banks and they involve deposits, loans and equity as well as private and government bonds (see de Grauwe, 1982; Aliber, 1984; Thomas and Wickens, 1987). Moreover, much of domestic banking activity involves firms and the finance of investment. In countries with less well-developed capital markets (i.e. in a majority of developed countries and in virtually all developing countries) banks are often the principal source of investment finance and frequently only they have access to international capital with which to finance domestic investment (see Folkerts-Landau, 1985, for a discussion of bank lending in development finance). In order to understand exchange rate determination for these countries it is necessary to take account of such institutional arrangements. In countries with well-developed capital markets the fact that the connection between the price of domestic assets and the exchange rate is imperfectly understood was glaringly revealed by the number of different explanations offered for the world-wide collapse of stock markets in October 1987 and the simultaneous realignment of exchange rates.

The aim of this paper is to construct a model of exchange rate determination which takes account of the role of banks both in international capital transactions and in providing finance for domestic investment. Firms are assumed to finance a proportion of their investment by bank loans and the rest from retained earnings. The thorny question of whether this is an optimal financial structure for the firm is not considered; we assume that sufficient imperfections exist to rule out the application of the Modigliani–Miller theorem. The demand for bank loans is by firms and is derived from an intertemporal model (which is an extension of that of Sundararajan, 1985) in which the net worth of firms is maximized. Investment is in physical capital which is used in the production of domestic output, thereby providing the model with an endogenous supply function (see Stockman and Svensson, 1987; Uctum, 1986, 1987; Zeiro, 1987). It is assumed that shares in each firm's equity can be purchased on the stock market and that there are a fixed number of shares, implying that raising investment finance by new issues is excluded. See Gavin (1986) for an alternative treatment of exchange rate determination with a stock market.

The model has six assets: cash, bank deposits, bank loans, equity, physical capital and foreign securities. In order to make the model tractable, and given the focus of our interest, we have assumed that domestic bank deposits and foreign securities are perfect substitutes and that the only domestic asset held by foreigners is bank deposits. We recognize that the last assumption especially is very strong but it reflects our emphasis on the role of banks in international capital transactions.

The paper is set out as follows. In section 4.2 we describe the model in detail, including a derivation of the firm's demand for loans, physical capital and the rate of return on equity. In section 4.3 we analyse the long-run properties of the model under the assumption of purchasing power parity. Our main concern is to determine the long-run behaviour of the exchange rate in response to changes in domestic and foreign monetary policy, demand shocks and the parameters that affect the financing decisions of the firm such as the proportion of investment financed by loans. We also examine the effect of changes in these variables on the stock market. The short-run behaviour of the exchange rate is analysed in section 4.4. A number of additional simplifying assumptions are made to make the analysis tractable. Some concluding remarks are offered in section 4.5 including a few speculative comments on some possible implications of our analysis for the stock market collapse of October 1987 and associated exchange rate movements.

4.2 THE MODEL

We make the following assumptions. The economy produces a single good which can be consumed, traded or used for domestic physical capital formation. Output is produced with a single factor of production, capital. Gross investment is financed partly through retained earnings and partly through bank loans, the proportions being determined exogenously. There are six assets: high-powered money, bank deposits, bank loans, foreign securities, physical capital and equity. Domestic bank deposits are assumed to be a perfect substitute for foreign securities and are the only domestic asset held by foreigners. Money is an imperfect substitute for bank deposits, equity and foreign securities. Finally, we assume that expectations are formed with perfect foresight.

The definitions of the variables are as follows:

π net operating profits
p price level
Q output
K stock of physical capital
I gross investment in physical capital
B new borrowing
R total outstanding debt
θ proportion of investment financed by borrowing
a amortization rate of debt
ρ internal rate of discount
q real shadow price of capital (Tobin's q)
V gross market value of the firm
s rate of return on equity
n price of a share
N number of shares
M stock of high-powered money
D bank deposits
L bank loans
k reserve ratio
i_D deposit rate
i_L loan rate
i^* rate of return on foreign securities
$\hat{e}$ expected exchange rate depreciation
y aggregate demand or income
p^* foreign price level
z autonomous demand

4.2.1 The firm

It is assumed that firms maximize discounted future net operating profits subject to equations determining capital accumulation, debt and new borrowing. Thus they maximize

$$\int_t^\infty \exp(-\rho x)\, \pi(x)\, dx \tag{4.1}$$

where

$$\pi = pQ(K) - pI - pc(I) + B - (a + i_L)R \tag{4.2}$$

subject to

$$\dot{K} = I - \delta K \tag{4.3}$$

$$\dot{R} = B - aR \tag{4.4}$$

and

$$B = \theta pI \tag{4.5}$$

$c(I)$ is the cost of installing new investment, $c' > 0$. Total debt outstanding R is derived as follows. A proportion $a(x)$ of new debt $B(t)$ in period t is repaid in period $t + x$ such that

$$\int_0^\infty a(x)\, dx = 1 \qquad a(x) \geqslant 0$$

and

$$a(x) = a \exp(-ax) \qquad a > 0$$

where a is a constant amortization rate. Debt outstanding after x periods is

$$\left[1 - \int_0^x a \exp(-au)\, du \right] B(t) = \exp(-ax)\, B(t)$$

Total debt understanding at time t is

$$R(t) = \int_0^t \exp[-a(t-x)]\, B(x)\, dx \tag{4.6}$$

which on differentiation yields (4.4). At the loan rate i_L total payments on interest and principal are $(a + i_L)R$ which is the last term in (4.2). Equation

(4.5) determines new borrowing as a proportion of gross investment. With perfect capital markets the Modigliani–Miller theorem implies that θ is indeterminate. We treat ρ as exogenous and examine the consequences of variations in θ. The Hamiltonian H associated with the optimization can be written

$$\exp(\rho t)\, H = pQ(K) - pI - pc(I) + B - (a + i_L)R + \mu(I - \delta K) \\ + \lambda(B - aR) + \gamma(B - \theta pI) \tag{4.7}$$

The first-order conditions for a maximum are

$$\exp(\rho t)\, dH/dI = -p(1 + c') + \mu - \gamma\theta p = 0 \tag{4.8}$$

$$\exp(\rho t)\, dH/dB = 1 + \lambda + \gamma = 0 \tag{4.9}$$

$$\exp(\rho t)\, dH/dK = pQ' - \mu\delta = \mu\rho - \dot{\mu} \tag{4.10}$$

$$\exp(\rho t)\, dH/dR = -(a + i_L) - \lambda a = \lambda\rho - \dot{X} \tag{4.11}$$

together with the three constraints (4.3)–(4.5). If i_L is assumed constant then

$$\lambda(t) = -(a + i_L) \int_t^\infty \exp[-(a + \rho)(t - x)]\, dx = -\frac{a + i_L}{a + \rho} \tag{4.12}$$

In practice i_L will vary in the short run, and so strictly (4.12) is appropriate only in the long run. Denoting the real shadow price of capital by $q = \mu/p$ (i.e. Tobin's q) from (4.10) we obtain

$$\dot{q} = (\rho + \delta - \dot{p}/p)q - Q' \tag{4.13}$$

If $c(I) = cI^2/2$ then $c' = cI$ and from (4.8), (4.9) and (4.12) we find that

$$I = [q + \theta(\rho - i_L)/(\rho + a) - 1]/c \tag{4.14}$$

From (4.4), (4.5) and (4.14) total firm debt is determined by

$$\dot{R} = \theta[q + \theta(\rho - i_L)/(\rho + a) - 1] - aR \tag{4.15}$$

This is also the demand for bank loans.
   The real market value of the firm is

$$V = qK \tag{4.16}$$

If there are a fixed number N of shares with price n then

$$V = nN \tag{4.17}$$

The rate of return on equity is

$$s = \dot{q}/q + \pi/pqK \tag{4.18}$$

or

$$s = \dot{n}/n + \pi/pnN \tag{4.19}$$

where $\dot{q}/q = \dot{n}/n$ is the expected capital gain on equity. This completes the specification of the firm.

4.2.2 Asset demands and banking sector

In a portfolio model with imperfect capital substitutability, it would be necessary to specify explicitly the demand for money, bank deposits, equity and foreign securities. But because we are assuming perfect substitutability between domestic bank deposits and foreign securities, and as equity is assumed to be held by domestic residents, we require only the following equations. First the demand for money, which is the sum of private demand and bank reserves, is

$$pm(i_D, s + \dot{p}/p, i + \hat{e}, y) + kD = M \tag{4.20}$$

with $m_1, m_2, m_3 < 0$ and $m_4 > 0$. Thus a higher deposit rate i_D, a higher rate of return on equity s and a higher rate of return on foreign securities adjusted for expected changes in the exchange rate $i^* + \hat{e}$ all reduce the demand for money. Higher total income y and reserve requirements kD increase it. Second, a balance sheet for banks is

$$(1 - k)D = L(i_L - i_D) \tag{4.21}$$

where k are reserve requirements. Third, an equation showing that loans L ($L' \geqslant 0$) are supplied to meet the debt requirements of firms is

$$R = L \tag{4.22}$$

The loan rate i_L is assumed to adjust to the margin sufficiently to induce banks to supply these loans (see de Grauwe, 1982; Thomas and Wickens, 1987). Fourth, an interest arbitrage condition reflecting the assumption of perfect substitutability between bank deposits and foreign securities gives

$$i_D = i^* + \hat{e} \tag{4.23}$$

4.2.3 The rest of the model

The model is completed by including an aggregate demand for goods

$$y = y(Ep^*/p, I, z) \tag{4.24}$$

with $y_1, y_2, y_3 > 0$ where Ep^*/p is the real exchange rate and z is autonomous demand. A balance of payments equation is not required because it is assumed that the only domestic asset held by foreign residents is bank deposits which are perfect substitutes for foreign securities and because wealth effects are excluded.

With such a large model analytical tractability has led us to adopt a number of simplifying assumptions. For example, it would be desirable to extend the asset structure of the model to permit foreign holding of other domestic assets. This would introduce an explicit demand for equity. Also in a model such as this it is natural to include wealth effects but we have not done so because this would require a balance of payments condition. Our analysis of the present model will be restricted to the long run, in which we ignore all short-run dynamics, and to the very short run, in which we assume that capital accumulation is too slow to need to be taken into account, prices are fixed and the goods market does not clear. In the short run our assumption regarding a constant future loan rate in determining λ in equation (4.12) may be a reasonably good approximation. We shall focus on the effects on the exchange rate and on the price of equity of domestic and foreign monetary policy as reflected by changes in the exogenous variables M, i^*, domestic fiscal policy z, the proportion of investment financed by borrowing θ, and the repayment of debt a.

4.3 THE LONG-RUN SOLUTION

We assume that a static equilibrium solution exists. From the model described in section 4.2 the long-run solution is described by (4.2), (4.5), (4.14), (4.16), (4.20)–(4.22), (4.24) and the following equations:

$$I = \delta K \tag{4.25}$$

$$B = aR \tag{4.26}$$

$$q = Q'/(\rho + \delta) \tag{4.27}$$

$$s = \pi/pqK \tag{4.28}$$

$$i_D = i^* \tag{4.29}$$

$$y = Q(K) \tag{4.30}$$

In order to obtain the solution for the main variables of interest E, p, s and n, first we consider the loans market. Equation (4.22) equates the demand and supply of loans. From (4.5) and (4.26) the long-run demand for loans is

$$R = \theta pI/a \tag{4.31}$$

Steady state investment is derived from (4.14) and (4.27) as

$$I = \frac{Q'(K)/(\rho + \delta) + \theta(\rho - i_L)/(\rho + a) - 1}{c} \tag{4.32}$$

Using (4.22), (4.31) and (4.32) loan market equilibrium implies that

$$L(i_L - i^*) = \frac{\theta p [Q'(K)/(\rho + \delta) + \theta(\rho - i_L)/(\rho + a) - 1]}{ac} \qquad (4.33)$$

from which we obtain

$$i_L = i(K, p) \qquad (4.34)$$

where

$$i_1 = \frac{\theta p Q''}{[acL' + \theta^2 p/(\rho + a)](\rho + \delta)} < 0$$

and

$$i_2 = \frac{c\theta I}{[acL' + \theta^2 p/(\rho + a)](\rho + \delta)} > 0$$

Substituting (4.32) into (4.30) gives

$$I = I(K, p) \qquad (4.35)$$

where $I_1 = [Q''/(\rho + \delta) - \theta i_L/(\rho + a)]/c$ is indeterminate but is almost certainly negative and $I_2 < 0$. From (4.23) and (4.33)

$$K = K(p) \qquad (4.36)$$

with $K' < 0$.

Real net revenue can also be expressed as a function of K and p. From (4.2), (4.5) and (4.26)

$$\pi/p = Q(K) - I - c(I) - \theta i_L I/a$$

Using (4.25) and the definition of $c(I)$ we have

$$\pi/p = Q(K) - [1 + c\delta K/2 + \theta i_L/a]\delta K = \pi(K, i_L) \qquad (4.37)$$

where $\pi_2 < 0$. If we assume that investment adds to net revenue then $\pi_1 > 0$. Eliminating i_L from (4.37) using (4.34) we obtain

$$\pi/p = \pi(K, p) \qquad (4.38)$$

with $\pi_1 > 0$ and $\pi_2 < 0$. From (4.16), (4.25), (4.27) and (4.31) the real value of the firm is

$$V = Q'(K)K/(\rho + \delta) = V(K) \qquad (4.39)$$

where $V' > 0$. Hence from (4.18) the price of a share is

$$n = V(K)/N \qquad (4.40)$$

From (4.28), (4.38) and (4.39) the rate of return on equity is

$$s = \pi(K, p)/V(K) = s(p) \qquad (4.41)$$

where the sign of $s' = [\pi_2 + K'(V\pi_1 - sV')]/V$ is indeterminate but is probably negative.

The price level is obtained from the money market equilibrium condition (4.20) after subtituting i_D from (4.29), s from (4.40), y from (4.30) and D from (4.21), (4.22), (4.25) and (4.31). Thus

$$M = pm[i^*, s(p), i^*, Q(K)] + k\theta p\delta K/a(1 - k) = M(K, p, i^*) \qquad (4.42)$$

with $M_2 > 0$, $M_3 < 0$ and M_1 indeterminate in general but unambiguously negative for $s' < 0$. Substituting K using (4.36) and solving (4.42) for p gives

$$p = p(M, i^*) \qquad (4.43)$$

with p_1, $p_2 > 0$ if $M_1 > 0$. It is interesting to note that (4.41) implies that money is not neutral in the sense that $dp/dM \neq 1$. The rate of return on equity is obtained from (4.41) and (4.43),

$$s = S(M, i^*) \qquad (4.44)$$

where S_1, $S_2 < 0$, and the price of shares from (4.36), (4.40) and (4.43):

$$n = n(M, i^*, N) \qquad (4.45)$$

The exchange rate can now be determined. From (4.24) and (4.25)

$$y(Ep^*/p, \delta K, z) = Q(K)$$

and hence

$$K = H(Ep^*, p, z) \qquad (4.46)$$

where H_1, $H_2 > 0$ if $Q' > \delta y_2$, i.e. if an increase in capital adds more to output supply than the extra replacement investment does to demand. Using (4.36), (4.43) and (4.46), the exchange rate is found to be

$$E = E(z, M, i^*, p^*) \qquad (4.47)$$

where E_1, $E_2 < 0$. The signs of E_2 and E_3 are the same as the sign of $pK'/H_1 + Ep^*/p$ which is indeterminate as $K' < 0$ and $H_1 > 0$. This ambiguity is in contrast with the conventional signs of E_2 and E_3 which are positive. It may be noted that the conventional analysis takes output as fixed, in which case $H_1 < 0$ and E_2, $E_3 > 0$ unambiguously.

The most likely results are summarized in table 4.1. Thus, expansionary domestic monetary policy, contractionary foreign monetary policy, domestic fiscal tightening and a fall in the foreign price level all cause a long-run depreciation of the exchange rate. The price level, the rate of return on equity and the price of shares are only affected in the long run by monetary shocks; a domestic monetary expansion or a foreign monetary contraction cause the price level to rise and the rate of return on equity and the price of shares to fall.

Table 4.1 Long-run multipliers

	z	M	i^*	p^*	N
E	−	+	+	−	0
p	0	+	+	0	0
s	0	−	−	0	0
n	0	−	−	0	−

4.4 THE SHORT-RUN SOLUTION

We wish to examine the impact effect on the exchange rate and the stock market of changes in the exogenous variables. We are therefore concerned with the immediate short run. It is assumed that over this period physical capital and the price level are fixed. As a result output is given and the goods market does not clear. It is assumed that expectations are formed using perfect foresight.

If we set $p = p^* = 1$ and $K = \bar{K}$ implying that $Q = Q(\bar{K}) = \bar{Q}$ and $q = \bar{q}$, the full model can be rewritten as equations (4.4), (4.18), (4.21)–(4.23) together with

$$B = \theta I \tag{4.48}$$

$$I = [\bar{q} + \theta(\rho - i_L)/(\rho + a) - 1]/c \tag{4.49}$$

$$V = \bar{q}\bar{K} \tag{4.50}$$

$$s = \pi/V \tag{4.51}$$

$$\pi = \bar{Q} - I - c(I) + B - (a + i_L)R \tag{4.52}$$

$$M = m(i_D, s, i^* + \hat{e}, y) + kD \tag{4.53}$$

with $m_1, m_2, m_3 < 0$ and $m_4 > 0$, and

$$y = y(E, I, z) \tag{4.54}$$

with $y_1, y_2, y_3 > 0$.

This system of equations can be reduced to two dynamic equations in E and R. First we consider the firm. Equations (4.22) and (4.23) can be solved to give

$$i_L = L^{-1}(R) + i^* + \hat{e} \tag{4.55}$$

with $L^{-1\prime} > 0$. Substituting (4.55) into (4.49) gives

$$\begin{aligned} I &= [\bar{q} + \theta(\rho - L^{-1}(R) - i^* - \hat{e})/(\rho + a) - 1]/c \\ &= J(R, i^* + \hat{e}, q) \end{aligned} \tag{4.56}$$

where $J_1 = -L^{-1}\theta/c(\rho + a) < 0$, $J_2 = -\theta/c(\rho + a) < 0$ and $J_3 = 1/c > 0$. From (4.4) and (4.56)

$$\begin{aligned} \dot{R} &= \theta I - aR \\ &= g(R, i^* + \hat{e}, q) \end{aligned} \tag{4.57}$$

where $g_1 = \theta J_1 - a < 0$, $g_2 = \theta J_2 < 0$ and $g_3 = \theta J_3 > 0$. Equation (4.57) is one of our two dynamic equations.

To obtain the second dynamic equation we eliminate y from (4.53) using (4.54) and I from (4.52) using (4.56). We find that (4.53) can be written

$$M = h(E, R, s, i^* + \hat{e}, q, z) \tag{4.58}$$

where

$$\begin{aligned} h_1 &= m_4 y_1 > 0 \\ h_2 &= k/(1-k) + m_4 y_2 J_1 \gtreqless 0 \\ h_3 &= m_2 < 0 \\ h_4 &= m_1 + m_3 + m_4 y_2 J_2 < 0 \\ h_5 &= m_4 y_2 J_3 > 0 \\ h_6 &= m_4 y_3 > 0 \end{aligned}$$

Taking a linear approximation to equations (4.57) and (4.58) enables us to write them as

$$\begin{bmatrix} -g_2/E & 1 \\ -h_4/E & 0 \end{bmatrix} \begin{bmatrix} \dot{E} \\ R \end{bmatrix} = \begin{bmatrix} 0 & g_1 \\ h_1 & h_2 \end{bmatrix} \begin{bmatrix} E \\ R \end{bmatrix} + \begin{bmatrix} 0 & g_2 & g_3 & 0 & 0 \\ h_3 & h_4 & h_5 & h_6 & -1 \end{bmatrix} \begin{bmatrix} s \\ i^* \\ q \\ z \\ M \end{bmatrix} \tag{4.59}$$

or

$$\begin{bmatrix} \dot{E} \\ \dot{R} \end{bmatrix} = \begin{bmatrix} -h_1 E/h_4 & -h_2 E/h_4 \\ -h_1 g_2/h_4 & g_1 - h_2 g_2/h_4 \end{bmatrix} \begin{bmatrix} E \\ R \end{bmatrix}$$

$$+ \begin{bmatrix} -h_3 E/h_4 & -E & -h_5 E/h_4 & -h_6 E/h_4 & E/h_4 \\ -h_3 g_2/h_4 & 0 & g_3 - h_5 g_2/h_4 & -h_6 g_2/h_4 & g_2/h_4 \end{bmatrix} \begin{bmatrix} s \\ i^* \\ q \\ z \\ M \end{bmatrix} \tag{4.60}$$

Denoting the matrix multiplying $(E\ R)'$ in (4.60) by A, we find that $\det(A) = -h_1 g_1 E/h_4 < 0$ and $\mathrm{tr}(A) = g_1 - (h_1 E + h_2 g_2)/h_4$ which is indeterminate in sign. Since $\det(A) < 0$ we have a saddlepoint solution.

The long-run solution is obtained from (4.59) as

$$\begin{bmatrix} E \\ R \end{bmatrix} = - \begin{bmatrix} h_3/h_1 & (h_4 - h_2 g_2/g_1)/h_1 & (h_5 - h_2 g_3/g_1)/h_1 & h_6/h_1 & -1/h_1 \\ 0 & g_2/g_1 & g_3/g_1 & 0 & 0 \end{bmatrix}$$

$$\begin{bmatrix} s \\ i^* \\ q \\ z \\ M \end{bmatrix} \tag{4.61}$$

Thus $dE/ds > 0$, $dE/dz < 0$, $dE/dM > 0$, the last being in the usual direction. The remaining derivatives are indeterminate. Given that $h_1 > 0$ and $g_1, g_2, h_4 < 0$, then if $h_2 > 0$ we have

$$dE/di^* = (g_2 h_2 - h_4 g_1)/h_1 g_1 > 0$$

This would require the effect on the demand for money of increased reserve requirements, which arise from additional borrowing, to dominate the effect of extra borrowing in lowering aggregate demand, which are a result of raising the loan rate and hence reducing investment. But if $h_2 < 0$, it is possible to have $dE/di^* < 0$. For

$$dE/dq = (h_2 g_3 - h_5 g_1)/h_1 g_1$$

$dE/dq < 0$ if $h_2 < 0$ and is otherwise indeterminate. In our analysis of short-run dynamic behaviour we shall therefore consider both $h_2 > 0$ and $h_2 < 0$. It may be noted that h_2 can be written

$$h_2 = k/(1 - k) - \theta m y L^{-1}/(\rho + a)c$$

Hence an important factor in the determination of the sign of h_2 is the response L' of the supply of loans to the margin between the loan rate and the deposit rate (equation (4.21)). If $L' \approx 0$, implying that the supply of loans is nearly independent of the margin, then $h_2 < 0$. But if L' is large, implying that there is virtually a perfectly elastic supply of loans and that the margin is almost fixed ($i_L \approx i^*$), then $h_2 > 0$.

4.4.1 Case 1: $h_2 > 0$

The dynamic behaviour of E and R in response to changes in the exogenous variables is obtained from (4.60). The slopes of the two equations for $\dot{E} = 0$ and $\dot{R} = 0$ are

$$\dot{E} = 0: \quad \partial E/\partial R = -h_2/h_1 < 0$$
$$\dot{R} = 0: \quad \partial E/\partial R = -h_2/h_1 + h_4 g_1/h_1 g_2 < -h_2/h_1 < 0$$

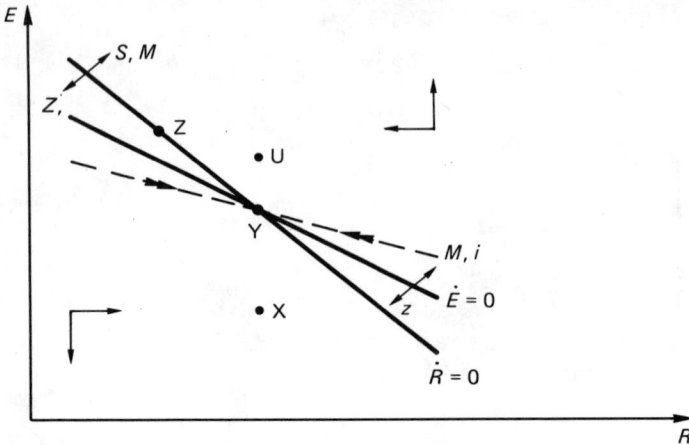

Figure 4.1   The dynamic behaviour of E and R in response to changes in the exogenous variables M, s, z and i^* when $h_2 > 0$

The solution is depicted in figure 4.1. The dotted line represents the saddle-path. The direction of shift of each line following an increase in an exogenous variable is indicated where it has been determined. The effect of an increase in M or s and a decrease in z is obtained by assuming that X is the original equilibrium and Y the new equilibrium. Since none of these variables appears in the long-run solution of R given by (4.61), R is unaffected by these changes and so X is vertically below Y. Thus, despite the saddlepoint solution, E jumps to its new equilibrium and R remains unaltered. An increase in i^* shifts only the $\dot{E} = 0$ line. If the original equilibrium is now taken as Y, the new equilibrium will be the point Z, implying that in the long run dE/di^* and dR/di^* are negative. In the short run the exchange rate jumps to the point U on the saddlepath through Z.

Thus a domestic monetary expansion results in a jump depreciation of the exchange rate as does a negative autonomous aggregate demand shock. An exogenous fall in the rate of return on equities causes a jump appreciation because it acts through the demand-for-money function like a domestic monetary contraction and causes an increase in the demand for money. There are no income effects arising from the collapse to offset the substitution effect on money holdings as there are in the long-run solution. Wealth effects, if included, would also reduce the demand for money. Of these only foreign monetary policy has any effect on the demand for loans and, because $n = (\bar{q}K + R)/N$, on the price of shares. A tightening of foreign monetary policy causes a fall in loans and the price of shares.

Turning to the effect of a change in q, we note that the direction of shift of the $\dot{R} = 0$ line is indeterminate. We shall therefore use the long-run solutions

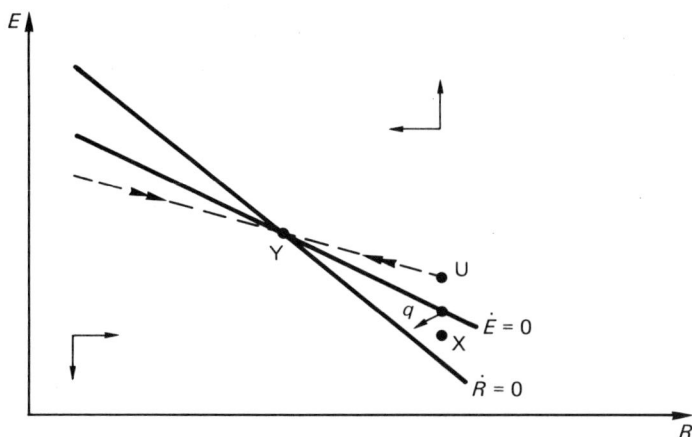

Figure 4.2   The dynamic behaviour of E and R in response to changes in Tobin's q when $h_2 > 0$

for q to determine the direction of shift of the $\dot{R} = 0$ line. When $h_2 > 0$ we find that $dE/dq < 0$ and $dR/dq > 0$ and therefore in the long run we require the directions of movement shown in figure 4.2. Thus, a decrease in q causes a shift from X to Y in the long run, with E jumping to U which is on the saddlepath through Y. This implies that there is no overshooting of the exchange rate which the jump depreciates initially. The demand for loans and hence the price of shares fall smoothly.

4.4.2 Case 2: $h_2 < 0$

The slope of the $\dot{E} = 0$ line is now positive and the slope of the $\dot{R} = 0$ line becomes indeterminate but is still less than that of the $\dot{E} = 0$ line. Although the slopes of the lines are different the outcome of changes in s, M and z are the same as before. We shall therefore focus on the effects of changes in i^* and q. First we consider the case where the gradient of the $\dot{R} = 0$ line is negative. This is depicted in figure 4.3.

An increase in i^* and a decrease in q cause the $\dot{E} = 0$ line to shift to the left. A change in i^* has no affect on the $\dot{R} = 0$ line, but a change in q does. Unfortunately, the direction of shift of the $\dot{R} = 0$ line is ambiguous, but since this does not affect the analysis (provided that the correct long-run results are maintained) we do not show a change in the $\dot{R} = 0$ line in the diagram. In contrast with the earlier analysis the exchange rate now overshoots. It jumps onto the saddlepath at U before converging to the new equilibrium at Y.

If the $\dot{R} = 0$ line has a positive slope then the analysis requires figure 4.4. The main difference is that in the long run we now have $\partial E / \partial i^* < 0$ instead

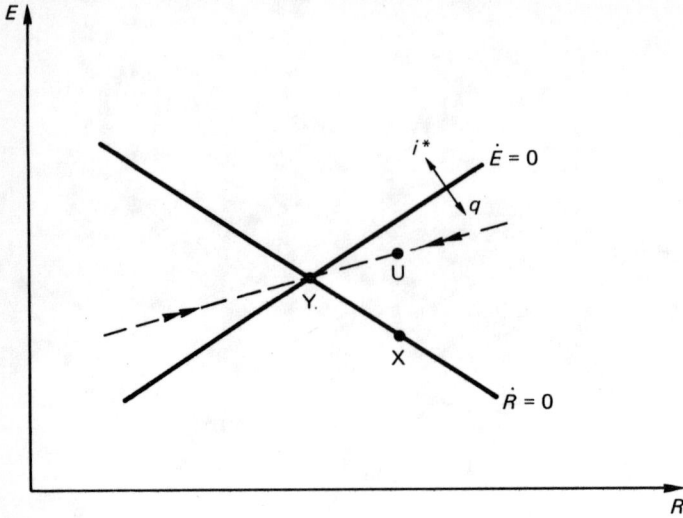

Figure 4.3   The dynamic behaviour of E and R in response to changes in i^* and Tobin's q when $h_2 < 0$ and the slope of $\dot{R} = 0$ is negative

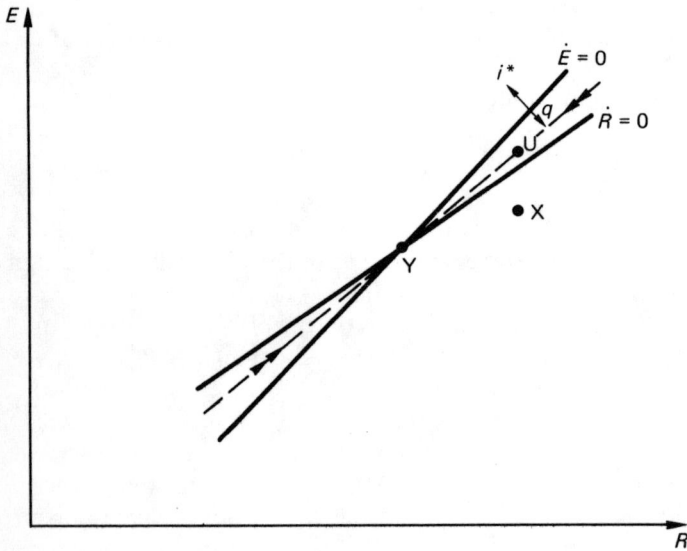

Figure 4.4   The dynamic behaviour of E and R in response to changes in i^* and Tobin's q when $h_2 < 0$ and $\dot{R} = 0$ has a positive slope

of > 0 and $\partial E/\partial q > 0$ instead of $\partial E/\partial q < 0$. Thus following an increase in i^*, or a decrease in q, the exchange rate again initially jump-depreciates but eventually it appreciates.

4.5 CONCLUSION

In this chapter we have attempted to extend the portfolio balance model of exchange rate determination. Instead of considering just money and bonds, we have introduced, in addition, bank deposits and loans, physical capital and equity. We have analysed the consequences for the exchange rate, the price of shares and the rate of return on equity of domestic and foreign money shocks and domestic demand shocks, together with several other factors. One of the purposes of this analysis is to examine the interconnections between these asset prices.

In order to make the analysis tractable, because of the generality of the model we have had to introduce various simplifying assumptions. This has enabled us to derive clear-cut results which would otherwise be indeterminate. Usually, we have tried to identify extra assumptions which lead to intuitively plausible results. For this reason it is most important to stress that different, and perhaps surprising, results occur if alternative assumptions are made. If we are seeking explanations of previously unaccountable events it may well be that our intuition is wrong and these alternative assumptions are correct. The model may then be able to provide the explanation we are seeking for these events. The correctness of the model and the validity of the assumptions we have made are ultimately an empirical matter. The model is sufficiently general to embrace a wide variety of possibilities. Indeed, the formation of a single model which possesses such a broad asset structure is itself a useful step forward in the search for the adequate fundamentals explanation of exchange rate movements.

In the long run, when prices and physical capital may be taken to be perfectly flexible, our results suggest that a domestic monetary expansion will cause a depreciation of the exchange rate and possibly a fall in the rate of return on equity, whilst a foreign monetary expansion will appreciate the exchange rate and cause an increase in the rate of return on domestic equity and the price of shares.

In the very short run, prices and physical capital may be taken as fixed. As a result, q and the rate of return on equity are also fixed. A domestic monetary expansion or a foreign monetary contraction cause an exchange rate depreciation without any overshooting. Both an exogenous increase in the rate of return on equity, which acts like a domestic monetary contraction and an exogenous decrease in q, possibly caused by a negative productivity shock, cause the exchange rate to jump-depreciate. Whilst the former has no effect on the price of shares, the latter does but in an unknown direction.

The model analysed in this chapter is best suited for an economy which does not have well-developed capital markets. Despite this, and despite the restrictive nature of our short-run analysis, it is tempting to use our results to comment on the stock market collapse in the USA (and in the rest of the world) of October 1987 and on the possibly related decline in the US dollar immediately afterwards. The long-run analysis suggests that a domestic monetary expansion and a foreign monetary contraction both cause an exchange rate depreciation and a rise in the price of shares. In the short run, however, they only affect the exchange rate. Of the exogenous variables we analyse, only q affects the price of shares, but the sign is ambiguous. Thus our analysis suggests that the US stock market collapse may not have been caused by monetary factors but by a change in q, the shadow price of capital. It also indicates that in the long run a domestic monetary contraction would help restore the price of shares. These conclusions are at best speculative. It remains to be seen whether they would still hold if the restrictions introduced for the sake of analytic tractability are removed. In particular, it is desirable to allow λ, the shadow price of borrowing, to be a fully dynamic variable. Among other things, this may introduce a short-run impact of monetary shocks on the price of shares and hence give a monetary explanation of the stock market collapse.

5 Uncovered Interest Parity, Exchange Rate Risk and Exchange Rate Dynamics

Vito Antonio Muscatelli, Andrew Stevenson and David Vines

5.1 INTRODUCTION

This paper is concerned with a small but important detail of exchange rate modelling under less than perfect capital mobility. We show in section 5.2 that there are two different specifications of the risk-adjusted uncovered interest parity condition, both of which are common in the literature. In one of these the expected change in the exchange rate is restricted to respond *ceteris paribus* one-for-one to changes in the interest differential between home and abroad, whilst in the other it is not. We seek to understand the theoretical basis for this restriction, and to explore its implications.

It will be shown in section 5.3 that these contrasting specifications are derived on the basis of two different, and extreme, assumptions regarding the nature of risk faced by the economic agent in an open economy. The implications of these alternative specifications for the risk-adjusted uncovered interest parity condition are considered in section 5.4, as well as the implications for exchange rate dynamics and for the specification of econometric models of exchange rate behaviour.

In conclusion we argue that each of the two extreme assumptions concerning the nature of risk will be more appropriate in some situations than in others. The nature of the risk faced by the economic agent in an open economy is likely to depend both on the financial structure of the country in question and on the underlying stance of economic policy, with the result that the appropriate form of the uncovered interest parity condition will similarly depend on these factors.

5.2 TWO CONTRASTING MODELS OF RISK-ADJUSTED UNCOVERED INTEREST PARITY

Most small-country portfolio models include three types of assets, namely domestic money (M) and bonds (B), which are denominated in domestic currency, and foreign bonds (F), denominated in foreign currency. Money is generally assumed to consist of non-interest bearing currency. We follow these two conventions. Our models will be fixed price ones, for simplicity. In addition we assume that all asset demands are homogeneous in wealth. Lastly, we also ignore any effect of real income in asset demand functions.

5.2.1 Model 1

The specification of (nominal) asset demands which is most general (in terms of the least number of cross-parameter restrictions) is one generally associated with Branson (e.g. Branson, 1977, 1979). This we call model 1:

$$M^d/W = \epsilon_0 - \epsilon_1 r - \epsilon_2(r^* + \dot{e}^e) \tag{5.1}$$

$$B^d/W = \xi_0 + \xi_1 r - \xi_2(r^* + \dot{e}^e) \tag{5.2}$$

$$EF^d/W = \eta_0 - \eta_1 r + \eta_2(r^* + \dot{e}^e) \tag{5.3}$$

where M, B and F are money, domestic bonds and foreign bonds respectively, E is the exchange rate expressed as the domestic currency price of foreign exchange, r and r^* are the interest rates on domestic and foreign bonds respectively and $\dot{e}^e$ is the expected rate of depreciation of the exchange rate.

The asset demands in equations (5.1)–(5.3) can be equated to given asset supplies in order to determine the rates of return. In particular, we may assume that $F^d = F$ and then invert equation (5.3) to obtain a risk-adjusted uncovered interest parity condition, which relates $\dot{e}^e$ to the interest differential between domestic and foreign assets:

$$\dot{e}^e = \frac{\eta_1}{\eta_2} r - r^* + \frac{EF}{W\eta_2} - \frac{\eta_0}{\eta_2} \tag{5.3'}$$

In this form of uncovered interest parity, the coefficient on the domestic interest rate is less than unity, since if foreign and domestic bonds are gross substitutes – as normally assumed – then $\eta_2 > \xi_2$, while $\eta_1 = \xi_2$ (cross-rates are the same for pairs of asset demands – a standard result in consumer demand theory), and so it necessarily follows that $\eta_2 > \eta_1$.

5.2.2 Model 2

An alternative specification of asset demands may be found in some port-folio models (see for example Dornbusch, 1980; Eaton and Turnovsky, 1983; Branson and Henderson, 1985; Smith, 1985). We call this model 2:

$$M^d/W = a_0 - a_1 r \tag{5.4}$$

$$B^d/W = b_0 + b_1 r - c_1(r^* + \dot{e}^e) \tag{5.5}$$

$$EF^d/W = c_0 - c_1 r + c_1(r^* + \dot{e}^e) \tag{5.6}$$

This may be viewed as a 'restricted' version of equations (5.1)–(5.3).

By analogy with the procedure used to obtain equation (5.3'), assuming $F^d = F$, we may invert equation (5.6) to yield a further risk-adjusted uncovered interest parity condition:

$$\dot{e}^e = r - r^* + EF/Wc_1 \tag{5.6'}$$

Notice how different (5.6') is from (5.3'). The coefficient on the home interest rate in (5.3') is different from that on the foreign interest rate, whereas in (5.6') they are identical. As Dornbusch (1980, 1983) points out, the correct specification of the risk premium in asset demands is a matter of great importance in modelling the exchange rate. For example, these dif-ferences in specification will be of significance in the estimation of empirical exchange rate models. Furthermore, as we shall see later, each of these specifications has its own implications for exchange rate dynamics.

It is not always apparent that these different forms of asset demand systems derive from different assumptions regarding the nature of the risk faced by the domestic investor. This is the purpose of the next section.

5.3 THE MICROFOUNDATIONS OF ASSET DEMANDS AND THE ALTERNATIVE RISK-ADJUSTED INTEREST PARITY CONDITIONS

One common starting point for portfolio theorists in deriving asset demands for the investor in an open economy (for example see de Macedo et al., 1984) is to assume that investors face uncertain nominal own-currency returns on both domestic bonds and foreign bonds and that the behaviour of the exchange rate is stochastic. As a result, the return on foreign bonds is uncer-tain for two reasons: the stochastic behaviour of the foreign interest rate and the stochastic behaviour of the exchange rate. Money is generally seen as a safe asset yielding a known fixed return (usually zero). We shall analyse a representative investor's portfolio choice in this particular scenario, using the tools of stochastic calculus introduced to portfolio theory by Merton (1971).

As is common, we assume that the investor possesses an instantaneous utility function which exhibits constant relative risk aversion. If we also assume that the percentage changes in asset prices follow geometric Brownian motion, we can then view the investor as maximizing the following objective function (see Merton, 1971; Malliaris and Brock, 1982; Branson and Henderson, 1985):

$$Q = E\left(\frac{dW}{W}\right) - \frac{1}{2} R\left[\text{var}\left(\frac{dW}{W}\right)\right] \tag{5.7}$$

where R is the coefficient of relative risk aversion, W is real wealth (which is equivalent to nominal wealth in our fixed price model) and E(.) and var(.) denote respectively the expectation and variance of a random variable. The reader should note the similarity between the objective function in (5.7) and the maximand obtainable by assuming an exponential utility function and normally distributed asset returns within the framework of a conventional Tobin–Markowitz mean variance approach (see for instance Bhattacharyya, 1979). In contrast with the above starting point, it is also possible to analyse the representative portfolio holder's choice in situations where domestic and foreign bonds have certain returns. In these circumstances the only assets which are risky to hold are foreign bonds, because of exchange rate risks. In such a scenario there is no apparent role for a zero-yield money asset, since it is entirely dominated by the riskless interest-bearing domestic bond B. The usual way in which money is incorporated in such systems (see Kouri, 1977; McCallum, 1983; Branson and Henderson, 1985) is to assume that the level of money balances enters the investor's objective function directly, in that these balances provide a service to the economic agent in terms of less time wasted in 'trips to the bank' (assuming that only money can act as a medium of exchange). We shall also examine the investor's choice in this second scenario.

As a result of explicitly adopting this assumption, Branson and Henderson (1985) modify objective function Q in equation (5.7) to the following:

$$Q = E\left(\frac{dW}{W}\right) - \frac{1}{2} R\left[\text{var}\left(\frac{dW}{W}\right)\right] + Z(M) \tag{5.7'}$$

where $Z(.)$ is an increasing concave function ($Z'(M) > 0$ and $Z''(M) < 0$). It would be more plausible to assume that Z (and hence Q) depends not on the level of money balances but on the ratio of money balances to nominal income, given that the objective is to model the transactions motive for holding money, and Branson and Henderson (1985) make this extension.

However, adding functions of the money–income ratio to our objective function (5.7), or even simply money balances as in (5.7′), leads to very complex asset demand functions.[1] As a result, for simplicity we have modified (5.7′) to the following objective function:

$$Q' = \mathrm{E}\left(\frac{\mathrm{d}W}{W}\right) - \frac{1}{2} R\left[\mathrm{var}\left(\frac{\mathrm{d}W}{W}\right)\right] + Z\left(\frac{M}{W}\right) \tag{5.8}$$

The assumption made here to simplify our results is that the utility derived from the transactions services which money provides depends on the proportion of wealth held in money balances.[2] We adopt the following simple formulation of $Z(.)$:

$$Z\left(\frac{M}{W}\right) = \alpha\left(\frac{M}{W}\right) - \frac{\beta}{2}\left(\frac{M}{W}\right)^2$$

This satisfies the requirement that $Z'(M/W) > 0$ and $Z''(M/W) < 0$.

5.3.1 The first set of assumptions about risk

The consumer's problem is to allocate optimal proportions of their wealth to the three assets at their disposal. These proportions are defined as follows:[3]

$$M = \mu W \tag{5.9}$$

$$EF = \lambda W \tag{5.10}$$

$$B = (1 - \lambda - \mu)W \tag{5.11}$$

Money is assumed to have a known (riskless) nominal return i_m (this may later be set equal to zero):

$$\mathrm{d}M/M = i_\mathrm{m}\mathrm{d}t \tag{5.12}$$

In accordance with our first set of assumptions about risk, we specify that the exchange rate and the returns on bonds follow stochastic processes of the type

$$\mathrm{d}B/B = i\mathrm{d}t + \sigma_b\mathrm{d}z_b \tag{5.13}$$

$$\mathrm{d}F/F = i^*\mathrm{d}t + \sigma_f\mathrm{d}z_f \tag{5.14}$$

$$\mathrm{d}E/E = \omega\mathrm{d}t + \sigma_e\mathrm{d}z_e \tag{5.15}$$

where the $\mathrm{d}z_i$ are Wiener processes. The means of these stochastic processes are i, i^* and ω respectively, and the variances are σ_b^2, σ_f^2 and σ_e^2 respectively. In order to find the mean and variance of $\mathrm{d}W/W$, so as to maximize the objective function Q, we apply Ito's lemma[4] to the definition of wealth

$$W = EF + B + M \tag{5.16}$$

to obtain

$$dW = dB + dM + FdE + EdF + dEdF \tag{5.17}$$

Substituting equations (5.9)–(5.16) into (5.17) we obtain the following expression for dW/W:

$$dW/W = [(1 - \lambda - \mu)i + \mu i_m + \lambda\omega + \lambda i^* + \lambda\rho_{ef}]dt + (1 - \lambda - \mu)\sigma_b dz_b + \lambda\sigma_e dz_e + \lambda\sigma_f dz_f \tag{5.18}$$

where ρ_{ij} denotes the covariance between the stochastic processes for i and j.
We can now find the expected value and variance of dW/W:

$$E(dW/W) = (1 - \lambda - \mu)i + \mu i_m + \lambda\omega + \lambda i^* + \lambda\rho_{ef} \tag{5.19}$$

$$var(dW/W) = (1 - \lambda - \mu)^2\sigma_b^2 + \lambda^2(\sigma_f^2 + \sigma_e^2 + 2\rho_{ef}) + 2(1 - \lambda - \mu)\lambda(\rho_{eb} + \rho_{ef}) \tag{5.20}$$

Substituting (5.19) and (5.20) into (5.8), setting $i_m = 0$ for simplicity, and maximizing (5.8) with respect to λ and μ, we obtain two equations in λ and μ which may be solved simultaneously to obtain expressions for μ and λ. We then obtain

$$\lambda = -\frac{i(R\gamma_1 + \gamma_0)}{R\gamma_0\delta_0\Delta} + (i^* + \omega)/R\delta_0\Delta + \gamma_1\gamma_2/\delta_0\gamma\Delta \tag{5.21}$$

$$\mu = -i\left[\frac{\gamma_1(R\gamma_1 + \gamma_0)}{\gamma_0^2\delta_0\Delta} + \frac{1}{\gamma_0}\right] + \frac{(i^* + \omega)\gamma_1}{\gamma_0\delta_0\Delta}$$
$$+ \frac{\gamma_1^2\gamma_2 R}{\gamma_0(\delta_0\gamma_0\Delta)} - \frac{\gamma_1}{\delta_0}\left(1 - \frac{\gamma_2}{\gamma_0}\right) + \frac{\delta_1}{R\delta_0} \tag{5.22}$$

where

$$\gamma_0 = \beta + R\sigma_b^2, \ \gamma_1 = \rho_{eb} + \rho_{ef} - \sigma_b^2, \ \gamma_2 = \alpha + R\sigma_b^2,$$
$$\delta_0 = \sigma_f^2 + \sigma_e^2 + \sigma_b^2 - 2\rho_{eb}, \ \delta_1 = \rho_{ef}, \ \Delta = 1 - R(\gamma_1^2/\delta_0\gamma_0)$$

We first examine the signs of the coefficients on i and $i^* + \omega$. Note that from (5.21) we require $\Delta > 0$ if the coefficient on the own-interest rate for foreign bonds is to be positive. This in turn implies that $R\gamma_1 + \gamma_0 = (\rho_{eb} + \rho_{ef})R + \beta > 0$ if the assumption of gross substitutability is to hold in (5.21). From equation (5.22) it then follows that for the three assets to be gross substitutes we also require

$$\gamma_1 < 0 \text{ and } \frac{\gamma_1(R\gamma_1 + \gamma_0)}{\gamma_0^2\delta_0\Delta} + \frac{1}{\gamma_0} > 0$$

By inspection of (5.21) and (5.22) we clearly see that in a general model where there is both interest rate risk (interest rates on domestic and foreign bonds are not known with certainty) and exchange rate risk (the rate of change of the exchange rate is not known with certainty) (a) the coefficients in our demand functions for EF will differ from each other, and (b) the coefficient on $r^* + \dot{e}^e$ in the demand function for M will not be equal to zero.[5] This situation corresponds to model 1 defined in equations (5.1)–(5.3). Given the assumptions outlined above for the three assets to be gross substitutes the coefficient signs will definitely be those outlined in equations (5.1)–(5.3). We can now obtain the risk-adjusted uncovered interest parity condition in this case by assuming that the demand for foreign assets equals the supply and by inverting equation (5.22). We obtain an equation of exactly the form of (5.3′):

$$\dot{e}^e = \frac{\eta_1}{\eta_2} r - r^* + \frac{\lambda_.}{\eta_2} - \frac{\eta_0}{\eta_2} \tag{5.23}$$

where explicit representations of the η_i may be obtained from (5.21) as

$$\eta_0 = \gamma_1 \gamma_2 / \delta_0 \gamma_0 \Delta$$
$$\eta_1 = (R\gamma_1 + \gamma_0)/R\gamma_0 \delta_0 \Delta > 0$$
$$\eta_2 = 1/R\delta_0 \Delta > 0$$

(The sign restrictions come from the parameter restrictions following equations (5.21) and (5.22).) From these coefficients, we can now infer that

$$\eta_1/\eta_2 = (R\gamma_1 + \gamma_0)/\gamma_0$$

and since $\gamma_1 < 0$ we have

$$\eta_1/\eta_2 < 1$$

thus confirming the parameter restriction discussed under equation (5.3′).

5.3.2 The second alternative set of assumptions about risk

In the case of the alternative scenario about risk, we now show that portfolio analysis yields asset demands of the type described in equations (5.4)–(5.6), with 'covered interest parity' condition (5.6′). Assume now that the interest rates on the two bonds are known and that the only uncertainty in the system stems from a stochastic exchange rate. Hence, we keep equation (5.15) but (5.13) and (5.14) become

$$dB/B = idt \tag{5.13′}$$

$$dF/F = i^*dt \tag{5.14′}$$

In this portfolio system the only role for a zero-yield money asset is that it offers transactions services, since it would otherwise be entirely dominated by the safe, interest-bearing domestic bond B. We can obtain the asset demand equations where the only risk faced by investors is exchange rate risk by substituting equations (5.13′) and (5.14′) for equations (5.13) and (5.14) in our previous analysis. Effectively, this alternative system of equations may be obtained by examining the effects on the γ_i and δ_i in equations (5.21) and (5.22) when we set σ^2_b, σ^2_f, ρ_{eb}, ρ_{ef} and ρ_{bf} equal to zero. From the definitions of these parameters, the effects on the γ_i and δ_i are as follows:

γ_0 falls to β, γ_1 rises to 0, γ_2 falls to α,
δ_0 falls to σ^2_e, δ_1 falls to 0.

Under these circumstances, the demand functions for foreign bonds and domestic money simplify to

$$\lambda = \frac{i^* + \omega}{R\sigma^2_e} - \frac{i}{R\sigma^2_e} \tag{5.21′}$$

$$\mu = -\frac{i}{\beta} + \frac{\alpha}{\beta} \tag{5.22′}$$

Notice that these asset demands have a structure which is identical with that of model 2 in equations (5.4)–(5.6). Firstly, note that the own-rate and cross-rate coefficients in the demand for foreign bonds have become equal. Secondly, we have obtained a demand for money which is independent of the foreign interest rate, as used by, for example, Eaton and Turnovsky (1983) and Smith (1985). As we move from a world with both interest and exchange rate risk to one where the only risk is exchange rate risk, the qualitative structure of our asset demand equations alters. Essentially, the investor's portfolio decision takes place in two stages: initially he finds the optimal portfolio division between assets denominated in foreign currency and domestic assets, and subsequently he finds the optimal subdivision between money and domestic bonds within the latter portfolio share.

We obtain the risk-adjusted uncovered interest parity condition in this case by assuming that the demand for foreign assets equals the supply and by inverting equation (5.21′) to obtain

$$\dot{e}^e = r - r^* + R\sigma^2_e\lambda \tag{5.24}$$

which has a coefficient of unity on the domestic interest rate r. Thus, our second set of assumptions about risk gives rise to an interest parity condition of exactly the form of equation (5.6′).

It is worth emphasizing that both these specifications of asset demands have been adopted in various models in the exchange rate literature. We have shown that the choice of one over the other depends on the assumptions made about the presence or absence of interest rate risk in addition to the presence of exchange risk. This point appears not to have been fully grasped so far in the literature. Dornbusch (1983b) emphasizes the importance of the specification of the demand for money in determining the risk premium on foreign bonds and hence exchange rate dynamics. Similarly, Branson and Henderson (1985) use a simpler model to that which yielded equations (5.21), (5.22), (5.21′) and (5.22′) to highlight the importance of our assumptions regarding risk in the specification of asset markets. However, the observations made by these workers, although useful, do not permit us to make a direct comparison of exchange rate dynamics in models where only exchange risk is present and in models where both interest and exchange risk exist. We cannot compare the behaviour of two exchange rate models which differ in that one imposes the restrictions (in terms of equations (5.1)–(5.3)) $\epsilon_2 = 0$ and $\eta_1 = \eta_2$, since we cannot at the same time make a *ceteris paribus* assumption regarding the ϵ_1 and ξ_1 parameters. The only proper way to compare models which make such different assumptions regarding risk is to examine the microfoundations of a general model such as that illustrated in (5.21) and (5.24) and to see how the ϵ_i, η_i and ξ_i coefficients vary as we move from one scenario to another.[6]

We now summarize the way in which the ϵ_i, η_i and ξ_i coefficients change as we move from a world with both interest and exchange risk to a world with exchange risk alone. This may be done by a comparison of equations (5.21) and (5.22) with equations (5.21′) and (5.22′) using the definitions for the γ_i and δ_i given above. As $\sigma^2{}_b$, $\sigma^2{}_f$, ρ_{eb}, ρ_{ef} and ρ_{bf} tend to zero, we can see that

ϵ_1 rises to a higher value ϵ_1^*, ϵ_2 falls to 0,
η_2 rises to a higher value η_2^*, η_1 rises to η_2^*,
ξ_1 rises to a higher value ξ_1^*, ξ_2 rises to η_2^*.

In describing our full exchange rate model below, we shall initially use the asset demands shown in equations (5.1)–(5.3), and subsequently we shall examine the effects on the dynamics of the exchange rate model when the parameter changes described above are imposed.

5.4 IMPLICATIONS

5.4.1 Implications for exchange rate dynamics

In this section we show that exchange rate dynamics will differ between model 1 and model 2.

An initial conjecture

We compare the instantaneous effect on the expected rate of exchange rate change of an exogenous increase in the ratio of money to total wealth. We show that this is definitely larger in the case of model 1 than in the case of model 2. Larger instantaneous effects on expected depreciation are likely, in

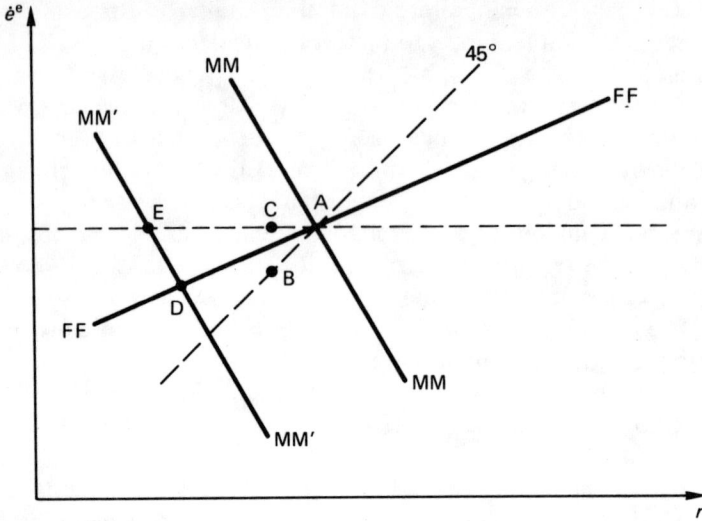

Figure 5.1   Model 1

a simple model, to be associated with a larger instantaneous exchange rate
overshooting with respect to long-run equilibrium. This provides the basis
for our conjecture: in a full exchange rate model, overshooting is likely to be
larger when domestic bonds are risky than when they are not.

Let us begin by examining the case of monetary expansion in model 1, with
the aid of figure 5.1. In figure 5.1 the foreign assets equilibrium locus FF
shows the combinations of r and $\dot{e}^e$ consistent with a given exogenous ratio of
foreign assets to wealth. Inspection of equations (5.3) and (5.23) shows that
FF has a slope of

$$\frac{\partial \dot{e}^e}{\partial r}\bigg|_{\lambda=\bar{\lambda}} = \frac{\eta_2}{\eta_1} = \frac{R\gamma_1 + \gamma_0}{\gamma_0} < 1$$

The money equilibrium locus MM shows the combinations of r and $\dot{e}^e$ consistent with a given exogenous ratio of money to wealth. It is downward
sloping. From equations (5.1) and (5.22), it has a slope of

$$\frac{\partial \dot{e}^e}{\partial r}\bigg|_{\mu=\bar{\mu}} = -\frac{\epsilon_2}{\epsilon_1} = \frac{\gamma_1(R\gamma_1 + \gamma_0)/(\gamma_0^2\delta_0\Delta + 1/\gamma_0)}{\gamma_1/\gamma_0\delta_0\Delta} < 0$$

Full asset market equilibrium is given by point A, where both the money
and foreign asset markets clear (the domestic bond market clearing by
residual). An exogenous increase in the ratio of money to wealth shifts MM
to MM'. (If we assume that this monetary expansion has been effected by
open-market purchases of domestic bonds, then the total wealth stock, and

therefore the ratios of foreign assets to wealth, is unchanged. Consequently, the FF line does not shift in this case.) The new equilibrium is at D where both $\dot{e}^e$ and r have fallen. More precisely, manipulation of equations (5.3) and (5.1) shows that

$$\Delta \dot{e}^e = -[1/(\epsilon_2 + \epsilon_1 \eta_2/\eta_1)]\Delta\mu \qquad (5.25)$$

By extensive manipulation of equations (5.21′) and (5.22′) we can express equation (5.25) in terms of the fundamental model parameters as[7]

$$\Delta \dot{e}^e = -[(\rho_{eb} + \rho_{ef})R + \beta]\Delta\mu \qquad (5.25')$$

Turning now to the more restricted case, as described by model 2 and set out in figure 5.2, we note that the slopes of MM and FF are significantly altered.

Inspection of equations (5.6) and (5.21′) shows that FF now has a slope of 45°, while the MM curve becomes vertical, as is apparent from equations (5.4) and (5.22′). Again, initial equilibrium is given by point A, and monetary expansion via open-market operations shifts MM to MM′, leaving FF unchanged. The new equilibrium is given by point B, and from equations (5.4), (5.21′) and (5.22′) we note that

$$\Delta \dot{e}^e = \Delta r = -\Delta\mu/a_1 \qquad (5.26)$$

Inspection of equation (5.22′) enables us to express this as

$$\Delta \dot{e}^e = -\beta\Delta\mu \qquad (5.26')$$

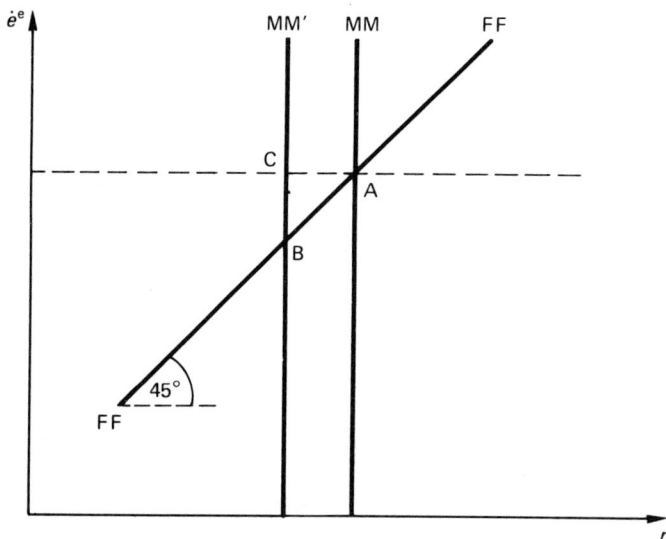

Figure 5.1   Model 2

Thus, by comparing (5.25′) and (5.26′) it clear that $\Delta \dot{e}^e$ is larger in the first case which provides the basis of our conjecture that exchange rate over-shooting is greater in model 1 than in model 2.

We now examine this conclusion in terms of figures 5.1 and 5.2. In model 2 (figure 5.2) the exchange rate must be expected to appreciate by an amount exactly equal to the immediate fall in the interest rate, which is given as precisely β. In contrast, in model 1 (figure 5.1) the exchange rate must unambiguously be expected to appreciate by more than in model 2 in response to the same monetary disturbance. This occurs because the interest rate coefficient ϵ_1 in the demand for money function is lower in model 1: the riskiness of bonds makes money and bonds less close substitutes, and there-fore the interest rate falls by more following a given monetary expansion. It will be noted that in model 1 it is also the case that $\eta \delta_1 / \eta_2 < 1$, which tends to offset the lower value of ϵ_1, since this means that any given fall in the interest rate has less effect on the expected rate of depreciation because the riskiness of domestic bonds also makes domestic and foreign bonds less close substitutes. However, the comparison of equations (5.25′) and (5.26′) clearly demonstrates that the first effect dominates. In terms of figure 5.1, point E is necessarily so far to the left of point C that the flatter slope of FF and the negative slope of MM′ (both of which serve to reduce the fall in $\dot{e}^e$ in model 1) cannot cause point D to lie higher than point B.

So far, we have focused on the role of the domestic interest rate and the expected rate of change of the exchange rate as the two endogenous variables which secure short-run asset market equilibrium, and this has enabled us to point to the likely overshooting characteristics of the exchange rate under different assumptions about risk. In the next section, we examine these issues within the framework of a more fully specified portfolio model.

A full model

We now use a simple fix-price portfolio balance model of the exchange rate to examine how the exchange rate dynamics change when we move from model 1 to model 2.

The model is written in deviation from equilibrium form to simplify matters. Lower case letters indicate logarithms (except for interest rates):

$$m - w = -\epsilon_1 r - \epsilon_2 (r^* + \dot{e}^e) \tag{5.27}$$

$$e + f - w = -\eta_1 r + \eta_2 (r^* + \dot{e}^e) \tag{5.28}$$

$$w = \pi_1 b + \pi_2 (e + f) + (1 - \pi_1 - \pi_2) m \tag{5.29}$$

Equations (5.27) and (5.28) capture the essence of equations (5.1) and (5.3), and we exclude equation (5.2) as only two asset market equilibria may be independently determined. Equation (5.29) is a log-linear approximation of the wealth identity, where the π_i represent the respective shares of assets in domestic wealth and are all assumed to be positive, so that the country is a net creditor in terms of holdings of foreign bonds (see Eaton and Turnovsky, 1983). Aggregate demand (and actual output) is given by

$$y = d_1 w + d_2 z \tag{5.30}$$

where (5.30) is a log-linear approximation to an expenditure function, with the d_i positive, and where z represents the current account surplus. The current account (and foreign asset accumulation process) is given by

$$df/dt = z = g_1 e - g_2 y \tag{5.31}$$

where interest payments on F are ignored for simplicity. We can write equations (5.27)–(5.31) as a second-order model in state space form by substituting out the non-dynamic endogenous variables y and r:

$$\begin{bmatrix} \dot{f} \\ \dot{e} \end{bmatrix} = \begin{bmatrix} a_{11} & a_{12} \\ a_{21} & a_{22} \end{bmatrix} \begin{bmatrix} f \\ e \end{bmatrix} + \begin{bmatrix} k_1 \\ k_2 \end{bmatrix} \tag{5.32}$$

where

$$a_{11} = -g_2 d_1 \pi_2/(1 + g_2 d_2)$$
$$a_{12} = (g_1 - g_2 d_1 \pi_2)/(1 + g_2 d_2)$$
$$a_{21} = a_{22} = \Omega_1 + \Omega_1 \pi_2(\eta_1/\epsilon_1 - 1)$$
$$k_1 = -g_2 d_1 \pi_1/(1 + g_2 d_2)b - g_2 d_2(1 - \pi_1 - \pi_2)/(1 + g_2 d_2)m$$
$$k_2 = \Omega_1 \pi_1(\eta_1/\epsilon_1 - 1)b - [(\pi_1 + \pi_2)\eta_1/\epsilon_1 + (1 - \pi_1 - \pi_2)]\Omega_1 m$$

and where

$$\Omega_1 = \frac{1/\eta_2}{1 + \eta_1\epsilon_2/\eta_2\epsilon_1} = \frac{\epsilon_1/\eta_1}{\epsilon_2 + \epsilon_1\eta_2/\eta_1}$$

If the determinant of the transition matrix, A say, in (5.32) is negative, the model satisfies the required saddlepoint condition. The determinant of A (given that $a_{22} = a_{21}$) can be found to be

$$\det(A) = (a_{11} - a_{12})a_{22}$$
$$= -\frac{g_1}{1 + g_2 d_2}\left[\Omega_1 + \Omega_1\pi_2\left(\frac{\eta_1}{\epsilon_1} - 1\right)\right]$$

The requirement that $\det(A) < 0$ is satisfied provided that $a_{22} > 0$, i.e. that the condition $\pi_2(\eta_1/\epsilon_1 - 1) > -1$ holds. We know that $0 < \pi_2 < 1$, and hence this condition will certainly be satisfied if $\eta_1/\epsilon_1 > 1$, i.e. provided that foreign and domestic bonds are closer substitutes than domestic bonds and money. Alternatively, the condition will be satisfied if foreign bonds only constitute a small part of total wealth (i.e. π_2 is small). This condition on relative substitutability and/or wealth composition is common in current-account-based models (see Eaton and Turnovsky, 1983) and ensures that the system is saddlepoint stable as opposed to globally stable.

The relationship between the non-predetermined (jump) variable and the predetermined variable is the following:

$$e(t) = -(c_{22})^{-1}(c_{21})f(t) \qquad (5.33)$$

where the c_i are elements of the left-eigenvector $[c_{21}\ c_{22}]$ corresponding to the unstable (positive) eigenvalue, which we call λ_1. We can solve for the elements of c from the equation

$$[c_{21}\ c_{22}](A - \lambda_1 I) = [0\ 0] \qquad (5.34)$$

where I is the identity matrix. Solving (5.34) by arbitrarily setting $c_{22} = 1$ we obtain

$$c_{21} = -a_{21}/(a_{11} - \lambda_1) \qquad (5.35)$$

From (5.33) we then find that the initial jump of the non-predetermined variable at time $t = 0$ is

$$\bar{e} - e(0) = -c_{21}[\bar{f} - f(0)] = [a_{21}/(a_{11} - \lambda_1)][\bar{f} - f(0)] \qquad (5.36)$$

where $\bar{e}$ and $\bar{f}$ are the new steady state values of e and f. Note that, given that we have assumed the equilibrium to be saddlepoint stable, it follows that $a_{21} > 0$ and $\lambda_1 > 0$. We also know that $a_{11} < 0$.

From equation (5.36) we then note that the degree of overshooting of the exchange rate is given by

$$\bar{e} - e(0) = [a_{21}/(a_{11} - \lambda_1)][\bar{f} - f(0)]$$

Following a monetary expansion, we know that the resultant depreciation will generate a temporary current account surplus leading to the domestic accumulation of foreign assets. Thus, $\bar{f} - f(0)$ must be positive. In addition, arising out of the conditions for the model to be saddlepoint stable, we know that $a_{21}/(a_{11} - \lambda_1)$ is negative, demonstrating that the exchange rate will overshoot in response to a monetary shock. Let us now consider how the degree of overshooting is affected as we move from model 1 to model 2.

The changing parameter values involved in reducing interest rate risk to zero leave a_{11} and a_{12} unaffected. Thus, we can focus our attention on what happens to $a_{21}\ (= a_{22})$, λ_1 and $\bar{f} - f(0)$ as we move to a world of exchange rate risk only.

The effect on equilibrium foreign asset holdings   Turning first to $\bar{f} - f(0)$, we need to examine $d\bar{f}/dm$, which is given by

$$d\bar{f}/dm = \frac{c_1}{a_{12} - a_{11}} - \frac{c_2 a_{12}}{a_{21}(a_{12} - a_{11})}$$

where

$$c_1 = -[g_2 d_1 (1 - \pi_1 - \pi_2)]/(1 + g_2 d_2)$$

and

$$c_2 = -\Omega_1[(\pi_1 + \pi_2)(\eta_1/\epsilon_1 - 1) + 1]$$

From the definitions of c_2 and a_{21} it may be seen that c_2 increases when a_{21} falls and vice versa. Thus, provided a_{21} falls when we move to the restricted (exchange risk only) model then, given that the other terms remain unchanged, $d\bar{f}/dm$ unambiguously falls, reducing the value of $\bar{f} - f(0)$ for a given initial value of foreign asset stocks. Below we will show that as we move to the restricted model a_{21} is indeed reduced in value. It then follows that monetary expansion increases foreign asset holdings by less in the restricted model, and therefore, other things remaining equal, it tends to increase the degree of exchange rate overshooting.

The intuition of this is that in the restricted model money and bonds are closer substitutes meaning that in long-run equilibrium, following monetary expansion, the home interest rate falls by less. This leads to a smaller demand for foreign assets (not withstanding the increase in the substitutability between home and foreign assets which is also involved in the move to the restricted model). But this in turn requires a smaller cumulation of current account surpluses which is consistent with a smaller exchange rate jump. To establish this conclusively, however, we must examine asset market adjustment in a little more detail.

Effect on speed of adjustment and asset demand coefficients   Note that, as we move to the restricted model, a_{11} remains unchanged. Examining λ_1 more closely, we note that

$$\lambda_1 = \tfrac{1}{2}\{(a_{21} + a_{1.}) + [(a_{21} + a_{11})^2 + 4a_{21}(a_{12} - a_{11})]^{1/2}\}$$

By inspection, we see that λ_1 and a_{21} must move in the same direction. Furthermore, it can be demonstrated that, as both a_{21} and λ_1 rise, the expression $a_{21}/(a_{11} - \lambda_1)$ must also rise. In this case, the effects of a higher set of demand parameters a_{21} on overshooting through the speed of adjustment dampens, but cannot entirely offset, the direct effect of a higher a_{21} itself.[8] Therefore, the key issue can be regarded as whether a_{21} rises or falls when we move to the restricted model. If a_{21} falls in the restricted model, then the absence of risk on domestic bonds reduces exchange rate overshooting, and our conjectures and intuitions set out above are confirmed. Let us now examine a_{21} in greater detail. From the definition of a_{21} we may rewrite it as

$$a_{21} = [(1 - \pi_2)\epsilon_1 + \pi_2 \eta_1]/(\epsilon_1 \eta_2 - \epsilon_2 \eta_1)$$

By reference to equations (5.21) and (5.22) we may rewrite this as[9]

$$a_{21} = R[\rho_{ef} + (1 - \pi_2)(\sigma^2_e + \sigma^2_f) + \rho_{eb}(2\pi_2 - 1)] + \pi_2\beta \qquad (5.37)$$

The question then reduces to whether eliminating interest risk from this model causes this expression to rise or fall. In fact, in the restricted model, this expression reduces to $R(1 - \pi_2)\sigma^2_e + \pi_2\beta$ as σ^2_f, ρ_{eb} and ρ_{ef} go to zero. If we subtract the latter expression from the right-hand side of equation (5.37), then the remainder is

$$R(\rho_{ef} + (1 - \pi_2)\sigma^2_f + \rho_{eb}(2\pi_2 - 1))$$

If the above expression is positive, it then follows that moving to the restricted model reduces a_{21} and therefore reduces the degree of exchange rate overshooting. It is clear that the remainder expression is indeed likely to be positive. Formally, a sufficient condition for overshooting to be reduced in the restricted model is that foreign assets constitute more than half the value of the portfolio. However, it should also be noted that the only negative term in the remainder expression is ρ_{eb}, which is significant when it is recalled that the gross substitutability assumption implies that variances dominate covariances in the structure of portfolio returns.

Comparing the results of this section with those of section 5.4.1, we can summarize the argument so far as follows. The results from our full model are not likely to overturn our conjecture that overshooting will be greater in the presence of interest risk. Indeed, allowing for the effects of equilibrium asset holdings and the speed of adjustment to equilibrium in our full model usually reinforces this result. The only exception to this statement appears to arise if the share of foreign assets in portfolios is very small, since in that case a given exchange rate change may cause a proportionate revaluation of foreign assets which is much larger than the associated proportionate revaluation of total wealth. It appears that this enables exchange rate changes to restore portfolio equilibrium with less overshooting.[10]

5.4.2 Implications for econometric studies of interest parity equations

It is common for econometric investigators to attempt to fit interest parity models of the kind shown in (5.6'), where simple interest differentials are taken to model movements in the exchange rate, thus imposing the restriction that the magnitude of the coefficient on the home interest rate should equal that on the foreign interest rate. However, in the presence of interest risk, a more general specification such as (5.3') would be more appropriate.

5.5 CONCLUSION

In this chapter we have shown that the appropriate form of the risk-adjusted uncovered interest parity condition in an exchange rate model depends crucially on the nature of the risk faced by the economic agent in an open economy. If domestic bonds are not risky then the appropriate form is as shown in equation (5.6'), in which the coefficients on the home interest rate and the foreign interest rate are equal to 1 and − 1 respectively. If domestic bonds are risky, however, then the appropriate form is as shown in equation (5.3') in which the magnitude of the coefficient on the foreign interest rate is unity but in which the magnitude of the coefficient on the domestic interest rate is less than unity.

Our findings have implications for exchange rate dynamics. In section 5.4 we showed that it will matter for exchange rate dynamics as to which of these interest parity equations is the appropriate one. In particular, in the case where both domestic and foreign bonds are risky, exchange rate over-shooting in response to monetary disturbances is greater than when only foreign assets are risky. In addition, our findings have important implications for the econometric investigation of exchange rates, as summarized in section 5.4.2.

Which of the two models and which of the two interest parity conditions shown in equations (5.3') and (5.6') is more likely to describe reality? It is our view that this depends upon the nature of the underlying shocks to an economy and the nature of the policy environment. If, for example, the authorities operate a policy of rigidly pegging the domestic interest rate, and letting the domestic money supply be endogenous, then the riskiness of domestic bonds will completely disappear. If, however, the domestic authorities fix the money supply, then the domestic interest rate will be endogenous and shocks to the domestic economy which change the demand for money will cause shocks to the domestic interest rate, and this will make domestic bonds risky. The *exact* degree of risk will depend upon the nature of the shocks impinging on the economy and the whole set of parameters of the economic system. It will certainly, however, be non-zero!

A richer model would, in fact, treat the riskiness of bonds (and hence the risk premium) as an endogenous phenomenon depending upon the degree to which the policy authorities stabilized the rate of interest, upon the nature of the shocks hitting the system, and upon the way these shocks propagate themselves into interest rate and exchange rate disturbances. We have not constructed such a model. Nevertheless, if the interest risk on domestic bonds is significant, then our arguments suggest that following points.

1 Econometric models of the exchange rate built along the lines of (5.6′)
   which neglect the influence of interest risk upon the risk premium and the
   interest parity condition are mis-specified.
2 Models which include equation (5.6′) will underestimate the degree of
   exchange rate overshooting.

Notes

1 Branson and Henderson (1985) derive a portfolio model where the objective
   function depends on M and on M/Y but where only exchange rate risk is present.
   However, it easy to show that in a more complex model like ours where both
   interest and exchange risk are present, the incorporation of M instead of M/W in
   the objective function yields interest rate coefficients which depend on the level
   of wealth, as well as the variances and covariances of the asset returns. A similar
   result would be obtained if M/Y were to be used instead, with parameters
   varying with the level of the income variable.
2 One possible justification for using wealth as a scaling variable for money
   balances in the objective function is that it may act as a proxy for income. But
   one must admit that, for some purposes, it may not be an accurate proxy. Its
   main attraction for us is that it provides tractable asset demand functions.
3 For simplicity we drop the superscript d from the asset demand functions in what
   follows.
4 A formal definition of Ito's lemma is provided by (inter alia) Malliaris and
   Brock (1982) and Branson and Henderson (1985).
5 It should be pointed out here that cross-rate effects will be the same for
   individual pairs of asset demands. Thus, for example, $\eta_1 = \xi_2$ in equations
   (5.1)–(5.3). This is a familiar result in consumer demand theory.
6 Branson and Henderson (1985), in contrast with our model, examine models
   with both interest and exchange risk (but without a transactions component of
   money demand), and contrast these models with models in which there is only
   exchange risk *and* a transactions demand for money. These two types of models
   are non-nested, and a comparison between them can only be qualitative. One
   cannot highlight the effects on an exchange rate model as we do in this paper as
   one cannot merely set ϵ_2 equal to zero and $\eta_1 = \eta_2$ and make a *ceteris paribus*
   assumption about the other parameters of the asset demand functions.
7 The expression in equation (5.27′) may be derived as follows. From (5.23) and
   (5.24) we see that

$$\eta_2/\eta_1 = \gamma_0/(R\gamma_1 + \gamma_0) > 0$$
$$\epsilon_1 = \gamma_1(R\gamma_1 + \gamma_0)/\gamma_0^2\delta_0\Delta + 1/\gamma_0 > 0$$

and

$$\epsilon_2 = -\gamma_1/\gamma_0\delta_0\Delta$$

It therefore follows that

$$\epsilon_2 + \epsilon_1\eta_2/\eta_1 = 1/(R\gamma_1 + \gamma_0)$$

We have already noted in the text that one of the requirements for gross substitutability is that $R\gamma_1 + \gamma_0 = (\rho_{eb} + \rho_{ef})R + \beta > 0$. The result of equation (5.27') follows directly from this.

8   This is a common feature of saddlepath rational expectations models such as this one. A similar observation could be made about the effect of a decrease in the interest elasticity of the demand for money in the Dornbusch (1976) model: it increases the degree of overshooting, but increases the speed of adjustment towards equilibrium.

9   We may derive the expression for a_{21} in the text as follows. From equations (5.21) and (5.22) we note that

$$\epsilon_1 = \gamma_1(R\gamma_1 + \gamma_0)/\gamma^2_0\delta_0\Delta + 1/\gamma_0$$
$$\epsilon_2 = -\gamma_1/\gamma_0\delta_0\Delta$$
$$\eta_1 = (R\gamma_1 + \gamma_0)/R\gamma_0\delta_0\Delta$$

and

$$\eta_2 = 1/R\delta_0\Delta$$

Substituting this into

$$a_{21} = [(1 - \pi_2)\epsilon_1 + \pi_2\eta_1]/(\epsilon_1\eta_2 - \epsilon_2\eta_1)$$

we obtain

$$a_{21} = (R\gamma_1 + R\delta_0 - \pi_2 R\delta_0 + \pi_2\delta_0)\gamma_0\delta_0\Delta/(\gamma_0\delta_0 - R\gamma^2_1)$$

Given that $\Delta = 1 - R\gamma^2_1/\gamma_0\delta_0$ it then follows that $a_{21} = R\gamma_1 + R\delta_0 - \pi_2 R\delta_0 + \pi_2\delta_0$, and given the definitions of γ_0, γ_1 and δ_0 given in the text it is apparent that we may rewrite this as

$$a_{21} = R[\rho_{ef} + (1 - \pi_2)(\sigma^2_e + \sigma^2_\epsilon) + \rho_{eb}(2\pi_2 - 1)] + \pi_2\beta$$

10   Our analysis in section 5.4.1 effectively ruled out the effect of exchange rate changes upon the proportion of foreign assets in wealth. This section shows that the partial asset market results obtained there can only be replicated by setting $\pi_2 = 1$: overshooting here depends on a_{21} which only simplifies to the term $(\rho_{eb} + \rho_{ef})R + \beta$ obtained in section 5.4.1 if we set π_2 equal to 1.

6 The Exchange Rate and the Current Account when Prices Evolve Sluggishly: A Simplication of the Dynamics and a Reconciliation with the Absorption Approach

Emmanuel Pikoulakis

6.1 INTRODUCTION

Models of the exchange rate and the current account under rational expectations, or perfect foresight, and sluggishly adjusting prices typically involve a relationship between at least three state variables. A minimum menu of the state variables involved includes two predetermined variables, namely the price of the domestic good and the stock of residents' holdings of net claims abroad, and one forward-looking variable, the exchange rate. Equilibrium in such models is typically a saddlepoint and the path that describes adjustments in the state variables and in the endogenous variables to disturbances which were previously unanticipated is a unique and stable saddlepath. A formal derivation of such a saddlepath requires the solution of a system of three difference or differential equations, and model-builders have hitherto resorted to simulation exercises for a description of adjustments along such a path. However, simulation exercises are not a very convenient tool of analysis nor are they very helpful for gaining an intuitive understanding of the characteristics of the saddlepath. Fortunately, as I shall show, when the object of analysis is a description of the qualitative characteristics of the saddlepath simulation exercises are not necessary. The qualitative characteristics of the saddlepath can be derived from phase diagrams drawn in a two-dimensional space defined by the two predetermined variables. Such phase diagrams are relatively easy to draw and the information they provide enhances intuition. To my knowledge this technique has not, hitherto, been applied systematically to this type of model and my main objective in writing this chapter is to illustrate some of its advantages.

More often than not open-economy models are cast in linear or, more frequently, in log-linear from at the outset. Imposing linearity at the outset rather than performing the linearization of an otherwise non-linear model can easily introduce pitfalls into the analysis with potentially serious consequences. Consider, for instance, the relationship between the current account and the goods market. When the market for goods clears, the current account surplus (deficit) equals the surplus (deficit) of domestic saving over domestic investment. In turn, the saving–investment relationship with the current account imposes certain restrictions on the relationship between the structural parameters of the IS equation and the structural parameters of the current account equation. Failure to observe these restrictions may lead to serious errors, and the possibility of committing such errors is always present when the IS equation is cast, at the outset, in a linear semi-reduced form as is the common practice. Accordingly, another objective of this chapter is to identify these restrictions and highlight the importance of observing them.

The structure of the chapter is as follows. In section 6.2.1 I present a log-linear model of the exchange rate and the current account which introduces three important dynamic extensions to the Mundell–Fleming model. These extensions involve the evolution, over time, of the price level, of the exchange rate and of the stock of residents' holdings of net claims abroad. The evolution of the price level reflects the gap of current output from its natural level along the lines of an augmented Phillips curve. The exchange rate is assumed to evolve along a perfect foresight path. Finally, residents' holdings of net claims abroad accumulate (decumulate) with a current account surplus (deficit). The model presented in 6.2.1 is 'superneutral'. In 6.2.2 I explain why superneutrality runs contrary to the principles of monetary economics and in 6.2.3 I allow for the possibility of a non-neutral inflation at the steady state by introducing real balances into aggregate demand via the government budget constraint. The government budget constraint dispenses with 'helicopter' money, allows for a richer menu of fiscal policies and highlights the fiscal implications of varying the rate of monetary growth. In section 6.2.4 I examine the stability conditions of the model and in 6.2.5 I look into the characteristics of the steady state in some detail. In the latter section I attempt a reconciliation of the Mundell–Fleming model with a saving–investment approach to the current account to highlight the restrictions on the parameters of the model that such a reconciliation requires and to show that the answer to certain questions crucially hinges on observing these restrictions. In section 6.3.1 I illustrate the steps required for the construction of phase diagrams in a two-dimensional space for an analysis of short-run and dynamic adjustment of the three state variables and of the endogenous variables along the stable saddlepath. Finally, to illuminate the advantages of phase diagrams over simulation exercises, in 6.3.3 I use these diagrams to illustrate an analysis of adjustments to a previously unanticipated pure fiscal expansion.

6.2. A MORE EXTENDED VERSION OF A MUNDELL–FLEMING MODEL

6.2.1 The structure of the model

$$y = -\gamma(r - Dp) + \delta(e + p^* - p) + \epsilon_1 g + \epsilon_2 F + \nu y^*$$
$$\gamma > 0,\ \delta > 0,\ \epsilon_1 > 0,\ \epsilon_2 > 0,\ \nu > 0 \quad (6.1)$$

$$m - p = ky - \lambda r \qquad\qquad k > 0,\ \lambda > 0 \qquad\qquad (6.2)$$

$$r = r^* + De \qquad\qquad\qquad\qquad\qquad\qquad\qquad (6.3)$$

$$Dp = \psi(y - \bar{y}) + \mu \qquad\qquad \psi > 0 \qquad\qquad\qquad (6.4)$$

$$\mu = D^+ m \qquad\qquad\qquad\qquad\qquad\qquad\qquad\qquad (6.5)$$

$$DF = -\theta y + f(e + p^* - p) + \sigma y^* + \epsilon_3 F \quad \theta > 0, f > 0, \epsilon_3 > 0, \sigma > 0 \ (6.6)$$

where y is the logarithm of the quantity of domestic product, $\bar{y}$ is the logarithm of the natural level of the domestic product, m is the logarithm of the nominal stock of domestic money, p is the logarithm of the price of the domestic good, e is the logarithm of the price of foreign currency in units of domestic currency, p^* is the logarithm of the price of the foreign good in foreign currency, r is the domestic nominal interest rate, r^* is the foreign nominal interest rate, y^* is the logarithm of the quantity of foreign product, g is the logarithm of government expenditure on the domstic good, μ is the core or trend rate of inflation and F is the stock of net claims of residents on non-residents measured in units of the domestic product. D is the differential operator so that, for example,

$$Dp = \frac{dp}{dt}$$

and D^+ is the right-hand side of the differential operator so that, for example,

$$D^+ m(t) = \lim_{T \to t} \frac{m(T) - m(t)}{T - t} \qquad T > t$$

Equation (6.1) is a version of an open-economy IS relation. Output, which is demand determined, is taken to be a decreasing function of the real interest rate but an increasing function of the relative price of the foreign good, of the level of production of the foreign good, of government spending on the domestic good and of resident holdings of net claims abroad. In what follows I shall take p^* to be fixed and by an appropriate choice of units I shall set it equal to zero. I shall take the influence of F on aggregate demand to reflect the effect of net property income from abroad and also to reflect a direct wealth effect. Equation (6.2) describes a textbook type LM relation. Equation (6.3) reflects the assumptions of perfect capital mobility, perfect substitutability between the domestic and the foreign bond and perfect foresight about the expected rate of depreciation of the exchange rate. Under these conditions risk-neutral speculators equate the uncovered interest differential in favour of the domestic economy to the rate of depreciation of the domestic currency. Equation (6.4) is a version of a Phillips curve. The excess of the current rate of inflation above the core rate is taken to rise proportionately with the excess of the current level of production above the natural level. Equation (6.5) identifies the core rate of inflation with the right-hand side time derivative of the money supply. This is one way of imposing short-run stickiness in the price level. Thus, even if the money supply were allowed to make discrete jumps the price level (although not its rate of change) would not. Equation (6.6) models the current account surplus as a decreasing function of domestic production but as an increasing function of the relative price of the foreign product, of the level of foreign production and of the real value of residents' net claims abroad. In this equation the coefficient ϵ_3 would be identified with the foreign interest rate r^* only if there were no wealth effects or disposable income effects in import demand.

6.2.2 Why inflation superneutrality is bad economics

The reader familiar with the influential writings of Buiter and Miller, especially their (1981), (1982) and (1983) papers, can easily verify that the model I have presented above shares one common characteristic with their 'basic' model and that is 'superneutrality'. Variations in the core rate of inflation that stem from variations in the rate of monetary growth are shown to be neutral in their long-run effects except for their effect on real balances. As I shall argue immediately below superneutrality runs contrary to a long-established body of monetary theory. It can also be particularly misleading in dealing with the macroeconomics of the open economy.

One tradition in monetary theory treats real balances like a consumers' durable good which yields a flow of services in the form of leisure or convenience. In this tradition it seems natural to include real balances in the utility function. Another tradition treats real balances like a producers' durable good which allows for a more efficient utilization of labour in the production of goods and services by reducing the labour requirement necessary to effect transactions. In this case it is natural to include real balances in the production function. In either case variations in real balances have 'real' effects since they influence tastes or technology and in either case superneutrality cannot hold. However, both these approaches have attracted criticism and it is for this reason that I find it more attractive to introduce real balances via the government budget constraint, a practice frequently used in the literature on money and growth. After all one cannot avoid the fact that inflation imposes a tax on those who hold real balances. In the case where the entire money stock is of the 'outside' variety the entire yield of the inflationary tax is appropriated by the government. However, there is a maximum to the amount of resources a government can extract through inflationary taxes, this maximum occurring at the point where the elasticity of the demand for real balances with respect to inflation is equal to unity. In general, a variation in the rate of inflation stemming from a variation in the rate of monetary growth will bring about a redistribution of resources between the public sector and the private sector at the steady state. To accommodate this redistribution of resources one or more determinants of private aggregate demand must adjust. In short, inflation cannot be superneutral.

6.2.3 Introducing the government budget constraint

To keep the analysis as simple as possible I shall be assuming that budget deficits are fully monetized and I shall write

$$G = T + \frac{\mathrm{d}M}{\mathrm{d}t}\frac{1}{P} = T + \mathrm{D}^+m\frac{M}{P} = T + \mu\frac{M}{P} \tag{6.7}$$

where G is the flow of government spending on the domestic good, T is the flow of tax revenue net of transfers and M/P is the stock of real balances. For simplicity I am assuming that there are no government expenditures on the foreign good. Since μ is effectively under the control of the monetary authorities and M/P is predetermined in the short run the government can choose to control either G or T but not both. In what follows I am assuming that the authorities choose to control the fraction of G to be financed by taxation. Denoting this fraction by h, I shall write

$$T = hG \qquad 0 < h < 1 \tag{6.8}$$

and therefore

$$G(1 - h) = \mu\frac{M}{P} \tag{6.9}$$

Taking logarithms to rewrite (6.9)

$$g = \hat{\mu} + m - p + \phi \qquad (6.10)$$

where $\hat{\mu}$ is the logarithm of μ and ϕ is minus the logarithm of $1 - h$.

An attractive feature of the budget contraint described by (6.10) is that it allows for an analysis of 'pure' fiscal policy, a policy in which expenditures and net taxes are varied so as to achieve a 'marginally balanced budget'. A pure fiscal expansion, for instance, is captured by a rise in ϕ. In this model a change in the rate of monetary growth has important fiscal implications. Without helicopter money a reduction in the rate of monetary growth, say, is identified with a reduction in the rate at which the monetary authorities extend interest-free credit (per unit of outstanding M) to the treasury to finance public spending. If the treasury were to adhere to a constant ϕ then public spending would reduce in the short run. However, in the long run real balances would rise and if the elasticity of the demand for money with respect to inflation were to exceed unity inflationary taxes would expand, permitting increased public spending at the steady state. At any rate the treasury can always choose to insulate public spending from monetary policy by varying ϕ to achieve a target of public spending.

6.2.4 An analysis of the stability of equilibrium

In what follows it will prove convenient and illuminating to work entirely in terms of the real interest rate, the real exchange rate or competitiveness, and liquidity (real balances). To this effect I shall define

$$i \equiv r - Dp \qquad c \equiv e - p \qquad \ell \equiv m - p$$

and I shall take (6.10) into account to rewrite the model as follows:

$$
\begin{aligned}
y = \; & -\gamma i + \delta c + \epsilon_1(\hat{\mu} + \ell + \phi) \\
& + \epsilon_2 F + \nu y^* \qquad \text{(IS)} \qquad (6.11)
\end{aligned}
$$

$$
\begin{aligned}
\ell = \; & ky - \lambda(i + Dp) \\
= \; & ky - \lambda i - \lambda\mu - \lambda\psi(y - \bar{y}) \qquad \text{(LM adjusted for inflation) (6.12)}
\end{aligned}
$$

$$i = r^* + Dc \qquad \text{(uncovered interest parity) (6.13)}$$

$$D\ell = -\psi(y - \bar{y}) \qquad \text{(Phillips curve)} \qquad (6.14)$$

$$DF = -\theta y + fc + \sigma y^* + \epsilon_3 F \qquad \text{(current account)} \qquad (6.15)$$

Letting a bar over a variable denote the steady state value of the variable,

$$\bar{y} = -\gamma\bar{i} + \delta\bar{c} + \epsilon_1(\hat{\mu} + \bar{\ell} + \phi) + \epsilon_2 F + \nu y^* \qquad (6.16)$$

$$\bar{\ell} = k\bar{y} - \lambda\bar{i} - \lambda\mu \qquad (6.17)$$

$$\bar{i} = r^* + D\bar{c} = r^* \tag{6.18}$$

$$D\bar{\ell} = 0 \tag{6.19}$$

$$DF = -\phi\bar{y} + f\bar{c} + \sigma y^* + \epsilon_3\bar{F} = 0 \tag{6.20}$$

Taking deviations from the steady state I shall write

$$y - \bar{y} = -\gamma(i - \bar{i}) + \delta(c - \bar{c}) + \epsilon_1(\ell - \bar{\ell}) + \epsilon_2(F - \bar{F}) \tag{6.21}$$

$$\ell - \bar{\ell} = (k - \lambda\psi)(y - \bar{y}) - \lambda(i - \bar{i}) \tag{6.22}$$

$$i - \bar{i} = Dc \tag{6.23}$$

$$D\ell = -\psi(y - \bar{y}) \tag{6.24}$$

$$DF = -\theta(y - \bar{y}) + f(c - \bar{c}) + \epsilon_3(F - \bar{F}) \tag{6.25}$$

Solving out $y - \bar{y}$ and $i - \bar{i}$ the dynamics are as follows:

$$\begin{bmatrix} D\ell \\ DF \\ Dc \end{bmatrix} = \begin{bmatrix} \dfrac{\psi(\gamma + \lambda\epsilon_1)}{B} & \dfrac{\psi\lambda\epsilon_2}{B} & \dfrac{\psi\lambda\delta}{B} \\ \dfrac{\theta(\gamma + \lambda\epsilon_1)}{B} & \dfrac{\epsilon_3 B + \theta\lambda\epsilon_2}{B} & \dfrac{fB + \theta\lambda\delta}{B} \\ \dfrac{1 + \epsilon_1(\psi\lambda - k)}{B} & \dfrac{\epsilon_2(\psi\lambda - k)}{B} & \dfrac{\delta(\psi\lambda - k)}{B} \end{bmatrix} \begin{bmatrix} \ell - \bar{\ell} \\ F - \bar{F} \\ c - \bar{c} \end{bmatrix} \tag{6.26}$$

The determinant of the coefficient matrix in (6.26) is given by $\psi(\delta\epsilon_3 - f\epsilon_2)/B$ where $B = \gamma(\lambda\psi - k) - \lambda$. As is done by Buiter and Miller I shall be assuming that $B < 0$. This corresponds to the intuitively appealing assumption that an autonomous increase (reduction) in aggregate demand will raise (reduce) output given competitiveness. Having assumed that $B < 0$ I shall also need to assume that $\delta\epsilon_3 - f\epsilon_2 < 0$ if the model is to possess a stable saddlepath. This proves an equally attractive assumption because it corresponds to the requirement that an increase (decrease) in F causes a deterioration (improvement) in the current account around the steady state. Having ruled out the existence of three stable roots there remains to rule out that all three roots are positive. To do this it will be sufficient to claim that the trace of the coefficient matrix is negative, which I do on empirical grounds.

To summarize, I am assuming that the determinant of the coefficient matrix in (6.26) is positive and that the trace of this matrix is negative on empirical grounds. These combined assumptions are sufficient to ensure that a model which possesses two variables predetermined in the short run, such as F and ℓ, and one forward-looking variable, such as c, has a unique and stable saddlepath.

6.2.5 The characteristics of the steady state: a reconciliation with the saving–investment approach

The model expressed by equations (6.16)–(6.20) can be written out more compactly to yield the following steady state solution:

$$
\begin{bmatrix} \bar{\ell} \\[2mm] \bar{F} \\[2mm] \bar{c} \end{bmatrix} =
\begin{bmatrix}
-\lambda & 0 & 0 & 0 & k & -\lambda \\[3mm]
\dfrac{-\lambda f\epsilon_1}{\Delta} & \dfrac{f\epsilon_1}{\Delta} & \dfrac{f\epsilon_1}{\Delta} & \dfrac{f\nu-\delta\sigma}{\Delta} & \dfrac{f(k\epsilon_1-1)+\delta\theta}{\Delta} & \dfrac{-f(\gamma+\lambda\epsilon_1)}{\Delta} \\[4mm]
\dfrac{\lambda\epsilon_1\epsilon_3}{\Delta} & \dfrac{-\epsilon_1\epsilon_3}{\Delta} & \dfrac{-\epsilon_1\epsilon_3}{\Delta} & \dfrac{-\nu\epsilon_3+\sigma\epsilon_2}{\Delta} & \dfrac{\epsilon_3(1-k\epsilon_1)-\theta\epsilon_2}{\Delta} & \dfrac{\epsilon_3(\gamma+\lambda\epsilon_1)}{\Delta}
\end{bmatrix}
\begin{bmatrix} \mu \\ \hat{\mu} \\ \phi \\ y^* \\ \bar{y} \\ r^* \end{bmatrix}
\qquad (6.27)
$$

In (6.27) $\Delta = \delta\epsilon_3 - f\epsilon_2$, which is negative by the stability assumption. Since the solution for steady state liquidity is straightforward, I shall focus attention on the joint determination of $\bar{F}$ and $\bar{c}$. To this effect, and to bring out more clearly the forces that determine the relation between $\bar{F}$ and $\bar{c}$ at the steady state, I shall make use of a diagram.

In figure 6.1 the GM locus, which is derived from equations (6.16)–(6.18), illustrates the combinations of competitiveness and of net claims abroad required to clear the market for the domestic good and the money market at the steady state. The position of this locus depends on the exogenously determined $\bar{y}$, y^* and r^* and on the policy instruments ϕ and μ (and $\hat{\mu}$). A unit rise in F raises aggregate demand by ϵ_2 units above the natural level of output. To restore aggregate demand to its natural level competitiveness must deteriorate by ϵ_2/δ units. In the same figure the $\dot{F} = 0$ locus, which is derived from equation (6.20), illustrates the combinations of competitiveness and of net claims abroad required to keep the current account in balance. A unit rise in $\bar{F}$ improves the current account by ϵ_3 units. To restore equilibrium in the current account competitiveness must deteriorate by ϵ_3/f units. By the stability condition the GM locus is steeper than the $\dot{F} = 0$ locus. Notice here that the position of the $\dot{F} = 0$ locus depends on the exogenously determined $\bar{y}$ and y^*. In what follows I shall only consider four types of shocks in the economy and their effects on the joint determination of

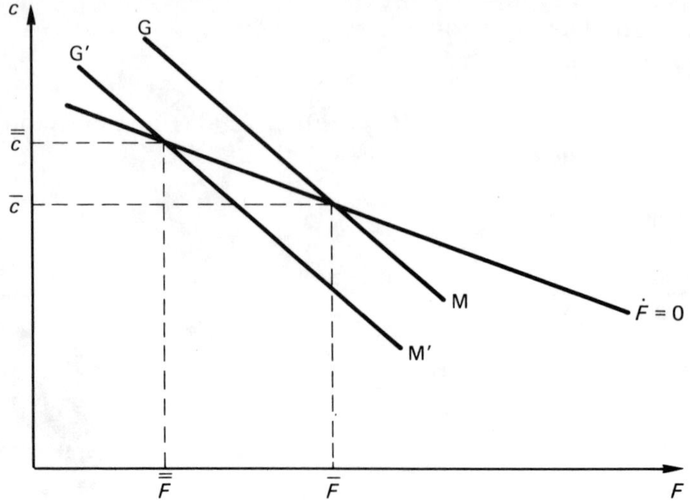

Figure 6.1   The joint determination of $\bar{F}$ and $\bar{c}$

competitiveness and of residents' net claims abroad at the steady state. These experiments will help to illustrate that the relationship between competitiveness, the trade balance and the current account at the steady state is a matter that depends on the type of shock.

Consider first a reduction in the rate of monetary growth. For brevity I shall only consider the case where the elasticity of money demand with respect to inflation exceeds unity around the steady state. In such a situation the proportion by which liquidity rises at the steady state exceeds the proportion by which the rate of monetary growth decreases. As a result inflationary taxes increase at the steady state and this enables an expansion of public spending. At any level of holdings of net claims abroad competitiveness must deteriorate to release enough resources from private use to public use to allow this redistribution of demand to take place and preserve aggregate demand at the natural level of output. In figure 6.1 the GM locus shifts down to the position occupied by, say, the G′M′ locus. To compute the magnitude of, say, the vertical shift we must take into account that $d\hat{\mu} = (1/\mu)d\mu$. This results in a vertical shift equal to $\epsilon_1/\delta(d\mu/\mu)(1 - \lambda\mu)$ in absolute terms. Notice that at the new steady state property income from abroad is reduced and the trade balance is therefore improved. Notice also that the improvement in the trade balance is associated with an improvement in competitiveness.

Consider next the effects of a pure fiscal expansion. In this model such a policy is captured by an increase in the instrument ϕ. At an unchanged level of competitiveness this policy results in excess demand. To restore aggregate demand to its natural level competitiveness must deteriorate sufficiently to reduce private demand by an amount just enough to offset the increase in public demand. Again the GM locus must shift down and the vertical distance by which it shifts amounts to $(\epsilon_1/\delta)\mathrm{d}\phi$. Except for steady state liquidity which remains unchanged, in all other respects the qualitative effects of such a policy reflect the effects of the previous policy. What the two policies have in common is an increase in absorption at a given level of competitiveness.

Next consider the effects of an increase in income abroad y^*. Figure 6.2 illustrates the case where the loss in competitiveness required to balance the current account is equal to the loss in competitiveness required to restore aggregate demand to its natural level. Formally, the GM locus shifts down by a vertical distance equal to $(\nu/\delta)\mathrm{d}y^*$ and the $\dot{F} = 0$ locus shifts down by a vertical distance equal to $(\sigma/f)\mathrm{d}y^*$, and $\sigma/f = \nu/\delta$ by assumption. As a result competitiveness deteriorates by $(\sigma/f)\mathrm{d}y^* = (\nu/\delta)\mathrm{d}y^*$ while residents' net claims abroad remain unchanged. Moreover the balance on net property income from abroad and the balance of trade remain at whatever level each of these balances attained at the previous steady state. This is an example where a shock in the economy leaves each component of the current account unchanged in spite of a deterioration in competitiveness.

Buiter (1987) asks whether an improvement in the current account or the trade balance at full employment requires a depreciation of the real exchange rate. The short answer he gives, and to which this model subscribes, is no.

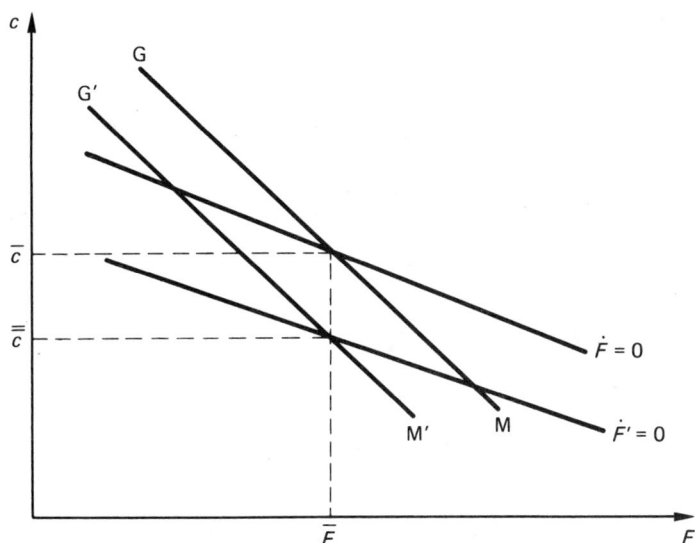

Figure 6.2   Adjustments in steady state competitiveness and residents' net claims abroad to an increase in foreign income when $\sigma/f = \nu/\epsilon$

Let me invert this question and ask whether a depreciation (appreciation) of the real exchange rate at full employment brings about an improvement (deterioration) in the current account or the trade balance. Figure 6.2 illustrates a case where the answer is no. To demonstrate that this result is not artificially contrived and to bring further insight into the forces that determine the relation between the current account, the trade balance and the real exchange rate at the steady state consider the fact that the current account records the difference between aggregate saving and aggregate investment. This fact imposes restrictions on some of the parameters of the model presented above. It also provides additional insight into the properties of the model. To illustrate this consider rewriting equations (6.1) and (6.6) in the following way:

$$S(Y - hG + r^*F, F) + G(h - 1) - I(i)$$
$$= X(Y - hG + r^*F, F, \tau, Y^*) + r^*F \qquad (6.28)$$

$$0 < S_1 < 1, S_2 < 0, I'(.) < 0, -1 < X_1 < 0, X_2 < 0, X_3 > 0, X_4 > 0$$

$$DF = X(Y - hG + r^*F, F, \tau, Y^*) + r^*F \qquad (6.29)$$

where

$$Y = \exp(y)$$
$$Y^* = \exp(y^*)$$
$$\tau = \exp(e - p) = \exp(c)$$

$S(.)$ is the desired private saving, $I(.)$ is the desired aggregate investment and $X(.)$ is the export demand less import demand valued in units of the domestic product.

Equation (6.28) is a version of the IS relation. In an *ex ante* sense, equilibrium in the market for the domestic product requires that aggregate (i.e. private plus public) saving less aggregate (i.e. private plus public) investment equals the surplus in the trade balance plus net property income from abroad. Private saving is taken to be an increasing function of disposable income and a decreasing function of residents' holdings of net claims abroad. Investment is taken to be a decreasing function of the real interest rate. Finally, the trade surplus is taken to be a decreasing function of disposable income and of residents' holdings of net claims abroad and an increasing function of competitiveness and of foreign income. The reader is asked to observe that, consistent with my previous analysis, I confine direct wealth effects to residents' holdings of net claims abroad and ignore valuation changes in these holdings.

Differentiating (6.28) and (6.29) and applying whatever log-linearizations are required to cast these equations in the form of (6.1) and (6.6) one obtains, among other results, that

1 $\delta\epsilon_3 - f\epsilon_2 < 0$ is satisfied only if $- S_2/r^* > S_1$,
2 $\epsilon_3 = X_2 + r^*(1 + X_1) < r^*$ and
3 $\sigma/f = \nu/\delta$.

The first result makes it clear that stability (of the saddlepath) requires a wealth effect in saving of sufficient strength to more than offset the income effect associated with variations in F. This is a rather standard finding reminiscent of the stabilizing role of wealth effects in macroeconomics. The second result states that a unit rise in residents' holdings of net claims abroad improves the current account at a rate which is less than the interest rate. This is not surprising when one takes account of the fact that a rise in F worsens the trade balance through a (disposable) income effect and a wealth effect. In fact if the wealth effect in import demand is sufficiently strong then a unit rise in F may cause a deterioration in the current account! Finally, the third result imposes a restriction on the relative magnitude of the coefficients σ, f, ν and δ. Thus, the assumption I made about the relative magnitude of these coefficients to illustrate the workings of figure 6.2 is validated. Let me dwell a little longer on this finding to impress the significance of the saving–investment approach to the current account analysis. To this effect consider figure 6.3.

In this figure the $\tilde{S} = 0$ locus describes the combinations of competitiveness and of residents' holdings of net claims abroad required to maintain aggregate saving and aggregate investment equal to zero at the steady state.

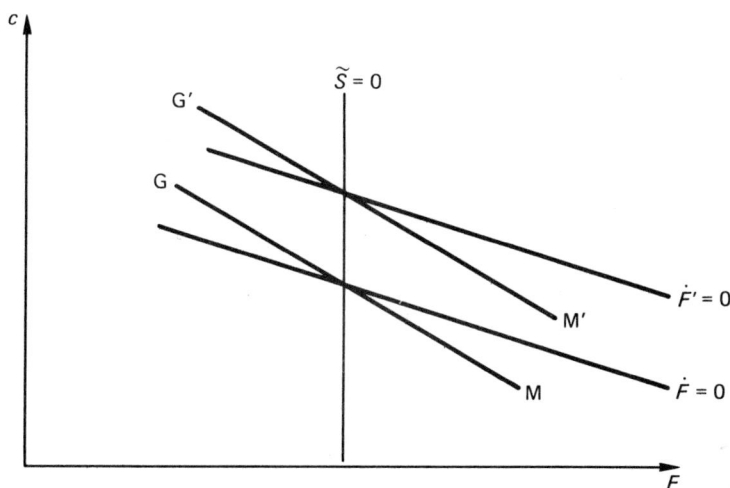

Figure 6.3   Steady state adjustments to a shift in preferences towards the foreign good at the expense of the domestic good

The locus is vertical because of the convenient assumption that F is valued in units of the domestic good so that variations in competitiveness do not have valuation effects. It shifts only if there is a shift in the propensity to save or to invest by the private or the public sector. Now consider a shift in residents' preferences towards the foreign good and at the expense of the domestic good. Such a shock cannot disturb the $\tilde{S} = 0$ locus. From a position of initial steady state described by the intersection of the GM locus with the $\dot{F} = 0$ locus the economy is placed, instantaneously, at the new steady state described by the intersection of the G'M' locus with the $\dot{F}' = 0$ locus. Again this is an instance when a depreciation of the real exchange rate at full employment has failed to improve (or deteriorate) the current account or the trade surplus. This is because the shock that brought about this depreciation has not disturbed any of the propensities to save or to invest.

6.3 A PHASE DIAGRAM ANALYSIS OF THE SADDLEPATH: AN ILLUSTRATION

How to construct such phase diagrams

Perhaps it has not been widely appreciated that when a model possesses one forward-looking and two short-run predetermined state variables, as is the case with the present model, the qualitative characteristics of the saddlepath associated with these variables can be conveniently obtained from phase diagrams constructed in a two-dimensional space. All that is required for the construction of such phase diagrams is an assumption about the numerical values of the structural parameters and the solution of the unstable root obtained from the parameter values. Accordingly when the object of the analysis is to ascertain the qualitative characteristics of the saddlepath in such a model, simulation excercises are not necessary. Moreover, phase diagrams enhance intuition – something which cannot be said with equal force about simulation exercises. In this section I shall first describe how to construct such diagrams and then I shall use these diagrams to illustrate adjustments to an unanticipated pure fiscal expansion.

Consider, first, the procedure for obtaining the normalized left-hand (row) eigenvector associated with the unstable root. Following Dixit (1980) I shall write

$$(M_{31} \quad M_{32} \quad -1) \begin{bmatrix} a_{11} - \rho_u & a_{12} & a_{13} \\ a_{21} & a_{22} - \rho_u & a_{23} \\ a_{31} & a_{32} & a_{33} - \rho_u \end{bmatrix} = (0 \ 0 \ 0) \qquad (6.30)$$

where ρ_u is the unstable root, a_{ij} $(i = 1,2,3, j = 1,2,3)$ is the ijth element of the coefficient matrix in the system of equations described in (6.26) and M_{31}, M_{32}

and -1 are the elements of the normalized left-hand (row) eigenvector associated with ρ_u.

Notice, next, that the stable path of the forward-looking variable can be uniquely determined by

$$c - \bar{c} = M_{31}(\ell - \bar{\ell}) + M_{32}(F - \bar{F}) \tag{6.31}$$

Substituting (6.31) back into the system of equations described by (6.26) one can write

$$D\ell = (a_{11} + a_{13}M_{31})(\ell - \bar{\ell}) + (a_{12} + a_{13}M_{32})(F - \bar{F}) \tag{6.32a}$$

$$DF = (a_{21} + a_{23}M_{31})(\ell - \bar{\ell}) + (a_{22} + a_{23}M_{32})(F - \bar{F}) \tag{6.32b}$$

$$Dc = (a_{31} + a_{33}M_{31})(\ell - \bar{\ell}) + (a_{32} + a_{33}M_{32})(F - \bar{F}) \tag{6.32c}$$

Let me rewrite (6.32a) and (6.32b), for convenience, as follows:

$$\begin{bmatrix} D\ell \\ DF \end{bmatrix} = \begin{bmatrix} \beta_{11} & \beta_{12} \\ \beta_{21} & \beta_{22} \end{bmatrix} \begin{bmatrix} \ell - \bar{\ell} \\ F - \bar{F} \end{bmatrix} \tag{6.33}$$

where

$$\beta_{11} = a_{11} + a_{13}M_{31} \qquad \beta_{12} = a_{12} + a_{13}M_{32}$$
$$\beta_{21} = a_{21} + a_{23}M_{31} \qquad \beta_{22} = a_{22} + a_{23}M_{32}$$

The intuitively obvious and yet remarkable fact about (6.33) is that the solution of the characteristic equation formed by the coefficient matrix in (6.33) yields the two stable roots. Accordingly one can construct a $D\ell = 0$ locus and a $DF = 0$ locus in (ℓ, F) space and use these loci to derive the characteristics of the paths of liquidity and of residents' holdings of net claims abroad along the stable path. Turning to equation (6.31) and setting $t = 0$ one can solve for the initial and discrete jump in competitiveness that is required to place the system on the stable path. Finally, turning to equation (6.32c) and setting $Dc = 0$ one can derive a locus of combinations of ℓ and F along which competitiveness is constant. Accordingly, this locus can serve to derive the motion of competitiveness along the stable path after the initial and discrete jump in this variable.

6.3.2 Adjustments following an unanticipated pure fiscal expansion: an illustration

To illustrate adjustments to this type of disturbance consider, first, the following parameter values.

1 Assumed parameter values:

$$\psi = 0.5, \qquad \delta = 0.5, \qquad \gamma = 0.5, \qquad k = 1, \qquad \lambda = 6$$
$$\epsilon_1 = 0.04, \qquad \epsilon_2 = 0.3, \qquad \epsilon_3 = 0.05, \qquad \nu = 0.3$$
$$\theta = 0.2, \qquad f = 0.3, \qquad \sigma = 0.18$$

2 The value of the unstable root associated with the above parameter values:

$$\rho_u = 0.154693$$

3 The elements of the normalized eigenvector associated with the unstable root:

$$M_{31} = 0.9867 \qquad M_{32} = -0.3260 \qquad M_{33} = -1$$

4 The slopes of the $D\ell = 0$, $DF = 0$ and $Dc = 0$ loci:

$$\left. \frac{d\ell}{dF} \right|_{D\ell = 0} = -\frac{\beta_{12}}{\beta_{11}} = -\frac{-0.0822}{-0.3700} = -0.2222$$

$$\left. \frac{d\ell}{dF} \right|_{DF = 0} = -\frac{\beta_{22}}{\beta_{21}} = -\frac{-0.0807}{0.1480} = 0.5453$$

$$\left. \frac{d\ell}{dF} \right|_{Dc = 0} = -\frac{a_{32} + a_{33}M_{32}}{a_{31} + a_{33}M_{31}} = -\frac{-0.0548}{-0.4133} = -0.1326$$

Let me now turn to figure 6.4 to describe the characteristics of the adjustment path associated with an unanticipated pure fiscal expansion. I am depicting a $DF = 0$ locus, a $Dc = 0$ locus and a $D\ell = 0$ locus going through point T which I take to describe the new steady state. Notice that the relative slopes of these loci reflect the assumed numerical values of the parameters. The analysis of the steady state presented above has revealed that a pure fiscal expansion reduces residents' holdings of net claims abroad whilst it

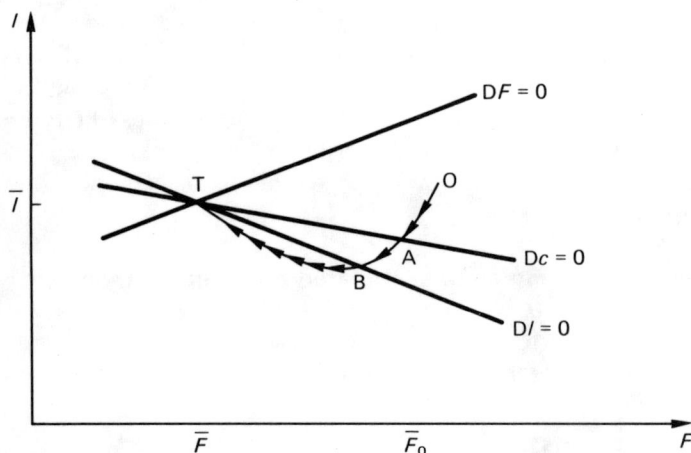

Figure 6.4 The characteristics of the stable path of l, F and c associated with an unanticipated pure fiscal expansion

leaves real balances unchanged. Thus, a point such as O can serve to describe the initial steady state. Since below (above) the $DF = 0$ locus $DF < 0 (> 0)$ and since above (below) the $D\ell = 0$ locus $D\ell < 0 (> 0)$, the path of liquidity and of residents' claims abroad can be described by the path marked by arrows which originates at O and terminates at T. Notice that along the entire path the current account is in deficit. Liquidity decreases over time until point B and then rises steadily to its original level. This path of liquidity implies that until point B inflation exceeds its trend rate and output exceeds its natural level. At point B output equals its natural level and inflation equals its trend rate. After point B output falls below its natural level to reach gradually some minimum level and then climbs back gradually to its natural level. Similarly, after point B inflation falls below its trend rate to reach gradually some minimum level and then climbs back gradually to its trend rate. Figure 6.5(a) and (b) illustrates these paths.

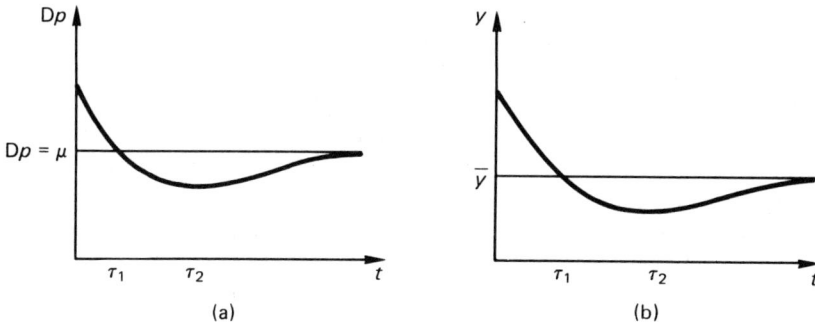

Figure 6.5   (a) The path of inflation; (b) the path of output

Finally, consider the path of the real exchange rate, focusing first on the initial, discrete, adjustment. Upon the announcement and the simultaneous implementation of the pure fiscal expansion the real exchange rate jumps below its new steady state since, by equation (6.31),

$$c_0 - \bar{c} = M_{32}(F_0 - \overline{F}) = -0.326(F_0 - \overline{F}) < 0 \qquad (6.34)$$

Moreover, this initial adjustment places the real exchange rate below its old steady state as well since

$$c_0 - \bar{c}_0 = -0.326(\overline{F}_0 - \overline{F}) + \bar{c} - \bar{c}_0$$

$$= -0.326\left(\frac{-f\epsilon_1}{\Delta} d\phi\right) + \frac{-\epsilon_1 \epsilon_3}{\Delta} d\phi$$

$$= d\phi (-0.029) < 0 \qquad (6.35)$$

where $\bar{c}_0$ denotes the old steady state real exchange rate.

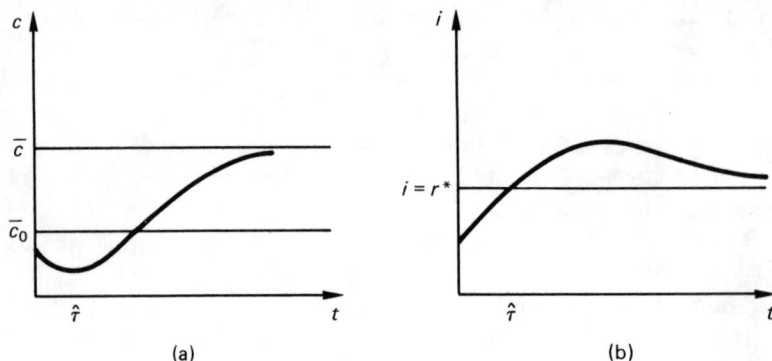

Figure 6.6   (a) The time path of the real exchange rate; (b) the time path of the real interest rate

Let us now focus attention on the path of the real exchange rate immediately after the initial discrete adjustment. Figure 6.4 reveals that until point A on the $Dc = 0$ locus the real exchange rate continues appreciating. At point A this appreciation stops and there follows a path along which there is a continuous depreciation until the new equilibrium is established. The reader should note that the path of the real exchange rate implies a path about the real interest rate. Figure 6.6(a) and (b) illustrates these paths. The reader should not be disturbed by the observation that the real interest rate initially falls. This is because the numerical values that I have assumed imply that $\lambda\psi - k > 0$ which, in turn, implies that the LM curve adjusted for inflation is downward sloping in (i,y) space.

6.4 CONCLUSION

To conclude, let us observe how well the above exercise captures recent behaviour of the American economy. The fiscal expansion in the USA, albeit not of the pure type, brought about a discrete appreciation of the dollar which continued for a while until the dollar began to depreciate. Meanwhile the US current account has shown persistent deficits. Let me also remark that a simulation exercise based on the assumed numerical values has verified the above analysis. As long as the structural parameters remain unchanged figure 6.4 can be used to describe adjustments to any type of shock. Simulation exercises are not necessary.

Part III
Foreign Exchange Market Efficiency

7 On the Bivariate Analysis of Speculative Efficiency in Forward Markets

Edmond Levy and A. Robert Nobay

7.1 INTRODUCTION

There exists, by now, a considerable body of empirical literature which seeks to evaluate the efficiency of forward markets in foreign exchange and related markets. Following Sargent (1979), one approach has been to consider efficiency within a time-series framework. Hansen and Hodrick (1980) propose an efficient test involving the cross-equation restrictions within a moving average representation. Hakkio (1981a) and Baillie et al. (1983b), to overcome the complexities that the procedure involves, work instead with finite-order autoregressive representations of spot and forward rates. Levy and Nobay (1986) extend the procedure to bivariate mixed autoregressive moving average (ARMA) representations.

In this paper we outline the bivariate mixed ARMA structure (section 7.2), and focus our discussion in section 7.3 on a key issue that is typically overlooked in the empirical application of time-series analysis. We consider the admissible structures of non-stationarity which the hypothesis of speculative efficiency permits, relating the discussion to the recent literature on co-integration. Sections 7.4 and 7.5, in turn, present empirical evidence for unit roots in spot and forward exchange rates and the co-integration of these series. In section 7.6 we consider the rate at which new information is absorbed within a rational expectations framework, which imposes restrictions on the parameters defining the moving average representation for spot and forward exchange rates. Concluding comments are offered in section 7.7.

A.R. Nobay acknowledges support from the H.G.B. Alexander Foundation, University of Chicago.

7.2 THE BIVARIATE TIME-SERIES FRAMEWORK

Let the vector y_t be defined as $y_t = (s_t, f_t)'$, where s_t and f_t are the spot and forward exchange rates determined at time t. We shall assume that the maturity of f_t is some $k > 0$ periods ahead. Speculative efficiency is the statement

$$f_t = E(s_{t+k}|\Omega_t^m)$$

where $E(s_{t+k}|\Omega_t^m)$ is the expectation of s_{t+k} conditional on Ω_t^m, the information set available to market agents. We shall assume that Ω_t^m contains the set $X_t = (s_{t-j}, f_{t-j})$, $j \geqslant 0$, and confine our attention to linear projections on X_t. Marginalizing on the set X_t gives

$$f_t = E(s_{t+k}|X_t). \tag{7.1}$$

Thus, under efficiency, the forward rate is interpreted as representing the optimal linear predictor of s_{t+k}, given X_t in the sense of minimizing the mean square error of the forecast.

Time-series analysis concerns the finding of stable rules or models for the innovation

$$\epsilon_t = y_t - E(y_t|X_{t-1}).$$

As we have confined attention to the set defined by X_t the models that subsequently arise are bivariate representations in which $E(s_{t+k}|X_t)$ will depend only on current and past s_{t-j} and f_{t-j} values. Thus the set of information upon which efficiency is examined corresponds to the majority of empirical work in this area.

When y_t is covariance stationary, the generalization of Wold's decomposition to multivariate processes allows us to write y_t in terms of current and past values of its one-step-ahead forecast errors as

$$y_t = \sum_{i=0}^{\infty} \Psi_i \epsilon_{t-i} = \Psi(L)\epsilon_t \tag{7.2}$$

where $\Psi_0 = I$ and L denotes the lag operator $L^k Z_t = Z_{t-k}$. Expression (7.2) is termed the moving average (MA) representation of y_t. The Ψ_is are 2×2 matrices satisfying

$$\sum_{i=0}^{\infty} \Psi_t \Sigma \Psi_i' < \infty$$

where $\Sigma = E(\epsilon_t \epsilon_t')$.

In practice, $\Psi(L)$ is approximated by a rational polynomial $\Phi(L)^{-1}\theta(L)$ and thus y_t is expressed as the bivariate ARMA process

$$\Phi(L)y_t = \theta(L)\epsilon_t. \tag{7.3}$$

Of course for $\theta(L) = I$ we have a pure autoregression (AR) model of previous studies. The number of restrictions that (7.3) will yield, as implied by (7.1), is finite given that the orders of the polynomials in $\Phi(L)$ and $\theta(L)$ are finite.

7.2.1 The restrictions

Define $\Phi(L)$ and $\theta(L)$ as

$$\Phi(L) = I - \Phi_1 L - \ldots - \Phi_p L^p$$
$$\theta(L) = I + \theta_1 L + \ldots + \theta_q L^q$$

then (7.3) has state variable form:

$$
\begin{bmatrix}
y_t \\
y_{t-1} \\
\vdots \\
y_{t-p+1} \\
\epsilon_t \\
\epsilon_{t-1} \\
\vdots \\
\epsilon_{t+q+1}
\end{bmatrix}
=
\begin{bmatrix}
\Phi_1 & \Phi_2 & \ldots & \Phi_p & \theta_1 & \theta_2 & \ldots & \theta_q \\
I & 0 & \ldots & 0 & 0 & 0 & \ldots & 0 \\
\vdots & & & \vdots & \vdots & \vdots & & \vdots \\
0 & 0 & I & 0 & 0 & 0 & \ldots & 0 \\
0 & 0 & \ldots & 0 & 0 & 0 & \ldots & 0 \\
0 & 0 & & 0 & I & 0 & & 0 \\
\vdots & \vdots & & \vdots & & \vdots & & \vdots \\
0 & 0 & \ldots & 0 & 0 & 0 & I & 0
\end{bmatrix}
\begin{bmatrix}
y_{t-1} \\
y_{t-2} \\
\vdots \\
y_{t-p} \\
\epsilon_{t-1} \\
\epsilon_{t-2} \\
\vdots \\
\epsilon_{t-q}
\end{bmatrix}
+
\begin{bmatrix}
\epsilon_t \\
0 \\
\vdots \\
0 \\
\epsilon_t \\
0 \\
\vdots \\
0
\end{bmatrix}
$$

or, with obvious notation,

$$'Y_t = BY_{t-1} + \zeta_t. \tag{7.4}$$

The vectors Y_t and ζ_t are $2(p + q) \times 1$ and the matrix B is $2(p + q) \times 2(p + q)$.

This reduction of our dynamic model (7.3) to the first-order AR system (7.4) will enable us to write the restrictions generated by condition (7.1) in terms of the matrix B alone. Denote e_i to be the $2(p + q) \times 1$ selection vector (a null vector apart from unity in the ith position). Noting that $E(Y_{t+j}|X_t) = B^j Y_t$, we may write condition (7.1) as

$$e_2' Y_t = e_1' B^k Y_t$$

or

$$(e_2' I - e_1' B^k)Y_t = 0. \tag{7.5}$$

Unless Y_t is a singular process (i.e. $E(Y_t Y_t')$ has less than full rank), (7.5) requires

$$r(\gamma)' = (e_2' I - e_1' B^k) = 0 \tag{7.6}$$

where $r(\gamma)$ is a $2(p + q) \times 1$ vector of restrictions on the parameter vector γ defining the non-trivial elements of B.

The vector $e_1'B^k$ expresses the optimal weights implied by the bivariate structure (7.3) for the forecast of s_{t+k} given X_t. Thus, (7.6) is the familiar statement that, aside from f_t which has weight equal to unity, the weight for every other state variable in Y_t is zero. Hence, f_t correctly reflects all available information in X_t relevant for s_{t+k}.

Typically studies using the bivariate methodology restrict attention to pure AR representations for y_t (see for example Hakkio, 1981a; Baillie et al., 1983b). Of course, the restrictions that arise will be a special case of (7.6) when $q = 0$ is imposed. It is therefore instructive to decompose (7.6) explicitly into terms relating to the AR component of the process and terms relating to the MA component.

Define matrices A, C and F as

$$A = \left[\begin{array}{c} \Phi_1 \ldots \Phi_{p-1} : \Phi_p \\ \hline I_{2(p-1)} \qquad : 0 \end{array} \right]$$

$$C = \left[\begin{array}{c} \theta_1 \ldots \theta_q \\ \hline 0 \end{array} \right]$$

$$F = \left[\begin{array}{c} 0 \qquad\quad : 0 \\ \hline I_{2(q-1)} : 0 \end{array} \right]$$

where A is $2p \times 2p$, C is $2p \times 2q$ and F is $2q \times 2q$. Thus B and B^k can be expressed in terms of these matrices as follows:

$$B = \left[\begin{array}{cc} A & : C \\ \hline 0 & : F \end{array} \right]$$

$$B^k = \left[\begin{array}{cc} A^k : \displaystyle\sum_{j=1}^{k} A^{k-j}CF^{j-1} \\ \hline 0 \quad : \qquad F^k \end{array} \right]$$

where $F^0 \equiv I_{2q}$, $A^0 \equiv I_{2p}$ and $F^m \equiv 0$ for $m \geqslant q$.

We may now express (6.7) as

$$(g_2'I - g_1'A^k) = 0 \tag{7.7a}$$

$$\sum_{j=1}^{k} g_1'A^{k-j}CF^{j-1} = 0 \tag{7.7b}$$

with g_i being the $2p \times 1$ selection vector. Hence with pure AR models only the $2p$ restrictions (7.7a) need be evaluated as $C = 0$. Note that in any event these restrictions involve only AR parameters. The additional $2q$ restrictions in (7.7b) arise solely because $q > 0$ and involve a mixture of AR and MA parameters. The advantage of allowing for mixed ARMA structures is that they may yield more parsimonious representations for the process $\{y_t\}$. The advantage over pure AR structures will be more apparent the closer the zeros in the MA determinantal polynomial, det $\theta(L)$, are to the unit circle.

Finally, note that it is also possible to derive the restrictions in terms of the MA representation implied by (7.3). From (7.4) the MA representations for s_t and f_t are

$$s_t = \sum_{i=0}^{\infty} e_1' B^i \zeta_{t-i}$$

and

$$f_t = \sum_{i=0}^{\infty} e_2' B^i \zeta_{t-2i}$$

Thus

$$s_{t+k} = \sum_{i=0}^{\infty} e_1' B^i \zeta_{t+k-i}$$

and hence the market forecast error $s_{t+k} - f_t$ has MA representation

$$s_{t+k} - f_t = \sum_{i=0}^{k-1} e_1' B^i \zeta_{t+k-i} + \sum_{j=0}^{\infty} (e_1' B^{k+j} - e_2' B^i) \zeta_{t-j}. \tag{7.8}$$

The condition that $s_{t+k} - f_t$ be orthogonal to X_t is just that the second part on the right-hand side of (7.8) be zero. Define $2(p + q) \times 1$ vectors $r_j(\gamma)$ by

$$-r_j(\gamma)' = r(\gamma)' B^j$$

for $j = 0, 1, \ldots$; thus $-r_0(\gamma) \equiv r(\gamma)$. From the structure of ζ_{t-j} we require that the (1,1), (1,2), (1,p + 1) and (1,p + 2) elements of $r_j(\gamma')$ be zero for $j = 0, 1, \ldots$. Thus, once a general test for $r_j(\gamma) = 0$ has been constructed, it is not difficult (computationally) to test these restrictions (see Levy and Nobay, 1986, for a derivation and application of the Wald test to a class of mixed ARMA representations).

It should be noted that if $r(\gamma) = 0$ then $r_j(\gamma) = 0$ for all $j \geq 0$ and the MA process for $s_{t+k} - f_t$ is of order $k - 1$. However, if $r(\gamma) \neq 0$ it is possible, by examining the restrictions on the MA representation for $s_{t+k} - f_t$, to determine the extent of the violation in terms of the innovations generating y_t.

7.3 NON-STATIONARITY AND CO-INTEGRATION

The previous discussion on the use of time-series analysis to derive testable restrictions as implied by the market efficiency hypothesis has presumed that the underlying vector process is stationary. Typically, however, time-series for spot and forward rates exhibit non-stationary characteristics. The usual approach to dealing with non-stationary vector processes has been to apply first differencing to each component in the vector as necessary. The decision to do this is often supported by prior inspection of the correlation properties of each individual component series, following conventional univariate tools of analysis.

Such an approach, however, has severe consequences for tests of the speculative hypothesis within a time-series framework. Firstly, as demon-strated by Levy and Nobay (1986) the additional restrictions, introduced by modelling in first differences, renders the finite bivariate AR representation incompatible with the speculative efficiency hypothesis. Secondly, the procedure does not exploit the information in the hypothesis itself – that of the close association between forward and spot exchange rates. This is paradoxical since the motivation for applying bivariate models is the main-tained hypothesis of an association between the time-series. Under the hypo-thesis of speculative efficiency, u_t in the equation

$$f_t = s_{t+k} + u_{t+k} \tag{7.9}$$

is a finite-order MA process. Given efficiency, any stable dynamic pattern in spot exchange rate series must be reflected in forward exchange rate series through (7.9). Efficiency implies that we should expect the forward rate to equal the spot rate in steady state and this should therefore be present in any model purporting to characterize the dynamic relationship between spot and forward exchange rates. A failure of an autoregressive representation formulated in only first differences of these variables is the absence of a steady state solution for f_t.

7.3.1 Co-integration

Consider the following simple bivariate process for $y_t = (y_{1t}, y_{2t})'$:

$$y_{1t} = \phi y_{1t-1} + \epsilon_{1t} \tag{7.10a}$$

$$y_{2t} = \phi y_{1t-1} + \epsilon_{2t} \tag{7.10b}$$

where $\epsilon_t = (\epsilon_{1t}, \epsilon_{2t})'$ is a 2×1 vector white noise process with $E(\epsilon_t \epsilon_t') = \text{diag}\{\sigma_1, \sigma_2\}$. The univariate models for the components of y_t are

$$(1 - \phi L)y_{1t} = \omega_{1t}$$
$$(1 - \phi L)y_{2t} = \omega_{2t}$$

where $\omega_{1t} = \epsilon_{1t}$ and $\omega_{2t} = \nu_t + \theta \nu_{t-1}$ and θ is the solution to the quadratic

$$\theta^2 + \left(\frac{1 + \phi^2}{\phi} + \frac{\sigma_1}{\sigma_2} \right)\theta + 1 = 0$$

satisfying $|\theta| < 1$. As ϕ tends to unity, both y_{1t} and y_{2t} will display non-stationary traits with Δy_{1t} and Δy_{2t} being stationary in the limit. But in this instance $y_{2t} - y_{1t} = \epsilon_{2t} - \epsilon_{1t}$ is stationary irrespective of the value for ϕ. Thus, at $\phi = 1$, $(\Delta y_{1t}, \Delta y_{2t})'$, $(\Delta y_{1t}, y_{2t} - y_{1t})'$ and $(\Delta y_{2t}, y_{2t} - y_{1t})'$ are all stationary vectors processes (the last two being linear transformations of each other). The system (7.10) expresses these components as

$$\Delta y_{1t} = \epsilon_{1t}$$
$$y_{2t} - y_{1t} = \epsilon_{2t} - \epsilon_{1t}$$
$$\Delta y_{2t} = \epsilon_{1t-1} + \Delta \epsilon_{2t}.$$

Of the three informations, that for $(\Delta y_{1t}, \Delta y_{2t})'$ is a non-invertible MA process. The other two transformations, however, have representations which do not feature this property. Estimating non-invertible processes is not a problem but the procedure is made unnecessary by adopting one of the other transformations. The example illustrates that whilst univariate representations of a vector process may be non-stationary, a linear combination of the components may be a stationary process. Following Granger (1981) such processes are termed 'co-integrated'. If true, then this observation imposes important constraints on the form a bivariate representation for $y_t = (s_t, f_t)'$ can take.

The extension to vector processes and theorems associated with their time-series representation is developed by Engle and Granger (1987).

A process $y_t = (y_{1t}, y_{2t})'$ is said to be co-integrated of order $(1,1)$ with co-integrating vector $\alpha = (1, -\lambda)'$ if each process must be differenced to achieve stationarity but the linear combination $y_{1t} - \lambda y_{2t}$ is stationary. The scalar λ (termed the 'co-integrating coefficient') reflects a need to take account of the units in which y_{1t} and y_{2t} are measured to induce stationarity. One example of immediate relevance to us here is given by Granger (1981, p. 128): when y_{2t} is the optimal linear forecast of y_{1t+k}, $k > 0$, based on the information set $\{y_{t-i}, i \geq 0\}$. The vector process y_t is then co-integrated with co-integrating coefficient $\lambda = 1$. The co-integratedness of $(s_t, f_t)'$ is then a direct implication of the efficiency hypothesis. To see this more clearly, subtract s_t from both sides of (7.9):

$$f_t - s_t = \Delta s_{t+k} + \Delta s_{t+k-1} + \ldots + \Delta s_{t+1} + u_{t+k}. \tag{7.11}$$

Hence whether s_t needs to be differenced to induce stationarity or not, $f_t - s_t$ is the sum of stationary components and is therefore itself stationary. Constraints are then imposed on the form of the bivariate representation for $y_t = (s_t, f_t)'$.

7.3.2 Specification under co-integration

We can always write (7.3) as

$$A(L)\Delta y_t + By_{t-1} = \omega_t, \tag{7.12}$$

where $\omega_t = \theta(L)\epsilon$, by suitable choice of $A(L)$ defined by

$$A(L) = \begin{bmatrix} 1 - \sum_{i=1}^{m} a_i L^i & - \sum_{i=1}^{m} b_i L^i \\ - \sum_{i=1}^{m} c_i L^i & 1 - \sum_{i=1}^{m} d_i L^i \end{bmatrix}$$

and with B a non-zero 2×2 matrix. If $\Phi(L)$ is of order p, then $A(L)$ is of order $m = p - 1$. When y_t is co-integrated of order $(1, 1)$, Engle and Granger prove that in (7.12) $A(L)$ has full rank and all zeros of $\det A(L)$ lie outside the unit circle and that B has rank equal to unity.

For the co-integrating vector $\alpha = (1, -1)'$, we can express matrix B as

$$B = \begin{bmatrix} \gamma_1 & -\gamma_1 \\ \gamma_2 & -\gamma_2 \end{bmatrix}$$

for some $\gamma_1, \gamma_2 \neq 0$. Strong evidence for co-integration then suggests estimation of the unrestricted error-correction representation

$$A(L)\Delta y_t - \begin{bmatrix} \gamma_1 \\ \gamma_2 \end{bmatrix} (f_{t-1} - s_{t-1}) = \omega_t \tag{7.12'}$$

Collecting terms, we can then write (7.12) in terms of our bivariate ARMA model as

$$\Phi(L)y = \begin{bmatrix} \left(1 - \sum_{i=1}^{m} a_i L^i \right)(1 - L) - \gamma_1 L, & - \sum_{i=1}^{m} b_i L^i (1 - L) + \gamma_1 L \\ - \sum_{i=1}^{m} c_i L^i (1 - L) - \gamma_2 L, & \left(1 - \sum_{i=1}^{m} d_i L^i \right)(1 - L) + \gamma_2 L \end{bmatrix} \begin{bmatrix} s_t \\ f_t \end{bmatrix} = \epsilon_t. \tag{7.13}$$

The restriction of co-integration now takes the form of $\Phi(1)$ having rank unity.

We find it convenient to adopt the following linear transformation of (7.13) given by

$$\begin{bmatrix} 1 & 0 \\ -1 & 1 \end{bmatrix} \Phi(L) \begin{bmatrix} 1 & 0 \\ -1 & 1 \end{bmatrix}^{-1} \begin{bmatrix} 1 & 0 \\ -1 & 1 \end{bmatrix} \begin{bmatrix} s_t \\ f_t \end{bmatrix} = \begin{bmatrix} 1 & 0 \\ -1 & 1 \end{bmatrix} \omega_t$$

or

$$\Psi(L) \begin{bmatrix} s_t \\ f_t - s_t \end{bmatrix} = v_t. \tag{7.13'}$$

The system (7.13') is equivalent to (7.12') but the restrictions underpinning co-integration are expressed now in terms of unit root restrictions on the AR polynomials, i.e. the structure of non-stationarity.

Let $\Psi_{ij}(L)$ denote the (i,j)th element of $\Psi(L)$; then

$$\Psi_{11}(L) = \left[1 - \sum_{i=1}^{m} (a_i + b_i)L^i \right] (1 - L) = \Psi_{11}^*(L)(1 - L)$$

$$\Psi_{12}(L) = - \sum_{i=1}^{m} b_i L^i (1 - L) + \gamma_1 L$$

$$\Psi_{21}(L) = \sum_{i=1}^{m} (a_i + b_i - c_i - d_i)L^i(1 - L) = \Psi_{21}^*(L)(1 - L)$$

$$\Psi_{22}(L) = \left[1 - \sum_{i=1}^{m} (b_i + d_i)L^i \right] (1 - L) + (\gamma_2 - \gamma_1)L$$

Thus we have

$$\begin{bmatrix} \Psi_{11}^*(L) & \Psi_{12}(L) \\ \Psi_{21}^*(L) & \Psi_{22}(L) \end{bmatrix} \begin{bmatrix} \Delta s_t \\ f_t - s_t \end{bmatrix} = v_t. \tag{7.14}$$

Note the following points. First, the restrictions that ensure that $\Phi(1)$ has rank unity, as required by co-integration, are $\Psi_{11}(1)$, $\Psi_{21}(1) = 0$ *and* $\Psi_{12}(1)$, $\Psi_{22}(1) \neq 0$. The condition $\Psi_{12}(1)$, $\Psi_{22}(1) \neq 0$ is equivalent to γ_1, $\gamma_2 \neq 0$ and translates to the absence of $1 - L$ as a factor for $\Psi_{12}(L)$ and $\Psi_{22}(L)$. The presence of such a factor is necessary for common first differencing to be appropriate. The condition $\Psi_{11}(1)$, $\Psi_{21}(1) = 0$, however, is required for the acceptability of both common first differencing and the co-integratedness of $(s_t, f_t)'$. Thus we may interpret the restrictions $\Psi_{12}(1) = 0$ and $\Psi_{22}(1) = 0$ as the marginal restrictions required for first differencing and the negation of co-integration as a property of the vector process. Second, the vector $(\Delta s_t, f_t - s_t)'$ is stationary given that $(s_t, f_t)'$ is co-integrated of order (1,1) with $\lambda = 1$. However, accepting (7.12) as the unrestricted model, the AR polynomials associated with its ARMA representations are such that $\Psi_{11}^*(L)$ and $\Psi_{21}^*(L)$ are polynomials in L of degree m, whereas $\Psi_{12}(L)$ and $\Psi_{22}(L)$ are of degree $m + 1$. On the other hand, those AR polynomials for $(s_t, f_t - s_t)'$ or $(s_t, f_t)'$ are all of degree $m + 1$.

The above discussion suggests the following sequential procedure in empirical application. Firstly, the orders of the bivariate ARMA model for the *levels* of spot and forward rates should be tentatively determined. In our earlier empirical study (Levy and Nobay, 1986), we adopted the identification procedure introduced by Tiao and Tsay (1983) to determine these orders. Then, a nested sequence of factoring unit roots from the AR polynomial for $(s_t, f_t - s_t)'$ can be undertaken to determine the structure of nonstationarity present in the data. Equivalently, we can examine the suitability of imposing certain stationarity-inducing pre-filters. Levy and Nobay (1988) provide necessary and sufficient conditions for a class of linear filters to be consistent with the hypothesis of speculative efficiency.

In the following two sections we illustrate our discussion above by examining for the presence and structure of unit roots in exchange rate data. The series are drawn from our previous study (Levy and Nobay, 1986) of speculative efficiency in exchange rate markets and a full description is given therein. Briefly, the series comprise weekly series for matched spot and one-month forward exchange rates for five major currencies quoted against the US dollar, with an effective sample size of 313 observations for each series.

7.4 EVIDENCE FOR UNIT ROOTS IN EXCHANGE RATE SERIES

In general, standard statistics such as t and F statistics are not valid under the null hypothesis that the AR representation in univariate models has one or more unit roots. Hence, it is necessary to apply formal tests for the presence of unit roots; see, for example, Fuller (1976), Dickey and Fuller (1979, 1981) and Hasza and Fuller (1979).

Suppose that $\{x_t\}$ has the AR representation

$$x_t = \phi_0 + \sum_{i=1}^{p} \phi_i x_{t-i} + \epsilon_t \qquad t = 1, \ldots, T \tag{7.15}$$

and $\{x_{+p+1}, x_{-p+2}, \ldots, x_0\}$ are known constants. Let, the characteristic equation of the AR process

$$z^p - \phi_1 z^{p-1} - \ldots - \phi_p = 0$$

have roots $\lambda_1, \ldots, \lambda_p$. Then we are interested in testing the null hypothesis that $\lambda_1 = \lambda_2 = \ldots = \lambda_d = 1$ and $|\lambda_i| < 1$ ($i = d+1, \ldots, p$). For $d = 1$ and $d = 2$ we have, respectively,

$$\Delta x_t = \phi_0 + \sum_{i=1}^{p-1} \alpha_i \Delta x_{t-i} + \epsilon_t \tag{7.16}$$

and

$$\Delta^2 x_t = \phi_0 + \sum_{i=1}^{p-2} \gamma_i \Delta^2 x_{t-i} + \epsilon_t. \tag{7.17}$$

Table 7.1 Sample autocorrelations for spot and forward exchange rates

Lag	WG		SW		FR		UK		CA	
	s	f	s	f	s	f	s	f	s	f
1	0.99	0.99	0.99	0.99	0.99	0.98	0.99	0.99	0.99	0.99
2	0.98	0.98	0.98	0.98	0.97	0.97	0.99	0.98	0.98	0.98
3	0.97	0.97	0.97	0.97	0.95	0.95	0.98	0.98	0.97	0.97
4	0.96	0.95	0.96	0.96	0.93	0.93	0.97	0.97	0.96	0.96
5	0.95	0.94	0.95	0.95	0.92	0.91	0.96	0.96	0.95	0.95
6	0.94	0.93	0.94	0.94	0.90	0.90	0.95	0.95	0.94	0.94
7	0.93	0.92	0.93	0.93	0.89	0.88	0.93	0.93	0.94	0.93
8	0.92	0.91	0.91	0.91	0.87	0.87	0.92	0.92	0.93	0.92
9	0.90	0.90	0.90	0.90	0.86	0.85	0.91	0.91	0.92	0.91
10	0.89	0.89	0.89	0.89	0.84	0.84	0.90	0.90	0.91	0.90
11	0.88	0.88	0.88	0.88	0.83	0.82	0.88	0.89	0.90	0.90
12	0.87	0.87	0.87	0.87	0.81	0.81	0.87	0.87	0.89	0.89
13	0.86	0.85	0.86	0.86	0.79	0.79	0.86	0.86	0.88	0.88
14	0.84	0.84	0.84	0.84	0.77	0.77	0.85	0.85	0.87	0.87
15	0.83	0.83	0.83	0.83	0.75	0.75	0.83	0.83	0.86	0.86
16	0.82	0.82	0.82	0.82	0.73	0.73	0.82	0.82	0.85	0.85
17	0.80	0.80	0.81	0.81	0.71	0.70	0.81	0.81	0.84	0.83
18	0.79	0.79	0.80	0.80	0.69	0.68	0.80	0.80	0.82	0.82
19	0.78	0.78	0.79	0.79	0.66	0.65	0.79	0.79	0.81	0.81
20	0.76	0.76	0.78	0.78	0.64	0.63	0.78	0.78	0.80	0.80

WG, West Germany; SW, Switzerland; FR, France; UK, United Kingdom; CA, Canada.

Fuller (1976) and Dickey and Fuller (1981) provide the test statistics τ_μ for testing (7.16) against (7.15), i.e. that the AR representation for x_t has one unit root. Hasza and Fuller (1979) provide the test statistic $\Phi_2(2)$ designed for testing (7.17) against (7.15), i.e. that the AR representation for x_t has two unit roots. These studies tabulate empirical percentiles for finite sample distributions obtained by Monte Carlo methods.

Table 7.1 reports the sample autocorrelation functions for spot and forward exchange rates whilst table 7.2 reports these for their first differences. The slow decay in every example autocorrelation function in table 7.1 suggests that both s_t and f_t are non-stationary across each currency. However, this appears not to be the case for their first differences, as shown in table 7.2. Such evidence is consistent with the belief that s_t and f_t have one unit root in their respective AR representation.

Direct evidence for the presence of a single root is provided in table 7.3. The final order p for the AR was chosen by reference to the various criteria indicated by Paulson (1984) and Lütkepohl (1985) together with an inspection of individual residual autocorrelations implied by each suggested

Table 7.2 Sample autocorrelations for first differences of spot and forward exchange rates

Lag	WG Δs	WG Δf	SW Δs	SW Δf	FR Δs	FR Δf	UK Δs	UK Δf	CA Δs	CA Δf
1	0.09	−0.07	0.08	−0.07	0.01	−0.06	0.00	−0.01	0.08	0.06
2	0.02	0.19	0.00	0.11	0.11	0.11	0.09	0.05	0.10	0.11
3	0.07	−0.06	0.05	0.02	0.04	0.03	0.03	0.08	0.00	−0.07
4	0.05	0.01	0.12	−0.10	0.01	0.03	0.12	0.07	−0.06	−0.04
5	−0.04	−0.01	−0.05	0.10	−0.03	−0.09	0.00	0.08	−0.10	−0.12
6	−0.11	−0.14	0.02	−0.05	−0.11	−0.13	0.03	−0.03	0.03	−0.03
7	0.00	0.09	0.01	0.06	0.00	0.03	0.06	0.08	−0.06	−0.03
8	0.09	−0.04	0.01	−0.04	0.01	−0.03	−0.02	−0.04	−0.03	−0.01
9	0.08	0.10	0.04	0.06	0.10	0.12	0.03	0.05	−0.09	−0.06
10	0.04	0.02	0.01	−0.01	0.07	−0.04	0.02	−0.02	−0.06	−0.08
11	0.00	0.13	0.03	0.07	0.06	0.17	−0.01	0.06	−0.02	0.05
12	0.12	−0.01	0.01	0.02	0.10	0.02	0.09	−0.03	0.13	0.00
13	0.02	0.00	0.03	−0.02	0.10	0.08	0.01	0.01	−0.06	0.04
14	−0.05	0.00	−0.05	−0.02	−0.04	0.07	−0.07	0.05	0.10	0.05
15	−0.04	−0.05	−0.06	−0.03	0.04	−0.06	−0.04	−0.07	−0.03	0.03
16	−0.03	−0.02	0.03	−0.05	−0.04	−0.04	−0.03	−0.02	−0.03	−0.01
17	0.03	−0.01	0.01	−0.01	0.04	0.02	0.01	−0.08	0.04	−0.02
18	−0.03	0.03	−0.07	0.04	−0.02	0.04	−0.06	0.05	0.04	0.03
19	−0.03	−0.05	0.00	−0.05	−0.01	−0.09	0.06	−0.01	0.00	0.02
20	0.06	0.06	0.09	0.06	0.04	0.05	0.00	0.06	0.02	0.01

WG, West Germany; SW, Switzerland; FR, France; UK, United Kingdom; CA, Canada.

AR representation. Modified Box–Pierce statistics for the chosen model at lags 15 and 30 are reported as $Q(15)$ and $Q(30)$.

The final two columns in table 7.3 present the statistics τ_μ and $\Phi_2(2)$. Each of these was evaluated on the basis of an $AR(p)$ representation for s_t and f_t as indicated in the previous column. The critical values for $\hat{\tau}_\mu$ for 1, 5 and 10 per cent levels of significance are given by Fuller (1976, p. 373, table 8.5.2) as, respectively, −3.46 (−3.44), −2.88 (−2.87) and −2.57 (−2.57) for a sample size of 250 (500). Those for $\Phi_2(2)$ are given by Hasza and Fuller (1979, p. 1116, table 4.1) as, respectively, 5.88 (5.81), 4.44 (4.41) and 3.79 (3.76) for a sample size of 250 (500). The statistics provide strong evidence for the presence of a single unit root in the AR representation of s_t and f_t. (In this and other tables, superscripts a, b and c denote significance at the 1, 5 and 10 per cent level respectively.) These findings support the results of Meese and Singleton (1982) and are consistent with the usual diagnostic-indicated first differencing to induce stationarity in $(s_t, f_t)'$.

Table 7.3 Tests for unit roots in the autoregressive representations of the logarithms of spot and forward exchange rates

Currency		p	$Q(15)$	$Q(30)$	τ_μ	$\phi_2(2)$
WG	s	1	20.65	27.94	-1.631	—
	f	3	16.32	26.08	-1.653	57.984[a]
SW	s	1	11.63	23.84	-1.568	—
	f	3	17.25	29.26	-1.613	68.885[a]
FR	s	3	16.57	25.60	-0.415	61.352[a]
	f	7	16.85[b]	29.17	-0.113	35.509[a]
UK	s	1	14.52	28.62	-1.045	—
	f	1	15.20	29.09	-1.038	—
CA	s	3	20.52[c]	27.39	-1.199	59.980[a]
	f	1	18.11	29.68	-1.239	—

WG, West Germany; SW, Swiss; FR, France; UK, United Kingdom; CA, Canadian.
[a] Significant at the 1 per cent level.

As we have seen earlier, however, although the existence of unit roots is necessary for the vector process $(s_t, f_t)'$ to require first differencing to induce stationarity, it is not sufficient. More specifically, such evidence is also consistent if s_t and f_t are co-integrated processes as necessitated by the speculative efficiency hypothesis, re-expressed as (7.11). It is therefore necessary to consider whether the data support a co-integrating structure. This is undertaken in the next section.

7.5 EVIDENCE FOR CO-INTEGRATION

Engle and Granger (1987) advance a two-stage approach to test for co-integration. Firstly the co-integration regression

$$s_t = \mu_1 + \lambda_1 f_t + v_{1t} \tag{7.18}$$

is formed. Given the super-consistency results of $\hat{\lambda}_1$, the least-squares estimate for λ_1, large sample sizes should provide a good estimate of the 'co-integrating coefficient' λ. The second stage is to test whether the residuals from the co-integrating regression are stationary. This can be carried out using the Dickey–Fuller tests above or by using the Durbin–Watson statistic as argued by Sargan and Bhargava (1983) and Bhargava (1986). The latter test has an advantage in that its distribution is invariant to nuisance paramters such as whether an intercept is included in (7.18).

In applying this procedure two issues need clarifying. Firstly, if $s_t - \lambda f_t$, Δs_t and Δf_t are stationary the residuals from (7.18) will have finite variance only if $\hat{\lambda}_1 = \lambda$. Secondly, co-integration could equally be investigated by regressing f_t on s_t,

$$f_t = \mu_2 + (1/\lambda_2)s_t + v_{2t} \tag{7.19}$$

giving an estimate λ_2 for λ. That is, if y_t is co-integrated then both $s_t - \lambda f_t$ and $f_t - (1/\lambda)s_t$ are valid as stationary processes. Ideally we would like $\hat{\lambda}_1 = \hat{\lambda}_2 = \lambda$.

On the first issue, recent evidence from Banerjee et al. (1986) show that the bias in the estimate of the co-integrating coefficient can be quite large for relatively simple models and for moderately large sample sizes. The response surface estimated from their Monte Carlo experiments relates this bias to deviations from unity of R^2 in the co-integrating regressions. Thus R^2 from co-integrating regressions should serve as a useful measure of accuracy. A high R^2 is also important for the second issue. The product of the R^2 statistics from (7.18) and (7.19) gives a measure of closeness of $\hat{\lambda}_1$ to $\hat{\lambda}_2$. More precisely, if this product is close to unity, $\hat{\lambda}_1$ is close to $\hat{\lambda}_2$ and the bias is close to zero.

The co-integrating regressions themselves are reported in table 7.4. The 5 per cent and 1 per cent lower and upper bound critical values are (0.257, 0.404) and (0.373, 0.538) respectively, as reported by Sargan and Bhargava (p. 157) for 100 observations. (For our sample size of 313 observations we can expect the critical values to be marginally smaller.) Thus the high Durbin–Watson statistics in table 7.4 indicate a clear rejection of the null hypothesis of a unit root in the residuals and thus favour co-integration. In addition, the high R^2 statistics suggest that λ_1 and λ_2 are approximately equal to unity as expected. Further support for co-integration is given in table 7.5 where we apply Dickey–Fuller test procedures for the presence of unit roots in the AR representation for $f_t - s_t$, thus constraining $\lambda = 1$. On the basis of these results together with those in table 7.3 we can conclude that $(s_t, f_t)'$ is co-integrated of order $(1,1)$.

Table 7.4 Co-integrating regressions

	$f_t = \lambda_1 s_t + v_{1t}$			$s_t = (1/\lambda_2)f_t + v_{2t}$		
Currency	λ_1	DW	R^2	λ_2	DW	R^2
WG	0.997	2.118	0.994	0.997	2.118	0.994
SW	0.994	2.082	0.995	0.994	2.082	0.995
FR	1.001	1.982	0.991	1.001	1.982	0.991
UK	0.997	1.735	0.992	0.997	1.735	0.991
CA	1.001	1.291	0.996	1.002	1.290	0.996

DW, Durbin–Watson; WG, West German; SW, Swiss; FR, French; UK, United Kingdom; CA, Canadian.

Table 7.5 Tests for unit roots in the autoregressive representations of $f_t - s_t$

Currency	p	$Q(15)$	$Q(30)$	τ_μ	$\Phi_2(2)$
WG	2	16.64	29.57	-10.457[a]	985.453[a]
SW	3	11.58	27.50	-8.044[a]	344.885[a]
FR	4	18.07[c]	30.36	-5.697[a]	191.140[a]
UK	5	9.25	20.78	-4.533[a]	129.154[a]
CA	4	13.51	28.12	-5.169[a]	156.665[a]

WG, West German; SW, Swiss; FR, French; UK, United Kingdom; CA, Canadian.
[a] Significant at the 1 per cent level.
[c] Significant at the 10 per cent level.

These reduced form tests for the co-integratedness of $(s_t, f_t)'$ confirm the view that the marginal two restrictions implied by the first differencing transformation over the depreciation/premium transformation are not supported by our data. Recall that a consequence of imposing such a transformation is the rejection of efficiency as a market condition driving the determination of forward exchange rates. One conclusion that follows from this evidence is that the undue reliance on univariate analysis by previous studies for determining the appropriate stationarity-inducing pre-filter has very probably resulted in the employment of over-differenced models. It is not surprising, therefore, that both Hakkio (1981a) and Baillie et al. (1983b) found that estimating adequate AR representations for first differenced data on spot and forward exchange rates sometimes required very large orders.

7.6 NEW INFORMATION AND THE FORWARD EXCHANGE MARKET

Time-series analysis in general terms revolves around the modelling of the MA representation of a given series. This representation expresses current variables in terms of current and past innovations. In the context of modelling spot and forward exchange rates, these innovations play an important role in our understanding of the degree to which current forward exchange rates respond to new information. Rational expectations imply that forward exchange rates are continually reflecting 'news', and hence impose certain restrictions on the parameters defining the MA representation for spot and forward exchange rates. This approach avoids the use of extraneous regressions, and their shortcomings noted earlier, to generate innovations, as represented in studies such as those of Edwards (1982a) and Bomhoff and Kortewegg (1983).

In section 7.2 we showed the test procedure from which to derive such innovations – see equation (7.8) and the related discussion. Under foreign exchange market efficiency, for a given future spot exchange rate, the relevant information concerning its value will be accumulated over the forward period as new information is received. This is reflected in the forecast error, and it is thus straightforward to derive the implied rate of absorption of new information by examining the time-series structure of the forecast error. Stockman (1978) carried out such an analysis for the early years of flexible exchange rates. We can consider whether any changes have occurred in the rate at which the market absorbs new information by examining the data set which is for a later period. We show below the framework in which such an analysis may be carried out.

The spot exchange rate on the Thursday of any week can be represented as its Tuesday value four weeks previously plus the sum of daily shocks between the two dates. Denote s_τ as the Tuesday value in any week and $s_{\tau+30}$ the subsequent Thursday value. Then we define shock $u_i (i = \tau + 1 \leqslant i \leqslant \tau + 30)$ as

$$s_{\tau+30} = s_\tau + \sum_{i=\tau+1}^{\tau+30} u_i$$

Let $a_{i\tau}$ denote the change in the spot rate on day i, $\tau + 1 \leqslant i \leqslant \tau + 30$, that was *unexpected* as of day τ, i.e.

$$a_{i\tau} = u_i - E(u_i | \Omega_\tau), \, i = \tau + 1, \ldots, \tau + 30$$

Using this notation, $s_{\tau+30} - E(s_{\tau+30} | \Omega_\tau)$ can be expressed as

$$s_{\tau+30} - E(s_{\tau+30} | \Omega_\tau) = \sum_{i=\tau+1}^{\tau+2} a_{i\tau} + \sum_{i=\tau+3}^{\tau+9} a_{i\tau} + \sum_{i=\tau+10}^{\tau+16} a_{i\tau} + a_{i\tau} \sum_{i=\tau+17}^{\tau+23}$$
$$+ \sum_{i=\tau+24}^{\tau+30} a_{i\tau}$$

where the $a_{i\tau}$s have been summed over weekly intervals.

The error term v_τ in the MA process can be defined by

$$v_\tau = \sum_{i=\tau+24}^{\tau+30} a_{i\tau}$$

Then

$$s_{\tau+30} - E(s_{\tau+30} | \Omega_\tau) = v_\tau + \theta_1 v_{\tau-7} + \theta_2 v_{\tau-14} + \theta_3 v_{\tau-21} + \theta_4 v_{\tau-28}$$

where

$$v_{\tau-i} = \sum_{i=\tau+24-j}^{\tau+30} a_{i\tau-j} \quad (j = 7, 14, 21, 28)$$

$$\theta_1 \;=\; \sum_{i=\tau+17}^{\tau+23} a_{i\tau} \;\; (v_{\tau-7})^{-1}$$

$$\theta_2 \;=\; \sum_{i=\tau+10}^{\tau+16} a_{i\tau} \;\; (v_{\tau-14})^{-1}$$

$$\theta_3 \;=\; \sum_{i=\tau+3}^{\tau+9} a_{i\tau} \;\; (v_{\tau-21})^{-1}$$

$$\theta_4 \;=\; \sum_{i=\tau+1}^{\tau+2} a_{i\tau} \;\; (v_{\tau-28})^{-1}$$

The θ_is have a useful economic interpretation. The first, θ_1, is the ratio of the sum of unanticipated shocks between $\tau + 17$ and $\tau + 23$ *at time τ* to the sum of unanticipated shocks between these same dates but *at time $\tau - 7$*. Thus $1 - \theta_1$ is the extent learned of these shocks between $\tau - 7$ and τ:

$$1 - \theta_1 \;=\; \frac{\displaystyle\sum_{i=\tau+17}^{\tau+23} [\mathrm{E}(u_i|\Omega_\tau) \;-\; \mathrm{E}(u_i|\Omega_{\tau-7})]}{\displaystyle\sum_{i=\tau+17}^{\tau+23} [u_i \;-\; \mathrm{E}(u_i|\Omega_{\tau-7})]}$$

Equivalently, leading by seven days, $1 - \theta_1$ represents the amount of information on the spot rate between $\tau + 24$ and $\tau + 30$ learned between τ and $\tau + 7$:

$$1 - \theta_1 \;=\; \frac{\displaystyle\sum_{i=\tau+24}^{\tau+30} [\mathrm{E}(u_i|\Omega_{\tau+7}) \;-\; \mathrm{E}(u_i|\Omega_\tau)]}{\displaystyle\sum_{i=\tau+24}^{\tau+30} [u_i \;-\; \mathrm{E}(u_i|\Omega_\tau)]}$$

Similarly, the definition θ_2 gives

$$1 - \theta_2 \;=\; \frac{\displaystyle\sum_{i=\tau+10}^{\tau+16} [\mathrm{E}(u_i|\Omega_\tau) \;-\; \mathrm{E}(u_i|\Omega_{\tau-14})]}{\displaystyle\sum_{i=\tau+10}^{\tau+16} [u_i \;-\; \mathrm{E}(u_i|\Omega_{\tau-14})]}$$

Thus $1 - \theta_2$ represents that amount of the sum of shocks on the spot rate between $\tau + 10$ and $\tau + 16$ learned by the market between $\tau - 14$ and τ. Equivalently, leading by 14 days, $1 - \theta_2$ is that amount of the sum of shocks between $\tau + 24$ and $\tau + 30$ learned between τ and $\tau + 14$:

$$1 - \theta_2 = \frac{\sum\limits_{i=\tau+24}^{\tau+30} [\mathrm{E}(u_i|\Omega_{\tau+14}) - \mathrm{E}(u_i|\Omega_\tau)]}{\sum\limits_{i=\tau+24}^{\tau+30} [u_i - \mathrm{E}(u_i|\Omega_\tau)]}$$

The argument can be similarly extended to θ_3 and θ_4 to give

$$1 - \theta_3 = \frac{\sum\limits_{i=\tau+24}^{\tau+30} [\mathrm{E}(u_i|\Omega_{\tau+21}) - \mathrm{E}(u_i|\Omega_\tau)]}{\sum\limits_{i=\tau+24}^{\tau+30} [u_i - \mathrm{E}(u_i|\Omega_\tau)]}$$

and

$$1 - \theta_4 = \frac{\sum\limits_{i=\tau+24}^{\tau+30} [\mathrm{E}(u_i|\Omega_{\tau+28}) - \mathrm{E}(u_i|\Omega_\tau)]}{\sum\limits_{i=\tau+24}^{\tau+30} [u_i - \mathrm{E}(u_i|\Omega_\tau)]}$$

Consider then a typical 30-day period beginning at γ. At the start of this period nothing is learned of

$$\sum_{i=\tau+24}^{\tau+30} a_{i\tau} = \sum_{i=\tau+24}^{\tau+30} [u_i - \mathrm{E}(u_i|\Omega_\tau)]$$

as, by definition, $\mathrm{E}(u_i|\Omega_\tau)$ represents all that is known of u_i. However, at the end of the first week, the market learns $1 - \theta_1$ of $\Sigma a_{i\tau}$ and at the end of weeks two, three and four the market learns an increasingly higher proportion $(1 - \theta_2, 1 - \theta_3$ and $1 - \theta_4$ respectively). Finally, a further two days more and all is revealed.

Table 7.6 displays conditional maximum likelihood estimates of θ_i ($i = 1$, . . ., 4) for the five exchange rates. The numbers in parentheses are standard errors and indicate that all coefficient estimates are significantly different from zero. The modified Box–Pierce statistics $Q(k)$ test the null hypothesis that the first k residual autocorrelations are jointly zero. Superscripts a, b and c again denote significance at, respectively, the 1, 5 and 10 per cent level. With $T = 313$ observations, an approximate 95 confidence interval for the null hypothesis that a residual autocorrelation is zero is given by $\pm 2/\sqrt{T} = (-0.113, 0.113)$. Table 7.6 reports those sample autocorrelations that exceed this interval. Generally an MA(4) representation is adequate for all but the French franc series.

Table 7.6 Fourth-order moving average model estimates for $s_t - f_{t-4}$

Currency	θ_1	θ_2	θ_3	θ_4	σ^2	$Q(10)$	$Q(20)$	$Q(30)$	Sample residual autocorrelations
WG	0.846 (0.035)	0.798 (0.038)	0.644 (0.038)	0.200 (0.034)	0.304×10^{-3}	17.865[b]	25.007[c]	28.112	Lag 4, 0.113
SW	0.791 (0.043)	0.815 (0.044)	0.745 (0.045)	0.201 (0.045)	0.500×10^{-3}	6.570	12.604	19.546	
FR	0.842 (0.037)	0.790 (0.043)	0.636 (0.041)	0.234 (0.035)	0.264×10^{-3}	17.640[b]	30.323[b]	39.012[b]	Lag 2, 0.113 Lag 6, −0.122 Lag 11, 0.136
UK	0.868 (0.044)	0.806 (0.050)	0.758 (0.048)	0.320 (0.042)	0.274×10^{-3}	13.327[b]	20.478	32.124	Lag 4, 0.125
CA	0.916 (0.051)	0.935 (0.056)	0.828 (0.053)	0.330 (0.052)	0.549×10^{-3}	3.750	16.330	21.791	Lag 14, 0.142

WG, West German; SW, Swiss; FR, French; UK, United Kingdom; CA, Canadian.
[b] Significant at the 5 per cent level.
[c] Significant at the 10 per cent level.

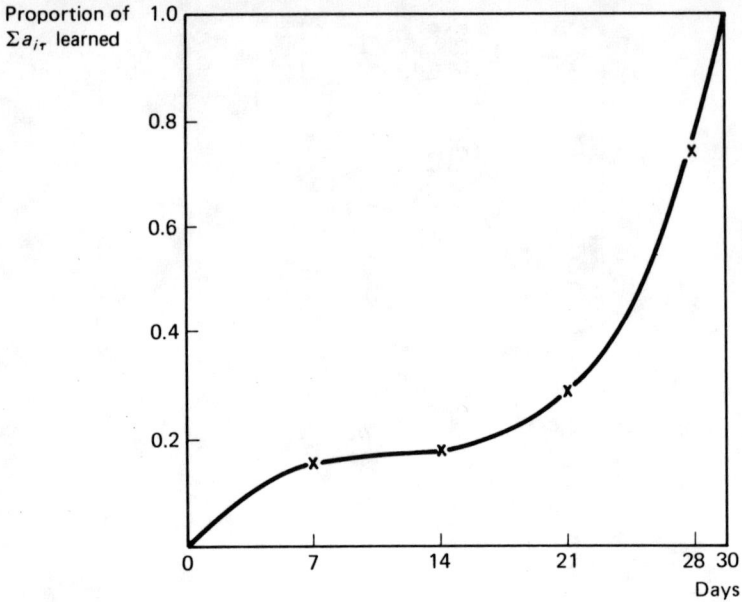

Figure 7.1 New information and the forward market learning curve: 1976–1981

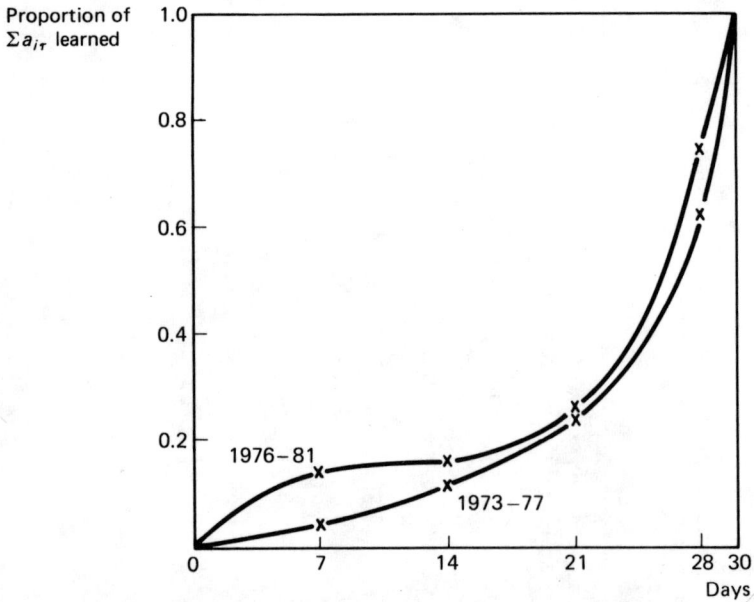

Figure 7.2 New information and the forward market learning curve: 1973–1977 and 1976–1981

Figure 7.1 presents the 'market learning curve' for Σa_{i_r} using the arithmetic average of each θ_i $(i = 1, \ldots, 4)$ across the five currencies. The resulting market percentage are $1 - \theta_1 = 0.157$, $1 - \theta_2 = 0.171$, $1 - \theta_3 = 0.278$, $1 - \theta_4 = 0.743$.

The study by Stockman (1978) was over a slightly broader set of exchange rates, which omitted FR, and over an earlier period (February 1973 to May 1977). There is therefore an overlap of four currencies: WG, SW, UK and CA. Averaging parameters across these currencies only, figure 7.2 compares the market learning curve implied by his parameter estimates with that for the estimates here. The figure clearly shows that over the two samples there has been some improvement, most notably in the first two weeks, in the rate at which new information is absorbed by the market. The early years of the flexible exchange rate period are generally regarded as turbulent. One would expect, as the results indicate, that over time the market would learn to adjust to new information. It would be instructive to undertake a sequence of innovation analysis to consider issues of learning and perhaps changes in exchange rate regimes.

7.7 CONCLUSION

This review of the time-series approach to evaluating speculative efficiency in foreign exchange markets has necessarily been a selective one. As the title would indicate, we have abstracted from a key question of the role of risk premia in markets. The issues raised in the context of speculative efficiency are nevertheless equally relevant in this wider area.

The joint hypotheses of rational expectations and speculative efficiency offer a powerful framework of analysis within time-series analysis. Our focus has been on the hitherto neglected issue of the structure of non-stationarity. We outline an integration of statistical approaches to stationarity-inducing filters with dynamic implications of the underlying hypothesis via the recent proposals on co-integration, with empirical illustrations. Finally, a consistent approach to the analysis of 'news' and information is outlined and examined.

8 Exchange Rates and News: A Vector Autoregression Approach

Laurence S. Copeland

8.1 INTRODUCTION

A series of papers testing the 'news' model of exchange rate determination have been published in recent years, according to which, given efficient markets and rational expectations, exchange rate innovations are related to unanticipated movements in a list of fundamental factors (Dornbusch, 1980; Frenkel, 1981; Edwards, 1982b, 1983; MacDonald, 1983b, 1985; Copeland, 1984a, b). Although in most cases the conclusions reached are broadly supportive of the news view, following the work of Pagan (1984) doubts have been cast on the methodology used in these tests. The problem, which this chapter attempts to remedy, arises as a result of inadequate modelling of the forecasting process for the news variables.

This chapter avoids the problems associated with the so-called two-step estimation technique by instead using a vector autoregression (VAR) approach to model the behaviour of the UK pound–US dollar and Deutschemark–US dollar exchange rates. The results, in the case of the German currency, are broadly consistent with a model in which the exchange rate reacts to surprises in the basic variables of the monetary model (e.g. Dornbusch, 1976; Frenkel, 1976), although for the UK the conclusion is not as clear. Attention is then turned to financial markets in an attempt to find better news variables, and a tentative model is proposed relating exchange rates to share prices as predictors of future levels of economic activity. However, this innovation does not significantly improve the fit of the equations, and it is concluded that a number of problems remain to be researched.

Helpful comments were received from the editors, and earlier versions also benefited from discussions with Charles Bean and Richard T. Baillie, none of whom can be held responsible for any remaining shortcomings in the paper.

The structure of this paper is as follows. In section 8.2 the foundations of the news model and the relevance of forward market efficiency are discussed. Section 8.3 outlines a testing procedure, the results of which are discussed in section 8.4. Finally, section 8.5 introduces a model of share prices and presents some results.

8.2 THE 'NEWS' MODEL AND THE EFFICIENCY OF THE FORWARD MARKET

In a seminal paper, Frenkel (1981) asserts that:

> In [asset] markets current prices reflect expectations. . . . The strong dependence of current prices on expectations about the future is unique to the determination of durable asset prices. . . . (p. 673)

To see the implications of this insight, consider the following general model:

$$s_t = \gamma z_t + b E_t \Delta s_{t+1} + v_t \qquad 0 < b < 1 \tag{8.1}$$

where s_t is the (logarithm of) the exchange rate (domestic currency price of dollars), z_t is a (possibly long) list of m 'fundamental' factors, some usually labelled 'real', others 'monetary', which affect the supply and demand for the currency and γ is an m-element coefficient vector. v_t is a zero-mean non-autocorrelated error term. The return to currency holders depends on the actual capital gain over the holding period – hence the expectations term in (8.1):

$$E_t \Delta s_{t+1} \equiv E_t s_{t+1} - s_t \tag{8.2}$$

Under rational expectations, (8.2) is the market's expected rate of depreciation between period t and $t + 1$, as forecast on the basis of the information available at time t (i.e. including a knowledge of the current exchange rate, so that $E_t s_t = s_t$.[1])

This model has the neat analytical solution for the expected exchange rate (Frenkel, 1981; Mussa, 1976)

$$E_t s_{t+j} = (1 + b)^{-1} \gamma \sum_k \beta^k E_t z_{t+j+k} \qquad \beta \equiv b(1 + b)^{-1} \tag{8.3}$$

and the usual conditions necessary to guarantee a unique non-explosive forward solution have been imposed.

Using (8.1), we can now rewrite (8.3) as

$$(1 + b)(s_t - E_{t-1} s_t) = \gamma(z_t - E_{t-1} z_t) + \gamma \sum_{k=1}^{\infty} \beta^k (E_t z_{t+k} - E_{t-1} z_{t+k}) + v_t \tag{8.4}$$

which expresses the innovation or unpredictable (and hence unpredicted) component in the exchange rate at time t as the sum of the innovation in (or news about) the elements of z_t plus a weighted sum of the extent to which expectations for all future periods have been revised between $t-1$ and t.

Equation (8.4), which is a completely general form of the news model,[2] contains only one observable variable, s_t itself. For empirical purposes, we need to specify the components of the vector z_t and the processes generating it. In principle, it should then be possible to solve for the expected exchange rate, making (8.4) directly testable by normal econometric methods.

In practice, however, it may be possible to short-circuit the problem of modelling the expected exchange rate if, with more or less complete forward markets for major currencies, we can write

$$f_t^{t+1} = a_t + s_{t+1}^e \tag{8.5}$$

where f_t^{t+1} is the (logarithm of)[3] the forward rate at t for contracts maturing at $t+1$. Equation (8.5) asserts that the relevant forward rate can be decomposed into a component reflecting the market expectation of the future spot rate plus another element a_t representing the sum of all the other relevant factors, including a risk premium if any exists.

The usual way to proceed from this point involves running regressions of the form

$$s_t = a + cf_{t-1}^t + w_t \tag{8.6}$$

and testing the joint hypothesis, often identified explicitly with forward market efficiency, that $a = 0$ and $c = 1$ (Frenkel, 1976; Frankel, 1980; Edwards, 1982b, 1983; and many others).[4]

However, our concern here is not efficiency *per se* but only the usefulness or otherwise of equations like (8.4) for testing the news hypothesis. To see what is required for this purpose alone, rewrite our news equation (8.4) as follows:

$$s_t = E_{t-1}s_t + \theta(\text{‘news’}) + v_t \tag{8.7}$$

where

$$\theta = (1+b)^{-1}\gamma$$

is an unknown vector of parameters – the coefficients which we are primarily concerned with estimating in this paper. Now, if the objective is to use the forward rate as a proxy for the expected spot rate in an empirical test of (8.7), the only conditions required are as follows.

1   The first term on the right-hand side of (8.5) satisfies

$$a_t = a_{t+s} = a \qquad\qquad \forall s$$

as in the efficiency test, equation (8.6). In other words, all we require is that any risk premium be constant, which, in turn, implies as a necessary but not sufficient condition that the joint process generating returns to currency speculation and to the relevant alternative investments be stable over the data period (see for example Grauer et al., 1976).[5]

2 In principle, we need not have a coefficient of unity on the forward rate. As long as c in (8.6) is a constant coefficient, the news equation is properly specified. However, it is difficult to see what interpretation to give to an equation where the forward rate is centred on a mean value of 90 per cent or, for that matter, 110 per cent of the expected spot rate – at least while the third necessary condition is satisfied.

3 The critical necessary condition is that w_t be serially uncorrelated. Notice that, subject to conditions (1) and (2), w_t is the sum of two types of stochastic disturbance. The first is a residual from the deterministic equation (8.5), a serially uncorrelated gap between the forward price of foreign currency and the exchange rate anticipated by the market in any period. A systematic component in this term would represent unexploited possibilities for profitable arbitrage. In research terms, it would mean either that the forward rate was an inadequate index of market expectations or that expectations were irrational or both.

The second component of w_t is the shocks associated with news. Now there are two kinds of reason why this component ought to be non-autocorrelated in non-overlapping data, one related to the definition of rational expectations and the second related far more to the nature of the foreign exchange market. The definitional reason is that the actual unobservable news variables have to be white noise – otherwise, under rational expectations, they cannot represent genuine news (i.e. surprises or innovations). However, if the market is inefficient, possibly as a result of transactions costs or other imperfections, it could be the case that expectations are rational (so the news variables are uncorrelated innovations) *but the spot rate only responds with a delay to any surprises.* In that case, we would have a situation where in any period t the exchange rate was influenced not only by the news that had accrued during t but also by news items from earlier periods $t-1, t-2. \ldots$

It follows that, if we were to find that *lagged* innovations had a role to play in the equation of interest, the result could be interpreted as indicating that expectations were irrational, or that the market was slow to react to news, or, of course, both. In terms of the simple model in equation (8.4), the relevant news may involve revisions to expectations about the fundamental variables at any or all *future* dates, but it cannot involve past innovations unless *either* expectations are not formed rationally *or*, conceivably, there are delays in the reaction to surprises, or both.[6]

In the present case, then, the most important conclusion is that the model as set out in equations (8.1)–(8.4) unambiguously requires that w_t be serially uncorrelated.[7] If this condition is not satisfied, then we are unable to use the forward rate as an indicator of the future spot rate, and an alternative approach will have to be found.

8.3 A TESTING PROCEDURE

If conditions (1), (2) and (3) are satisfied, it seems straightforward to proceed by modelling the processes generating the news variables explicitly, typically fitting an autoregressive integrated moving average equation or possibly a theory-based single-equation model, and using the estimated innovations in a test of (8.4), the 'equation of interest'. However, it has recently become clear that this two-step approach, which was followed by Edwards (1982b, 1983), Copeland (1984a, b), MacDonald (1985) and others, is potentially subject to a number of criticisms on econometric grounds.

In the first place, there may well be correlation between the news variables, resulting from structural relationships in the domestic macroeconomy.[8] Second, if there are non-surprise variables figuring in the true exchange rate equation, they may well be correlated with the residuals at the first stage and hence with the error term in the (mis-specified) second-stage equation.

Even if mis-specification of the exchange rate equation (the equation of interest) can be ruled out, Pagan (1984) demonstrates that, unless it can be guaranteed that the news variables are orthogonal to the whole set of past levels of the explanatory variables (i.e. to the information set upon which the innovations are conditioned), the estimated standard errors will be biased.[9]

The general remedy seems to be to use the technique of VAR.[10] This methodology avoids the econometric pitfalls, since it results in surprise variables each of which is guaranteed to be orthogonal to all the exogenous variables, not simply to its own past history.

As far as economic theory is concerned, a multivariate submodel is obviously closer to the spirit of rational expectations than a univariate model – for any variable, if a superior forecast can be achieved by using a multivariate rather than a univariate model, the rational agent will do this. However, although it would be possible to build a multivariate structural model to generate the surprise series, the problem of modelling variables like interest rates and income would take us far from the central issue of exchange rate determination. In addition, the original argument used by Sims (1980) in favour of the VAR approach seems valid here: the agnostic view is appropriate in a situation where we can claim little a priori knowledge of the structure of the macroeconomy. In particular, it seems unwise to prejudge the exogeneity or otherwise (even in the 'weak' sense of Engle et al., 1983) of what were referred to in section 8.2 as fundamental variables. In terms of (Granger) causality, there is at least the possibility, not to say likelihood, of two-way causality between money and any or all of the other variables.[11]

Consider the following system:

$$s_t = a + cf_{t-1}^t + \Theta\tilde{x}_t + v_t \tag{8.8}$$

$$\begin{bmatrix} 1 - A(L) & B(L) \\ C(L) & I - D(L) \end{bmatrix} \begin{bmatrix} f_t^{t+1} \\ x_t \end{bmatrix} = \begin{bmatrix} e_t \\ u_t \end{bmatrix} \tag{8.9}$$

where L is the lag operator, i.e. $Lx_t = x_{t-1}$, and $A(L)$, $B(L)$ etc. are polynomials in the lag operator so that

$$A(L) = a_1L + a_2L^2 + a_3L^3 + \ldots + a_ML^M$$

and so on. x_t is the $K \times 1$ vector of explanatory variables, with the tilde denoting innovations. The coefficient matrix in (8.9) is of order $(K + 1) \times M(K + 1)$, where M is the maximum lag length of the VAR. We assume that v_t, e_t and u_t are mutually contemporaneously uncorrelated.[12] Provided that they are white noise, the K residuals in u_t are themselves the news variables – in other words, if the model is correctly specified, we can rewrite (8.8) as

$$s_t = a + cf_{t-1}^t + w_t \tag{8.10}$$

where

$$w_t = \theta u_t + v_t$$

The null hypothesis that news variables have no part to play in exchange rate determination is then

$$H_0: \Theta = 0$$

The system made up of the VAR in (8.9) augmented by equation (8.10) has the following residual covariance matrix under the news hypothesis:

$$\Omega = \begin{bmatrix} \Sigma_{ww} & \Sigma_{we} & \Sigma_{wu} \\ \Sigma_{ew} & \Sigma_{ee} & \Sigma_{eu} \\ \Sigma_{uw} & \Sigma_{ue} & \Sigma_{uu} \end{bmatrix} \tag{8.11}$$

Thus point estimates of the elements of Θ can be extracted from

$$\Sigma_{wu}\Sigma_{uu}^{-1}$$

as is done by Edwards (1983). Furthermore, unbiased estimates of the standard errors in the equation of interest can be derived in straightforward fashion.[13]

Efficiency would require estimation of the complete system (i.e. (8.9) and (8.10)) by three-stage least squares (3SLS). In practice, however, there proved to be little difference between the system estimates and single-equation ordinary least squares (OLS), which is not surprising considering that we are dealing with what is almost, but not quite, a simple VAR (for which, of course, OLS and 3SLS are equivalent).

8.4 RESULTS

The system (8.8) was estimated with monthly data for the UK and West Germany from January 1977 to January 1984.[14] In both cases, the 'foreign country' is the USA, and all explanatory variables are measured relative to the USA.[15]

In the spirit of the literature on news, no reference has been made so far to the question of what variables to include as fundamentals. Tests of the efficient market hypothesis have frequently used a very restricted set of explanatory variables – typically, interest rates or forward premia alone. The tendency to use high frequency data, following the methodology introduced by Hansen and Hodrick (1980), has severely limited the field of choice, since only financial data are available on a weekly basis. This disadvantage is not necessarily very serious in efficiency testing, particularly when the conclusion is against efficiency, as has usually been the case in recent studies. If inefficiencies can be demonstrated even with respect to a very limited data set, the conclusion must hold good *a fortiori* for a more general data set.[16]

However, where, as here, the intention is to investigate the way exchange rates are determined, the data set should preferably be unlimited – or at least limited only by theoretical considerations. Unfortunately, however, theory is of virtually no help in guiding the choice of news variables. To see that this is the case, suppose the true model has the bilateral exchange rate determined by the expected price ratio for the two countries – in other words, suppose the expected real exchange rate is constant (as in Roll, 1979; and Adler and Lehman, 1983). Now if price levels are determined in a straightforward manner by the respective demand-for-money functions, it follows that the exchange rate at any point in time depends simply on expected relative money stocks, expected real incomes and so on. Even in this ultra-simple scenario, the list of news variables is potentially very long, for two distinct reasons. First, as was clear from the outset of the rational expectations revolution, rational agents will not be limited in their notional modelling of the economic environment by the macroeconomist's arbitrary distinction between exogenous and endogenous variables. Thus, if the publicly available information set includes current and past values of all relevant variables, the market's expectations with respect to the money supply, for example, may well be conditioned on the value of a number of variables, some normally regarded as economic, some non-economic (political, sociological etc.), some observable and some unobservable and even unmeasurable.

But this is not all. Even if we could be sure of the true process driving the money supply, it might still be the case that, in a world where the agent's information set is both incomplete and costly to expand, expectations are conditioned on signals from pure news variables, i.e. variables of no other relevance than as signals. In other words, in this type of world *a variable need play no causative role to serve as news* – all that is required is that it provides a reliable, although probably noisy, signal about the future path of the variable being forecast.[17]

However, even if we could be sure that, say, the money supply had a causative role to play, we could not with confidence say anything about the likely size of the coefficient on money stock innovations, nor even about its sign. Unexpected money stock increases might, for example, generate expectations of a future tightening, leading to an apparently perverse sign on the relevant coefficient.[18]

Subject to these caveats, a sensible starting point appears to be the variables figuring in the monetary model of the exchange rate: relative money stocks, income and interest rates (see, for example, Dornbusch, 1976; Frenkel, 1976).[19]

Three money supply definitions were used: M0 for base money (for the UK and USA only), M1 for narrow money and M3 for broad money. Both T-bill and Eurocurrency deposit rates were used for relative interest rates. The obvious proxy for national income is the index of industrial production, although its shortcomings are probably particularly severe over the present data period because of the well-documented shift in the composition of UK and US national income away from manufacturing and towards services.

As can be seen from the first four columns of table 8.1, the results for the UK are poor by any standards.[20] In the first place, there is clear evidence of autocorrelation in the residuals from the equation of interest.[21] In spite of this, none of the news variables appears with a significant coefficient over the period as a whole, and the situation is only slightly better over the subperiod.

The results for Germany (columns 6–9) are noticeably more encouraging, with only slight evidence of autocorrelation and some support for the view that interest rate innovations play a major part in moving the Deutschemark–US dollar exchange rate. In fact, the negative coefficient on relative T-bill rates and Eurocurrency deposit rates, when taken in conjunction with the (albeit insignificant) negative sign on relative money stocks, is consistent with the view that increases in German interest rates relative to the USA are most often associated with previously unanticipated monetary tightening and, consequently, Deutschemark appreciation. Surprisingly, equations in T-bill rates explain up to a quarter of the unanticipated movement $s_t - f_{t-1}^t$, in the spot rate and the null hypothesis that the news coefficients are zero can be rejected very decisively.

Table 8.1 The index of industrial production for the UK and Germany from January 1977 to January 1984

| | UK | | Germany | | Dependent variable: exchange rate innovation | | | |
| | | | | | UK | | Germany | |
	ER	TB	ER	TB	ER	TB	ER	TB
Constant	0.001	0.006	0.010	0.006	6.17×10^{-10}	-5.02×10^{-10}	5.68×10^{-11}	3.94×10^{-11}
S.E.	0.003	0.013	0.018	0.003	1.50×10^{-3}	1.40×10^{-3}	1.90×10^{-3}	1.71×10^{-3}
t ratio	0.29	0.49	0.56	1.78	4.11×10^{-7}	3.59×10^{-7}	2.99×10^{-8}	2.30×10^{-8}
Money stock	0.169	−0.055	−0.424	−0.340	0.215	0.069	−0.377	−0.294
S.E.	0.483	0.480	0.361	0.299	0.250	0.235	0.22	0.18
t ratio	0.35	−0.11	−1.18	−1.14	0.86	0.29	−1.75	−1.64
Industrial prod	0.070	0.048	−0.015	0.010	0.070	0.048	−0.182	−0.026
S.E.	0.095	0.093	0.321	0.269	0.051	0.048	0.20	0.17
t ratio	0.73	0.52	−0.05	0.04	1.35	1.02	−0.93	−0.16
Relative interest rate	ER	TB	ER	TB	ER	TB	ER	TB
Coefficient	−0.003	−0.003	−0.010	−0.019	−0.003	−0.003	−0.010	−0.019
S.E.	0.003	0.003	0.004	0.004	0.002	0.002	0.003	0.002
t ratio	−1.20	−1.12	−2.25	−5.20	−1.85	−1.71	−3.67	−8.24
Forward rate	1.000	1.009	1.000	0.994				
S.E.		0.020		0.024				
t ratio		49.70		42.27				

R^2	0.97	0.02	0.97	0.02	0.96	0.09	0.97	0.26	0.06	0.04	0.24	0.47
Durbin–Watson	1.36	1.35	1.39	1.37	1.96	1.97	1.88	1.89	1.97	2.05	1.72	2.00
Autocorrelation tests												
LM(3)	4.31	4.17	3.68	4.14	1.02	0.92	0.70	0.64	0.23	0.36	1.06	0.86
$F_{(3, 74)}$	0.01	0.01	0.01	0.01	0.39	0.43	0.56	0.59	0.87	0.79	0.37	0.46
LM(6)	2.76	3.43	2.41	3.46	0.71	0.64	0.43	0.38	0.12	0.30	1.04	0.54
$F_{(6, 68)}$	0.02	0.01	0.04	0.01	0.64	0.69	0.86	0.89	0.99	0.93	0.41	0.78
LM(9)	1.93	3.32	1.78	3.41	0.56	0.50	0.62	0.54	0.23	0.7	0.85	1.01
$F_{(9, 62)}$	0.06	0.00	0.09	0.00	0.83	0.87	0.78	0.84	0.99	0.71	0.57	0.44
F-stat (3, 80)	0.63	0.63	0.50	0.51	2.67	2.70	9.45	9.56	1.68	1.24	8.32	24.40
News hypothesis	0.60	0.60	0.68	0.68	5.3×10^{-2}	5.1×10^{-2}	2.0×10^{-5}	1.8×10^{-5}	1.80×10^{-1}	3.00×10^{-1}	6.9×10^{-5}	4.0×10^{-8}

Money stock, M3 relative to USA (logarithms). Interest rates: ER, Eurocurrency; TB, T-bill rate (per cent per annum). SER, standard error. F-stat is for testing the joint hypothesis that all coefficients of news variables equal zero (significance in bottom row). LM(n) is the value of the Lagrange multiplier test statistic for autocorrelation of order AR(n) or MA(n).

However, some doubt is cast on the results for both countries by the fact that one of the key assumptions discussed in section 8.2 is probably invalid, at least as far as the UK is concerned. Specifically, although in the standard test of forward market efficiency (equation (8.6)) the point estimates of the slope coefficient were invariably less than two standard deviations from unity, there remained significant residual autocorrelation, of first order or higher.[22] Nor is this result very surprising. The growing literature on forward market efficiency testing has more often than not reached a similar conclusion. For example, Boothe and Longworth (1986) summarize the situation as follows:

> The empirical evidence indicates that speculative efficiency does not hold and therefore *it should serve as a simplifying assumption in modelling only when it is not critical to the results.* (italics added). (p. 146)

Broadly similar conclusions were reached by Hansen and Hodrick (1980), Baillie et al. (1983b) and a number of others.

An obvious solution would be to use the lagged spot rate itself as a proxy for the expected rate $E_{t-1}s_t$, an approach that could be justified by the frequently cited fact that exchange rate movements tend to be well approximated by a random walk. Alternatively, the spot rate could be incorporated in the VAR to generate innovation series that are orthogonal to the full information set, including the lagged news variables and the lagged exchange rate itself. Although both approaches were tried, with broadly similar results, it still proved difficult to generate non-autocorrelated residuals with the first method. Hence, the results reported in the last four columns of table 8.1 are for a VAR including the spot exchange rate.

The noticeable feature of the UK results in columns 10 and 11 is the near-complete elimination of autocorrelation from the residuals, a result that applied equally to the unreported money supply definitions as well as the longer data period. Surprisingly, interest rate innovations play a significant part in explaining the unanticipated change in the exchange rate, and even the income proxy contributes, albeit with an insignificant coefficient. By contrast with Germany, both the money supply and the income variables appeared with a positive coefficient in all the equations estimated, so that positive innovations were associated with unexpected sterling depreciation. As far as the money supply is concerned, this could reflect simply the impact of news on inflation expectations, as in a straightforward interpretation of the monetary model. However, the significant positive coefficient on income is problematic. One possibility is that, for the relatively small proportion of national income represented by the index of industrial production, the traditional Keynesian view of 1950s vintage is still appropriate: output is (unexpectedly) high when the exchange rate is (unexpectedly) low, and hence competitiveness is high. At the same time, the demand for money depends on a (total) national income largely composed of non-industrial goods and services which are either non-traded or traded on non-price-competitive markets.

The results for Germany in the last two columns are satisfactory, although there is some suspicion of high-order autocorrelation.[23] In general, the news variables explain a remarkably high proportion of the unexpected variation in the Deutschemark relative to the dollar. The results for money and interest rates are broadly consistent with the policy adjustment process familiar from the UK (Smith and Goodhart, 1985) and USA (Cornell, 1982): in the aftermath of unexpected growth in the German money stock, market agents anticipate a policy correction, with the result that the Deutschemark appreciates during the month. Concurrently, the interest rate differential moves in favour of Germany.

The coefficient on the income variable is more difficult to interpret. On the one hand, a negative coefficient is consistent with an interpretation of the news model as a restatement in terms of innovations of the monetary model. On the other hand, this view is completely inconsistent with the signs on money and interest rates in the same equations. A more plausible explanation would be to argue by extension of the policy adjustment hypothesis that, the more economic activity exceeds expectations, the greater the pressure to operate a restrictive monetary policy. Putting the matter differently, the more buoyant the domestic economy turns out to be, relative to anticipations, the firmer the resolve of the monetary authorities to resist pressure to expand the money supply and/or to cut interest rates. This interpretation is certainly consistent with press and media comment on market sentiment in both countries in recent years.

8.5 THE EXCHANGE RATE AND THE STOCK MARKET INDEX

The difficulty in interpreting the income variable suggests the need for an alternative to the index of industrial production. In this section, we experiment with a news variable very much in the spirit of Frenkel's original approach, which emphasized that new information is reflected more or less instantaneously in security markets. So far, there have been few attempts to relate exchange rates to other financial variables, although in recent years stock market indices have frequently been studied alongside exchange rates in the context of money supply announcement effects (e.g. Cornell, 1982). However, Copeland (1984b) used an index of UK oil share prices as a measure of market expectations with respect to future oil revenues. More recently, Solnik (1987) explicitly regressed exchange rates on stock returns and found a relationship he called 'fairly weak'. He concluded that the linkage may appear tenuous either because 'stock returns are a poor proxy for real economic growth'[24] or for the reasons related to competitiveness which were mentioned in section 8.4 in the context of the index of industrial production. In any case, as Solnik observed in conclusion, serious investigation of the relationship must await a more fully specified model.

For present purposes, consider the following *ad hoc* model of share prices in an efficient market under rational expectations and risk neutrality:

$$P_t = \pi \sum_{J=0}^{\infty} \lambda^{-J} E_t y_{t+J} \qquad 0 < \pi < 1, \lambda > 1 \tag{8.12}$$

The assumption underlying (8.12) is that the level of share prices P_t is determined by the present value of future corporate earnings.[25] π is the (constant) expected proportion of profits in national income, and the appropriate discount rate is $\lambda - 1$, which is known with certainty.[26]

Now if we rewrite (8.2), separating the income variable from the other fundamentals,

$$s_t = \bar{\gamma} \bar{z}_t + \gamma y_t + b E_t \Delta s_{t+1} + v_t \tag{8.13}$$

where the parameter vector $\bar{\gamma}$ is now of dimension $m - 1$ and γ is simply a scalar coefficient, we can proceed to solve for the exchange rate in terms of share prices and the components of z other than income, denoted $\bar{z}$. Using the abbreviation

$$\tilde{x}_{t+J} \equiv E_t x_{t+J} - E_{t-1} x_{t+J}$$

which is the current period's revision to expectations with respect to period $t + J$, we arrive at the following solution for the exchange rate:

$$\tilde{s} = \frac{\bar{\gamma}}{1 + b} \tilde{z}_t + \frac{\bar{\gamma}}{1 + b} \sum_{J=1}^{\infty} \beta^J \tilde{z}_{t+j}$$

$$+ \frac{\gamma}{\pi(1 + b)} \tilde{P}_t + \frac{\gamma}{b\pi\lambda} (\lambda\beta - 1) \sum_{J=1}^{\infty} \beta^J \tilde{P}_{t+J} + v_t \tag{8.14}$$

From this solution, three points are clear. First, if the coefficient γ on national income is negative, so should be the coefficient on the current stock market innovation.[27] Second, the coefficient on stock prices ought in principle to be greater in absolute value than that on national income. For example, if the profit share π is around one-quarter, the coefficient on current stock market news ought to be about four times as great as that on national income.[28]

Finally, note that if, by chance, we had the discount rate equal to the reciprocal of the expectation elasticity b then it would follow that

$$\lambda\beta = 1$$

making the coefficient on all future innovations zero in (8.14). In this, albeit unlikely, eventuality, the current value of the share price could be said to neatly summarize the whole term structure of expectations with regard to future levels of economic activity.

Table 8.2 gives the results of rerunning the exchange rate equation using the log difference between broadly based stock market indices as the income proxy (see the appendix for details). For the UK, a proxy for oil revenue expectations was used, as was done by Copeland (1984b). According to conventional market wisdom in the late 1970s and early 1980s, any news which was felt to presage a rise in the value of UK oil production, whether as a result of higher world petroleum prices or of higher North Sea output, would be associated with sterling appreciation. If the shares in the oil companies quoted on the London stock market trade at prices which reflect the present value of the proportion of profits in North Sea output, then, by similar arguments to those employed to justify using the general share index, we can introduce the *Financial Times* Index of Oil Share Prices as an explanatory variable.

In the UK equations, the null hypothesis of zero coefficients on the news variables can be decisively rejected, at least when M1 and M3 definitions are used. Nevertheless, the coefficient on the share price variable is erratic, as is that on the oil share index.[29] The major contribution comes from interest rate innovations, which as before are negatively associated with the dependent variable.

Finally, although the results for Germany are by and large highly satisfactory, it is obvious, comparing the results in table 8.2 with those in the last two columns of table 8.1, that the fit is not improved by the new proxy for income, which is insignificant in all four equations reported.

8.6 CONCLUSION

In this paper a version of the news model of exchange rates for two currencies, the pound sterling and the Deutschemark, has been tested. The results are erratic in the former case, but provide strong support for the model in the latter. However, the attempt to introduce stock market prices into the model is, at best, only partially successful.

A number of reasons could be adduced to explain the failure of stock prices to add much to the explanation of exchange rate movements. At the theoretical level, the model of share prices outlined in the last section relies on a number of unrealistic assumptions, not least with regard to market attitudes to risk. Moreover, no attempt was made to incorporate the relationship between interest rates and share prices, although, of course, both variables were included in the VAR. Nonetheless, by failing to impose any structure on that relationship, it is possible that an important linkage

Table 8.2 The index of stock prices for the UK and Germany from January 1977 to January 1984 with exchange rate innovation as the dependent variable

	UK						Germany			
Constant	5.72×10^{-10}	-5.35×10^{-10}	6.42×10^{-10}	8.24×10^{-10}	2.09×10^{-10}	1.66×10^{-9}	2.68×10^{-12}	7.95×10^{-12}	2.96×10^{-14}	2.74×10^{-12}
S.E.	1.27×10^{-3}	1.32×10^{-3}	1.26×10^{-3}	1.20×10^{-3}	1.38×10^{-3}	1.11×10^{-3}	1.94×10^{-3}	1.73×10^{-3}	1.97×10^{-3}	1.78×10^{-3}
t ratio	4.50×10^{-7}	-4.05×10^{-7}	5.10×10^{-7}	6.87×10^{-7}	1.51×10^{-7}	1.50×10^{-6}	1.38×10^{-9}	4.59×10^{-9}	1.50×10^{-11}	1.54×10^{-9}
Money defn	M0	M1	M3	M0	M1	M3	M1	M3	M1	M3
Coefficient	-0.152	0.276	0.409	-0.315	0.223	0.284	0.335	-0.407	0.016	-0.218
S.E.	0.171	0.190	0.211	0.197	0.205	0.208	0.22	0.17	0.22	0.17
t ratio	-0.89	1.45	1.94	-1.60	1.09	1.37	1.55	-2.43	0.07	-1.30
Share index	0.005	-0.137	-0.089	0.062	-0.020	-0.084	-0.089	0.051	-0.073	-0.059
S.E.	0.052	0.063	0.067	0.054	0.066	0.057	0.08	0.07	0.08	0.08
t ratio	0.09	-2.19	-1.32	1.16	-0.30	-1.49	-1.06	0.71	-0.97	-0.78
Relative interest rate	ER	ER	ER	TB	TB	TB	ER	ER	TB	TB
Coefficient	-0.003	-0.006	-0.004	-0.001	-0.005	-0.004	-0.010	-0.011	-0.012	-0.015
S.E.	0.002	0.002	0.002	0.002	0.002	0.002	0.003	0.002	0.003	0.002
t ratio	-1.65	-2.79	-1.91	-0.67	-2.46	-2.57	-4.00	-5.13	-4.64	-6.06

FT-OIL	−0.062	−0.115	−0.036	−0.030	−0.148	0.028				
	0.044	0.045	0.042	0.038	0.043	0.040				
t SER ratio	−1.40	−2.54	−0.86	−0.81	−3.49	0.71				
R^2	0.07	0.20	0.10	0.09	0.18	0.09	0.17	0.27	0.21	0.32
Durbin–Watson	2.19	2.09	2.14	2.02	2.13	2.06	1.89	1.81	1.96	2.01
Autocorrelation tests										
LM(3)	2.13	1.60	0.57	2.01	1.05	0.85	0.81	0.58	0.41	1.54
$F_{(3, 74)}$	0.10	0.20	0.63	0.12	0.38	0.47	0.49	0.63	0.74	0.21
LM(6)	1.24	1.50	0.32	1.76	1.03	1.38	0.45	0.44	0.28	0.84
$F_{(6, 68)}$	0.3	0.19	0.92	0.12	0.42	0.23	0.84	0.85	0.94	0.54
LM(9)	1.16	1.63	0.31	1.52	0.98	1.07	0.43	0.36	0.62	0.84
$F_{(9, 62)}$	0.33	0.13	0.97	0.16	0.47	0.4	0.92	0.95	0.78	0.58
F-stat (4,80)	1.46	4.91	2.25	1.88	4.52	2.07	5.42	9.76	7.28	12.34
News hypothesis	0.22	0.00137	0.0701	0.12	0.0024	0.093	1.9×10^{-3}	1.4×10^{-5}	2.2×10^{-4}	1.0×10^{-6}

Share index, equity prices (logarithms, relative to USA); M0, M1, M3, money stock definitions (logarithms, relative to USA); FT-OIL, UK index of oil share prices (logarithms).

See also notes to table 8.1.

between the stock market and exchange rates has been suppressed.

Another potential explanation of the poor fit lies in the possibility that stock markets are themselves inefficient. The consensus in favour of weak and, more debatably, semi-strong form efficiency has broken down in recent years, as the growing volume of published work applying variance-bounds tests has for the most part concluded in favour of inefficiency (e.g. Grossman and Shiller, 1981; Leroy and Porter, 1981; Shiller, 1981; although see also Kleidon, 1986).[30] Furthermore, even if share prices are efficient with respect to corporate earnings, problems in using them as predictors for the level of activity could arise from the changing share of profits in national income.[31]

Finally, the serial correlation reported in equations involving the forward rate could well be explained by the unjustified imposition of a constant risk premium. If the true unobservable risk premium follows an ARMA process or depends on other variables which admit a Wold representation, the residual autocorrelation will only be eliminated by explicitly taking account of this fact (e.g. Taylor, 1988a).

The traditional call for further research is particularly appropriate in the present case because, while the VAR approach seems to be a convenient starting point, one is left with the feeling that it has been taken as far as is useful in this chapter. A number of major limitations are evident. The lack of structure makes the results difficult to interpret and the rapid exhaustion of degrees of freedom rules out testing some plausible hypotheses (e.g. those involving absolute rather than relative values of the news variables). The problems encountered in arriving at white noise residuals may in any case be suggestive of the need to countenance a non-linear formulation.

Appendix

All data are unadjusted for seasonal variation. Data on exchange rates, interest rates and stock prices are averages of bid and offer rates at close of trade on the third Friday of the month.

Money supply and interest rate series are taken from the *Bank of England Quarterly Bulletin* and the *Financial Times* (UK), the *Federal Reserve Bulletin* (USA) and the *Bundesbank Monthly Statistics* and *IMF International Financial Statistics* (Germany).

Industrial production indices are taken from *OECD Main Economic Indicators* and cover all industries.

The UK pound–US dollar (Deutschemark–US dollar) spot rate is entered as the logarithm of the sterling (Deutschemark) price of dollars. Forward rates are for the appropriate 30-day contracts.

General stock market indices are entered as the difference between the logarithms of the FT Actuaries All-Share Index and the S&P Composite for the UK equations. The FT Oil Share Index is for subgroup 51 of the FT Actuaries Indices, currently covering 17 stocks in the sector.

Notes

1 Note that this particular formulation of rational expectations is not unique. Apart from the more or less standard assumption that e_t is in the information set dated t, which is hardly contentious, it also involves the premises that (a) the relevant conditioning information is actually dated t (i.e. that the decision to hold or not to hold currency is updated at least as frequently as the observation interval and furthermore is synchronized with it) and (b) that the holding period is equal to the observation interval, so that only the rate of depreciation over the immediately succeeding period affects the net demand. These are logically separate assumptions. The first might hold and the second might not if, for example, the holding period is normally two months but half the portfolios are reallocated each month.

    Alternatively, it could be argued that arbitrage will ensure that these conditions are always satisfied, irrespective of the portfolio behaviour of ultimate wealth owners. The problem with this approach is that, not only does it presuppose an adequate supply of arbitrage funds, it is also hard to see how it can leave any significant role for domestic money demand variables to play in exchange rate determination.

2 Wolff (1986) gives a more detailed derivation.

3 It is normal to formulate these relationships in logarithms to avoid problems with Jensen's inequality.

4 Although see for example Boothe and Longworth (1986) for a discussion of these tests.

5 In particular, we do not need to insist on a zero risk premium, a condition which is often, wrongly, thought necessary.

    It should be noted that the concern here is purely with the conditions necessary for the forward rate to serve as a proxy for the expected future spot rate. Almost any pattern of variation could be justified in theoretical terms (see for example Stockman, 1978, or Domowitz and Hakkio, 1985).

6 Delays in the market response to news might be consistent with a partial adjustment mechanism in the demand for money, for example. At any rate, this particular possibility is not pursued here.

7 In other words, if, as is often the case, market efficiency is taken as implying the absence of a risk premium – and there is really no reason why it should – it is not a necessary condition. However, in so far as efficiency implies that prices are not systematically biased by transaction costs etc., we require the forward exchange market to be efficient if it is to be of any use as a proxy for expectations.

8 Notice that, in the present case, there are a number of reasons to suspect non-zero cross-correlations between the innovations from different univariate regressions and between innovations from one (univariate) regression and the

regressors in another. For example, one would expect there to be correlation between innovations in the economic activity series and money supply news – possibly including lags, if activity levels are 'sticky' (see for example Sargent, 1976).

9   Pagan (1984) also shows that if the objective were to perform tests of the hypothesis that the coefficients on expected values are zero (as Barro (1977) does, for example), the two-step standard error estimates would be biased downwards, making the tests too conservative. For further discussion of some of these and related issues, see Pagan and Hall (1983).

10   The idea of using VAR was suggested by Pagan in correspondence with the author.

11   However, it has to be admitted that this kind of agnostic attitude sits very uncomfortably alongside the rational expectations assumption. It is a paradox of rational expectations that ordinary economic agents behave as if they know the true model, while the applied econometrician approaches research as if he knows very little – virtually nothing, in the case of the VAR model-builder.

For present purposes, the most plausible way of resolving the paradox is to rely on the existence of important variables which are omitted because they are unobservable and/or unmeasurable. So, for example, it could be argued that, at any moment, market agents know very well the direction of causality between the money stock and, say, interest rates, thanks to their close observation of day to day developments in financial markets and to the pronouncements emanating from the monetary authorities themselves.

12   Since all the variables in (8.8) and (8.9) – s, f and x – are likely to be non-stationary (see, for example, Meese and Singleton, 1983), valid inference is only possible if the error terms v_t, e_t and u_t are stationary. This in turn implies that s and f, f and x must be co-integrated (e.g. Granger, 1986; Hendry, 1986). In the same literature it is also suggested that differencing the series in order to eliminate non-stationarity may be inappropriate in the context of a VAR, because of the omission of error-correction terms – which is, of course, unavoidable in the present situation.

13   As can be verified by applying the methodology of Bean (1986) to the present case, to derive the result that the asymptotic covariance of the estimates is given by

$$\Omega_{we} \otimes \Sigma_{uu}^{-1}$$

where the first term in the Kronecker product is the 2×2 matrix in the upper left-hand corner of (8.11).

14   The UK results were estimated for the full floating rate period, starting in January 1973, and separately from 1977 onward. There are two reasons for splitting the period at 1977. First, because data for Germany were only available from January 1977, it was felt desirable to provide a basis for comparison between the UK and German results over the same data period. Second, there are a number of reasons to suspect a shift in the relationship in the late 1970s: instability in domestic demand-for-money functions, the 1979 change in US monetary control techniques, the emergence of the UK as a net oil exporter, along with the 1979 oil price shock, and so on. In the event, the fit for the UK

over the longer period was no better than from 1977, so only the post-1977 data are reported here.

15 All variables are entered in natural logarithms except interest rates which are in per cent per annum. For more details, see the appendix.

16 At a given frequency, that is. I am grateful to one of the editors for pointing out that it is quite possible to find in a restricted data set (e.g. a weekly price series) apparently unexploited profit opportunities which disappear when daily or intra-daily observations on a wider data set are examined.

17 As a trivial example, a pronouncement by the authorities on future monetary policy may be a very important news variable (though somewhat difficult to quantify). But it certainly cannot be said to cause the subsequent money supply change.

Of course, what is called here a pure news variable would still play a causal part in the Granger sense of the term – if, that is, it could be quantified in the first place.

18 For evidence on the so-called policy anticipation hypothesis, see Urich and Wachtel (1981), Cornell (1982), Urich (1982), Smith and Goodhart (1985).

19 In addition, some of the equations included a series for the trade balance, although the results are not reported here since it appeared to make no significant contribution. The fact that no role could be found for trade balances might be explained, very tentatively, in a number of ways. First, it could be simply that (multilateral) trade balances are of little relevance to (bilateral) exchange rates, at least for the UK and Germany. Alternatively, it could be the case that the trade balance is perceived as a poor proxy for the current balance. Perhaps a more plausible explanation would be that the exchange rate is deter-mined in any case by movements on (short-term) capital account which are largely independent of the current account situation.

In any case, no firm conclusions are warranted. In the first place, trade balances are quite highly correlated with the other variables, meaning that news about the trade balance may be to a greater or lesser extent embodied in news about the other variables. Also, the addition of trade balances to the four variables already included in the VAR made it impossible to estimate over the full 12 lags, at least in the case of Germany. This in turn made it virtually impossible to arrive at uncorrelated residuals.

20 Table 8.1 reports M3 equations only. The results using M0 and M1 (for the UK) and M1 (for Germany) were broadly similar and are not reported.

21 The persistent autocorrelation is not necessarily damning for the news hypothesis, since it could simply be indicative of the need to estimate a higher-order VAR than the twelfth-order VAR used here. Unfortunately, limitations on computer memory made it difficult to expand the number of lags much beyond 12. Another possibility would be to include moving average error terms. The problem with the VAR moving average (VARMA) approach in the present case is that it is extremely awkward to estimate, starting from a twelfth-order VAR. Degrees of freedom are rapidly exhausted, as is computer space.

Practical problems apart, one further difficulty is that the benefits of the VAR approach, referred to earlier in this section, are somewhat diluted by a VARMA approach because the moving average polynomial may be of different order in each of the equations. For the same reason, it is not clear whether there are any benefits to be achieved in the present context by searching for a parsimonious representation of the news variables.

22   The results of actually running efficiency tests like (8.6) tended to suggest low (first or third) order autocorrelation in the error term w_t. Results are not reported simply because they are broadly consistent with the far more sophisticated tests carried out by other researchers (see below).

23   The suspicion arose only with regard to M3 equations.

24   For evidence on the hypothesis that stock returns forecast changes in the level of economic activity, see Fama (1981) and Geske and Roll (1983). Pearce and Roley (1985) investigate the relationship between stock prices and (announced) news about economic activity.

25   Although, if we can safely ignore personal taxation, we can invoke the model of Modigliani and Miller (1963) to justify replacing cash flows by dividends.

26   Obviously, this assumption sits uncomfortably inside a model involving interest rate surprises. In fact, it could be relaxed simply by redefining λ as the expectation of one divided by one plus the discount rate and changing the sign of the exponent in (8.12) – provided that we impose the condition that the covariance between λ and y is zero.

It is also possible to derive a formulation similar to (8.12) without imposing risk neutrality. Under highly restrictive assumptions about the utility function, cash flows are discounted at a rate which is the sum of a rate of time preference and a risk premium, in the form of the marginal rate of intertemporal substitution (see Copeland and Stapleton, 1987).

27   The same is not necessarily the case for expectation revisions with respect to future stock prices, since the sign of these coefficients depends on the sign of $\lambda\beta - 1$.

28   Of course, since net industrial output is itself well under half of the gross domestic product, this conclusion cannot be stated nearly as unambiguously when comparing coefficients on the index of industrial production with those on stock market indices.

29   Excluding the oil share variable from the equation did not substantially change the conclusions with respect to the general share index, but it did worsen the overall fit.

30   Although Marsh and Merton (1984) question the practice of basing variance-bounds tests on dividend streams, which are obviously smoothed, rather than on the underlying cash flows.

31   The undeniable fact that profits do vary as a proportion of gross domestic product is not, on its own, a major problem for the model in section 8.4, since we only need the expected level of profitability to be constant – in other words, deviations about the long-run level must be (a) serially uncorrelated and (b) uncorrelated with the other variables in the model.

9 Some Survey-based Tests of Uncovered Interest Parity

Ronald MacDonald and Thomas S. Torrance

9.1 INTRODUCTION

At the heart of a number of important theoretical models of exchange rate determination (see *inter alia* Dornbusch, 1976; Frankel, 1979a; Buiter and Miller, 1981) is the condition of uncovered interest parity (UIP): the yield on a home country bond should equal that on an equivalent foreign asset, adjusted for the expected change in the exchange rate. The UIP condition is thought to be a more appropriate building block for a model of exchange rate determination than purchasing power parity (PPP), which has demonstrably not held during the recent floating experience (thus the early flex-price monetary models were jettisoned as models of exchange rate determination, largely because key equations used in their derivation, i.e. PPP, were invalid). But is it? A number of researchers have indicated that UIP has not, in fact, held for the recent float (this research is discussed more fully in section 9.2). The problem, however, with the extant tests of UIP is that they are tests of a joint hypothesis and therefore it is difficult to discern whether a rejection of a null is due to imperfect bond substitution, as a consequence of risk aversion, or the irrationality of speculators. Clearly which element is responsible for rejection has important theoretical and policy implications.[1] In this paper we present some new tests of the UIP condition which provide single hypothesis tests of the relationship: such tests rely on the use of survey data on the exchange rate expectations of foreign exchange market participants for four currencies against the US dollar.

The outline of the remainder of this paper is as follows. In section 9.2 we present a brief review of the extant evidence pertaining to the UIP condition. Data series and definitions are given in section 9.3. A methodology for discerning whether rejection of UIP is due to risk aversion or irrationality is also presented in section 9.3, as are our empirical results. The paper closes with a summary and conclusions.

9.2 UNCOVERED INTEREST PARITY: THE EXTANT EVIDENCE

The UIP condition may be stated formally as

$$s^e_{t+j} - s_t = \Delta s^e_{t+j} = i_{t+j} - i^*_{t+j} \tag{9.1}$$

where s denotes the natural logarithm of the spot exchange rate (home currency per unit of foreign currency), s^e_{t+j} represents the expectation of the exchange rate, formed in period t, for period $t+j$, Δ denotes the first difference operator, i_{t+j} denotes the interest rate on a bond purchased in period t which matures in $t+j$ and an asterisk denotes a foreign magnitude. Condition (9.1) will hold if investors regard the domestic and foreign assets underlying i and i^* as perfect substitutes and there are no impediments to international capital movements.

Two types of tests of (9.1) have been conducted in the literature. The first is indirect in so far as it posits that if covered interest parity holds,

$$f^{t+j}_t - s_t = i_{t+j} - i^*_{t+j} \tag{9.2}$$

then the forward premium $f^{t+j}_t - s_t$ should be equal to the expected change in the exchange rate (where f denotes the natural logarithm of the forward rate):

$$f^{t+j}_t - s_t = \Delta s^e_{t+j} \tag{9.3}$$

A large number of researchers have sought to test equation (9.3) by assuming that expectations are formed rationally and examining whether the forward premium is an optimal predictor of the change in the exchange rate. The main conclusion to emerge is that the forward premium is an inefficient predictor of the change in the exchange rate, because of either the existence of a time-varying risk premium or the irrationality of agents' expectations (see MacDonald, 1988, and MacDonald and Taylor, this volume, for a further discussion).

Direct tests of the UIP are less commonplace in the literature. With rational expectations and risk neutrality, such a test would amount to testing the interest differential as an optimal predictor of the rate of depreciation. Such a test might involve, for example, estimating a regression relationship of the form

$$s_t = \alpha_0 s_{t-n} + \alpha_1 (i - i^*)_{t-n} + v_t \tag{9.4}$$

where the joint hypothesis of risk neutrality and the rationality of expectations implies that α_0 and α_1 should equal minus and plus unity respectively and that v_t should be a stochastic process, orthogonal to past information.

Hacche and Townend (1981) test equation (9.4) for sterling's effective exchange rate over the period July 1972 to February 1980 and find that a priori constraints on α_0 and α_1 are supported by the data. The error ortho-gonality property, however, was not supported by the data: lagged values of domestic credit expansion and the change in the exchange rate proved to be statistically significant (similar results for the UK pound–US dollar rate, February 1973 to December 1980, are reported in Davidson, 1985). Similarly, Loopesko (1984), in testing the error orthogonality property, found that it did not hold for the majority of currencies studied. Taylor (1987c) tests UIP using the bivariate vector autoregression (BVAR) approach. He uses a data base covering spot and forward dollar exchange rates against the French franc, Italian lira, Dutch guilder, Deutschemark, UK pound and Japanese yen, as well as the appropriate Eurodeposit rates, for six and twelve months' maturities for the period July 1979 to December 1986. UIP is easily rejected in both maturities for all exchange rates with the exception of the US dollar–Deutschemark. Similar results are obtained using Deutschemark and UK pound bilateral rates (constructed assuming triangular arbitrage conditions), except that UIP cannot be rejected for UK pound–lira in either maturity. Cumby and Obstfeld (1981) estimate whether the error term v_t in equation (9.4) is in fact white noise when $n = 1$ by using Box–Pierce and likelihood ratio tests on $s_t - s_{t-1} - (i - i^*)_{t-1}$ for six bilateral dollar exchange rates (weekly data for the period 5 July 1974 to 27 June 1980). For only one exchange market, the US dollar–UK pound, is it demon-strated that the residuals are white. Cumby and Obstfeld rationalized these deviations from UIP by suggesting the existence of a variable risk premium (a further rejection of UIP is given in Cumby and Obstfeld, 1984).

However, one problem with the above tests is that they are testing the joint hypothesis of UIP *and* the rationality of expectations. Clearly rejection of the joint hypothesis could be due to some form of irrationality or the existence of a risk premium. The decision as to which it is depends very much on a researcher's prejudices. However, the recent availability of survey data on agents' expectations allows determination of whether the failure of the UIP condition, noted in the above studies, is due to irrationality or risk aversion or both. In section 9.4 we discuss this concept in a little more detail.

9.3 DATA DESCRIPTION AND THE RISK PREMIUM: SOME SURVEY-BASED EVIDENCE

Our basic survey data were supplied by Money Market Services Ltd of London (MMS(UK)). They consist of expected exchange rates against the US dollar of the Deutschemark, the Japanese yen, the UK pound and the Swiss franc. In line with the usual convention, the original data on the UK pound were in the form of the number of dollars per pound, while in the case of the other three currencies the data specified the number of the units in question per dollar.

From the various sets of survey data of the four expected exchange rates against the dollar provided by MMS(UK), we utilize the series of two-weekly data running from 12 July 1982 to 13 April 1987, both dates inclusive, which give the expected spot rates four weeks later. (In the case of the expected Swiss franc rates, the data terminate on 28 April 1986). Since the sample period embraces a period in which all the currencies in question were depreciating against the US dollar and a period in which they were all appreciating, we considered it important to examine the properties of our models for both these periods separately. Accordingly, our first subsample, for all four currencies, runs from 12 July 1982 to 18 February 1985. Our second subsample for the Deutschemark, the Japanese yen and the UK pound runs from 4 March 1985 to 13 April 1987, while in the case of the Swiss franc the second subsample ends at 28 April 1986.

In collecting these data, MMS(UK) sought the views of approximately 30 major financial institutions, many of them large banks, situated both in the City of London and in the main financial centres of continental Europe. The data we employ here consist of a set of the median values of two-weekly surveys conducted every other Monday and done with the aim of ascertaining dealers' forecasts of the relevant closing London rate on the Monday of four weeks hence.[2]

Our data on spot exchange rates and on interest rates are taken from the *Financial Times*. For each currency the spot rate is the mid-market London closing rate on the Monday at the start of each two-weekly period that falls into the overall survey period. The interest rates we use are the appropriate four-week Euro-rates published in the *Financial Times* as prevailing at the close of the London financial markets on each relevant Monday. On the matter of the choice of interest rates, the fact that we use Euro-rates, including four-week Euro-sterling rates (as opposed to some four-week 'onshore' sterling rates), ensures that all five series of rates are homogeneous in their institutional attributes.

Consider the regression equation

$$\Delta s_{t+2} = \alpha_0 + \beta_1(i - i^*)_t + u_{t+2} \tag{9.5}$$

where the rational expectations substitution $\Delta s_{t+2} = \Delta s_{t+2}^e - u_{t+2}$ has been utilized. In an estimated version of (9.5) α_0 is expected to be zero, β_1 unity and the error term orthogonal to the information set. In table 9.1 we present estimates of this equation for our four currencies and three data samples: the broad conclusion to emerge from these results is that in a number of cases β_1 differs significantly from unity and this, combined with the significance of the constant term, results in a rejection of the joint hypothesis.

Insight into why β_1 deviates from unity in table 9.1 may be seen in the following way. If we define the risk premium term θ_t, we have

Table 9.1 The uncovered interest parity condition with rational expectations

$$\Delta s_{t+2} = \alpha_0 + \beta_1 (i - i^*)_t$$

		α_0	β_1	R^2	$t\beta_1 = 1$	$\chi^{\alpha=0}_{\beta_1=1}$	DF
BP	Full	0.013	−7.299	0.18	−4.30	18.68(0.00)	120
		(3.57)	(5.08)				
		(3.57)	(3.78)				
	1	0.014	−2.289	0.01	—	13.08(0.00)	64
		(4.35)	(0.81)				
		(3.34)	(0.77)				
	2	0.048	−17.262	0.08	—	6.02(0.05)	54
		(1.72)	(2.25)				
		(1.38)	(1.69)				
DM	Full	−0.038	−11.883	0.12	4.00	13.94(0.00)	120
		(4.38)	(4.05)				
		(3.63)	(3.68)				
	1	−0.021	−8.406	0.07	1.97	7.51(0.02)	64
		(1.51)	(2.21)				
		(1.15)	(1.76)				
	2	−0.007	6.606	0.01	—	12.19(0.00)	54
		(0.38)	(0.79)				
		(0.38)	(0.76)				
JY	Full	−0.027	−8.052	0.06	2.71	7.78(0.02)	120
		(3.80)	(2.76)				
		(2.77)	(2.41)				
	1	−0.019	−6.819	−0.04	—	2.45(0.29)	64
		(1.48)	(1.58)				
		(1.08)	(1.34)				
	2	−0.008	9.197	0.02	—	11.89(0.00)	54
		(0.69)	(1.10)				
		(0.63)	(1.11)				
SF	Full	−0.044	−9.552	0.10	2.74	8.88(0.01)	96
		(3.34)	(3.34)				
		(2.30)	(2.48)				
	1	0.001	−1.352	0.00	—	5.48(0.06)	65
		(0.08)	(0.34)				
		(0.08)	(0.33)				
	2	−0.073	−16.222	0.04	—	6.34(0.04)	29
		(1.61)	(1.06)				
		(1.84)	(1.28)				

BP, UK pound–US dollar; DM, Deutschmark–US dollar; JY, Japanese yen–US dollar; SF, Swiss franc–US dollar; R^2, coefficient of determination; DF, degrees of freedom; χ, a linear Wald test with a chi-squared distribution. The numbers in parenthesis next to the statistics are marginal significance levels; the numbers in parenthesis immediately below the point estimates are OLS t ratios and the second set of numbers in parenthesis are t ratios calculated using Hansen's method of moments (the latter allow for conditional heteroscedasticity and the MA 1 error process implied by the overlapping contracts). Full denotes the full sample and 1 and 2 denote subsamples 1 and 2 respectively (see text for definitions).

$$(i - i^*)_t = \Delta s^e_{t+2} + \theta_t \tag{9.6}$$

Equation (9.6) will be relevant if agents are risk averse and therefore have to be compensated for taking open positions in foreign currency, at time t, by a risk premium θ_t. In using (9.6) we may decompose the plim of β_1 in (9.5) into

$$\beta_1 = \frac{\text{cov}[u_{t+2}, (i - i^*)_t] + \text{cov}(\Delta s^e_{t+2}, \theta_t)}{\text{var}(i - i^*)_t} \tag{9.7}$$

Following Frankel and Froot (1986a), β_1 may be written as

$$\beta_1 = 1 - \beta_{\text{re}} - \beta_\theta \tag{9.8}$$

That is, β_1 is equal to unity (the null) minus a term β_{re} due to the failure of rational expectations to hold and minus a term β_θ due to the existence of a risk premium, where

$$\beta_{\text{re}} = \frac{\text{cov}[u_{t+2}, (i - i^*)_t]}{\text{var}(i - i^*)_t}$$

$$\beta_\theta = \frac{\text{var}(\theta_t) + \text{cov}(\Delta s^e_{t+2}, \theta_t)}{\text{var}(i - i^*)_t}$$

The availability of independent information on expectations permits us to determine whether deviations of β_1 from unity are due to risk aversion or irrationality or both. We now turn to estimates of β_{re} and β_θ for our chosen currencies and sample periods.

In table 9.2 we report our estimates of β_{re}. Such estimates are obtained by regressing the survey forecast error $s^e_{t+2} - s_{t+2}$ on the interest differential, i.e.

$$s^e_{t+2} - s_{t+2} = \alpha_{\text{re}} + \beta_{\text{re}}(i - i^*)_t + u_{t+2} \tag{9.9}$$

A test of rationality may be performed by testing whether $\alpha_{\text{re}} = \beta_{\text{re}} = 0$. Interestingly, eight (out of 12) of the point estimates of β_{re} are significantly different from zero at the 95 per cent level (on the basis of the method-of-moments standard errors) and a number of estimates of α_{re} are also statistically significant. There appears to be no consistently clear pattern of irrationality across exchange markets or subsamples. Thus, although the point estimates of β_{re} are significant for all four exchange markets, the significance of subsample results varies between currencies. Not surprisingly, given the above, the joint null hypothesis $\alpha_{\text{re}} = 0$ and $\beta_{\text{re}} = 0$ is rejected at the 95 per cent level or better for all cases except the full-sample Japanese yen.

Our estimates of the β_θ term are obtained in the following way. As we have noted, the derivation of (9.5) relies on the absence of a time-dependent risk premium. This assumption, however, may be explicitly tested by estimating the following equation by ordinary least squares (OLS):

$$\Delta s^e_{t+2} = \rho_0 + \rho_1(i - i^*)_t + v_{t+2} \tag{9.10}$$

Table 9.2 Regression-based tests of rational expectations

$$s^e_{t+2} - s_{t+2} = \alpha_{re} + \beta_{re}(i - i^*)_t$$

		α_{re}	β_{re}	R^2	$\chi^{\alpha=0}_{\beta=0}$	DF
BP	Full	−0.014	8.201	0.18	19.63(0.00)	120
		(3.65)	(5.29)			
		(3.69)	(3.74)			
	1	−0.015	2.108	0.01	12.93(0.00)	64
		(4.44)	(0.70)			
		(3.38)	(0.65)			
	2	−0.066	23.009	0.13	7.23(0.02)	54
		(2.24)	(2.81)			
		(1.85)	(2.15)			
DM	Full	0.033	12.307	0.11	14.69(0.00)	120
		(3.47)	(3.84)			
		(2.90)	(3.68)			
	1	0.015	8.985	0.07	17.22(0.00)	64
		(1.05)	(2.23)			
		(0.89)	(2.00)			
	2	−0.006	−10.408	0.02	6.18(0.04)	54
		(0.30)	(1.14)			
		(0.29)	(1.04)			
JY	Full	0.018	7.406	0.04	4.58(0.10)	120
		(2.39)	(2.37)			
		(1.83)	(2.13)			
	1	0.005	4.732	0.02	5.97(0.05)	64
		(0.33)	(1.04)			
		(0.27)	(0.99)			
	2	−0.005	−15.539	0.05	10.64(0.00)	54
		(0.44)	(1.78)			
		(0.45)	(2.08)			
SF	Full	0.041	10.606	0.11	12.63(0.00)	96
		(2.88)	(3.48)			
		(1.92)	(2.56)			
	1	−0.015	0.611	0.00	9.98(0.01)	65
		(0.74)	(0.16)			
		(0.58)	(0.13)			
	2	0.018	30.329	0.09	9.44(0.01)	29
		(2.02)	(1.68)			
		(2.95)	(2.63)			

For definitions see table 9.1.

If agents are risk neutral it is expected that $\rho_1 = 1$. In fact a test of $\rho_1 = 1$ is equivalent to a test of $\beta_\theta = 0$, since

$$\rho_1 = 1 - \frac{\text{var}(\theta_t) + \text{cov}(\Delta s_{t+2}^e, \theta)}{\text{var}(i - i^*)_t} \qquad (9.11)$$

$$= 1 - \beta_\theta$$

or

$$\beta_\theta = 1 - \rho_1$$

Our estimates of ρ_1, and therefore by implication β_θ, are presented in table 9.3. Note that in the majority of cases the point estimates of ρ_1 are insignificantly different from zero and, of those that are statistically significant, all but one are more than two standard errors away from unity (on the basis of the $t_{\rho 1} = 1$ statistic, calculated using the method-of-moments standard errors). The only point estimate favourable to the hypothesis $\beta_\theta = 0$ is that for the UK pound over the full sample; however, this result is not robust with respect to the sample split. The conclusion to emerge from the results in table 9.3 is that part of the failure of equation (9.5) to hold may be traced to the existence of a risk premium.

9.4 CONCLUSION

Previous tests of UIP have been hampered by the jointness of the hypothesis under consideration. Thus all the extant empirical research on UIP relies on the assumption of rational expectations. In this paper we have used survey data to determine whether it is the rational expectations or the risk neutrality leg of the joint hypothesis that is responsible for the often-cited rejection of the UIP condition. We find that rejection is due to problems with both legs of the joint hypothesis: foreign exchange market agents do not appear to be 'rational' and they require the incentive of a risk premium in order to be persuaded to hold foreign bonds. Clearly our findings have important implications for exchange rate models which rely on the simple UIP condition for their derivation and also for the operation of macroeconomic policy: to the extent that the 'irrationality' noted above is reflected in excessive exchange rate volatility,[3] there is a potential role for stabilizing central bank intervention, perhaps of a co-ordinated type.

Notes

We are grateful to Mr Raymond Attrill of Money Market Services Ltd of London for his help in providing us with the expectational survey data used in this paper.

Table 9.3 Regression-based tests of perfect substitutability

$$\Delta s^e_{t+2} = \rho_0 + \rho_1(i-i^*)_t$$

		ρ_0	ρ_1	R^2	$t\rho_1=1$	$\chi^{\rho_0=0}_{\rho_1=1}$	DF
BP	Full	−0.001 (1.35) (2.11)	0.901 (2.34) (1.90)	0.04	−0.21	4.78(0.09)	120
	1	−0.001 (1.72) (1.69)	−0.181 (0.29) (0.30)	0.00	—	5.85(0.05)	64
	2	−0.018 (2.36) (2.97)	5.747 (2.63) (3.19)	0.11	2.17	9.61(0.01)	54
DM	Full	−0.006 (1.91) (1.39)	0.424 (0.47) (0.41)	0.00	—	9.99(0.01)	120
	1	−0.005 (1.48) (1.46)	0.579 (0.57) (0.58)	0.00	—	14.63(0.00)	64
	2	−0.013 (2.07) (1.75)	−3.802 (1.31) (1.13)	0.03	—	3.72(0.15)	54
JY	Full	−0.008 (4.59) (4.44)	−0.646 (0.82) (0.96)	0.01	—	28.08(0.00)	120
	1	−0.015 (4.48) (4.58)	−2.088 (1.91) (2.19)	0.05	3.24	32.42(0.00)	64
	2	−0.014 (4.38) (5.63)	−6.342 (2.88) (3.18)	0.13	3.68	38.79(0.00)	54
SF	Full	−0.003 (0.54) (0.44)	1.054 (0.76) (0.70)	0.01	—	5.55(0.06)	96
	1	−0.013 (1.96) (1.78)	−0.741 (0.59) (0.50)	0.01	—	14.49(0.00)	65
	2	0.035 (1.17) (2.36)	14.107 (1.40) (2.47)	0.06	2.29	5.58(0.00)	29

For definitions see table 9.1.

MacDonald acknowledges financial assistance from the Scottish Economic Society.

1 Thus if UIP fails due to risk aversion the portfolio balance model of the exchange rate is appropriate and not the monetary model. This in turn has the policy implication that sterilized foreign exchange market intervention will be efficacious. If, however, rejection is due to speculation which is excessive relative to the information set, then there may be a role for foreign exchange market intervention to attenuate exchange rate movements.

2 This expectational series contains a small number of missing observations, corresponding to public holidays. To obtain expectation points for these missing values we regressed the survey data expectations against the series of current spot rates and a constant up to the break point. The point estimates were then used to obtain any subsequent missing expected values.

3 See MacDonald and Torrance (1988c) for a further discussion of the extrapolative nature of exchange rate expectations for the sample periods considered in this paper.

Part IV
Open Economy
Macroeconomics

10 Crowding-out and Pulling-in of Fiscal Policy under Fixed and Flexible Exchange Rates

Robin Bladen Hovell and Christopher Green

10.1 INTRODUCTION

The theory of the small open economy has been intensively investigated over the last two decades. The objectives of this chapter are, to some extent, those of recapitulation and synthesis of standard neo-Keynesian models which build on the work of Mundell (1963b) and Fleming (1962). A short list of such models might include those of Turnovsky (1972, ch. 9), Argy and Salop (1979), Dornbusch and Fischer (1980), Frenkel et al. (1980), Branson and Buiter (1983), Ahtiala (1984) and Kawai (1985). A closer look at these and related papers reveals that the complexity of a small open economy is such that it is difficult to build theoretical models which are simultaneously general, comprehensible and interesting. Investigators are typically obliged to make relatively arbitrary simplifying assumptions in order to focus on the questions of interest. Thus, Turnovsky mainly analyses a model with perfect capital mobility and fixed exchange rates. Argy and Salop focus on supply-side issues but assume perfect capital mobility; Dornbusch and Fischer and Branson and Buiter have analysed models in which wealth effects are fully specified but the former assume fixed real incomes while the latter mainly assume perfect capital mobility and fixed product prices. Frenkel et al. ignore wealth effects as does Ahtiala; the focus of their papers is on clarifying 'monetarist' and 'Keynesian' views of balance of payments determination. Kawai's contribution also assumes perfect capital mobility.

Our concern in the present chapter is with the implication of different

We thank Ron MacDonald, Mark Taylor and participants in the Manchester research seminar for their helpful comments on an earlier draft of this chapter.

monetary policy regimes in the short run. Our analysis includes five distinctive features. First, the supply side of the model determines domestic product prices and retail prices, allowing for an effect of exchange rate changes on domestic prices. Second, we provide for less than perfect capital mobility. Third, we propose an eclectic scheme for the treatment of expectation formation which forces us neither to ignore expectations altogether, as do some economists, nor to assume rational expectations, as do the rest. Rational expectations may be a satisfactory assumption for the medium term but it appears to us to be distinctly doubtful as a representation of the rather short-run period with which the Mundell–Fleming model is concerned. Fourth, we consider a wider range of monetary policy regimes than is common in such models. In particular, we investigate the strategies of targeting, respectively, money, the exchange rate, the nominal interest rate, the real interest rate, and the foreign uncovered interest differential. As a convenient way of unifying the discussion of these policy regimes we investigate the different degrees of crowding-out (or 'pulling-in') of government spending under each of the different regimes. Fifth, in order to make the analysis relatively accessible, we have developed a geometric technique which provides for the analysis of simultaneous variations in output and prices under different monetary regimes. This geometry makes comparisons between regimes intuitively clearer than does the more usual grinding out of multipliers, and it appears to us to be a natural extension of Mundell's well-known diagrams.

The chapter is organized as follows. The structure of the model is outlined in sections 10.2–10.4, where we discuss the main assumptions and compare the model with the familiar Mundell–Fleming framework. In section 10.5 we develop the geometric technique for analysing the model which also shows the manner in which the standard Mundell–Fleming results are modified in the presence of variable prices. In sections 10.6–10.8 we set out the different monetary policy options available to the authorities and discuss multiplier magnitudes and the crowding-out of fiscal policy under fixed and flexible exchange rates. A summary and concluding comments are contained in section 10.9.

10.2 THE MODEL

The model has standard open-economy IS–LM features and is set out as follows:

$$Y = H\left(Y, r - \frac{P^e}{P} + 1, \frac{E}{Q}\right) + X\left(\frac{E}{Q}\right) + G \tag{10.1}$$

$$\frac{M}{P} = L(Y, r) \tag{10.2}$$

$$M = M_{-1} + sB + D \tag{10.3}$$

$$B = QX\left(\frac{E}{Q}\right) - EZ\left(Y, \frac{E}{Q}\right) + F\left(r - r^* - \frac{E^e}{E} + 1\right) \tag{10.4}$$

$$Q = U(Y,E) \tag{10.5}$$

$$P = Q^\alpha E^{1-\alpha} \tag{10.6}$$

The variables are defined as follows: Y, domestic income; H, total private expenditure on domestic goods; X, total exports; G, government spending (taxes are set to zero for simplicity but could easily be included); Z, imports (Y, H, X, G and Z are all defined at constant prices); M, the nominal quantity of money; B, overall balance on the balance of payments; D, the autonomous part of domestic credit expansion (DCE); F, net capital inflow; Q, the price of domestically produced goods and services ($q \equiv \ln Q$); P, retail price index ($p \equiv \ln P$); E, spot exchange rate (the price of foreign currency) ($e \equiv \ln E$); r, nominal interest rate; r^*, foreign interest rate (foreign prices are normalized at unity). P^e and E^e refer to the expectation formed in the current time period of P and E in the next time period. Thus $r - P^e/P + 1$ is the real interest rate and $r - r^* - E^e/E + 1$ is the uncovered foreign interest differential.

The derivatives of the functions and coefficients are signed as follows:

$$1 > H_1 > 0 \qquad H_2 < 0 \qquad H_3 > 0 \qquad X' > 0 \tag{10.1'}$$

$$L_1 > 0 \qquad L_2 < 0 \tag{10.2'}$$

$$0 \leqslant s \leqslant 1 \tag{10.3'}$$

$$X' > 0 \qquad H_1 > Z_1 > 0 \qquad Z_2 < 0 \qquad \infty > F' > 0 \tag{10.4'}$$

$$U_1 > 0 \qquad U_2 > 0 \tag{10.5'}$$

$$0 < \alpha < 1 \tag{10.6'}$$

Equation (10.1) shows income to be the sum of domestic private expenditures, foreign expenditures on domestic goods, and government purchases. Equation (10.2) is the demand for money. The signs of the derivatives in these equations are standard. Equation (10.3) is the money supply identity which shows the current money stock to be equal to the sum of the (predetermined) previous period's stock (M_{-1}) and the new money originating from the balance of payments (B) and autonomous DCE (D); s is a sterilization parameter, complete sterilization occurring when $s = 0$ and no sterilization when $s = 1$. Equation (10.4) gives the balance of payments. We make the simplifying assumption that the real interest rate has no effect on imports.[1] Capital flows are assumed to respond to the differential between the domestic and foreign interest rate adjusted for the expected change in the exchange rate.[2] We also assume that capital mobility is less than perfect ($F' < \infty$), giving some scope for an independent interest rate policy.

The supply side of the economy is summarized by equations (10.5) and (10.6). The latter is simply a Cobb–Douglas price index with weights α, $1 - \alpha$ being given by the shares of expenditures on domestic and foreign goods at some base date. Equation (10.5) could be justified in a number of ways. We prefer to think of it as a reduced form representation of the labour market. Contract wages are determined by retail prices,[3] whereas actual wages differ from those in the contract as the level of income affects the amount of short-time or overtime worked. Domestic product prices are marked up over wages. Eliminating wages from this scheme yields equation (10.5).

The exact specification of the model could, no doubt, be debated. Small changes of specification (such as the inclusion or exclusion of price expectations in specific equations) would make no essential difference to the analysis. The main specification issue would appear to involve our treatment of wealth effects, and this we now explain briefly. Our concern in the analysis is with a single time period which is sufficiently short that wealth effects arising from the net acquisition or disposal of assets and liabilities can be ignored. Thus, the stock of wealth is not included explicitly as an argument in asset demand functions, and we do not distinguish sharply between 'stock' and 'flow' views of the capital account of the balance of payments (see note 2). We assume that stocks of assets in the previous period are predetermined. By adding to these stocks (possibly endogenous) current flows, we obtain the current period's stocks. From the viewpoint of the mathematics, an equilibrium of the model is static, but the economics imply that the equilibrium is temporary, for the economy will evolve over time as the stocks of assets and liabilities which are predetermined in the model change from period to period (see Tobin, 1979). Strictly, we should model the entire process, but this is a complex problem and would take us too far from our immediate objectives.

10.3 EXPECTATIONS

Although the analysis is comparative static throughout, we shall be comparing equilibria which have different price levels and exchange rates and therefore probably different expectations of future values of these variables. It is well known that a change in, say, the actual exchange rate will probably induce some change in exchange rate expectations. To manage this in an eclectic way, we propose to use the concept of the elasticity of expectations which shows the proportionate response of expectations to a change in the underlying variable. For the price level

$$\pi \equiv \frac{\partial \ln P^e}{\partial \ln P} \geqslant 0$$

For the exchange rate

$$\eta \equiv \frac{\partial \ln E^{e}}{\partial \ln E} \geq 0$$

In the static one-period framework, we can represent different expectation formation schemes as follows:

Static expectations	$\pi = 0; \eta = 0$
Regressive expectations	$\pi < 1; \eta < 1$
Extrapolative expectations	$\pi > 1; \eta > 1$

It is sensible to impose the assumption of consistency by which we simply mean that agents form expectations with the help of the price index ((10.6) which, unlike the behavioural relations, is objective information) and that therefore

$$P^{e} = (Q^{e})^{\alpha}(E^{e})^{1-\alpha} \tag{10.7}$$

Using lower-case letters for natural logarithms, taking logs on both sides of (10.6) and (10.7) and differentiating gives

$$\frac{dp^{e}}{dp} = \frac{\alpha\, dq^{e} + (1-\alpha)\, de^{e}}{\alpha\, dq + (1-\alpha)\, de} \tag{10.8}$$

Using the elasticity definitions and $\mu \equiv \partial \ln Q^{e}/\partial \ln Q$ in (8.10) and rearranging gives

$$\pi = \frac{\alpha\mu\, dq/de + (1-\alpha)\eta}{\alpha\, dq/de + 1-\alpha} \tag{10.9}$$

Equation (10.9) shows the relation which must hold between π and η if agents are able to compute the retail price index. The exact relation will obviously depend on agents' perceptions of the linkages between foreign and domestic prices (dq/de). By manipulating (10.9) it is easily seen that the assumption of consistency does not impose any strong restrictions on the value of π and η. In particular, we do not require $\pi = \eta$, nor do we require that π and η lie on the same side of unity. It is worth emphasizing, therefore, that any combination of values of π and η could be plausible in the short run, particularly if agents are faced with the problem of determining whether a particular shock to the system is temporary or permanent.

What constitute plausible values of these elasticities will depend in part on the long-run environment within which we assume the short-run model to be embedded. If, for example, the core inflation rate in the domestic economy is positive and equal to that in the rest of the world,[4] it could be sensible to assume $\eta < 1$ and $\pi > 1$. For exchange rate expectations, an element of regressivity $(\eta < 1)$ is probably plausible; for the price *level*, static or extrapolative expectations $(\pi \geq 1)$ may be more plausible.

10.4 THE MUNDELL–FLEMING FRAMEWORK

When set within the Mundell-Fleming framework, our model has two basic versions – a fixed exchange rate regime with variable foreign reserves and a flexible exchange rate regime with constant foreign reserves. The fiscal policy instrument is government spending, and it is convenient to let the monetary policy instrument be domestic credit expansion, assuming in other words that there is no sterilization.[5]

As a main object of the present exercise is to study different monetary rules, it is convenient to reduce the equation system (10.1)–(10.6) to three relationships involving real income, the nominal interest rate and the exchange rate. To save space, in general we shall not analyse the behaviour of the price level explicitly, but similar exercises could be carried out involving prices instead of real income. We therefore eliminate M between (10.2) and (10.3), use (10.5) and (10.6) to eliminate prices from equations (10.1), (10.2) and (10.4), and totally differentiate the remaining three equations to work out the standard comparative static multiplier effects of an increase in government spending with fixed DCE. The equation systems for the fixed and flexible exchange rate regimes can be written out in full as follows: for a fixed exchange rate

$$\begin{pmatrix} a_{11} & a_{12} & 0 \\ a_{21} & a_{22} & a_{24} \\ a_{31} & a_{32} & a_{34} \end{pmatrix} \begin{pmatrix} dY \\ dr \\ dB \end{pmatrix} = \begin{pmatrix} dG \\ 0 \\ 0 \end{pmatrix} \tag{10.10}$$

and for a flexible exchange rate

$$\begin{pmatrix} a_{11} & a_{12} & a_{13} \\ a_{21} & a_{22} & a_{23} \\ a_{31} & a_{32} & a_{33} \end{pmatrix} \begin{pmatrix} dY \\ dr \\ de \end{pmatrix} = \begin{pmatrix} dG \\ 0 \\ 0 \end{pmatrix} \tag{10.11}$$

Here

$$1 - H_1 + \frac{U_1\alpha}{Q}\left[\alpha^{-1}\sigma(H_3 + X') - H_2(1-\pi)\frac{P^e}{P}\right] = a_{11} > 0$$

$$- H_2 = a_{12} > 0$$

$$- \left[H_2(1-\pi)\frac{P^e}{P}(1-\alpha\psi) + \sigma\psi X'\right] = a_{13} < 0$$

$$L_1 + L(.)\frac{U_1\alpha}{Q} = a_{21} > 0$$

$$L_2 = a_{22} < 0$$

$$(1-\alpha\psi)L(.) = a_{23} > 0$$

$$- \frac{s}{P} = a_{24} < 0$$

$$Z_1 - \frac{\theta U_1}{Q} \qquad\qquad = a_{31} > 0$$

$$-\frac{F'}{E} \qquad\qquad = a_{32} < 0$$

$$\psi\theta - \frac{F'}{E}\frac{E^e}{E}(1 - \eta) \qquad\qquad = a_{33} < 0$$

$$\frac{1}{E} \qquad\qquad = a_{34} > 0$$

and

$$\frac{E}{Q} \qquad\qquad \equiv \sigma > 0$$

$$1 - U_2\sigma \qquad\qquad \equiv \psi \geqslant 0$$

$$\frac{X(.)}{\sigma} - X' + Z_2\sigma \equiv \theta < 0$$

The signs of the parameters in equations (10.10) and (10.11) are generally straightforward to determine. ψ is zero or greater provided that the elasticity of domestic prices with respect to foreign prices ($U_2\sigma \equiv \partial q/\partial e$) is not greater than unity, and $\theta < 0$ is needed to satisfy the Marshall–Lerner conditions. These two conditions unambiguously sign all the parameters except those involving expectations elasticities. Of these, $\pi \leqslant 1$ is sufficient to guarantee $a_{11} > 0$; if $\pi > 1$, we shall assume that it is not so large as to make $a_{11} < 0$. Similarly $\eta < 1$ is sufficient to guarantee $a_{33} < 0$; if $\eta > 1$, we shall assume that it does not change the sign of a_{33}. For a_{13}, $\pi > 1$ would be needed to guarantee that $a_{13} < 0$; in practice, it is rarely necessary to sign a_{13} explicitly, although on occasion it is helpful for expositional purposes to assume $a_{13} < 0$.

We shall denote determinants of the equation systems as $\Delta(i,j)$, i referring to the exchange rate regime and j to the monetary policy regime. Equations (10.10) and (10.11) correspond to fixed (e) and flexible (B) exchange rates and constant DCE (D). The signs of the determinants are, for fixed rates,

$$\Delta(e,D) < 0$$

and for flexible rates

$$\Delta(B,D) > 0$$

$\Delta(e,D)$ is guaranteed negative but the sign of $\Delta(B,D)$ is ambiguous. Although we can appeal to Samuelson's (1947) correspondence principle to require that $\Delta(B,D)$ be positive, it is in any event most unlikely that $\Delta(B,D)$ will be negative. This can be seen by observing that the condition that $\Delta(B,D)$ be positive is equivalent to requiring that the full equilibrium effect of a devaluation under otherwise fixed exchange rates is to improve the overall balance of payments. The channels by which a devaluation works can be classified into four groups.

1 The direct current account effect: an improvement in competitiveness improves the current balance provided that the Marshall–Lerner conditions are satisfied.
2 The direct capital account effect: given some regressivity in exchange rate expectations, a devaluation sets up an expectation of a partial revaluation and induces a capital inflow.
3 Indirect effects which improve the balance of payments: for example, a devaluation increases the price level, reduces real cash balances and thus raises the nominal interest rate. This improves both the current account (by depressing incomes) and the capital account (through a capital inflow).
4 Indirect effects which 'perversely' worsen the balance of payments: the main such effect is that the rise in exports expands demand and hence imports. However, an expansion of demand also raises interest rates and improves the capital account. Thus, the expansion in demand only worsens the overall balance if capital flows are relatively interest inelastic and the marginal propensity to import relatively high (or if the LM schedule is flatter than the balance of payments (BB) schedule).

$\Delta(B,D)$ would be negative only if the perverse effects of an exchange rate change were sufficiently large to offset the customary effects, making for an improvement in the balance of payments. As this possibility seems remote, $\Delta(B,D) > 0$ is plausible as well as being required for stability.

10.5 GEOMETRIC ANALYSIS

Before studying the multipliers of the model, it will prove useful to develop the technique for analysing the model geometrically. Consider equations (10.10) and (10.11) with the exchange rate and reserve flows (temporarily) fixed. We then have three relationships between income and nominal interest rate given by

$$a_{11} \, dY + a_{12} \, dr = 0 \tag{10.12}$$

$$a_{21} \, dY + a_{22} \, dr = 0 \tag{10.13}$$

$$a_{31} \, dY + a_{32} \, dr = 0 \tag{10.14}$$

Equation (10.12) shows the combinations of income and the interest rate consistent with simultaneous equilibrium in the product market and the labour market. We call this relation the ISP curve because each point on the curve corresponds to a different price level as well as to a different combination of income and the interest rate. The ISP curve is unambiguously steeper than the usual IS curve drawn for a constant price level because, with flexible prices, a part of an increase (say) in aggregate nominal demand results in higher prices, whereas with fixed prices the entire increase in nominal demand is reflected in higher real income. In other words, the difference between the ISP curve and the IS curve is due to the fact that the former reflects an upward-sloping and the latter a horizontal supply schedule. Similarly, equation (10.13) is dubbed the LMP curve. LMP is steeper than LM as any increase (say) in real income is associated with an increase in prices to maintain labour market equilibrium. Thus, the demand for money increases by more than if prices were fixed and it takes a larger rise in the interest rate to restore money market equilibrium.

These relationships are drawn in figure 10.1 where we also carry out the classroom exercise of increasing the level of government spending. This is represented by a shift in IS to IS' and in ISP to ISP'. We can then show the increase $Y_0 Y_1$ in the level of real income with fixed prices, given by the inter-

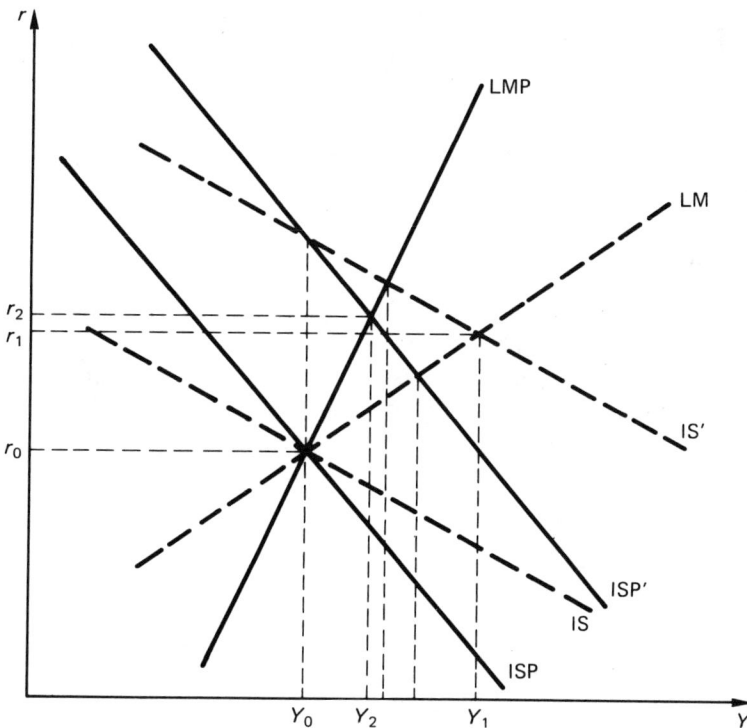

Figure 10.1   Increase in government spending with constant money supply

section of IS' and LM, and the increase $Y_0 Y_2$ which occurs with flexible prices, given by the intersection of ISP' and LMP. The latter is, of course, smaller and we can identify the amount of crowding-out of private spending due to the rise in the price level as $Y_2 Y_1$. This, in turn, can be divided into two components. The first is an expenditure effect: with a constant exchange rate, higher prices tend to reduce exports and, in so far as there is any regressivity in price expectations, higher prices lower inflation expectations and crowd out private spending by raising the real interest rate. The second is the Keynes' effect: higher prices reduce real cash balances and crowd out private spending by raising the interest rate. It is worth observing that, although the transmission process of higher prices involves a change in the interest rate, the crowding-out is due to the price change, not the interest rate changes which may follow. This can be seen by noting that although in figure 10.1 the flexible price level multiplier produces a higher interest rate (r_2) than the fixed price level multiplier (r_1), it is equally possible for the flexible price level multiplier to generate a lower interest rate.[6]

Analogous reasoning leads us to label equation (10.14) the BBP schedule which shows combinations of income and the rate of interest consistent with equilibrium in the labour market and in the balance of payments. As before, BBP is steeper than BB in (r, Y) space. However, for familiar reasons, the BBP schedule may be steeper or flatter than the LMP schedule. It is often assumed that the interest elasticity of capital flows is relatively large in comparison with the interest elasticity of demand for money, implying that BBP is flatter than LMP, the extreme case of perfect capital mobility being associated with a horizontal BBP schedule.

To complete the geometry, we incorporate changes in exchange rates and reserves. Exchange rate changes will shift all three schedules and reserve flows shift the LMP and BBP schedules. To manage this systematically, we proceed in an analogous manner to Mundell by developing the aggregate demand (XXP) and external balance (FFP) schedules.

The aggregate demand schedule shows combinations of real income and the exchange rate consistent with equilibrium in all markets except the balance of payments. We obtain this schedule by setting dG to zero and eliminating dr between the first two rows of equation (10.11) to obtain

$$
\left. \frac{dY}{de} \right|_{\text{XXP}} = \frac{\overset{-}{a_{13}} - \overset{+}{a_{12}} \overset{+}{a_{23}}/\overset{-}{a_{22}}}{\underset{+}{a_{11}} - \underset{+}{a_{12}} \underset{+}{a_{21}}/\underset{-}{a_{22}}}
\tag{10.15}
$$

with the parameters signed as shown. Clearly, the slope of XXP depends on the sign of the numerator. The denominator is unambiguously positive, showing that a rise in income reduces the net excess demand for goods (i.e. expenditures increase by less than income). However, the effects of a devaluation are ambiguous.

1 *Expenditure effects* (given by a_{13}) are expansionary: the improvement in competitiveness expands exports ($\sigma\psi X'$ in a_{13}) and, in so far as price expectations are extrapolative, the real interest rate will fall as the exchange rate falls and increases the price level ($H_2(1 - \pi)(P^e/P)(1 - \alpha\psi)$ in a_{13}). If these expenditure effects are dominant, then $dY/de > 0$ and it will take a devaluation to restore equilibrium after a rise in income.

2 The Keynes' effect (given by $a_{12}a_{23}/a_{22}$) is contractionary as it raises the interest rate because of the fall in real cash balances. If this effect is dominant then $dY/de < 0$ and it will take a revaluation to restore equilibrium after a rise in income.

In general, the more rapidly is a devaluation reflected in domestic prices, the more the Keynes effect will tend to be dominant. Here, the price effect adds an important element of ambiguity to the Mundell–Fleming set-up. When prices are fixed, the aggregate demand schedule is always positively sloped.

In a similar way, the external balance schedule shows combinations of real income and the exchange rate consistent with equilibrium in all markets except that for domestic expenditures and is obtained by eliminating dr between the last two rows of equation (10.11):

$$\frac{dY}{de}\bigg|_{FFP} = -\frac{(\overset{-}{a_{33}} - \overset{-}{a_{32}}\overset{+}{a_{23}}/\overset{-}{a_{22}})}{(\underset{+}{a_{31}} - \underset{-}{a_{32}}\underset{+}{a_{21}}/\underset{-}{a_{22}})} \qquad (10.16)$$

The numerator is unambiguously positive, showing that apart from expenditure effects a devaluation improves the balance of payments. The ambiguity of the denominator is straightforward: $-a_{31}/a_{32}$ is the slope of the BBP schedule, whereas $-a_{21}/a_{22}$ is the slope of the LMP schedule. If the

Table 10.1 Configurations of the economy

	Expenditure effects dominate Keynes effect	Keynes effect dominates expenditure effects
LMP steeper than BBP (interest-elastic capital flows)	(i) $dY/de\|_{XXP} > 0$ $dY/de\|_{FFP} < 0$	(ii) $dY/de\|_{XXP} < 0$ $dY/de\|_{FFP} < 0$
BBP steeper than LMP (interest-inelastic capital flows)	(iii) $dY/de\|_{XXP} > 0$ $dY/de\|_{FFP} > 0$	(iv) $dY/de\|_{XXP} < 0$ $dY/de\|_{FFP} > 0$

LMP schedule is steeper than the BBP schedule the denominator is negative, meaning that an increase in income improves the balance of payments as the capital account improves more than the current account deteriorates. Accordingly, a devaluation must be accompanied by a fall in income to maintain balance of payments equilibrium and $dY/de < 0$. The reverse is true when the LMP schedule is flatter than the BBP schedule.

Thus, there are two principal sources of ambiguity in the structure of the economy. The first is due to the impact of price changes and to whether relative price changes (expenditure effects) are more important than absolute price changes (the Keynes effect). The second is the familiar problem of the relative magnitudes of the interest and income elasticities of the demands for money and bonds which generate the relative slopes of the LMP and BBP schedules. These ambiguities give rise to four possible configurations of the economy summarized in table 10.1. In each configuration the effects of fiscal policy may be analysed under a variety of monetary regimes. It is to these regimes that we now turn.

10.6 MONETARY REGIMES

In previous papers on this subject, monetary policy was typically represented by some polar regime such as a constant money supply or constant nominal interest rate. With perfect capital mobility, the choice is between constant money supply and constant exchange rate (see Poole, 1970; Parkin, 1978; Artis and Currie, 1981). With less than perfect capital mobility, however, the authorities have an extra degree of freedom. They can choose both the exchange rate regime (fixed or flexible) and the domestic monetary regime (constant DCE or constant nominal interest rate). A variable which is held 'constant' is, of course, to be interpreted as a variable which is targeted by the monetary authorities. In the present paper we propose a modest but significant expansion in the range of possible monetary regimes. We consider the two standard exchange rate regimes and, under each of these, four different domestic monetary regimes. This makes eight policy regimes in all, as set out in table 10.2.

Under fixed exchange rates, the degree of sterilization obviously has an impact on fiscal multipliers, the two polar cases being constant DCE and constant money supply. Under flexible exchange rates, the two policies are identical as foreign reserves are constant.

A constant nominal interest rate is feasible under fixed and flexible exchange rates with less than perfect capital mobility. A constant real interest rate been proposed, on occasion, as an alternative policy in an environment in which product prices are variable. A natural extension of this idea to a small open economy is to maintain a constant differential between

Table 10.2 Monetary regimes

Flexible exchange rate		Fixed exchange rate	
1 Domestic credit		5 Domestic credit	
expansion	$dD = 0$	expansion	$dD = 0$
2 Nominal interest rate	$dr = 0$	6 Money supply	$dM = 0$
3 Real interest rate	$dR = 0$	7 Nominal interest rate	$dr = 0$
4 Foreign interest		8 Real interest rate	$dR = 0$
differential	$dC = 0$		

$R \equiv r - P^e/P + 1; \; C \equiv r - r^* - E^e/E + 1.$

domestic and foreign (nominal) interest rates adjusted for the expected change in the exchange rate. Clearly, under a (credibly) fixed exchange rate, such a constant foreign interest differential is equivalent to a constant nominal interest rate.

We interpret both the constant real interest rate and the constant foreign interest differential as modified interest rate targets. The authorities are assumed to adjust the nominal interest rate instantaneously to achieve the desired constant real interest rate or interest differential. We assume that the authorities are able to use objective information about price and exchange rate expectations in order to set the nominal interest rate at the appropriate level. This is a rather artificial assumption, though not wholly implausible (see Blanchard and Wyplosz, 1981). Provided that such information is available, we are not obliged to impose such a strong assumption as complete rationality in order to make the policies operational. These regimes are not so much 'realistic' as illustrative of the range of options which are, in practice, open to the monetary authorities, and, we would argue, are rather more suggestive of plausible operating procedures. Thus, it makes more sense to think of the authorities manipulating the nominal interest rate to achieve some objective such as a prespecified real interest rate than to achieve some arbitarily defined constant value.

10.7 GOVERNMENT EXPENDITURE MULTIPLIERS WITH CONSTANT DOMESTIC CREDIT EXPANSION

10.7.1 Flexible exchange rates

Figure 10.2 analyses the effects of an increase in government spending with constant domestic credit expansion for each of the four configurations of the economy discussed above. In each case, the increase in spending is shown as a shift of the ISP locus to ISP'. The aggregate demand schedule shifts from

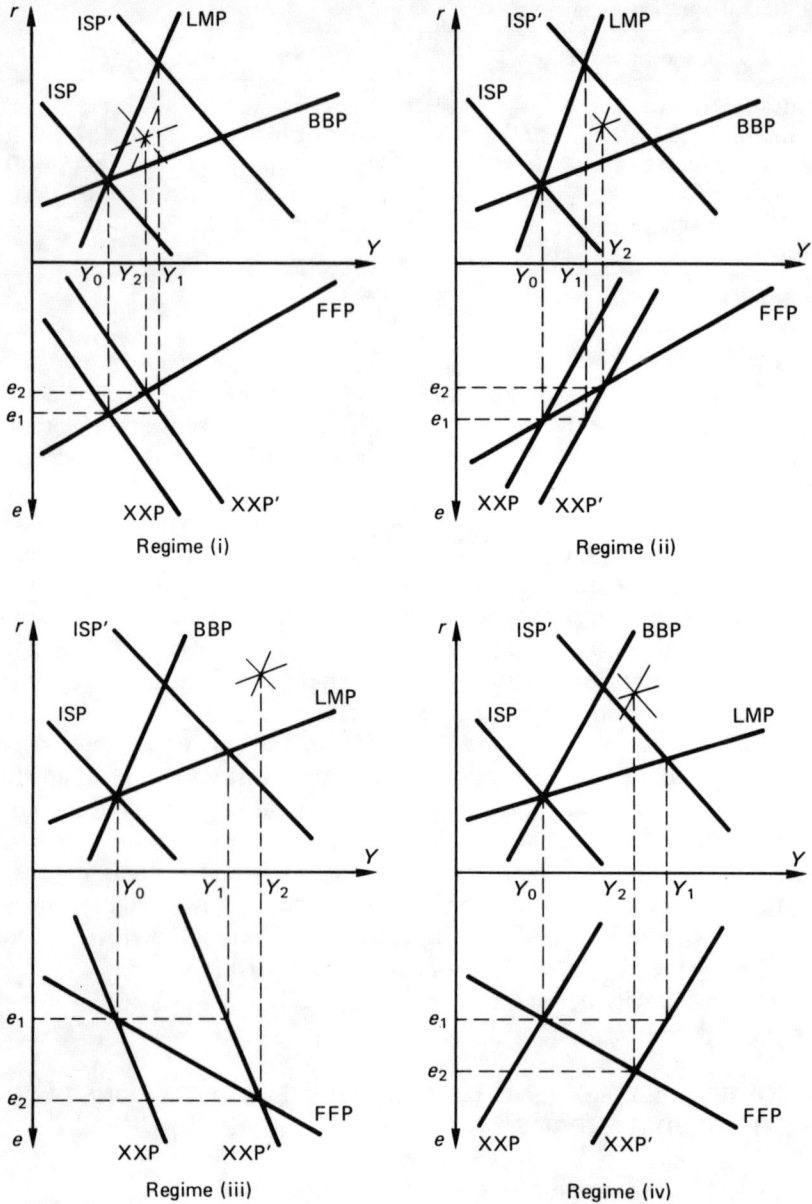

Figure 10.2   Crowding-out: flexible exchange rate and constant domestic credit expansion

XXP to XXP', a distance determined by the intersection of ISP' and LMP. Under flexible exchange rates, the external balance locus is unaffected by government spending changes and so the full equilibrium levels of income and the exchange rate (Y_2 and e_2) are given by the intersection of FFP and XXT'. As ISP', LMP and BBP are each drawn for a given exchange rate, the exchange rate change will shift these loci until they reach the full equilibrium which is shown by the intersection of the broken lines in (Y, r) space. The closed-economy equilibrium Y_1 is given by the intersection of ISP' and LMP – this is the change in aggregate demand for given exchange rate and reserve flows. Subsequent changes in income result from the exchange rate change, and therefore the difference between Y_1 and Y_2 shows the crowding-out or pulling-in of private expenditures which can be attributed to the movement in the exchange rate. Clearly, the amount of such crowding-out is determined by the slopes of both the aggregate demand and the external balance schedules.

Figure 10.3, regime (i), illustrates the standard Mundell–Fleming case in which, with relatively mobile capital, a fiscal expansion leads to an appreciation of the exchange rate and some crowding-out of private spending. In the present model, however, fiscal policy is never wholly crowded out even when international capital is perfectly mobile. With perfect capital mobility, BBP is horizontal and FFP is steeper than before, but not vertical as it is when prices are fixed. The appreciation of the exchange rate reduces domestic prices and therefore provides some expansionary influence through the increase in the real quantity of money (the Keynes effect). To put it another way, the nominal appreciation of the currency is greater than the real appreciation, and it is only the real appreciation which crowds out spending. Figure 10.2, regime (iii), shows the other standard case in which international capital is relatively immobile. In this case, fiscal policy leads to a depreciation of the currency and therefore pulls in private spending, implying that the open-economy multiplier is larger than the closed-economy multiplier.

The other two panels of figure 10.2 show less conventional cases which the introduction of variable prices makes possible. If the *expenditure effects* of an exchange rate change are weak and the *Keynes' effect* is strong (if, that is, the real exchange rate change is small relative to the nominal exchange rate change), then the aggregate demand schedule may be negatively sloped. In this case, an appreciation of the exchange rate will pull in private spending (figure 10.2, regime (ii)) and a depreciation will crowd out spending (figure 10.2, regime (iv)).

10.7.2 Fixed exchange rates

The effects of fiscal policy conducted under a fixed exchange rate regime are illustrated in figure 10.3 for each of the four configurations discussed above. However, with the exchange rate fixed, we note two important modifications to the previous analysis. First, the supply side of the economy is considerably simplified. With the removal of the linkage between the price of domestically produced goods and the exchange rate, the price level and rate of inflation are determined solely by domestic demand pressures. Second, the domestic monetary authorities may engage in sterilization policies designed to offset, more or less completely, the monetary consequences of the balance of payments. Moreover, changes in the level of foreign reserves brought about by an improvement or deterioration of the economy's external position will cause a shift of the BBP schedule.

As before, the impact of a fiscal expansion is shown as a shift of the ISP schedule to ISP' and as a movement of the aggregate demand schedule to XXP'. With the exchange rate fixed, the external balance schedules BBP and FFP respond to the change in foreign reserves and shift to BBP' and FFP' while, to the extent that the domestic monetary authorities do not sterilize, the balance of payments imbalance will feed through into the domestic supply of money. Under a policy of constant domestic credit, the degree of sterilization is zero and the consequent monetary adjustment shifts LMP and XXP to LMP' and XXP' respectively. The full equilibrium level of income is therefore given by Y_2 and the difference between Y_1 and Y_2 indicates the crowding-out or pulling-in of private sector expenditures attributable to the monetary adjustments induced by the balance of payments surplus or deficit.

Figure 10.3, regime (i), illustrates the case of a relatively high degree of capital mobility. In the extreme case of perfect mobility, the BBP schedule becomes horizontal and fiscal policy has its maximum effect upon domestic output, although the multiplier response is still smaller than that encountered in the Mundell–Fleming framework because of the effect of higher prices on international competitiveness and the real value of cash balances. Reducing the degree of capital mobility increases the degree of crowding-out in the model as the interest rate is able to increase. In comparison with the closed-economy equilibrium at Y_1, the degree of crowding-out or pulling-in depends upon the relative slopes of the LMP and BBP schedules. Thus, under configuration (i) where the LMP curve is steeper, the surplus on the balance of payments relaxes monetary conditions and pulls in private expenditures in comparison with the closed-economy equilibrium at Y_1. The reverse is true of the opposite configuration of the LMP and BBP schedules (figure 10.3, regime (iii)) since the resultant deterioration of the balance of

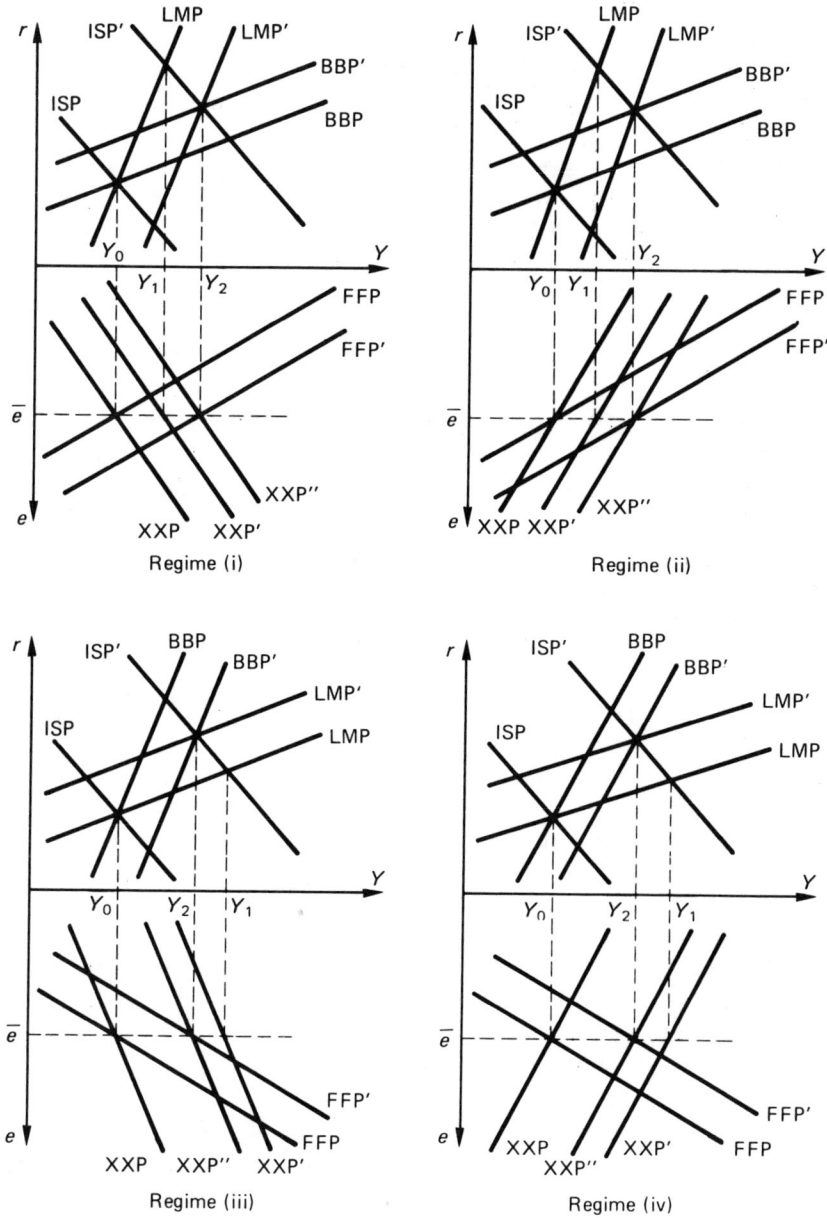

Figure 10.3 Crowding-out: fixed exchange rate and constant domestic credit expansion

payments serves to reduce the domestic money supply. Moreover, even if the degree of capital mobility is zero (the BBP schedule is vertical), fiscal policy continues to have some effect upon the level of output in the short run, the new higher income level being financed by a loss of foreign reserves which obviously cannot continue indefinitely.

In the fixed exchange rate case, configurations (ii) and (iv) are similar to (i) and (iii) respectively. Because the exchange rate is fixed, there are no independent external pressures on domestic prices which therefore always tend to move in the same direction as domestic output. Accordingly, expenditure and cash balance effects are always mutually reinforcing rather than offsetting as they may be in the flexible rate case.

10.8 CROWDING-OUT UNDER ALTERNATIVE MONETARY REGIMES

10.8.1 Flexible exchange rates

Clearly, it would be tedious to analyse each of the monetary regimes appropriate to flexible exchange rates for all four possible configurations of the economy. We have already analysed the regime of constant DCE and two simple arguments will show that the three remaining regimes automatically simplify the structure of the economy in a straightforward way.

First, regimes (2), (3) and (4) can be interpreted as regimes of monetary accommodation in which DCE is endogenously adjusted to achieve the desired interest rate target. In all three cases the LMP curve is horizontal, although in regimes (3) and (4) it is adjusted upwards or downwards depending on the endogenous variations in prices or the exchange rate. Second, we noted two conflicting influences of the exchange rate on real income: the expenditure effect by which a devaluation tends to expand real income; and the Keynes effect by which it tends to reduce income. It is intuitively obvious, therefore, that in a regime of monetary accommodation in which the authorities aim at an interest rate target, the money supply will be adjusted so as to offset the effects of price changes on real cash balances. Accordingly, the Keynes effect will automatically be stifled and the expenditure effect will always be dominant.

The first point means that we can confine our attention to configurations in which the LMP locus is flatter than the BBP locus and the second limits us to configurations in which the XXP locus is positively sloped, i.e. to configuration (iii) in table 10.1. Furthermore, these same considerations show that the effect of increased monetary accommodation is to rotate the FFP locus clockwise and the XXP locus counterclockwise, i.e. so that they lie closer together. These effects are shown more fully in figure 10.4 which compares the fiscal multiplier for constant DCE with that for a constant

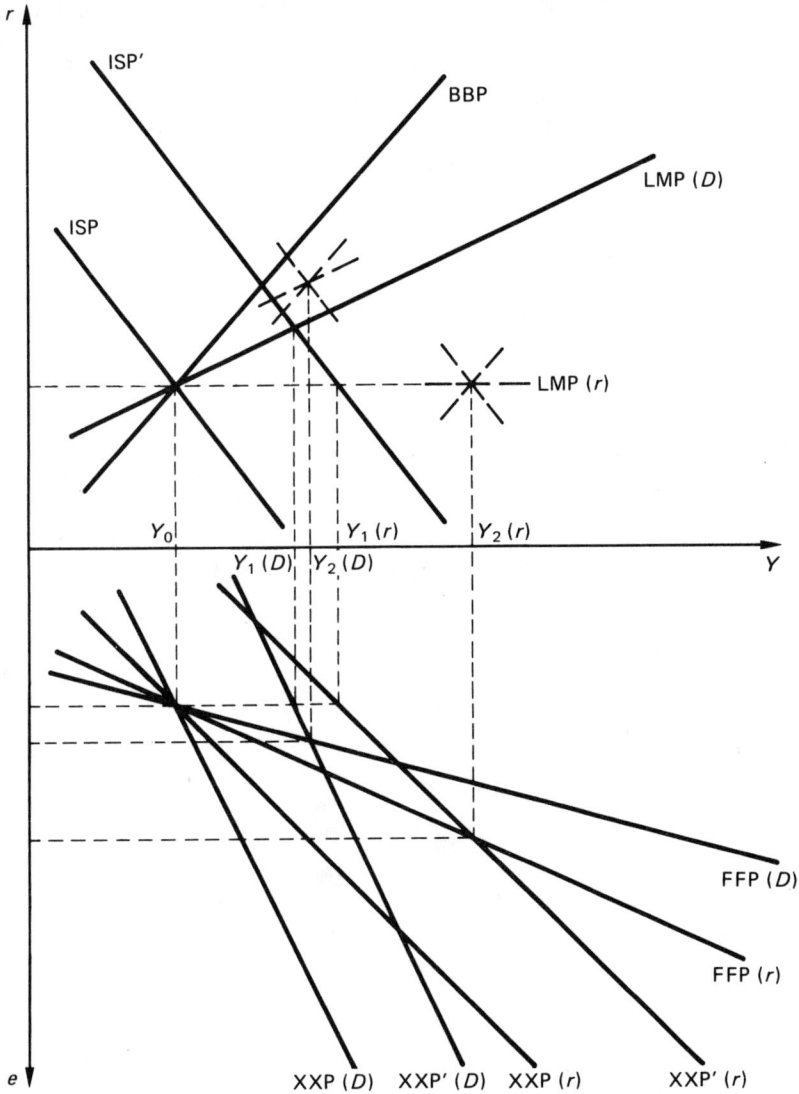

Figure 10.4 Crowding-out: flexible exchange rate, constant domestic credit expansion (*D*) or constant nominal interest rate (*r*)

nominal interest rate. In this diagram XXP(i), FFP(i) are the aggregate demand and external balance loci with $i = D$ representing constant DCE and $i = r$ the constant interest rate. A fiscal expansion is shown as a shift in the ISP curve to ISP'. Clearly, the corresponding shift in the aggregate demand schedule is greater under a regime of monetary accommodation than for constant DCE. The balance of payments deficit induces a depreciation in the exchange rate which is greater under the fixed interest rate than fixed DCE policy. The full equilibrium level of income under each regime is shown as $Y_2(i)$. As we would expect, a fixed nominal interest rate produces less crowding-out than fixed DCE. Not only does the constant interest rate produce less direct (interest rate) crowding-out but it also pulls in more expenditures indirectly by inducing a larger depreciation of the exchange rate than under fixed DCE.

Similar arguments apply to the two remaining monetary regimes. However, in each case the actual out-turn will also depend on the elasticity of expectations as this will determine the direction (as well as the magnitude) of movement of the nominal interest rate. For illustrative purposes, since the results are quite similar in each case, we shall assume that the elasticity π of price expectations exceeds unity and the elasticity η for the exchange rate is less than unity. Figure 10.5 compares the outcomes under the three interest rate regimes: constant nominal rate r; constant real rate R; and constant foreign differential C. Here we also distinguish the ISP(r) and ISP(R) loci. The former shows combinations of nominal interest rate and real income consistent with product and labour market equilibria; the latter shows the same equilibria in terms of the real interest rate and real income.[7] An increase in real income increases the price level and, with $\pi > 1$, expected inflation increases. To restore product market equilibrium will therefore require a smaller decrease in the nominal interest rate than in the real rate as a part of the decrease in the real rate is achieved by the increase in expected inflation. Accordingly, ISP(R) is steeper than ISP(r). The reverse is true when $\pi < 1$.

A similar argument will show that with $\pi > 1$ the FFP and XXP loci will rotate to lie further apart under a fixed real rate of interest than under a fixed nominal rate. In effect, it takes a smaller change in the nominal interest rate to achieve a given change in the real interest rate because a part of the work is done by the change in inflation expectations. Correspondingly, therefore, a *less* accommodating monetary policy is required to peg the real interest rate because an element of accommodation is already provided by the increase in inflation expectations as income expands. Exactly the reverse applies for $\pi < 1$.

In contrast, when the foreign differential is pegged a depreciation of the exchange rate sets up the expectation of a partial appreciation (under regressive expectations) and, for a given nominal interest rate, increases the real differential. This provides an element of monetary disaccommodation.

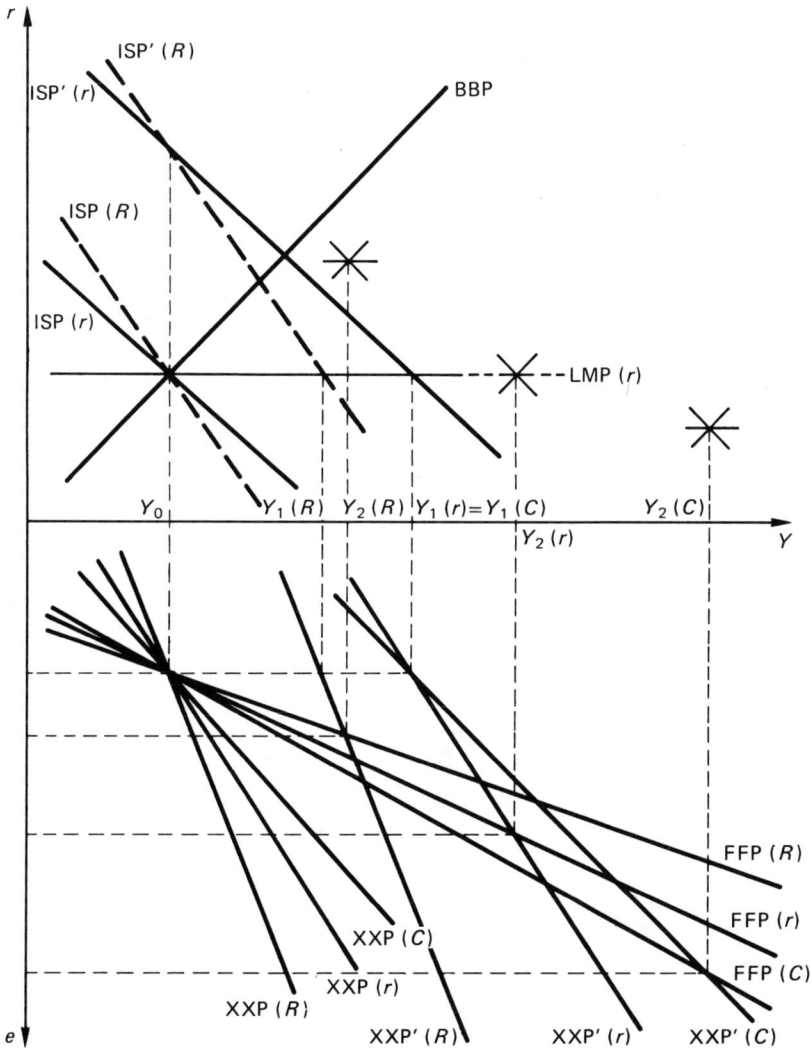

Figure 10.5 Crowding-out: flexible exchange rate, constant nominal interest rate (r), constant real interest rate (R) or constant uncovered differential (C)

The slopes of the ISP, LMP and BBP schedules are the same as under a constant nominal interest rate.

Clearly, therefore, with $\pi > 1$ and $\eta < 1$ the multipliers for a fiscal expansion can be ranked in the following order: the largest multiplier occurs with a constant foreign differential; next is the constant nominal interest rate; and the smallest multiplier occurs with a constant real interest rate. However, the analysis highlights the crucial importance of expectations. If $\pi < 1$ and $\eta > 1$, the rankings are exactly reversed. Moreover, constant DCE provides a smaller multiplier than a constant nominal interest rate, but may provide a larger or smaller multiplier than a constant real interest rate (when $\pi > 1$) or a constant foreign differential (when $\eta > 1$).

10.8.2 Fixed exchange rates

With the exchange rate fixed and expected to remain so for the immediate future we remove a major channel from the transmission mechanism for the crowding-out or pulling-in of private expenditures subsequent to a fiscal expansion. The relevant monetary regimes are those numbered 5–8 in table 10.2. It would be tedious to analyse each regime in detail. We therefore summarize the results and omit the geometry. The interested reader can easily perform these and other geometric exercises for himself or herself or refer to Bladen Hovell and Green (1982) for a more detailed analysis.

Consider, first, the constant money and constant DCE regimes. We note that the open-economy multiplier under constant money coincides with the closed-economy multiplier under constant DCE. Therefore the relative magnitude of the multiplier responses under these regimes in an open economy depends on the effect of the fiscal stimulus on the balance of payments. If LMP is flatter than BBP the balance of payments will deteriorate and constant DCE will lead to higher interest rates and more crowding-out than constant money. If, however, LMP is steeper, then the opposite conclusions will result.

As we have seen, under an interest rate policy some degree of monetary accommodation occurs. Thus, with a constant nominal interest rate, the income multiplier is always larger than with either constant money or constant DCE. Both constant money and constant DCE generate crowding-out through a higher rate of interest and this is prevented when the authorities peg the interest rate.

The effects of fiscal policy under a constant real interest rate depend, as before, on the elasticity of expectations. If $\pi > 1$ a fiscal expansion increases inflation expectations and this puts downward pressure on the real interest rate. The nominal interest rate therefore has to rise to preserve the real interest rate target and this produces a lower multiplier than if the nominal interest rate were constant. Evidently the reverse is true if $\pi < 1$.

10.9 CONCLUSION

In this chapter we have been concerned to examine the effects of fiscal policy within the context of a simple model of a small open economy which can allow for simultaneous variations in real income, product prices, asset prices and the exchange rate. The standard results relating to the effectiveness of fiscal policy under fixed and flexible exchange rates were summarized and it was shown how these results are modified by the introduction of alternative monetary regimes.

Under flexible exchange rates, with regressive expectations, a constant real interest rate or foreign differential is a more accommodating policy than is a constant nominal interest rate. With extrapolative expectations, a constant nominal rate is more accommodative. A policy of constant DCE is in general less accommodative than any of the other policies. However, strongly extrapolative expectations could render both the real interest rate and foreign differential policy less accommodative than constant DCE.

When the exchange rate is fixed, the relative ranking of the constant nominal interest rate and constant real rate continues to depend upon the elasticity of expectations in the same way as under flexible exchange rates. Constant money or DCE will give rise to a smaller multiplier than both a constant nominal interest rate and a constant real interest rate, unless in the latter case expectations are strongly extrapolative. However, constant DCE will be more or less accommodating than a constant money supply, depending upon the relative interest elasticities of capital flows and the demand for money.

Finally, we can observe that the standard proposition concerning the relative effectiveness of fiscal policy under fixed and flexible exchange rates is weakened when prices are variable. In particular, when international capital is relatively mobile (BBP is flatter than LMP) and prices are fixed, the standard result is that fiscal policy is more effective under fixed exchange rates than under flexible rates. When prices are variable, however, our results indicate that it is conceivable that fiscal policy is more effective under a flexible exchange rate regime.[8] If domestic prices adjust relatively quickly to exchange-rate-induced changes in import costs and it therefore takes a relatively large nominal change in the exchange rate to achieve a given real change, an appreciation of the exchange rate may have an expansionary rather than a contractionary effect (see figure 10.2, regime (ii)). A fiscal expansion which induces an appreciation of the exchange rate may therefore have a larger multiplier effect than a fiscal expansion with no change in the exchange rate.

Notes

1   This is largely for convenience but could be because the import good can only be consumed whereas the home good can be either consumed or invested. This avoids some sign ambiguities which typically are eliminated in any event by assumptions needed to guarantee the stability of the system. See Turnovsky (1977, ch. 10).

2   We reconcile this with asset choice theory by assuming that the stock of foreign-held domestic bonds in the previous period is predetermined. Given the previous period's stock, the demand for the current period's stock is equivalent to the net purchases of (flow demand for) domestic bonds. In practice, for most countries, the real time period over which a *ceteris paribus* increase in the domestic interest rate can attract a continuing inflow of foreign capital is probably rather short. Conceptually, however, the assumption that interest rate differentials determine capital flows is similar in kind to the assumption that other asset stocks in the model are predetermined.

3   We recognize that this formulation is *ad hoc*, although it is similar to other models of this kind. Note that very little is gained by introducing the rate of inflation through a standard Phillips curve relationship for we would then treat past prices as predetermined with the same general results as are obtained with equation (10.5). See Turnovsky (1977, ch. 10).

4   Note that this would not in any way alter our comparative statics; it would merely require a particular normalization for current and past foreign prices and past domestic prices.

5   As sterilization is not required under flexible exchange rates and impossible under perfect capital mobility, no sterilization is a natural assumption for the basic model as it can be sustained irrespective of the exchange rate regime or capital market assumption.

6   If the expenditure effect is stronger than the Keynes effect, so that ISP is steeper relative to IS than is LMP relative to LM, then the fixed price interest rate r_1 will exceed the flexible price interest rate r_2.

7   The loci are normalized so that initially the expected inflation rate is zero; however, strictly this is a normalization and not an assumption.

8   Under perfect capital mobility, however, this result is only possible for a relatively implausible combination of values of the expectations elasticities, i.e. $\eta > 1$ and $\pi < 1$.

11 Do Floating Exchange Rates Insulate?

Patrick Minford

11.1 INTRODUCTION

According to a view widely held in the early 1970s and still highly influential, floating exchange rates would to a very large extent insulate the floating economy against foreign shocks. This view is neatly encapsulated in the Mundell–Fleming (Fleming, 1962; Mundell, 1963b) model of a small open economy, which underlies a great deal of applied work in international macroeconomics.

In the model, portfolio capital is perfectly mobile, and so domestic interest rates R are equal to foreign interest rates R^* plus expected depreciation of the exchange rate (and a risk premium which we treat as exogenous and will ignore); this gives us a horizontal FF curve in (R, y (domestic income)) space. The curve shifts up or down with expected depreciation. Domestic prices are sticky, responding to excess demand for output; we treat them as fixed in the short run so that their behaviour is only relevant in pushing the economy to its long-run (vertical Phillips curve) position. We complete the short-run model with a standard IS and LM curve. The LM curve is treated as in a closed economy (the effect of the exchange rate on domestic prices being neglected). The IS curve is modified for the open economy by the effect of the real exchange rate (competitiveness) and world output and trade on net export volumes. Expected depreciation, finally, is assumed to be zero under fixed rates (implying that occasional parity changes are unanticipated) and also under floating rates (implying static expectations). Figure 11.1 illustrates the model.

The main point is now quickly made. Under fixed rates the LM curve adjusts (as indicated by the arrows) to the IS–FF intersection through reserve changes which shift the money supply instantaneously under perfect capital mobility, sterilization being useless. Any foreign shocks, which alter foreign output y^*, prices p^* or interest rates R^*, will impact on our economy. A rise in y^* or p^* shifts the IS curve to the right along the FF curve. A fall in R^*

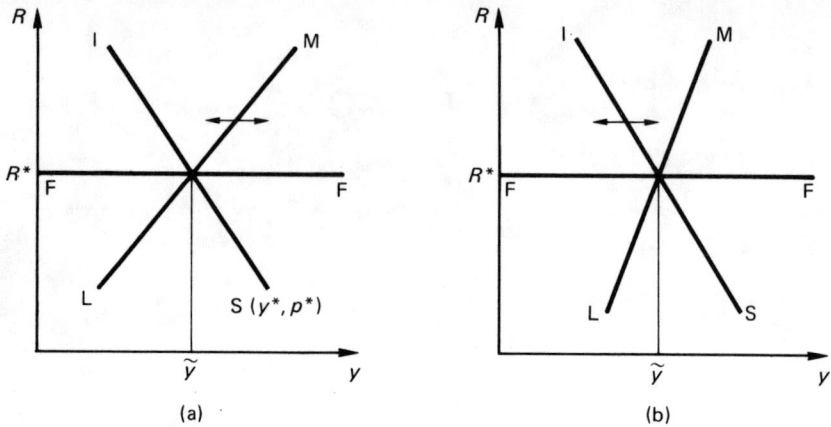

Figure 11.1   Mundell–Fleming model: (a) fixed rates; (b) floating rates

shifts FF down the IS curve. (As for domestic policy, the well-known Mundell–Fleming result that fiscal policy is effective and monetary policy impotent is immediate.)

But under floating rates, it is now the IS curve which adjusts, as the exchange rate rises or falls to clear the foreign exchange market, to the LM–FF intersection. y^* and p^* now no longer impact on y. In addition, a fall in R^* in response to foreign monetary stimulus will still have an impact on y but it will be perverse and contractionary, and if, as drawn here and usually assumed, the interest elasticity of domestic money is small (or if it is neutralized by accommodation of domestic money) it can be ignored. In this case, insulation is effectively total. (Domestic policy exhibits the Mundell–Fleming reversal of fiscal and monetary roles: fiscal policy is now impotent, monetary policy effective.)

For completeness, we should note that in the long run the Phillips curve drives y back to $\bar{y}$; under fixed rates this occurs because changing p changes competitiveness, shifting the IS curve, and under floating changing p shifts the LM curve.

The influence of this model can be judged by its subsequent lineage. It was taken over, with the addition of regressive expectations (which also turned out to be rational) by Dornbusch (1976), whose model in turn has been widely used in the construction of floating rate models. For example, a very recent international model by J.B. Taylor (1986) is exactly of this type – like Mundell–Fleming models with rational expectations as in the model due to Dornbusch and overlapping wage contacts to give price stickiness.

The paradox is that the Mundell–Fleming insulation property does not appear to tally with the facts of the floating rate system. The evidence is clear that under floating rates economies are if anything vibrating more closely together than under fixed rates (e.g. Camen, 1987). There are a number of possible answers to this paradox. One is that the Mundell–Fleming model is wrong on insulation. Another possibility suggested by Swoboda (1983) and Genberg et al. (1988) is that there have been *common* (not country-specific) shocks under floating – insulation is then irrelevant, although possibly still correct.

In this chapter we argue for the first view, on the grounds that the insulating properties of the Mundell–Fleming model are an artefact of the simplifying assumptions made in the exposition above. The key simplification seems to be that on expectations. Recent models in the Mundell–Fleming lineage have tended to adopt rational expectations. This, combined with the well-known slowness of net exports to respond to exchange rates, implies that the FF curve moves substantially and rapidly in response to shocks; consequently when y^* or p^* move the IS curve, the FF curve adjusts in the short run. A further modification, which turns out to be important once the FF curve is liberated by this expectations mechanism, is the sensitivity of domestic prices to the exchange rate; this enables the LM curve to move in the short run. A rise in R^*, which causes a depreciation of the spot exchange rate, will therefore now raise domestic prices and shift the LM curve to the left, reducing y in a normally signed spillover. In what follows, we consider first how a two-country world could be acceptably modelled under fixed and floating rates. It turns out that floating adds an extra set of feedbacks, namely via the exchange rate, but in so doing does not alter the basic structure of interdependence between the other variables in the model; it is as if in cinematic terms a filter of unknown type is placed in front of a camera lens. However, it is not possible a priori to say in this case which way the extra feedbacks will modify the interdependences (how the filter lens modifies the colours of the picture); it is an empirical matter, to which we turn in section 11.2. Two models are examined: the Taylor model, which is New Keynesian, and the Liverpool model, which is New Classical. It is found in both models that there is surprisingly little difference between interdependence under fixed and floating rates (such a result was reported in an earlier paper by Taylor for his model).

11.2 A STYLIZED TWO-COUNTRY MODEL

11.2.1 The nature of interdependence under fixed and floating rates

Leaving the money market on one side, our two countries will each have a goods market supply and demand, and there will be a common foreign exchange market clearing condition, given by uncovered interest parity (UIP – 11.5):

$$y = \sigma_1 p + \sigma_2 \text{RXR} \ldots \qquad \text{(supply, home)} \qquad (11.1)$$

$$y = -\delta_1 r - \delta_2 \text{RXR} - \delta_3 p + \delta_4 y^* \ldots \qquad \text{(demand, home)} \qquad (11.2)$$

$$y_F = s_1 p^* - s_2 \text{RXR} \ldots \qquad \text{(supply, abroad)} \qquad (11.3)$$

$$y_F = -dr^* + d_2 \text{RXR} - d_3 p^* + d_4 y \ldots \qquad \text{(demand, abroad)} \qquad (11.4)$$

$$r = r^* + \alpha \text{RXR} \qquad \text{(foreign exchange, UIP)} \qquad (11.5)$$

We write equation (11.5) in terms of real interest rates and the real exchange rate RXR, assume that the current RXR is observable and assume approximate monotonic first-order saddlepath dynamics. Then (11.5) gives us a simple direct relationship between the real interest differential and RXR. We examine only impact effects in this model and so all variables are to be considered as 'surprises' – deviations from the previous period's expectation. Notice that all the effects on trade are subsumed into the demand curve for goods; this demand curve also has prices entering because of real balance effects on spending. All variables except interest rates (fraction per annum) and RXR (fractional deviation from a base date) are logarithms. An ellipsis indicates omitted exogenous variables and lagged terms. Substitution of (11.5) into (11.2) to eliminate r allows us to write both demand curves as functions of r_F, RXR, own prices and the other country's income. The goods market is illustrated in figure 11.2.

The system to this point has seven endogenous variables ($y, y^*, p, p^*, r, r^*,$

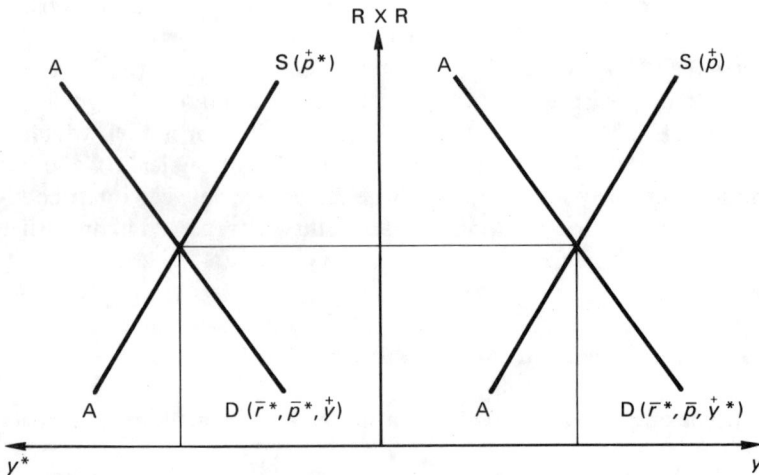

Figure 11.2 Two-country goods markets

and RXR) but only five equations. To close it we must of course add the monetary sector.

We choose to represent this by three more equations. First, we introduce a world LM curve: world supply of money is equated with world demand for money (a weighted average of the two countries' demands). World supply is a weighted average of the two countries' supplies under floating rates; under fixed rates it may be determined by the reserve currency country (i.e. under Bretton Woods, the US essentially), but other rules relating money supply to intervention are conceivable. We shall discuss this important issue further below.

Second, we have a world *differential* LM curve; the difference between the two countries' money supplies is equated with the difference between their money demands. Under fixed rates, this equation is satisfied by reserve movements which alter money supplies endogenously; any inequality gives rise to a (tiny) interest differential which causes 'infinite' reserve movements until money supplies have altered to eliminate the offending inequality.

Finally, we introduce the definition of the real exchange rate as the nominal rate S plus the price differential $p - p_F$. (S is the price of the *home* currency, so a rise is an appreciation.)

So we have

$$m_w(= wm + (1 - w)m^*) = - w\mu_1 r - (1 - w)m_1 r^* + wp$$
$$+ (1 - w)p^* + w\mu_2 y + (1 - w)m_2 y^* \qquad (11.6)$$

$$m - m^* = - \mu_1 r - m_1 r^* + p - p^* + \mu_2 y - m_2 y^* \qquad (11.7)$$

$$RXR = S + p - p^* \qquad (11.8)$$

Now consider how to close the *fixed* rate system. $m - m^*$ is recursively fixed by (11.7); so we can ignore (11.7) and $m - m^*$. S is exogenous in (11.8). We can therefore rewrite (11.8) as

$$p = p^* + RXR - S \qquad (11.9)$$

This indicates the well-known property that, other than real (or fixed) nominal exchange rate movements, prices at home are determined by foreign prices.

We can now substitute for p in our home goods markets from (11.9). We can also think of (11.6), world money markets, determining r^*, the rest of the world (ROW) interest rate, subject to numerous feedbacks from p^*, y, y^* and RXR.

Now figure 11.3 represents our fixed rate world. p_F and RXR move around until AS = AD at home and abroad. Notice that the new home AS and AD curves are now flatter than before because RXR enters p.

If we now turn to floating, we can treat S as recursively determined by

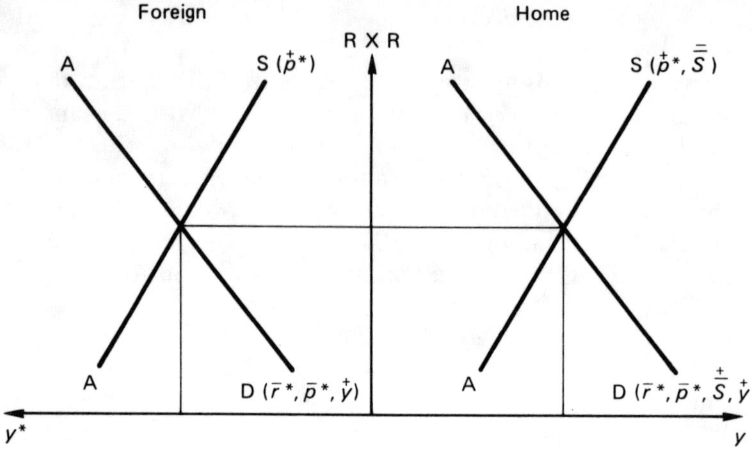

Figure 11.3   Two-country goods markets – fixed rates

(11.8); it enters in no earlier equation. However, p is now determined by (11.7) as

$$p = (m - m^*) + p^* + \mu_1 \alpha \text{RXR} + (\mu_1 + m_1)r^* - \mu_2 y + m_2 y^* \quad (11.10)$$

This equation now gives us the familiar floating independence of monetary policy to fix the home price level. The first three terms in (11.10) correspond to the first three terms in (11.9). $m - m_F$ is the analogue of $- S$; monetary excess corresponds under floating to a depreciation under fixed. However, the coefficient on RXR is not in general equal to unity because it reflects money demand (μ_1) and system dynamics (α). The remaining three terms reflect money demand behaviour. Hence home prices are determined by an extra set of relationships, those of money demand interacting with the system dynamics. This extra set is the added filter mentioned above, whose effect is to complicate interactions in a way that we cannot assess a priori. We can merely note the parallelism of structure: substituting for p from (11.10) gives us figure 11.4 under floating.

The slope of the AD curve which, for given p, was

$$\frac{\delta y}{\delta \text{RXR}} = -(\delta_1 \alpha + \delta_2)$$

now becomes probably flatter:

$$\frac{\delta y}{\delta \text{RXR}} = - \frac{\delta_1 \alpha + \delta_2 + \delta_3 \mu_1 \alpha}{1 - \delta_3 \mu_2}$$

Although we assume that it does not, it may even flip over and slope up if the

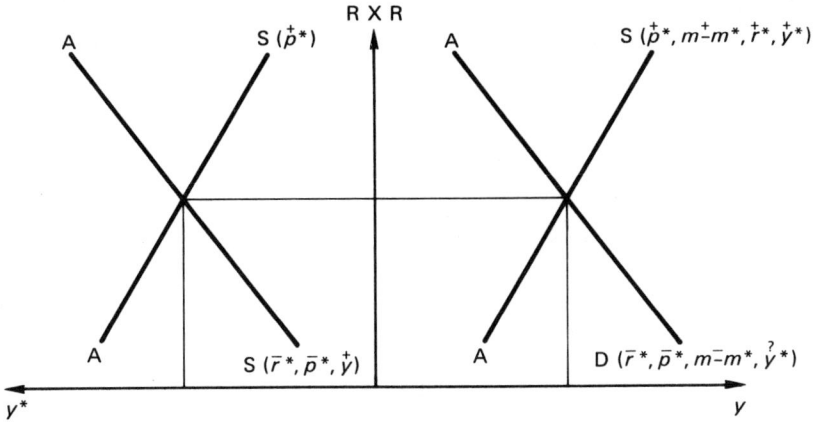

Figure 11.4 Two-country goods markets – floating rates

real balance effects are powerful (δ_3). Note too that the sign on $y^*(\delta_4 - \delta_3 m_2)/(1 - \delta_3 \mu_2)$ is now indeterminate, because of the real balance effect.

The AS curve slope changes from

$$\frac{\delta y}{\delta \text{RXR}} = \sigma_2$$

to

$$\frac{\delta y}{\delta \text{RXR}} = \frac{\sigma_2 + \sigma_1 \mu_1 \alpha}{1 + \sigma_1 \mu_2}$$

which may go flatter or steeper. Finally notice the extra terms now in aggregate supply compared with the fixed rate case.

In short, floating *complicates* but it does not add to or subtract from interdependence.

11.2.2 Are there independent monetary shocks under fixed rates?

It might be said that monetary shocks in non-reserve currency countries (NRCCs) cannot affect the world money supply under fixed rates. So fixed rates remove one set of shocks from the system altogether. Only monetary shocks in the reserve currency country matter and are transmitted elsewhere. This would be so if rates were rigidly fixed and reserve currency countries did not allow their money supply policies to be affected at all by the credit policies in NRCCs; this implies that as credit is created in an NRCC, reserve currency countries must *contract* their own credit in order to neutralize the effect of NRCC credit on world money. Such is in principle the role of a reserve currency under fully fixed rates. However, under Bretton Woods this was not usually the behaviour followed; certainly rates were not fixed immutably, and the USA, the major reserve currency, could not freely fix world monetary policy (for example in the late 1960s when Germany was strongly opposed to American expansionist policies it acted as a restrictive force).

It is more plausible to model monetary shocks by NRCCs as occurring through the medium of parity changes (S). For example, Germany by revaluing periodically enabled itself to achieve a slower growth in money and prices, and so to influence the world money supply. A change in S operates by shocking the home AS and AD curves in the same direction as do $m - m^*$ shocks under floating rates (see figures 11.3 and 11.4). It then becomes an empirical matter how often these S shocks occur – compared with $m - m^*$ shocks – and how they are transmitted. To this and other empirical issues we now turn.

Empirical evidence on transmission from the Taylor model

In his recent paper, Taylor reported the results of applying a variety of shocks to his quarterly world model. The Taylor model is essentially of the type set out above with the exception that the real balance effects on demand (δ_3 and d_3) are zero. Its New Keynesian provenance with staggered wage contracts generates dynamics that are approximately monotonic, from inspection of the simulations; the root appears to be around 0.8 (in quarterly data), implying rather rapid convergence (near total in three years) and it is similar under both fixed and floating rates. The staggering of contracts, however, implies that price and inflation dynamics are neither faster nor slower than the real visible dynamics. (Under the New Classical Liverpool model the dynamics apply to real variables only; nominal variables or components of variables adjust immediately, once the shock has been observed.)

Given the similarity of dynamics under our two regimes, we can evaluate the relative patterns of transmission (own effect and spillover effect) by recording only the impact effect in year 1. We look at inflation and output effects only.

Table 11.1 reproduces Taylor's (1986) reported results and shows direct and spillover effects in year 1 of a US monetary and fiscal shock (the effects are approximate, taken by eye off Taylor's graphs). Own US effects are not much different. But there is a clear difference of spillovers under floating rates. Output spillovers are smaller in absolute size under floating rates and for the fiscal shock the spillover differs in sign, being small and

Table 11.1 Taylor model comparisons of fixed and floating rates

	Floating	Fixed	Comment
US money shock (permanent rise of 3 per cent in money supply level), year 1 effects			
USA	$y = 0.84$	$y = 0.89$	No change
ROW	$y = 0.05$	$y = 1.1$	Spillover larger under fixed
USA	$p = 0.40$	$p = 0.40$	No change
ROW	$p = -0.03$	$p = 0.45$	Spillover larger under fixed
US fiscal shock (permanent rise in government spending by 1 per cent of GNP), year 1 effects			
USA	$y = 1.2$	$y = 1.45$	No change
ROW	$y = 0.22$	$y = -1.0$	Changed direction of spillover
USA	$p = 0.48$	$p = 0.41$	No change
ROW	$p = 0.20$	$p = -0.25$	Changed direction of spillover
Supply shocks everywhere (stochastic wage shocks), full period 1987 first quarter to 1989 fourth quarter, standard deviation, percentage difference			
USA	$y = 0.94$	$y = 0.84$	No change
ROW	$y = 0.64$	$y = 2.93$	Spillover larger under fixed
USA	$p = 2.52$	$p = 2.51$	No change
ROW	$p = 0.81$	$p = 0.88$	No change

positive instead of the large negative value under fixed. Price spillovers are also smaller in absolute size under floating rates, and differ in sign.

To make sense of this, we turn to our figures for the Taylor case, treating the 'home' quadrant as the small ROW (figures 11.5 and 11.6). Since $\delta_3 = 0$ in Taylor's model, the home AD slope will not change under floating rates; there is therefore also no transmission through to AD, so that p^* and $m - m^*$ do not affect the position of the AD curve.

The essence of the difference under the US fiscal shock (figure 11.5) is that the ROW AS curve shifts further to the right under floating rates as the exchange rate *fall* in ROW stimulates a price *rise*.

Under the US monetary shock (figure 11.6), the AS curve this time shifts slightly *leftwards* under floating, because the *rise* in ROW exchange rates slightly more than offsets the direct upward pressure of US prices on the ROW domestic price level.

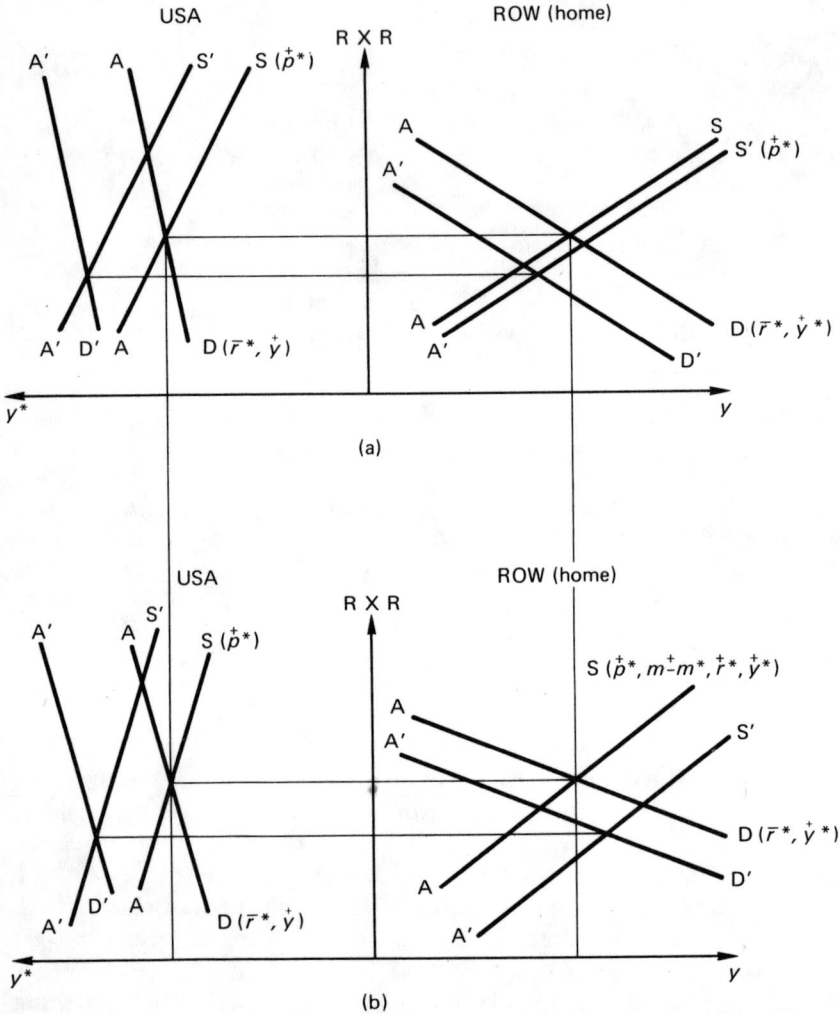

Figure 11.5 Taylor model: effects of US fiscal shock (a) for fixed rates and (b) for floating rates. Note that r^* and p^* rise by approximately the same amount under fixed and floating rates

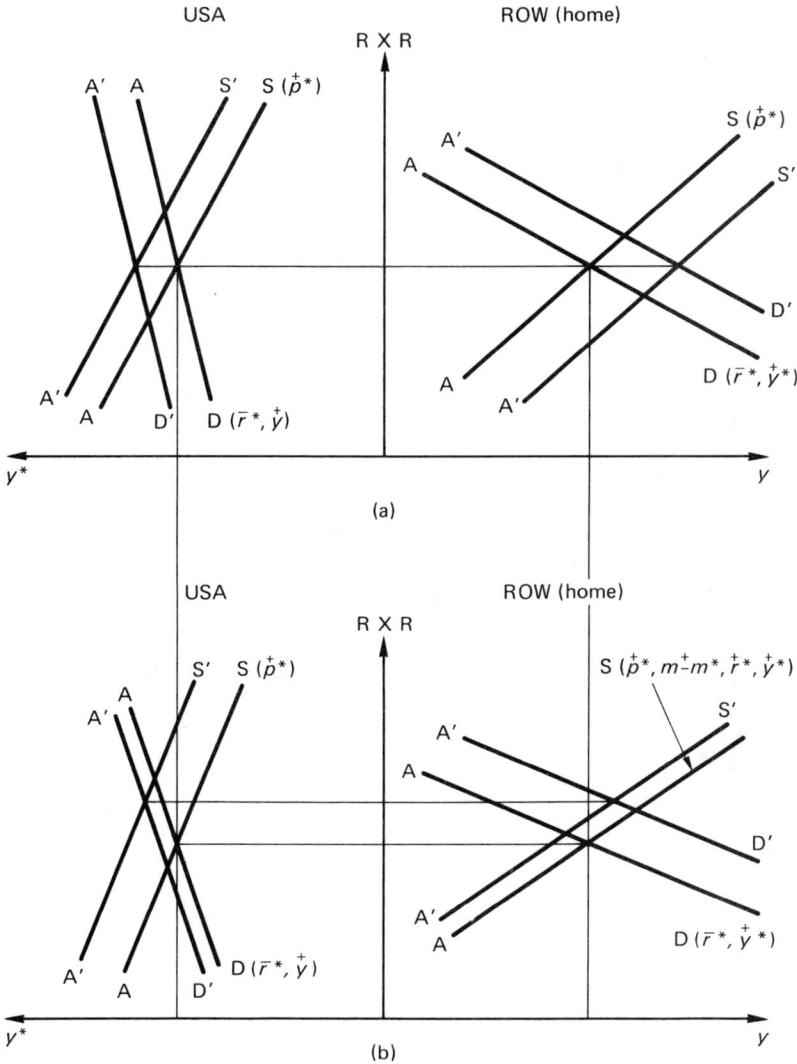

Figure 11.6   Taylor model: effects of US monetary shock (a) for fixed rates and (b) for floating rates. Note that r^* and p^* rise by approximately the same amount under fixed and floating rates

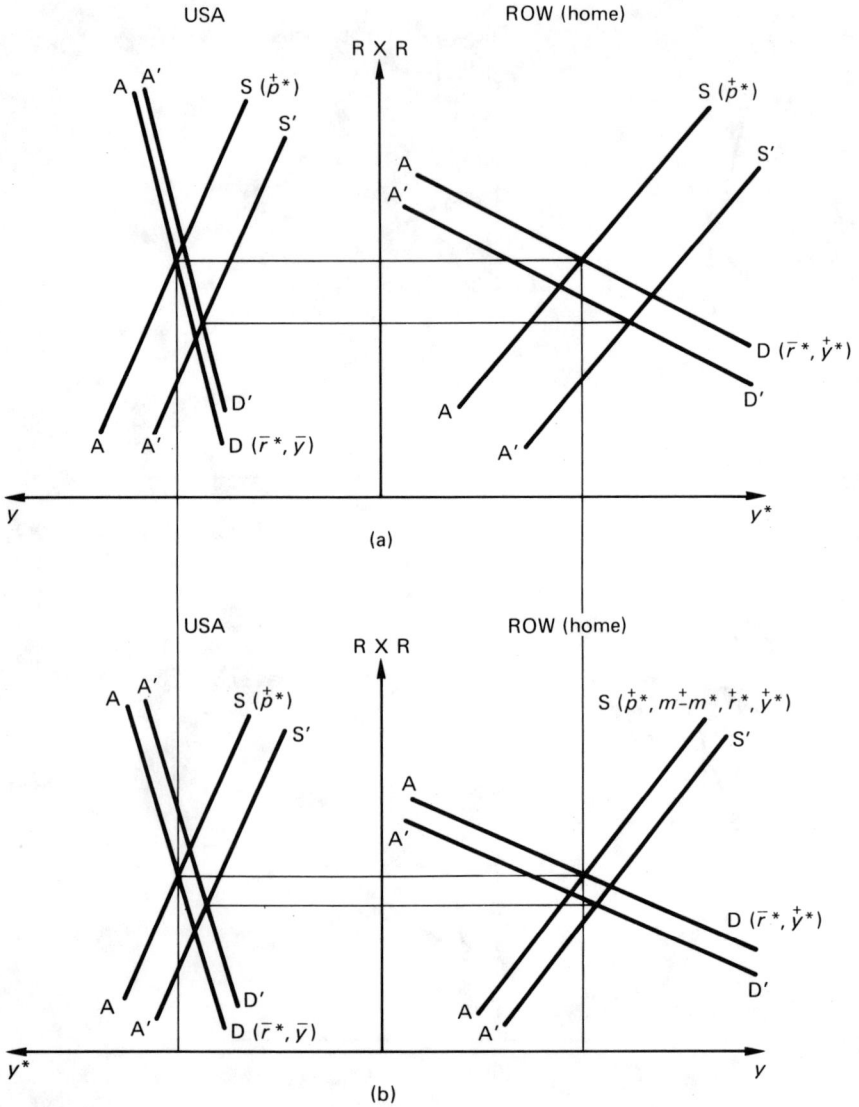

Figure 11.7 Taylor model: effects of US supply shock (a) for fixed rates and (b) for floating rates. Note that r^* and p^* rise both under fixed and floating rates

Table 11.1 also shows the standard deviation of the effects of *universal* stochastic supply shocks (representative shocks to wage equations are applied from the first quarter of 1987 to the fourth quarter of 89). We cannot therefore isolate spillover effects: the figures include own effects (of own supply shocks) plus spillover effects of others' supply shocks in each case. But they appear to suggest that output spillovers are higher under fixed rates for the ROW but not for the USA. Price spillovers are no different across regimes for either the ROW or the USA. Can we again suggest why ROW should suffer higher supply shock spillovers? Figure 11.7 illustrates the problem for a US supply shock. Again the reason is the differential behaviour of the ROW AS curve, as the ROW exchange rate rises in response to the rise in US prices and the fall in US interest rates.

Table 11.2 Liverpool model – year 1 response to foreign shocks under fixed and floating rates

(a) Supply shocks

	US supply shock (10 per cent temporary one-year fall in US output supply)		Non-US supply shocks[a] (10 per cent temporary one-year rise in real exchange rates)	
	Floating	Fixed	Floating	Fixed
Output y				
USA	$(-5.3)^b$	$(-5.5)^b$	−0.40	−0.34
Canada	−0.8	−0.8	−0.05	−0.78
Japan	−0.5	−0.4	−0.08	−0.03
Germany	−2.1	−2.3	−0.36	−0.24
France	−1.6	−1.8	−0.21	−0.16
Italy	−1.1	−1.3	−0.16	−0.15
UK	−1.3	−1.3	−0.20	−0.18
Average	−1.23	−1.35	−0.23	−0.23
Prices p				
USA	$(3.2)^b$	$(3.3)^b$	0.43	0.28
Canada	0.2	0.6	0.50	0.27
Japan	0.4	1.2	0.41	0.41
Germany	2.1	0.8	0.29	0.33
France	0.7	0.6	0.28	0.29
Italy	3.3	0.6	1.07	0.43
UK	0.8	0.7	0.10	0.32
Average	1.2	0.8	0.45	0.33

[a] Each entry shows average response to shock in non-US foreign countries (i.e. excluding USA and own country).
[b] US response to own supply shock.

In short, the Taylor model does appear to have some of the Mundell–Fleming insulation properties. Transmission appears to be reduced by the floating rate; but it still exists, albeit attenuated.

Empirical evidence on transmission from the Liverpool model

The Liverpool model is New Classical; it operates on annual data. Real balance effects are powerful (δ_3, d_3), an additional channel for transmission compared with Taylor's model since foreign shocks affect domestic prices and so real balances. The dynamics (reflecting adjustment costs) are also approximately monotonic under floating rates, but with a root of around 0.7 (annual) convergence takes much longer (around eight years for 95 per cent) than in the Taylor model for real variables. (The nominal components of

Table 11.2 *cont'd*

(b) Monetary shocks

	US monetary shock (2 per cent once-and-for-all rise in money supply)		Non-US monetary shocks[a]	
	Floating	Fixed	Floating	Fixed
Output y				
US	$(0.58)^{b}$	$(1.2)^{b}$	0.06	0.35
Canada	0.05	0.27	−0.06	−0.02
Japan	0.05	0.48	0.004	0.14
Germany	0.25	0.71	0.08	−0.01
France	0.18	0.91	0.03	0.26
Italy	0.13	0.56	0.03	0.25
UK	0.15	0.24	0.04	0.02
Average	0.13	0.53	0.03	0.14
Prices p				
US	$(1.65)^{b}$	$(1.17)^{b}$	−0.08	0.01
Canada	−0.23	0.43	−0.40	0.10
Japan	−0.21	0.83	−0.27	0.19
Germany	−0.24	0.65	−0.05	0.14
France	−0.13	0.70	−0.12	0.18
Italy	−0.48	1.28	−0.44	0.39
UK	−0.10	0.61	−0.07	0.14
Average	−0.23	0.75	−0.20	0.16

[a] Under floating, each country raises money supply by 2 per cent once and for all; under fixed, each devalues (trade-weighted basis) by 2 per cent once and for all. Each entry shows average response to shock in non-US foreign countries (i.e. excluding own and US shocks).
[b] US response to own shock.

nominal variables as noted above move immediately to compensate for changes in anticipated money.) Under fixed rates, the root is similar.

Table 11.2 shows (year 1) impact effect comparisons for supply shocks and monetary shocks; it shows effects on a 'home' country (left-hand side) of foreign shocks only.

What is immediately striking is that, for *supply* shocks, transmission is extraordinarily similar under fixed and floating rates. Home prices react slightly more to foreign supply shocks under floating because the exchange rate movement reinforces the shock. Figure 11.8 illustrates this.

The cases are very similar because r^* rises while y^* falls so that the AS curve under floating moves only a little more than under fixed. So ROW

Table 11.2 *cont'd*

(c) Fiscal shocks

	US fiscal shock (1 per cent of GDP rise in government spending for five years)		Non-US fiscal shock[a] (i.e. 1 per cent of GDP rise in government spending for five years)	
	Floating	Fixed	Floating	Fixed
Output y				
US	(0.45)[b]	(0.68)[b]	0.00	0.23
Canada	0.16	−0.17	0.12	0.05
Japan	0.00	0.02	0.04	0.25
Germany	0.05	−0.30	0.15	0.24
France	0.10	0.16	0.12	0.41
Italy	0.02	0.15	0.08	0.31
UK	−0.01	−0.04	0.02	0.11
Average	0.05	−0.03	0.08	0.23
	Floating	Fixed	Floating	Fixed
Prices p				
US	(0.45)[b]	(0.56)[b]	0.45	0.09
Canada	0.55	0.15	0.15	0.17
Japan	0.45	0.30	0.09	0.35
Germany	−0.12	0.22	−0.16	0.25
France	0.14	0.25	−0.01	0.29
Italy	−0.04	0.47	−0.23	0.59
UK	0.04	0.22	−0.02	0.25
Average	0.17	0.27	0.04	0.28

[a] Each entry shows average response to shock in non-US foreign countries (i.e. excluding USA and own country).
[b] US response to own shock.

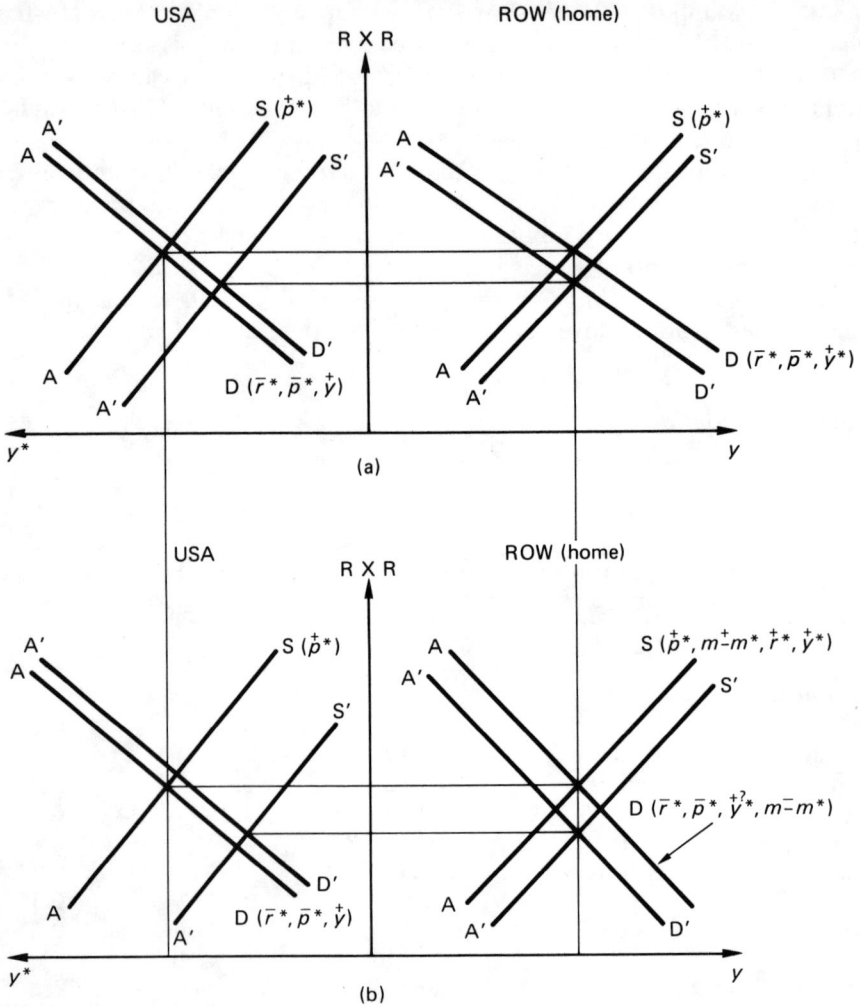

Figure 11.8 Liverpool model: effects of US supply shock (a) for fixed rates and (b) for floating rates. Note that r^* and p^* rise in both cases but under fixed rates r^* rises slightly more

RXR depreciates a little more under floating, reinforcing a little the transmission of the price rise in the USA. Similar comments could be made about the effects of non-US foreign supply shocks: the real exchange rate moves more under floating, and so does the home price, but output is similarly affected. This contrasts with the Taylor model where output is less affected under floating and prices behave much the same under either regime.

Turning to monetary shocks, there is evidence of the Mundell–Fleming effect, as in the Taylor model (figure 11.9). Home prices react negatively to foreign money shocks and this greatly dampens the output reaction compared with that under fixed rates. Under fixed rates the monetary shocks are devaluations, which cause positive output and price reactions abroad. What we find here is that under floating output transmission of monetary shocks is small, whereas under fixed it is significant.

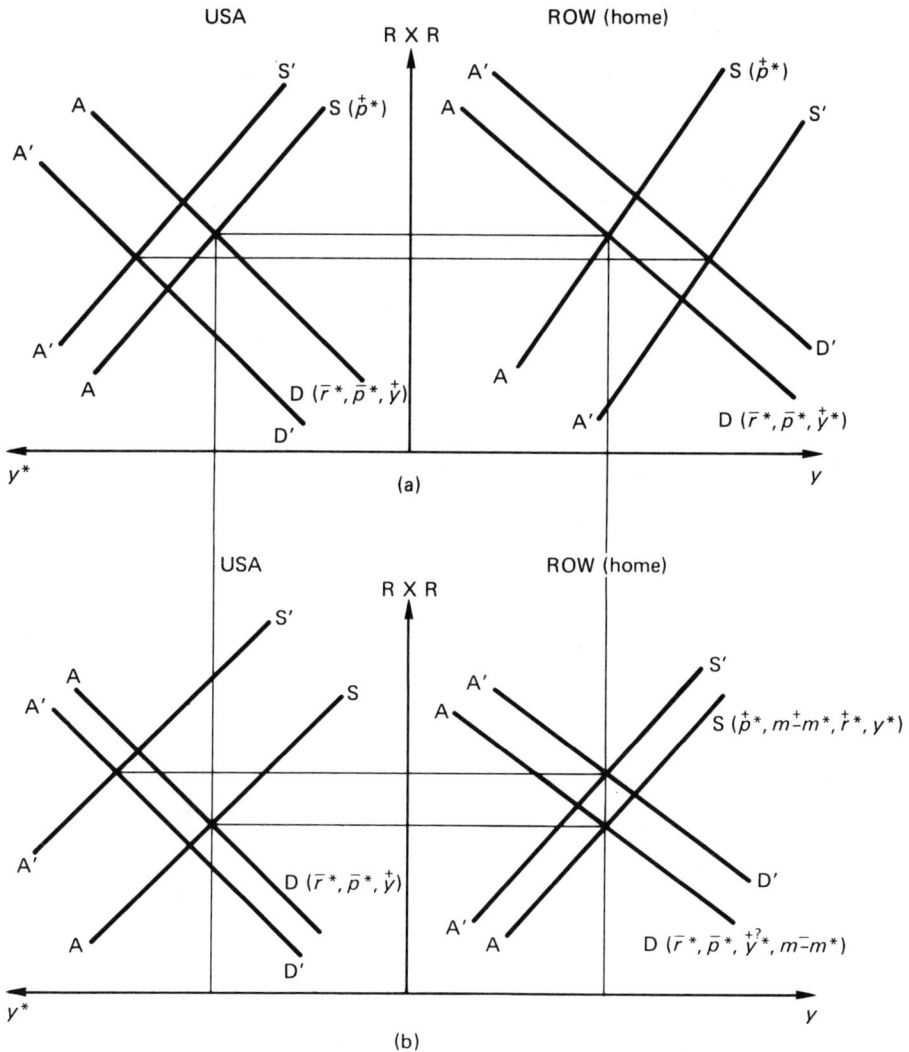

Figure 11.9   Liverpool model: effects of US monetary shock (a) for fixed rates and (b) for floating rates. Note that p^* rises and r^* falls in both cases

Last, we consider fiscal shocks in the Liverpool model. (The shock administered is a five-year rise in government spending by 1 per cent of gross domestic product). Here we find virtually no transmission of US shocks under either regime. The reason for this is that real interest rates rise by so much, because of the size of the USA relative to the world capital market,

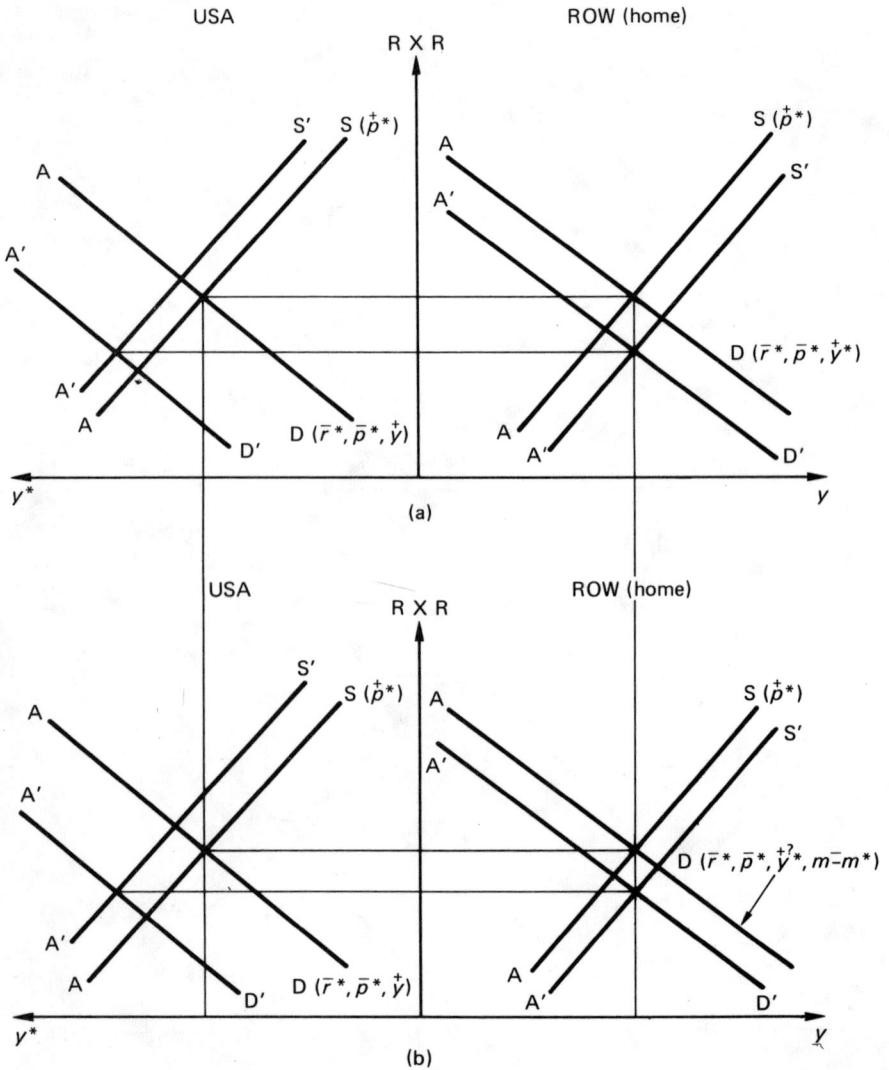

Figure 11.10 Liverpool model: effects of US fiscal shock (a) for fixed rates and (b) for floating rates. Note that r^* and p^* rise in both cases

that foreign expansion via trade multipliers and price spillovers on the supply curve is 'crowded out' by higher real rates (see figure 11.10): the ROW AD curve is shifted left so that, in spite of a rightward AS curve shift, output changes little. Notice the usual result (as in the Taylor model) that the US real exchange rate appreciates (RXR falls).

When we turn to non-US fiscal shocks, the effects are more conventional. The output spillovers are always positive (because world real interest rates are little affected) but less so under floating; this is because price spillovers are reduced by nominal exchange rate appreciation in the reflating countries, so the AS curve does not shift and there is only the shift in AD to provide the spillover.

As with monetary shocks, we can find here a certain Mundell–Fleming effect. Fiscal shock spillovers on output are in general lower under floating than under fixed rates.

So in the Liverpool model, as in Taylor's, there is a Mundell–Fleming style reduction in the output transmission of fiscal and monetary shocks. But this does not carry over to supply shocks, which generate approximately equal output spillovers under both regimes.

11.3 CONCLUSION

We have examined the output transmission of domestic shocks under fixed and floating rates through the eyes of two modern multi-country descendants of the Mundell–Fleming model: one New Keynesian (Taylor); one New Classical (Liverpool). With its ideal classroom simplicity, the Mundell–Fleming model asserts *zero* transmission under floating rates as against the usual transmission via aggregate demand (trade multipliers and competitiveness effects) under fixed rates. The Taylor and Liverpool models adulterate this simplicity in two key ways: expectations are rational (not static as in the Mundell–Fleming model) and import prices shift the LM curve (via effects on consumer prices). The two models are further differentiated from each other by overlapping nominal contracts (Taylor) and wealth effects on demand (Liverpool).

Both models show tendencies towards the Mundell–Fleming result for fiscal and monetary shocks; they predict that under floating rates output spillovers are attenuated, although by no means zero. For supply shocks, the Taylor model predicts attenuation of the spillovers, though much less than for fiscal or monetary shocks, and the Liverpool model predicts essentially the same output spillovers for supply shocks under floating as under fixed rates. By implication, the world is *not* pure Mundell–Fleming, in spite of certain tendencies that that simplified model usefully identifies.

Our original question was how far the continued high degree of world economic integration under floating rates can be accounted for by the transmission of domestic shocks. This paper suggests that this transmission will retain an important role *either* if a major source of domestic shocks under floating has been the supply side *or* if domestic fiscal and monetary shocks under floating have been much larger than under fixed rates. Both these possibilities have some plausibility, the first because of the extent of oil price volatility since 1972, and the second because of the much increased cross-country differentials in money supply growth and budget deficits under floating rates (suggesting that individual 'reflation'/'deflation' validated by devaluation/revaluation may have been rarer under fixed rates, as indeed intended by Bretton Woods, than under its floating-rate-validated counterpart). Proper consideration of these possibilities lies beyond the scope of this paper. But a reasonable working hypothesis at this stage is, I suggest, that we do not need to postulate an upsurge in *common* shocks under floating to account for the stylized facts of the world business cycle.

12 Some Issues Concerning the Long-run Credibility of the European Monetary System

Michael J. Artis and Mark P. Taylor

12.1 INTRODUCTION

There now exist a number of studies which demonstrate that the exchange rate mechanism (ERM) of the European Monetary System (EMS) has been instrumental in improving both the stability and the predictability of intra-ERM exchange rates, both real and nominal (see for example the European Commission, 1982; Padoa-Schioppa, 1983; Ungerer et al., 1983; Rogoff, 1985; Ungerer et al., 1987; and Artis and Taylor, 1988). In a recent paper, Artis and Taylor (1988) also demonstrate that the credibility effects of the ERM are such that, far from having purchased this reduction in exchange rate volatility at the expense of greater variation in interest rates, there is in fact some evidence of *reduced* interest rate volatility amongst ERM members. However, while the ERM may be seen to have achieved certain short- to medium-term objectives, it is not immediately obvious whether certain other longer-run objectives have been attained, nor, indeed, whether the long-run credibility of the EMS has been established beyond doubt. This is the motivation for the present paper.

In particular, in this paper we examine the issues of exchange rate *misalignment* and currency substitutability within the ERM. While the immediate and formal objective of the ERM is the stabilization of member countries' *nominal* exchange rates, since the EMS is an exchange rate mechanism of a customs union it must be expected, if it is to survive in the long run,

Any views expressed in this paper are those of the authors and should in no way be construed as representing the views or policies of the Bank of England, past or present. Michael Artis acknowledges financial support received from the Sloan and Ford Foundations administered by the Centre for Economic and Policy Research under its programme 'Macroeconomic Interactions and Policy Design in Interdependent Economies'.

to ensure that member countries' competitiveness is protected; otherwise, the protection-reducing achievements of the customs union must be called into question as countries seek to restore their terms of trade. This is to suggest that, at the same time as the immediate and formal objective of the system is to stabilize *nominal* rates of exchange, its inner long-run rationale involves a requirement on *real* rates of exchange. This fundamental ambiguity accounts for the what Goodhart (1986) has termed 'unholy alliance' of those advocating British participation in the ERM, between those who seek to consolidate the counter-inflation gains of recent years (by targeting the German mark–UK pound rate essentially) and those who wish to protect the competitiveness of sterling from the devastating over-appreciation of the 1980–1 period. The difference, stressed by Williamson (1985), between the concepts of exchange rate *volatility* and *misalignment*, is important here. Volatility is a 'high frequency' concept referring to movements in the exchange rate over comparatively short periods of time. Misalignment, on the other hand, refers to the capacity for an exchange rate to depart from its fundamental equilibrium value over a protracted period of time. For the reasons given by Williamson it seems fair to argue that the greater welfare significance attaches to the diminution of misalignment than to the reduction of volatility where there is (perhaps surprisingly) little evidence to support the view that volatility is welfare reducing.[1]

The issue of intra-ERM currency and financial asset substitutability is also important. Following Canzoneri (1982), we can say that the creation of a successful exchange rate union converts external shocks affecting member countries asymmetrically into symmetric shocks; if the permanence of the union is credible, one member's currency is as good as another's and an external shock inducing a flight of capital into, say, the mark, should affect the franc and lira in the same way, relieving pressure on the cross-rates. Indeed, a diminution of the exposure of German competitiveness to sentiment against the US dollar was apparently a major motivation of German interest in the founding of the EMS (Ludlow, 1982).

The remainder of the paper is set out as follows. In section 12.2 we describe our tests for long-run misalignment and report some empirical results using them. In the following section we discuss methods of testing for asset and currency substitutability on the basis of the uncovered interest rate parity condition and we report further empirical results. A final section concludes.

12.2   REAL EXCHANGE RATES AND THE EUROPEAN MONETARY SYSTEM: RANDOM WALK OR DRAGGING ANCHOR?

Arguments for joining the ERM may hinge on the targeting of either the real or the nominal exchange rate. Although EMS realignments have probably made less than full adjustment for price level differences, one would expect the longer-run consequences of ERM membership to entail convergence on some form of purchasing power parity (PPP), at least against other ERM currencies; indeed this can be viewed as a measure of policy convergence. Thus, as we noted in our introductory section, the long-run survival of the system would seem to depend upon long-run preservation of competitiveness, so that member countries are not continually tempted to try and restore their terms of trade to more favourable levels.

In fact, however, there exists a whole literature which suggests that deviations from PPP, as measured by the real exchange rate, can generally be characterized as martingale or, more particularly, random walk behaviour. Seminal papers in this context are those of Roll (1979), who proposed a martingale PPP hypothesis based on efficient international goods arbitrage, and of Adler and Lehmann (1983), who derive similar conclusions based on considerations of efficient cross-border bond arbitrage. Indeed, if the expected exchange rate depreciation over a given period is just equal to the expected inflation differential, the real exchange rate must follow a random walk.

We propose to examine the long-run implications of the EMS by testing for unit roots in real exchange rates. Since the real exchange rate can be viewed as the deviation from PPP, if some form of (relative or absolute) PPP is to hold in the long run, the real exchange rate must be characterized by a stationary process. If the real exchange rate is non-stationary, there is no tendency for it to settle down at any particular level, even in the long run. Thus, PPP deviations – the degree of misalignment – will tend to get larger and larger over time.

12.2.1 Testing for unit roots in real exchange rates

The specific hypothesis under examination is that the real exchange rate is characterized by a stochastic process with a unit root. Denote the real exchange rate c, and suppose that it is generated in discrete time according to

$$c_t = c_{t-1} + u_t \tag{12.1}$$

where the error sequence u_t may be weakly dependent and heterogeneously distributed but satisfies certain weak regularity conditions (see Phillips, 1987). This assumption concerning the error process is quite important for two reasons. Much previous empirical work on this topic may be confounded because of implicit assumptions made concerning the error process in the random walk specification, i.e. that it is independently and identically distributed (iid). A number of workers, notably Cumby and Obstfeld (1984) and Domowitz and Hakkio (1985), have noted the presence of conditional heteroscedasticity (more particularly autoregressive conditional heteroscedasticity) in exchange rate innovations. In addition, the 'peso problem'

(Krasker, 1980) suggests that a perceived small probability of a large discrete change in the exchange rate (such as an expected devaluation), which does not materialize in-sample, may induce serial dependence into the forecast errors. In the present paper we therefore apply unit root tests which are non-parametric with respect to nuisance parameters and which therefore allow for weakly dependent and heterogeneously distributed forecast errors. Secondly, it may well be that the real exchange rate follows some general autoregressive moving average (ARMA) process with a unit root rather than a pure random walk,

$$(1 - L) A(L) c_t = B(L)v_t$$

(where A(.) and B(.) are scalar polynomials in the lag operator L), which can be written in the form (12.1) with

$$u_t = A^{-1}(L) B(L) v_t$$

Thus, although we apparently test for a pure random walk, the results may in fact detect non-stationarity in higher-order processes.

In order to test the unit root hypothesis with iid errors, Dickey and Fuller (1981) and Fuller (1976) propose tests based on the ordinary least-squares (OLS) regression:

$$c_t = \mu + \beta(t - T/2) + \alpha c_{t-1} + u_t \tag{12.2}$$

where T is the sample size and the null hypothesis is

$$H_o: (\mu, \beta, \alpha) = (0, 0, 1) \tag{12.3}$$

Under the maintained hypothesis that the error sequence is iid, Fuller (1976) and Dickey and Fuller (1981) derive the limiting distributions of the standard t-statistics for the individual null hypotheses $\alpha = 1$, $\mu = 0$, $\beta = 0$ (these statistics will not be distributed as t under the null because of the presence of a unit root) and use Monte Carlo methods to construct estimates of their finite sample empirical distributions. We denote these Dickey–Fuller statistics as t_α, t_μ and t_β respectively. Phillips and Perron (1986) propose an amendment of these statistics to allow for weakly dependent and hetero-geneously distributed errors (see Phillips and Perron, 1986). We denote these amended statistics t^*_α, t^*_μ and t^*_β respectively.

If the error sequence is in fact iid, then the Dickey–Fuller and Phillips–Perron procedures will be asymptotically equivalent. Phillips and Perron show that the tables of critical values tabulated by Fuller (1976) and Dickey and Fuller (1981) can be used for the Phillips–Perron statistics. At a significance level of 5 per cent, the approximate rejection regions for both the Dickey–Fuller and Phillips–Perron statistics are as follows (for a sample size of around 100):

$$t_\alpha, t^*_\alpha: \{t \mid t < -3.45\}$$

$$t_\mu, t^*_\mu: \{t \,\|\, |t| > 3.42\}$$
$$t_\beta, t^*_\beta: \{t \,\|\, |t| > 3.14\}$$

Although these statistics test the individual hypotheses $\alpha = 1$, $\mu = 0$ and $\beta = 0$ respectively, since they are constructed under the joint null hypothesis (12.3) they should reflect *any* departure from the joint null.

12.2.2 Empirical results for tests for misalignment

Monthly (end of the month) data on bilateral US dollar exchange rates were taken from the IFS data tape for the period January 1973 to December 1986. Bilateral rates against the German mark and UK pound were also constructed by assuming a triangular arbitrage condition. Real exchange rates were constructed by deflating by the wholesale price index (also from the IFS

Table 12.1 Testing for unit roots in real exchange rates

$$c_t = \mu + \beta(t - T/2) + \alpha c_{t-1} + u_t$$

Exchange rate	Period	t^*_α	t^*_μ	t^*_β
DMK–DKR	Pre-EMS	2.55	−0.81	−2.70
	Post-EMS	1.01	−0.23	−0.26
DMK–BFR	Pre-EMS	2.64	−0.78	−2.72
	Post-EMS	0.98	−0.24	−0.30
DMK–FFR	Pre-EMS	2.75	−0.86	−2.68
	Post-EMS	0.97	−0.21	−0.25
DMK–ITL	Pre-EMS	2.66	−0.84	−2.69
	Post-EMS	0.98	0.25	−0.26
DMK–NGL	Pre-EMS	2.61	−0.83	−2.71
	Post-EMS	0.98	−0.22	−0.26
DMK–US$	Pre-EMS	2.81	−0.77	−2.11
	Post-EMS	1.04	−0.27	−0.31
DMK–CN$	Pre-EMS	2.59	−0.84	−2.65
	Post-EMS	0.97	−0.26	−0.25
DMK–JPY	Pre-EMS	2.63	−0.83	−2.70
	Post-EMS	0.99	−0.24	−0.26
DMK–UK£	Pre-EMS	2.65	−0.82	−2.72
	Post-EMS	1.08	−0.29	−0.30

DMK, German mark; DKR, Danish kroner; BFR, Belgian franc; FFR, French franc; ITL, Italian lira; NGL, Dutch guilder; US$, US dollar; CN$, Canadian dollar; JPY, Japanese yen; UK£, UK pound.
t^*_α, t^*_μ, t^*_β are the Phillips–Perron test statistics for the null hypotheses $\alpha = 1$, $\mu = 0$, $\beta = 0$.
Approximate rejection regions at the 5 per cent level are $(t^*_\alpha \,|\, t^*_\alpha < -3.45)$, $(t^*_\mu \,|\, |t^*_\mu| > 3.42)$ and $(t^*_\beta \,|\, |t^*_\beta| > 3.14)$ respectively.

tape). The currencies used included six ERM members – German mark, Danish kroner, Belgian franc, French franc, Italian lira and Dutch guilder – and four non-ERM members – US dollar, UK pound, Japanese yen and Canadian dollar. Using the test procedures outlined above, we tested for the presence of unit roots in real bilateral exchange rates against the mark, pre- and post-EMS.[2] The results are given in table 12.1.

Interestingly, in no case, either pre- or post-EMS, can the null hypothesis of a pure random walk with zero drift be rejected at standard levels of significance. These results are potentially quite damaging to the case for EMS membership: there appears to have been no movement towards a stabilization of competitiveness amongst ERM members, even in a long-run sense. The results are, in fact, consistent with persistent and growing degrees of exchange rate misalignment.

However, there are a number of remarks which should be made concerning these results. Firstly, the results reported by Artis and Taylor (1988) show a very definite reduction in intra-ERM exchange rate volatility after March 1979, using an identical data base. This can be interpreted as a reduction in the (average) variance of the disturbance term u_t in (12.1). Thus, one interpretation of these results is that, although the ERM has not been able to put a halt to the tendency for exchange rates to become misaligned, it has been successful in reducing the rate at which the degree of misalignment grows. Put another way, the ERM appears to have increased exchange rate predictability. Secondly, it might be argued that the data period over which the ERM has been observed is too short to enable one to infer the very long-run properties of the system: in spectral analysis terms, it may be the case that the low frequency components are not particularly evident in the data collected in date.[3] Thirdly, it may be that PPP is not the appropriate yardstick by which to measure exchange rate misalignment in a world characterized by substantial real shocks. The period of operation of the EMS has seen an inordinate number of these, ranging from the second Organization of Petroleum Exporting Countries (OPEC) oil shock to large swings in fiscal stances and real interest rates. These factors themselves may have caused shifts in equilibrium real exchange rates and perhaps should be controlled in tests of this kind.[4]

12.3 CURRENCY SUBSTITUTABILITY AND RISK PREMIA

12.3.1 Testing for substitutability

One way of testing for substitutability between financial assets is to look for significant risk premia.[5] Although, at least in principle, it is possible that the configuration of asset demand and supply is such that the risk premium is apparently zero between two currencies whose assets are, in fact, less than perfect substitutes in agents' portfolios, a non-zero risk premium nevertheless is evidence of imperfect substitutability. Simply put, a zero risk premium is a necessary but not a sufficient condition for perfect substitutability. Non-substitutability should be detected as deviations from a simple (non-risk-adjusted) uncovered interest parity (UIP) condition. The UIP theorem states that the interest differential between two financial assets, identical in every relevant respect except currency of denomination, should be exactly offset by the expected rate of change of the exchange rate between the relevant currencies over the period of maturity. Under the maintained hypothesis of rational expectations, the UIP condition may be written

$$\rho_t + E(e_{t+n}|I_t) - e_t = i_t - i^*_t \tag{12.4}$$

where e_t is the (logarithm of the) domestic price of foreign currency, i_t is the interest rate on the domestic security with n periods to maturity, an asterisk denotes a foreign variable and ρ_t denotes the (possibly time-varying) risk premium. If, for example, ρ_t is positive, agents require a premium for holding the domestic security over and above the expected depreciation-adjusted interest differential.

Because of the difficulty in obtaining observed expectations of the future spot rate, empirical tests of UIP have generally relied on indirect evidence by assuming covered interest parity, i.e. that the forward exchange premium is equal to the interest differential which, together with UIP and rational expectations, then implies the optimality of the forward rate as a spot rate predictor. In contrast with early work by Frenkel (1981), a number of studies have rejected the simple UIP condition using this indirect method (Hansen and Hodrick, 1980; Hakkio, 1981a; amongst others).

We propose, however, to test currency substitutability directly by inferring the optimal conditional forecast of the future spot rate from the time-series properties of the data, using a method originally developed by Sargent (1979) to test the rational expectations model of the term structure of interest rates. Since this methodology is by now well known, we shall give only a brief discussion. For further details see, for example, Taylor, 1987c.

Setting the risk premium in (12.4) identically equal to zero (i.e. assuming perfect substitutability) the UIP condition becomes

$$E(e_{t+n}|I_t) - e_t = i_t - i^*_t \tag{12.5}$$

If the one-period rate of depreciation Δe_t and the interest differential together form a linearly indeterministic, jointly covariance stationary process, then the multivariate form of a statistical theorem known as Wold's decomposition (Hannan, 1970) implies that the process has a unique infinite-order moving average representation. For a suitably chosen value of j, this can be approximated in finite samples by a jth order bivariate vector auto-regression. This can be written[6,7]

$$\begin{pmatrix} \Delta e_t \\ i_t \end{pmatrix} - i^*_t = \sum_{i=1}^{j} \begin{pmatrix} \alpha_i \\ \gamma_i \end{pmatrix} \Delta e_{t-i} + \sum_{i=1}^{j} \begin{pmatrix} \beta_i \\ \delta_i \end{pmatrix} (i - i^*)_{t-i} + \begin{pmatrix} \epsilon_t \\ \eta_t \end{pmatrix} \quad (12.6)$$

where the innovations process $w_t = (\epsilon_t \, \eta_t)'$ is vector white noise:

$$E(w_t \, w'_{t-i}) = \begin{cases} \theta, i = 0 \\ 0, i \ne 0 \end{cases}$$

In companion form the model is

$$Z_t = \Phi Z_{t-1} + \nu_t \quad (12.7)$$

where

$$\Phi = \begin{bmatrix} \alpha_1 & \alpha_2 & \cdots & \alpha_{j-1} & \alpha_j & \beta_1 & \beta_2 & \cdots & \beta_{j-1} & \beta_j \\ \hline & I_{j-1} & & & 0 & & 0 & & & 0 \\ \hline \gamma_1 & \gamma_2 & \cdots & \gamma_{j-1} & \gamma_j & \delta_1 & \delta_2 & \cdots & \delta_{j-1} & \delta_j \\ \hline & 0 & & & 0 & & I_{j-1} & & & 0 \end{bmatrix}$$

$$Z_t = (\Delta e_t, \ldots, \Delta e_{t-j+1}, (i - i^*)_t, \ldots, (i - i^*)_{t-j+1})'$$
$$\nu_t = (\epsilon_t \, 0 \ldots 0 \, \eta_t \, 0 \ldots 0)'$$

Using the first-order formulation (12.7), it is then easily shown that

$$E(e_{t+n} - e_t | \Lambda_{t-1}) - E(i_t - i^*_t | \Lambda_{t-1})$$

$$= \left(h' \sum_{k=1}^{n} \Phi^{k+1} - g' \Phi \right) Z_{t-1} \quad (12.8)$$

where Λ_{t-1} is an information set consisting of only lagged values of the rate of depreciation and the interest differential and h and g are $2j$-dimensional selection vectors with unity in the first and $(j + 1)$th elements respectively and zeros elsewhere. However, taking expectations of the UIP condition under perfect substitutability (equation (12.4)) with respect to Λ_{t-1} implies that (12.8) should be identically equal to zero. Hence, the perfect substitutability restrictions are

$$h' \sum_{k=1}^{n} \Phi^{k+1} - g' \Phi = 0 \quad (12.9)$$

One way of testing these restrictions is to estimate the unrestricted system by OLS and construct a Wald test statistic. Since this is an asymptotic test, however, we also computed likelihood ratio and Lagrange multiplier statistics for the restrictions as a cross-check (see Taylor, 1987c, for details on the construction of these statistics).

12.3.2 Empirical results for substitutability tests

Monthly (end of the month) data on six-month Eurodeposit interest rates were taken from the *Financial Times*. In order to ensure compatibility, the exchange rate data used in this section were also taken from this source. The ERM currencies considered were the German mark, France franc, Italian lira and Dutch guilder; the non-ERM currencies were the US dollar, UK pound and Japanese yen.

The order of the vector autoregressions was chosen using the method outlined by Taylor (1987c). Basically, this involves balancing criteria such as whiteness of residuals, likelihood ratio tests on lag restrictions and minimization of the Akaike information criterion (Akaike, 1973).

Table 12.2 gives the results of testing for perfect substitutability between the German mark and the other currencies examined during the period of operation of the EMS. Whatever test statistic is used, the results are qualitatively identical. As one might have expected, the dollar and the mark are close substitutes and the simple UIP condition (zero risk premium) cannot be rejected for these currencies. However, there are massive rejections of perfect substitutability between the mark and both the yen and sterling. Perhaps the most striking finding, however, is the strong evidence of non-substitutability between the mark and the other ERM currencies. In particular, the simple UIP condition is rejected for the Dutch guilder–German mark exchange rate, which is perhaps slightly surprising since the US dollar–German mark and the US dollar–Dutch guilder exchange rates are often seen as moving in tandem.

Given that the assumption of rational expectations formed part of the maintained hypothesis in the tests outlined and applied above, one possible interpretation of these findings is that market participants do not in fact efficiently process and act upon all available information. However, since typical participants in foreign exchange and asset markets are highly motivated professionals with access to potentially vast information sets literally at the touch of a button, this might appear a rather unattractive option. Indeed, many economists who would demur at the rational expectations hypothesis in general would accept it as a useful working hypothesis when applied to foreign exchange or asset markets – such a view forms the basis, for example, of the 'partly rational' models of Dornbusch (1976) or Blanchard (1981b).

Thus, the results of this section suggest that the EMS has *not* been successful in eliminating the vulnerability of the cross-rates of its members *vis-à-vis* the mark to swings in sentiment against the dollar.[8]

Table 12.2 Wald, likelihood ratio and Lagrange multiplier tests for the perfect substitutability restrictions: six-month maturity

Exchange rate	Chosen value of n	R_1^2	R_2^2	Q_1	Q_2	$L(n-1)$	$L(n+1)$	Wald statistic	Likelihood ratio statistic	Lagrange multiplier statistic
FFR–DMK	1	0.10	0.71	26.16	22.77	—	5.48	13.96	12.94	11.03
				(0.45)	(0.65)		(0.24)	(0.001)	(0.0015)	(0.004)
ITL–DMK	1	0.01	0.66	34.87	28.65	—	6.91	88.15	60.13	52.31
				(0.11)	(0.33)		(0.14)	(0.00)	(0.00)	(0.00)
NGL–DMK	3	0.36	0.64	5.25	30.47	8.49	6.97	268.70	135.83	116.68
				(0.99)	(0.17)	(0.07)	(0.14)	(0.00)	(0.00)	(0.00)
US$–DMK	2	0.09	0.66	19.21	26.10	18.26	3.55	5.99	5.84	5.64
				(0.79)	(0.40)	(0.001)	(0.47)	(0.20)	(0.21)	(0.23)
UK£–DMK	1	0.16	0.80	20.79	19.43	—	1.61	595.85	249.85	138.71
				(0.75)	(0.82)		(0.00)	(0.00)	(0.00)	(0.00)
JPY–DMK	2	0.08	0.87	12.53	33.63	14.51	5.67	506.54	427.03	310.16
				(0.98)	(0.12)	(0.006)	(0.22)	(0.00)	(0.00)	(0.00)

Period of estimation is July 1979 to December 1986, truncated as necessary because of lags. R_1^2 and R_2^2 denote the coefficients of determination for the rate of depreciation and interest differential regressions respectively; Q_1 and Q_2 are the corresponding Ljung–Box statistics evaluated at 27 autocorrelations and are asymptotically central chi-squared variates under the null of white noise residuals, with $27 - n$ degrees of freedom. $L(n-1)$ is a likelihood ratio statistic for a vector autoregression of order $n - 1$ (VAR$(n-1)$) against the alternative VAR(n), whilst $L(n+1)$ tests VAR(n) against VAR$(n+1)$: each is an asymptotically central chi-square variate with four degrees of freedom, and was constructed with a finite sample correction for degrees of freedom as suggested in Sims (1980). The Wald, likelihood ratio and Lagrange multiplier statistics for the rational expectations restrictions are each asymptotically central chi-square under the null with $2n$ degrees of freedom; figures in parentheses denote marginal significance levels in all cases.

12.4 CONCLUSION

Previous empirical studies of the ERM of the EMS have generally focused on whether or not it has attained certain short- to medium-term objectives. More particularly, a number of studies have highlighted the effectiveness of the ERM in enhancing the stability and predictability of member countries' exchange rates, both real and nominal, while in a recent paper Artis and Taylor (1988) demonstrate that these countries have also enjoyed reductions in interest rate volatility, probably due to the enhanced credibility of their exchange rate policy. In this paper, we have examined two issues crucial for the longer-run credibility of the EMS: the degree of intra-ERM asset substitutability and the ability of the EMS to correct long-term misalignment of exchange rates. In both cases, our results are disappointing. The ERM has not, apparently, been successful in rendering member countries' financial assets perfect substitutes or in establishing long-run convergence on some form of PPP. Both these findings are worrying since it is easy to imagine the stock of credibility which the EMS has earned being dissipated as sophisticated and forward-looking international capital markets begin to focus on the longer-run stability properties of the EMS.[9] However, our investigation can only really be described as tentative rather than definitive.[10]

Notes

1 To be more precise, what has been tested is whether exchange rate volatility appears to be trade reducing. While a study by Akhtar and Hilton (1984) found that it was so for US–German trade, comparable studies by the Bank of England (1984) and the International Monetary Fund (1983) failed to confirm this finding for alternative trade flows, time periods and volatility measures. Recent work by Cushman (1986), however, has discovered evidence of volatility effects on trade when 'third country' effects are controlled for (e.g. US dollar–German mark volatility may affect US–UK trade).

2 In each case, the logarithm of the real rate was normalized to zero at the beginning of each test period.

3 A closely allied point relates to the possibly poor power characteristics of the extant tests for random walk behaviour of exchange rates (see for example Hakkio, 1986). Monte Carlo evidence presented by M.P. Taylor (1986) does suggest, however, that a certain class of tests closely related to those used here (the augmented Dickey–Fuller test) may have very high power to reject a false null against a whole range of stationary local alternatives.

4 We are grateful to Emil-Maria Claasen and Eric Perée for pointing this out.

5 The notion of substitutability discussed and tested for in this section really relates to *asset* substitutability. It seems clear that if 'a franc is as good as a mark' then mark and franc Eurodeposits should be perfect substitutes. This is slightly

different to the currency substitution hypothesis of Girton and Roper (1981) and others, where a basket of currencies is held in order to hedge against exchange rate risk.

6 Note that the vector autoregressive representation (12.6) implicitly assumes that the moving average representation has zero deterministic part. In all the empirical work, the data were transformed to mean deviation form, which is equivalent to including constants in the vector autoregressions.

7 Note that this formulation does not directly contradict our earlier reasoning that the exchange rate approximates a random walk – the coefficient matrix may be sparse. Also, although we do not allow for heteroscedastic disturbances in this section, results obtained using the heteroscedastic-robust vector autoregressive tests developed by Taylor (1987b) yielded qualitatively identical results with those reported below.

8 Radaelli (1987) provides corroborating evidence of non-substitutability between the franc and the mark over this period by estimating a particular parameterization of the risk premium suggested by Frankel (1982b). From an examination of movements in the onshore–offshore differential, Radaelli also suggests that market participants may have been reasonably accurate in forecasting the timing of realignments. This is quite important in the present context since otherwise our results may suffer from the peso problem (Krasker, 1980). In order to be absolutely sure that our results are not dominated by the peso problem, we are currently engaged in research which separates the data into 'turbulent' and 'non-turbulent' periods.

9 One interpretation of the international stock market crash of October 1987 is that the markets were worried by the apparent unwillingness of the USA to impose a 'transversality condition' on the international monetary system by taking measures sufficient to curb the US federal budget deficit and hence to reduce the large US current account deficit. This affords an example of the markets' ability to discipline policy-makers.

10 In particular, further work might concentrate on replicating our tests for intra-ERM risk premia with full allowance for the peso problem and on testing for currency misalignment whilst allowing for the impact of the various real shocks which have occurred over the period.

13 What are the Risks in Co-ordinating Economic Policies Internationally?*

Andrew J. Hughes Hallett

13.1 INTRODUCTION

The theoretical case for the international co-ordination of economic policy is now well established. The work of Hamada (1976) and others has shown that independent policy-making is generally suboptimal. In a world where domestic policies have significant spillover effects on other economies, where economies are to different degrees sensitive to external shocks and where governments typically have more policy targets than instruments, co-operation is required to reach an efficient outcome.

The gains from co-ordinating economic policies internationally have always been presented in terms of 'efficiency' gains in a certainty equivalence framework: a set of policies can be found which makes at least one country better off, in terms of its own objectives, without making any other country worse off. The major criticism of recent work aimed at designing co-operative policies for the industrialized economies, and at identifying the sources and extent of those gains, has been that the results are thought to be highly model dependent. This is a major obstacle since policy-makers are typically uncertain about the policy responses of the economies which they are attempting to steer: if the true economic structure is imperfectly understood, the models used will be subject to a large degree of uncertainty and error. However, empirical estimates have shown that the gains from co-ordination are likely to be fairly small.[1] Hence these potential errors impose very substantial risks on the policy-making process, and Feldstein (among others) has argued that countries should not co-ordinate their policies rather than run the risk that model errors will turn all the co-ordination gains into co-ordination losses.

However, there is no obvious reason why co-ordinated policies are necessarily more sensitive to these errors than non-co-operative policies, and policy-makers evidently do believe that they should capture the co-ordination gains if they can. In this chapter therefore we compare co-operative and non-co-operative policies for the USA and the rest of the Organization for Economic Co-operation and Development (ROECD) in the context of seven prominent models. We consider cases in which both countries agree on a model and that model is the true one; in which the countries agree on a model (from the set of seven) but some other model is the true one; and in which the countries disagree about the model. We also include the exchange rate in the welfare function of the two countries involved. This introduces a very direct conflict of interest, since one country's rise is another's fall, and it produces welfare gains from co-ordination which are significantly larger than previous research had suggested.

The implication is that co-operation on the shared exchange rate target may be vital, in terms both of policy improvements and of suppressing the risks imposed by model errors and model disagreements. It turns out that co-ordinated policies can be found which produce gains (over non-co-operative policies) which are robust to model errors. But the downside risks in those policies are not always small, i.e. the gain may be maintained but the co-ordinated and non-co-operative policies as a pair may be badly affected by model errors. This suggests that we need relatively simple policy rules which are robust to model errors, and that co-ordinating exchange rates may be a simple way of delivering the majority of the co-ordination gains without the associated risks from model error. We therefore contrast this approach with a straightforward 'fixed rules' approach as a way of co-ordinating policies while containing risks.

13.2 THE POLICY PROBLEM: SPECIFICATION AND QUALIFICATIONS

13.2.1 Non-co-operative and co-operative policy design

In this chapter we consider a world of two economic blocks each possessing two policy instruments: fiscal and monetary. The fiscal policy instrument is government expenditure; the monetary policy instrument is not specified but is calibrated by the stock of a targeted monetary aggregate, usually M1.

The non-co-operative outcome studied is the simple Nash equilibrium. Each country has a vector of targeted variables. Define y_t^A as the vector of deviations of country A's targets from their ideal values at time t. Then $y^{A'} = (y_1^{A'} \ldots y_T^{A'})$ is the vector of deviations over the decision periods $1, \ldots, T$. Similarly let $x^{A'} = (x_1^{A'} \ldots x_T^{A'})$ be the vector of deviations of country A's instruments from their ideal values.

We can now define a loss function

$$w^A = (y^{A'} C^A y^A + x^{A'} E^A x^A) \qquad (13.1)$$

where C^A and E^A are positive-definite symmetric matrices. This loss function will be minimized subject to a set of linear constraints

$$y^A = R_{AA} x^A + R_{AB} x^B + s^A \qquad (13.2)$$

where R_{AA} and R_{AB} are matrices containing submatrices of dynamic multipliers and s^A represents the sum of non-controllable (exogenous and potentially random) influences on y^A. If the instrument values of the other player B are treated as given, the first-order conditions yield a set of linear reaction functions:

$$x^A = -(R'_{AA} C^A R_{AA} + E^A)^{-1} R'_{AA} C^A (R_{AB} x^B + s^A) \qquad (13.3)$$

Meanwhile country B will have a loss function $w^B = (y^{B'} C^B y^B + x^{B'} E^B x^B)$ and will face the constraints $y^B = R_{BA} x^A + R_{BB} x^B + s^B$. Hence a reaction function for B, analogous to (13.3), can be solved simultaneously with (13.3) to yield the Nash equilibrium values x^A and x^B. This equilibrium is, in general, not optimal even among the set of possible non-co-operative outcomes. But it is an equilibrium in the sense that, given that each player presumes that the other policy-maker will continue what he is currently doing, then no one has any incentive to change policy instruments.

Yet what if policy-makers believed that their opponents would change policy as a result of their own policy changes? In a multiperiod game that is only what each player should expect to happen since it is exactly what he himself is doing. Player A would now conceive of his policy problem as finding the values of x^A such that

$$\frac{\partial w^A}{\partial x^A} + \left(\frac{\partial y^A}{\partial x^B} \frac{\partial x^B}{\partial x^A} + \frac{\partial y^A}{\partial x^A} \right)' \frac{\partial w^A}{\partial y^A} = 0 \qquad (13.4)$$

Of course equation (13.4) depends on the value of x^B, and player A must recognize that his rival will simultaneously be choosing x^B to satisfy the first-order conditions (for x^B) corresponding to (13.4). Solving this pair of first-order conditions will then lead to a conjectural variations equilibrium which is not in general unique but which has a solution that is Pareto-superior to the simple Nash equilibrium. Examples of empirical studies of gains to co-operation using conjectural variations non-co-operative equilibria will be found in the papers by Hughes Hallett (1986a, b). But, in the absence of any pre-assigned 'rules of the game', it is not clear which equilibrium concept should be used. The Nash concept is adopted here as the conventional one, used in the majority of other empirical studies of co-ordination policy.

Finally co-operative outcomes are calculated by minimizing the 'collective' loss function

$$w = \alpha w^A + (1 - \alpha)w^B \qquad 0 < \alpha < 1 \tag{13.5}$$

subject to the constraints represented by (13.2) and its counterpart for y^B. A fundamental question concerns the value of α. Various bargaining models have been proposed in the theoretical literature (see Hughes Hallett, 1986b, for a comparison of several). For most of the comparisons in this chapter, we have set $\alpha = \frac{1}{2}$. However, we also compute outcomes for other α values to check the robustness of those comparisons to other dominant co-operative solutions.

13.2.2 The models

The seven models used in this exercise are drawn from the group of 12 that were reported for a Brookings conference in March 1986 (Bryant et al., 1988). A standardized set of macroeconomic policy actions in the USA was simulated and the results for the US economy and for the ROECD were reported. Parallel results were then given for ROECD policy actions. We use matrices of dynamic multipliers from that exercise and treat them as invariant to the level of economic activity. This procedure would of course falsify the properties of a non-linear model but most investigators argue that these linearization errors are insignificant *in terms of policy choice*. Finally each model uses the same standardized baseline so that the differences in optimized policies due to model variations do not become confused with changes owing to different definitions of the baseline position.

13.2.3 A benchmark objective function

For the sensitivity analysis, a benchmark objective function has to be specified as a point of comparison. No attempt was made to infer 'as if' parameters for this objective function from the actual setting of policy instruments in the recent past, as Oudiz and Sachs (1984) do. That would only be legitimate if there were just one model which the policy-makers believe since the 'as if' parameters will be dependent on the model used to generate them. Since our purpose is to estimate the size of the gains from co-operation across a range of models, the 'as if' procedure would bias the results towards one model and might exaggerate the differences between models and their projected outcomes.

A 'plausible' parameterization of a standard quadratic utility function was used for each country across all models. Each country sets its own priorities and ideal values. The arguments in the hypothesized utility functions were gross national product (GNP) growth, the rate of consumer price inflation, the (nominal) exchange rate and the balance of foreign trade. Movements in policy instruments were penalized to prevent excessive movements in the instruments. Parameters of this benchmark objective and the standardized baseline are shown in the appendix.

13.2.4 Some neglected issues

Policies and their effects are considered over a period of six years. Nonetheless, the approach is not fully dynamic as it considers only 'open-loop' strategies, which are set at the beginning of the six years and not subsequently modified. The question of how best to revise policies in the light of past performance, when policy-makers realize that their model of the economy has been in error, lies beyond the scope of this chapter because it involves designing joint revisions to the policies and the model's parameters. (To do that requires the active learning techniques described by Kendrick, 1981.)

Similarly we do not go into the robustness of co-operative or non-co-operative policies to errors in the initial information sets, external shocks or objective function parameters (this is done in Hughes Hallett, 1987b, 1987c). Nor do we examine the potential for time-inconsistent behaviour by the policy-makers. The solutions here represent a reputational equilibrium because both countries have the opportunity to renege and, if they are rational, they will recognize that if they *both* renege then they will *both* be made worse off. In that case the incentive to renege vanishes (Oudiz and Sachs, 1985) and building a reputation becomes internalized as part of the decision-making process.

13.3 THE GAINS TO CO-OPERATION IN SEVEN MODELS

The results of optimal non-co-operative and co-operative policy-making according to our sample of seven models are collected in tables 13.1–13.4. All results are computed using the initial (1985) information set and they are not revised thereafter. These results therefore represent the options as they would have appeared to policy-makers when the fundamental decision of which model to use had to be taken. The co-operative solution is one in which the welfare of each region receives equal weight. That turns out to be in the set of solutions which dominates the non-co-operative Nash equilibrium for all models.

13.3.1 Where the models agree

Table 13.1 summarizes the expected outcomes of co-operative and non-co-operative policy-making, focusing on the size and distribution of the expected gains from co-operation. Table 13.2 compares the average (fiscal

Table 13.1 Gains to co-operation in seven multicountry models

Model strategy	Conventional models				RE models		
	MCM	EEC	OECD	LINK	MSG	MINI	Taylor
Non-co-operation							
w_{US}	678.46	480.44	441.74	551.35	1264.94	1003.89	1298.05
w_{RO}	1345.58	766.50	1085.25	750.57	1469.00	1085.74	1390.47
Co-operation[a]							
w_{US}	323.6	382.2	386.8	366.26	228.7	294.3	89.4
w_{RO}	450.6	492.0	460.1	470.4	362.2	482.8	174.5
Dominant α range	0.15–0.9	0.26 to 0.85	0.27 to 0.9	0.1 to 0.85	0.1 to 0.9	0.1 to 0.9	0.1 to 0.9
Bargaining power (α values for the USA)							
Nash	0.62	0.59	0.65	0.54	0.50	0.47	0.46
Harsanyi	0.48	0.49	0.49	0.49	0.49	0.50	0.45
Gains to co-operation measured in equivalent GNP annual growth rate units							
w_{US}	4.1%	2.3%	1.7%	3.1%	6.6%	5.6%	7.1%
w_{RO}	6.2%	3.7%	5.3%	3.7%	6.8%	5.3%	7.1%
Proportion of that gain due to exchange rate co-ordination alone[b]							
w_{US}	0.59	0.55	1.17	0.66	0.95	0.82	0.89
w_{RO}	0.23	0.20	0.12	0.44	0.89	0.97	0.89

[a] In co-operative policy, α = 0.5.

[b] If all policy variables contributed equally to co-ordination these proportions would all be 0.167. w_{US}, loss-function value for USA; w_{RO}, loss-function value for ROECD.

Table 13.2 Average policy instrument values under non-co-operation and co-operation

| | United States | | | | | | ROECD | | | | | |
| | $\dot{M}$ | | | G | | | $\dot{M}$ | | | G | | |
	Nash	Co-op	Change	Nash	Co-op	Change	Nash	Co-op	Change	Nash	Co-op	Change
MCM	5.48	5.20	−0.28	19.50	19.22	−0.28	4.62	6.14	1.52	20.96	21.50	0.54
EEC	5.75	5.46	−0.29	17.52	17.59	0.07	5.55	4.74	−0.81	22.15	23.56	1.41
OECD	6.20	7.75	1.55	18.27	20.44	2.17	5.33	5.83	−0.01	20.93	22.96	2.03
LINK	5.90	4.89	−1.01	17.28	17.12	−0.16	5.84	4.51	−1.33	22.86	22.69	−0.17
MSG	5.46	4.61	−0.85	18.55	19.69	1.14	6.94	3.96	−2.98	21.28	22.86	1.58
MINI	5.77	4.04	−1.73	18.45	17.19	−1.26	5.54	4.27	−1.67	22.99	21.58	−1.41
Taylor	5.31	5.84	0.53	18.72	19.27	0.55	7.51	6.49	−1.02	22.32	22.32	0.00
Mean	5.69	5.40	−0.29	18.32	18.64	0.32	5.90	5.07	−0.90	21.93	22.50	0.66
S.D.	0.30	1.19		0.75	1.33		0.99	0.96		0.87	0.75	
C of v (%)	5.34	22.04		4.07	7.13		16.78	18.97		3.97	3.33	

$\dot{M}$, average annual rate of money growth per cent; G, average government expenditure, per cent of GNP, both at constant prices; Nash, non-co-operative solution, open-loop Nash equilibrium; Co-op, co-operative solution, $\alpha = 0.5$; Change, difference between co-operative and Nash instrument setting; C of V, coefficient of variation.

Table 13.3 Average policy values over six years in the non-co-operative solution

Model	US targets				ROECD targets		
	GṄP	$\dot{P}$	TB	E/R	GṄP	$\dot{P}$	TB
MCM	3.36	4.22	−77.07	−6.81	1.87	2.52	66.45
EEC	2.05	2.51	−93.31	−7.01	3.12	−0.24	58.68
OECD	3.25	3.37	−73.87	−5.90	1.35	1.16	70.41
LINK	4.34	1.24	−101.28	−10.01	3.84	3.47	59.72
MSG	1.62	4.07	−85.37	−3.04	4.16	2.02	50.96
MINI	3.19	4.32	−67.32	−8.37	4.13	3.67	52.63
Taylor	2.18	4.00	−74.82	−2.77	4.10	3.24	52.45

GṄP, percentage rate of GNP growth per year; $\dot{P}$, annual rate of increase in consumer prices; TB, net real trade balance in \$bn; E/R, US dollar divided by a weighted average of other OECD currencies.
All variables expressed as annual percentage changes, except TB (1985 \$bn).

Table 13.4 Average policy values over six years in the co-operative solution ($\alpha = \frac{1}{2}$)

Model	US targets				ROECD targets		
	GṄP	$\dot{P}$	TB	E/R	GṄP	$\dot{P}$	TB
MCM	4.86	1.84	−84.3	−0.36	4.26	2.82	55.6
EEC	3.82	2.97	−73.08	−3.96	3.95	2.39	52.64
OECD	3.63	2.55	−101.13	−4.33	4.31	2.56	57.63
LINK	3.58	2.03	−72.47	−0.53	5.11	2.32	57.55
MSG	3.29	4.43	−90.68	−4.57	3.43	1.63	54.55
MINI	4.43	3.80	−83.09	−3.32	4.26	4.20	53.06
Taylor	3.86	3.32	−83.44	−5.95	4.79	2.56	56.59

Variables defined as in table 13.3.

and monetary) policy interventions needed to achieve those outcomes, while tables 13.3 and 13.4 set out the corresponding expected target values. The results agree on the following general points.

1 The expected gains to co-operation are fairly large, perhaps three to four times larger than previous estimates. About three-quarters of those gains are due to the exchange rate's direct contribution to the objective functions.[2] Co-ordination of the exchange rate is therefore the crucial

factor in co-ordinating policies generally, and for the US economy in particular.

2   All models agree on a dominant range of co-operative policies ($0.27 < \alpha < 0.85$).

3   They substantially agree on relative bargaining powers. The Harsanyi bargaining model, for instance, suggests a mean α value for the USA of 0.48 (with a standard deviation of only 0.02).

4   The models clearly agree more on the likely target outcomes under each strategy than they do on the interventions needed to achieve those outcomes (tables 13.3 and 13.4 versus table 13.2).

5   The results from the rational expectations models consistently produce results which are distinct from the results of conventional models, there being greater similarity between the within-group results than between the rational expectations and conventional models.

6   There is always greater similarity between the results generated by different models under co-operative policy-making than under a non-co-operative policy regime.

7   Holtham and Hughes Hallett (1987) show that all the models agree on lower activism in the policy interventions, and smaller fluctuations in the targets, under a co-operative policy regime. Co-operation therefore implies greater continuity in the policies and smoother target trajectories.

13.3.2   Where the models disagree

For the USA the average policy settings over six years are *more* diverse across models in the co-operative solution than at the non-co-operative equilibrium (table 13.2); the standard deviation of instrument settings across models is higher under co-operation. This is particularly marked for monetary policy. The average intervention values, on the other hand, change rather little with co-operation. For the ROECD the picture is reversed. Both government expenditures and monetary growth become more uniform with co-operation.

There is considerable diversity in the nature of the policy changes in the move to co-operation. On balance both countries switch from monetary to fiscal expansion; government expenditures are increased on average while monetary growth is reduced. This switch is quite marked in the ROECD but it is marginal for the USA. However, the consensus picture masks some significant disagreements. Government expenditure in the USA increases in four of the models and decreases in the other three; co-operation increases government expenditure in the ROECD in four models, reduces it in two and leaves it unchanged in one. Monetary growth in the USA is reduced by co-operation in five models and increased in two; it is generally decreased in the ROECD – only one model gives faster ROECD money growth in consequence of co-operation. There is therefore a genuine consensus for monetary tightening in both areas but the 'consensus' for increased government expenditures is really only the result of averaging.

What about changes in *relative* policy settings between the two areas? The average reduction in monetary growth is greater in the ROECD than in the USA, and five of the seven models imply relatively greater monetary restriction in the ROECD. The average expansion of government expenditures is likewise greater in the ROECD, but only three of the seven models actually show the ROECD to be the more expansionary. There is therefore a consensus on monetary policy, both in terms of the direction of adjustment (contraction) and in terms of who bears the burden of that adjustment (the ROECD). But, although the average outcome is expansion by the ROECD, any genuine consensus on fiscal policy is elusive on either score.

Among the target variables, all models show that the move to co-operation would secure greater output growth and a smaller dollar depreciation together with smaller exchange rate movements. On average the US trade deficit is increased, while the ROECD's surplus is unchanged. Co-operation also leads to less inflation in the USA and more in the ROECD; but there are some cases where co-operation also implies higher inflation for the USA (in the EEC, LINK and MSG models). The uniformity of these results is clearly higher across rational expectations models than it is across conventional models. There is also greater uniformity in the US variables than in their ROECD counterparts. Co-operation uniformly yields faster growth in the USA and ROECD, but the ROECD's gain is usually smaller.

13.3.3 The gains from co-ordination

Estimates of the gains from co-operation vary substantially across models, ranging from 12 to 93 per cent for the USA and from 35 to 87 per cent for the ROECD (table 13.1). Removing the exchange rate components of these calculations only reduces the variability moderately.[3] However, if the variation in the estimated co-operative gains is large, so is the difference between the mean of these results and the results of previous studies. Table 13.1 shows that the gains to co-ordination would be 'worth' the equivalent of about 3–5 per cent extra GNP growth per year for the USA and about 4–6 per cent extra GNP growth for the ROECD if all other variables were to remain fixed on some pre-assigned path.[4] This is large compared with the estimated 0.5 per cent a year for the USA and 1.3 per cent a year for the EEC (Hughes Hallett, 1986a).

These gains have been estimated with the essentially arbitrary choice of $\alpha = \frac{1}{2}$. Economic theory has produced a wide range of optimal bargaining models based on a variety of behavioural assumptions. Several of these models have been used to generate rational bargains between the USA and

ROECD, and table 13.1 reports results for two of them. The Nash co-operative bargaining model is the conventional approach and it corresponds to picking α to maximize the product of the co-operation gains over the best non-co-operative outcomes (which is said to minimize the risk of breakdown because it distributes the gains in proportion to bargaining power, as measured by the losses incurred by not making a deal). A second possibility is the Harsanyi model which maximizes the sum of the co-operative gains over the non-co-operative outcomes (like the economic surplus measure of welfare analysis).

In this case, the Nash and Harsanyi models yield values of 0.55 and 0.48, with standard deviations of 0.07 and 0.02 respectively. The Harsanyi model, in particular, is extremely insensitive to model changes. Hence there is really no risk that the two countries would fail to agree on a bargain over their relative contributions or the distribution of the gains just because they are uncertain about the model. But it is true that there is more variation in the results between types of bargains than there is across different economic models using one type of bargain. This suggests that it would be comparatively easy to secure agreement on some criteria (e.g. joint gains) but more difficult on others (e.g. that no country should gain too much over the others).

13.4 THE RISKS IMPOSED BY MODEL UNCERTAINTY

A comparison of the outcomes under non-co-operative and co-operative policies shows that they are more uniform across models in the co-operative case (tables 13.3 and 13.4). The expected outcomes of an optimized co-operative policy are therefore less sensitive to model changes than their non-co-operative counterparts; this holds for *all* the target variables in both countries. Hence you would expect (across alternative information sets) smaller differences in policy performance from model changes when you co-operate than when you do not. How useful this result is depends on your attitude to risk. If you are not concerned by the risk that policies generated by one model might produce bad results in a world where some other model is actually 'true', then it matters less under co-operation which set of policies (and hence which model) is chosen even when those models disagree about the nature of the optimal interventions. But it is most unlikely that policy-makers would actually be so risk neutral.

The difficulty here is that we have so far considered only *ex ante* sensitivities, i.e. by how much the policy-makers would want to change their policies if each model were selected in turn. That shows the different outcomes when each model actually turns out to be 'true', but not what would happen under different model *errors*. If one is risk averse, a better evaluation of the possible outcomes is something like the expected outcome (evaluated now across different models) of the policy sets generated by each model in turn. That kind of calculation involves *ex post* sensitivities, which show how much the policy outcomes would change if policies, computed using one model and information set, were applied to a world where another model and information set actually turns out to be true. It could be disastrous to look at the potential gains when the chosen model happens to be true, but not at the potential losses when the chosen model is 'wrong'.

We therefore need to consider *ex post* robustness, with the aim of minimizing the sensitivity of the expected outcomes of the chosen policy to model errors. The standard way to do this is to compute expected outcomes when the policy packages which are optimal for each model in turn are evaluated according to each of the other models in the 'sample' (Chow, 1981; Hughes Hallett and Rees, 1983; Becker et al., 1986). This is the only practical way we have of simulating, *ex ante*, what might happen if the world

Table 13.5 Payoff matrix for optimal non-co-operative (Nash) results: absolute robustness

Reality	Maintained model						
	LINK	OECD	EEC	MCM	Taylor	MSG	MINI
LINK	551.4	1116.1	858.5	5580.0	7706.1	8624.2	6203.5
	750.6	2234.5	720.3	8403.8	7103.4	8511.5	6103.3
OECD	846.7	441.7	829.7	7586.7	15881.8	14574.9	7371.2
	854.5	1085.3	1028.5	10183.9	16306.6	15766.4	7904.2
EEC	688.8	488.0	480.4	4778.6	3745.6	3334.4	3503.2
	873.7	3403.7	766.5	9463.6	4214.5	4915.1	3360.7
MCM	484.8	382.6	428.6	678.5	3258.1	4000.3	1086.6
	701.1	908.6	571.7	1345.6	3552.2	4484.8	1474.5
Taylor	523.3	371.8	391.8	683.5	1298.1	1067.4	393.0
	727.1	1223.5	631.6	2631.6	1390.5	1422.1	552.7
MSG	686.7	477.8	574.9	771.4	2313.5	1265.0	270.1
	836.6	946.6	660.9	1288.6	2413.7	1469.0	527.1
MINI	477.4	334.2	326.7	1565.7	3115.5	2505.2	1003.9
	601.6	1566.5	414.2	3253.6	3014.0	2866.2	1085.7
Minimax	846.7*	1116.1	858.5	7586.7	15881.8	14574.9	7371.2
	873.7*	3403.7	1028.5	10183.9	16306.6	15766.4	7904.2

The cell in the upper row relating to each model is the loss-function value for the USA; the lower row is the loss-function value for the ROECD.
Columns are 'maintained' model; rows denote the model corresponding to 'reality'. The asterisk denotes the maintained model which minimizes (for each decision-maker separately) the maximum losses risked under the different possible outcomes considered.

behaved differently from the maintained model. Of course, it is an act of considerable faith to suppose that the available models represent all the possible states of the world. The difficulty is not simply the expense of adding more models, but the fact that we cannot know in principle what other specifications should be included.

Tables 13.5 and 13.6 show the payoff matrices under non-co-operative and co-operative policy regimes. Each column shows the expected value of the USA and ROECD loss functions using the optimized policies from the indicated maintained model when the 'true' state of the world is given by the model named in each row. The diagonal elements therefore show outcomes when the maintained model is correct; the other elements show the outcomes under various potential model errors. The final two rows (marked 'minimax') repeat the largest US and ROECD elements in each column, i.e. the worst outcome which could be sustained when each model in turn is maintained.[5]

The payoff matrices presented in tables 13.5 and 13.6 are subsets of much

Table 13.6 Payoff matrix for co-operative $(\alpha = \frac{1}{2})$ results: absolute robustness

Reality	LINK	OECD	EEC	MCM	Taylor	MSG	MINI
			Maintained model				
LINK	366.3	1759.1	860.6	819.7	946.5	2081.6	2104.4
	470.7	2984.4	851.7	958.3	1028.3	1935.8	2142.3
OECD	1148.4	386.8	1939.3	495.5	903.8	1222.6	2794.1
	11050.0	460.1	12415.8	3667.7	19117.7	6152.2	9000.1
EEC	1283.7	4660.5	382.2	1028.9	1291.5	3081.7	3452.9
	2497.9	3061.8	492.0	1318.0	1768.9	2431.6	3587.7
MCM	16087.6	6077.0	7707.2	323.6	3774.6	3704.6	10263.8
	9741.5	4236.1	22475.5	450.8	1729.4	12827.6	5497.7
Taylor	7730.4	2615.2	4447.8	405.4	89.4	2513.8	8850.3
	2249.3	3181.7	1549.7	492.4	174.5	638.8	1394.6
MSG	4761.9	828.0	758.5	507.9	387.5	228.7	2483.9
	9291.4	5052.2	8539.9	858.1	2436.4	362.2	957.9
MINI	1206.1	779.5	1991.5	751.7	515.2	467.6	294.3
	1787.6	2264.5	3668.0	1013.9	775.5	1137.9	482.8
Minimax	16087.6	6077.0	7707.2	1028.9*	3774.6	3704.6	10263.8
	11050.0	5052.2	22475.5	3667.7*	19117.7	12827.6	9000.1

The asterisk denotes the maintained model which minimizes (for each decision-maker separately) the maximum losses risked under the different possible outcomes considered.

larger possible matrices. Since we are examining the risks implied by model uncertainty, and not uncertainty about the model which other policy-makers might choose, tables 13.5 and 13.6 report only the range of possible outcomes when both policy-makers believe in the same model at any time. This gives payoff matrices with 49 cells. If the policy-makers believe in different models, one or both of which could differ from the true model, each payoff matrix would have 343 cells. In practice, such disagreements about the model could well exist and we examine separately any extra risks which that might introduce (see tables 13.8 and 13.9 below).

13.4.1 No co-operation

Suppose that policy-makers have diffuse priors – they are not dogmatic – and that they are risk averse and therefore wish to use a minimax criterion for selecting the model and policy combination. If they do not wish to co-operate but assume, at least to start with, that their opponents will believe the same model as they, both the US and the ROECD policy-makers would select the LINK model and its associated policy package. That would be a stable result from considering just this restricted set of possibilities.

13.4.2 Co-operation

Suppose, instead, that policy-makers have a prior commitment to co-operation and are looking for the best model on which to proceed. The MCM model clearly dominates on the minimax outcome criterion (table 13.6). In fact it is one of only three models that yield an expected positive return to co-operation, assigning each model equal prior probabilities. (Table 13.7 shows the difference between the matrices in tables 13.5 and 13.6.) The other models are Taylor and MSG, each of which predicts a relatively poor outcome to non-co-operative policy-making. This distinction appears to be due to the fact that exchange rate multipliers are larger than average in these models.

Finally, co-operative policies entail greater downside risks for the USA than does non-co-operation with four of the maintained models. The risks are more serious for the ROECD where co-operation implies greater downside risks in six out of seven models. In fact the maximum losses possible with non-co-operative policies based on LINK are less (for both countries) than the maximum losses risked under co-operation based on any model. This illustrates the most significant result of this section: although non-co-operative policies cannot secure all the gains available through co-operative policies, they do not run the risk of very large downside losses either.

Table 13.7 Payoff matrix showing the percentage gains to co-operation (the difference between tables 13.6 and 13.5 as a percentage of the values in table 13.5): the relative robustness of co-operation

Reality	Maintained model						
	LINK	OECD	EEC	MCM	Taylor	MSG	MINI
LINK	33.6	−57.6	−0.2	88.9	87.7	75.9	66.1
	37.3	−33.6	−18.2	88.6	85.5	77.3	64.9
OECD	−35.6	12.4	−133.7	93.5	94.3	91.6	62.1
	−1193.2	57.6	−1107.2	64.0	−17.2	61.0	−13.9
EEC	−86.4	−855.0	20.4	78.5	65.5	7.6	1.4
	−185.9	10.0	35.8	86.1	58.0	50.5	−6.8
MCM	−3218.4	−1488.3	−1698.2	52.3	−15.9	7.4	−844.6
	−1289.5	−366.2	−3831.3	66.5	51.3	−186.0	−272.9
Taylor	−1377.2	−603.4	−1035.2	40.7	93.1	−135.5	−2152.0
	−209.4	−160.0	−145.4	81.3	87.5	55.1	−152.3
MSG	−593.4	−73.3	−31.9	34.2	83.3	81.9	−819.6
	−1010.6	−433.7	−1192.2	33.4	−0.9	75.3	−81.7
MINI	−152.6	−133.2	−509.6	52.0	83.5	81.3	70.7
	−197.1	−44.6	−785.6	68.8	74.3	60.3	55.5
Minimax	−3218.4	−1488.3	−1698.2	34.2*	−15.9	−135.5	−2152.0
	−1289.5	−433.7	−3831.3	33.4*	−17.2	−186.0	−272.9

A positive value implies a gain from co-operation over non-co-operation, and a negative value implies a loss.
The asterisk denotes the maintained model which maximizes the minimum gain (or minimizes the largest possible loss) from co-operation under the different possible outcomes considered.

13.4.3 Co-operative gains

Table 13.7 shows the gains from policy co-ordination in the same payoff matrix form. There are 48 entries (out of 98) where that co-operation would produce worse outcomes than non-co-operative policies as a result of using the wrong model. Since we are not working with the complete 343-cell matrix, this shows that model uncertainty is, if anything, a greater obstacle to policy co-operation than model disagreements. However, there is no country bias; 23 of the losses apply to the USA and 25 to the ROECD.

Nevertheless the losses risked are relatively large: only nine of them are actually smaller than the co-operative gains obtained when policy-makers manage to pick the correct model. Moreover the risks of suffering a loss are concentrated on the conventional models: the MSG and Taylor models are fairly safe (with two or three losses) while LINK, EEC or OECD are highly risky (with 11 or 12 losses out of 14).

Finally the MCM is the only model which continues to yield significant gains to co-operation whichever model turns out to be true. Whether this constitutes an argument for using MCM depends on one's priors and attitude to risk because, although MCM guarantees co-operative gains, non-co-operative policies on LINK would carry lower downside risks. An agnostic or strongly risk-averse policy-maker might therefore prefer to use LINK and not co-operate at all.

The risks highlighted in this section are all evaluated with co-operative policies based on an arbitrary choice of $\alpha = \frac{1}{2}$. Would those perceived risks change with alternative bargains? Taking the most popular bargaining model (Nash, with the α values given in table 13.1), only two extra gains and one extra loss were generated in table 13.7. Hence the estimated risks are extremely robust to the type of bargain struck.

13.5 THE RISKS IN MODEL DISAGREEMENT

To what extent does the possibility that policy-makers may disagree about which model to use increase the risks that they face? Does the risk of model disagreement change any of the conclusions in the previous section?

13.5.1 The disagreement scenario

Tables 13.8 and 13.9 display the objective function values for the USA and ROECD when policy-makers decide to use different models to generate optimal non-co-operative and co-operative policies. In the non-co-operative case, to say that the USA maintains LINK and the ROECD maintains MCM, for example, means that the USA derives its optimal reaction function from the LINK model and the ROECD its reaction function from the MCM model, and the two reaction functions are then solved simultaneously to yield the policy values. These values can then be simulated through each model in turn to provide the outcomes reported in table 13.8. In the corresponding co-operative scenario of table 13.9, neither country is explicit about the model it uses when making its policy proposals. So the USA would use LINK multipliers to represent its own target responses, while the ROECD uses the MCM multipliers for its targets. The co-operative bargain is then created by minimizing (13.5) subject to a mixed set of restrictions

Table 13.8 Payoff matrix for non-co-operative policies with disagreement over the models

		Maintained models											
		US LINK	EEC	MINI	MCM	EEC	MINI	MCM	LINK	MINI	MCM	LINK	EEC
Reality		RO MCM	MCM	MCM	LINK	LINK	LINK	EEC	EEC	EEC	MINI	MINI	MINI
LINK	w_{US}	259.2	305.6	325.1	3915.2	365.0	346.6	379.5	358.2	336.8	346.2	269.2	368.8
	w_{RO}	488.3	565.6	547.4	630.2	496.9	458.5	628.5	697.0	621.3	446.5	423.6	453.9
EEC	w_{US}	501.9	281.5	277.0	5214.0	315.1	300.8	266.3	462.5	192.8	320.9	476.0	278.2
	w_{RO}	481.6	446.1	450.3	1004.0	372.8	367.2	490.9	564.3	485.2	429.0	322.7	318.3
MCM	w_{US}	1502.5	1807.5	727.9	10975.0	3683.7	2322.7	935.0	2465.7	1333.9	758.2	2032.4	2316.9
	w_{RO}	2190.3	2844.7	1253.2	7405.4	6834.7	4212.4	3719.0	6166.9	3958.1	2944.6	4125.6	5166.1
MINI	w_{US}	1238.8	1294.9	590.1	4805.7	2731.4	1873.0	527.5	1659.9	534.7	700.5	1659.8	1652.9
	w_{RO}	1419.0	1633.0	869.9	2237.7	2803.1	2000.1	861.3	1809.3	850.4	828.7	1527.6	1664.6
Minimax[a]	w_{US}	1502.5*	1807.5*	6203.0	10975.0*	3683.7*	6203.0	5580.0	2465.7*	6203.0	5580.0	2032.4*	2316.9*
	w_{RO}	9463.0	9463.0*	9463.0	7405.4*	6834.7*	4212.4*	3719.0*	6166.9*	3958.1*	6103.0	6103.0	5166.1

[a] The maximum loss which each country could sustain by maintaining the model named at the column head (first row, USA's model; second row, ROECD's model) (from tables 13.5 and 13.6, adjusted to the subset of four models).
* The maximum loss is supplied by model disagreement.

Table 13.9 Payoff matrix for co-operative ($\alpha = \frac{1}{2}$) policies with disagreement over the models

		Maintained models											
US: Reality	RO:	LINK MCM	EEC MCM	MINI MCM	MCM LINK	EEC LINK	MINI LINK	MCM EEC	LINK EEC	MINI EEC	MCM MINI	LINK MINI	EEC MINI
LINK	w_{US}	297.9	335.8	333.6	406.2	421.4	367.2	423.9	471.9	368.0	357.0	329.3	445.1
	w_{RO}	511.1	575.3	553.3	534.3	593.0	510.7	604.9	747.1	577.9	453.6	457.2	460.3
EEC	w_{US}	555.8	310.4	285.6	430.4	391.7	333.7	329.2	680.9	229.7	342.2	566.5	361.1
	w_{RO}	483.6	457.5	462.1	493.8	495.6	442.0	476.2	616.6	430.2	445.5	359.7	345.6
MCM	w_{US}	1934.9	3580.0	3792.0	2630.0	4063.0	2886.0	1879.0	3640.7	2241.0	1681.0	2551.6	2994.0
	w_{RO}	3181.5	5061.0	4437.0	5085.0	8514.0	5454.0	4663.0	8671.1	5234.0	3050.0	5619.4	6915.0
MINI	w_{US}	2015.7	3464.0	887.0	5297.0	7961.0	4808.0	1950.0	3239.0	1872.0	1242.0	2528.3	4343.0
	w_{RO}	2149.3	3780.0	1241.0	5534.0	8105.0	5015.0	2185.0	3211.1	207.0	1373.0	2363.7	4314.0
Minimax[a]	w_{US}	16087.6	7707.2	10263.8	5297.0*	7061.0*	10263.8	1950.0*	16087.6	10263.8	1681.0*	16087.6	4343.0
	w_{RO}	1318.0*	5061.0*	4437.0*	9741.5	9746.5	9741.5	22475.5	22475.5	22475.5	5497.0	5619.4*	4314.0

[a] See the notes to table 13.8.

$$\begin{bmatrix} y^A \\ y^B \end{bmatrix} = \begin{bmatrix} R^A_{AA} & R^A_{AB} \\ R^B_{BA} & R^B_{BB} \end{bmatrix} \begin{bmatrix} x^A \\ x^B \end{bmatrix} + \begin{bmatrix} s^A \\ s^B \end{bmatrix} \tag{13.6}$$

in the notation of (13.2), where the superscript on each R matrix indicates which model generated the policy multipliers. This is the procedure adopted by Frankel and Rockett (1988), but it obviously represents a lower level of co-operation than if countries introduce their models explicitly into the negotiations so that in effect they bargain about the various policy–model *combinations* represented in table 13.6.

Rather than reproduce all the 294 disagreement cases which belong to tables 13.8 and 13.9, we report results for a subset of four models. MCM and LINK are included because they are the least-risk choices (so far) for co-operative policy-making and non-co-operative policy-making respectively. The next best performer in tables 13.5 and 13.6 was the EEC model, and the best of the rational expectations models was MINI. That subset gives 48 cases to consider, and 96 entries in tables 13.8 and 13.9. The final double row in each table repeats the element which is largest in either the corresponding column of that table or the associated column of table 13.5 or 13.6 based on the same subset of four models, i.e. the worst outcome that each country could experience while maintaining the indicated model from the subset of four. These results understate the risks of a bad outcome to the extent that one of the three excluded models might produce even worse results if it was included as 'reality', but any such differences were small enough to have no impact on the conclusions.

13.5.2 Non-co-operative policies

The most obvious feature of table 13.8 is that disagreement over the model can add significantly to the risks which policy-makers face in a non-co-operative environment. Taking minimax as the selection criterion, 14 out of 24 entries in the final double row show that disagreement produces a worse outcome with a given pair of maintained models than would agreement to adopt either model from that pair. Interestingly disagreement produces all these bad outcomes from the case where MCM is 'true'. In fact, by contrast with table 13.5, the outcomes when either LINK or EEC are reality are uniformly better under disagreement than agreement; those when MINI is reality are roughly the same, while those when MCM is reality are all rather worse under disagreement. So the incidence of risk is very unevenly spread across alternative states of the world, but more evenly spread over the different combinations of maintained models. This means that uncertainty is more serious than disagreement over the model: policy-makers can do rather little to control the risks caused by uncertainty either over the 'true' model or over which model their opponents will choose.

In this case the USA would best maintain LINK, and the ROECD MINI since (in ignorance of each others' intentions) the USA could only *expect* to suffer a loss of 2465 at worst and the ROECD a loss of 6103 – rather than the larger maximum losses if they unilaterally adopted other models. In practice, that model combination would actually yield losses of 2033 and 6103 for the USA and the ROECD, which is slightly better than the USA would expect but a long way short of the maximum losses of 688 and 873 if they could both agree to use LINK.[6] Once again, we see that disagreement over the model exaggerates the losses risked quite significantly. On the other hand, disagreement yields an unstable solution here. If the USA knew or suspected that the ROECD would choose MINI then the USA would choose MINI too (to reduce its loss to 1003, and that of the ROECD to 1085 at the same time). Similarly if the ROECD knew that the USA would choose LINK, then it would do so too (reducing its loss to 750, and that of the USA to 551). So policy-makers, who are sophisticated enough to perform this kind of analysis, are rather unlikely to pick a model disagreement solution – or, which comes to the same thing, the incentives to go for a full information exchange about models and information but to continue to pick policies in a non-co-operative manner are large. Tacit co-operation in the form of information exchanges leading to agreement over the model can obviously cut down the risks very substantially. The question is whether that approach is an adequate substitute for full co-ordination.

13.5.3   Co-operative policies

Turning now to the co-operative case (table 13.9), disagreement over the model appears to offset some of the risks of model uncertainty: the entries in table 13.9 are smaller than the corresponding row of table 13.6 for LINK, EEC and MCM (but not MINI). This happens because mixing the constraints, as in (13.6), introduces some characteristics from another possible model, and the combination of two models together tends to produce results 'closer' to the various alternative realities than either of those models could have done individually. Hence co-operation reduces the risks faced by policy-makers through risk sharing. However, those risk reductions, while significant in themselves, are not very useful because the losses in table 13.6 were large to start with and consequently the results in table 13.9 remain worse than their counterparts in table 13.8 in all but eight out of 96 cases. Sometimes these differences are small and could be cured by an alternative bargain (α value), but more often the margins are really quite large. Finally, model disagreement evidently exaggerates the risks facing policy-makers less under co-operation than under non-co-operation – only 8 out of 24 of the maximum losses in table 13.9 arise through disagreement, compared with 14 out of 24 in table 13.8.

Under this regime, both the USA and the ROECD would want to use MCM because both would *expect* to lose less than with any other choice irrespective of which model the other chose to use. At worst the USA expects to get 5297 and the ROECD 5061. In practice that choice would yield 1028 and 1318 respectively – which is now better than the best non-co-operative outcomes when the possibility of disagreement over the model is recognized but not as good as when they 'agree to agree' to an information exchange but not to co-operate. Moreover, this co-operative choice of MCM is a stable outcome: neither side has any incentive to deviate unilaterally. Once again we see how much model disagreement exaggerates the risks, and that a powerful way of reducing those risks is to co-operate on picking a model (even if it turns out to be false).

Thus co-operation works best if it involves negotiating an agreed model at the same time, and the potential losses increase very sharply if this is not done. However, even that is not as good as information exchanges on the model plus non-co-operative policies. So, as far as handling risk is concerned, non-co-operative policies without model agreement are worst; then co-operation without agreed models; then co-operation without agreed models; and finally non-co-operative policies on an agreed model. Hence the key to risk reduction is to at least agree on the model rather than on a policy bargain; that can remove much of the downside risks even if it fails to capture all the upside gains.

13.5.4 Simple (fixed) policy rules

One simple way of avoiding the inevitable uncertainties due to model specification errors is to follow fixed (simple) policy rules. Many investigators have argued that highly developed decision rules, such as those being operated here, are not robust enough to be operated reliably where there is a substantial uncertainty about the true economic responses (or about the correct specification of the different planning priorities for that matter). Fixed policy rules, they argue, give nearly as good a performance on average, but without the attendant downside risks.[7] Fixed rules also simplify matters. Not only do policy-makers avoid any complicated decision procedures designed to reduce the possible risks from model errors or model disagreements, they do not even have to maintain any formal model or any information gathering network.

Table 13.10 sets out the results of applying fixed policy rules to each of the seven original models. The instruments have been set to their ideal values throughout: government expenditures in the USA fall by 1 per cent of GNP each year (from 20 to 15 per cent, to eliminate the current US budget deficit); government expenditures in the ROECD remain at their historical value of 22 per cent of GNP; and monetary growth is constant at 5 per cent in the

Table 13.10 Objective function values for fixed rule policies

	Model						
	MCM	OECD	EEC	LINK	MGS	MINI	Taylor
w^*_{US}	1924.2	1144.9	938.2	1005.7	1417.8	1150.6	1545.5
w^*_{RO}	1753.9	1844.6	924.1	1047.6	1553.9	1095.0	1524.3

USA and 6 per cent in the ROECD. This is a scenario of fiscal conservatism and Friedmanite neutral monetary growth. It is not the only possible fixed rule scenario, but it is the obvious one since it represents the optimal policy when the priorities on reaching the targets are reduced (Hughes Hallett, 1979). Hence other fixed rules are unlikely to perform very much better.

The objective function values in table 13.10 show significant losses compared with the non-co-operative outcomes of the conventional models in table 13.1, but smaller losses for the rational expectations models. Naturally comparison with the co-operative outcomes of table 13.1 reveals even greater losses, since a fixed rule is unaffected by the policy regime and cannot hope to capture any of the co-ordination gains. Thus fixed rules show a poor performance in that they are quite unable to come close to the gains of well-designed policies. However, fixed rules eliminate the downside risks of model uncertainty and disagreements most effectively; the outcomes in table 13.10 show losses several times smaller (for every model) than the potential losses recorded in tables 13.8 and 13.9. The worst losses due to model errors are therefore eliminated at the cost of not being able to capture the gains achieved by getting the model right.

The fact that these outcomes are more robust than either the non-co-operative or the co-operative results shows that policy conflicts, whether fully exploited in the non-co-operative case or partially resolved in the co-operative case, greatly increase the risks faced by policy-makers. However, these results do not constitute grounds for adopting fixed rules since the risk of sustaining large losses can also be eliminated by carefully selecting the model. In table 13.10 the maximum losses, whichever model turns out to be 'true', are 1924.2 for the USA and 1844.6 for the ROECD. This is worse than maintaining non-co-operative policies in the LINK, OECD or EEC models for the USA (but better than the other four) and worse than using non-co-operative policies in the LINK and EEC models for the ROECD (but better than the remaining five models). So *both* countries can eliminate risks better, whilst also retaining the possibility of securing upside gains when their model turns out to be right, if they adopt the LINK (or EEC) models and non-co-operative policies.

Thus fixed rules are not effective here because the risks can be eliminated better by choosing the appropriate model and non-co-operative policies. However, the robustness argument against co-operation remains since the latter cannot eliminate the risks so effectively, although it does offer significantly larger upside gains. So the security–ambition trade-off is genuinely between co-operative and non-co-operative policies rather than between optimal versus fixed or simple policy rules.

13.6 SPECIFYING AIMS FOR A SHARED TARGET: THE EXCHANGE RATE PRIORITIES

13.6.1 Other sources of risk

Policy-makers face two other sources of uncertainty. The first is unanticipated shocks or prediction errors in the main exogenous (non-controllable) variables. The second is the possibility that each policy-maker may specify their opponent's preference function wrongly and consequently base their policy calculations on a false prediction of the opponent's decisions.

The risks imposed by prediction errors have been analysed by Hughes Hallett (1987b). Although both countries may be sensitive to such errors, co-operative policies are disturbed less than non-co-operative policies. Moreover the relative robustness of co-operative policies *increases* with the degree of uncertainty. Optimal policy revisions on a closed-loop basis are an option open to both countries and, apart from selecting the lower risk strategy (co-operation), there is nothing the countries can do to avoid such prediction errors.[8]

The risks posed by mis-specifying the priorities in the opponent's objective function are examined by Hughes Hallett (1987c). They turn out to be considerably smaller than the risks posed by model uncertainty or model disagreement. This holds true for all objective function parameters except that assigned to the exchange rate target. Varying the priority given to exchange rate stability produced disturbances which were, if anything, larger than those from model errors (tables 13.5–13.9). Table 13.A2 in the appendix reproduces these results, and the disturbances from the next most sensitive priority parameter, to make the point.

13.6.2 Shared targets

The crucial distinction here is that the exchange rate is a *shared* target but the others are not. This introduces a very direct conflict of interest: one country's exchange rate rise is another's fall.[9] As a result the exchange rate priority dominates all others in terms of the sensitivities generated. However, there is a second reason for picking the exchange rate out for special attention. Unlike disagreements over the expectations for exogenous events, which are just another form of prediction error that cannot be controlled, 'disagreements' over priorities imply a form of uncertainty which could be avoided if the specifications were announced. It is hard to specify the preferences of others without extensive consultation and there is always the uncertainty that other countries might have announced aims different from their true intentions in order to secure some strategic advantage. A third reason is that policy-makers can easily disagree over their ideal path for a shared target. If they set incompatible exchange rate targets, the gains from co-operation will certainly increase, because where there is disagreement about the desired path policy-makers will waste instrument 'power' in a vain effort to push against each other (Canzoneri and Henderson, 1987).

The consequences of mis-specifying or disagreeing over the specification of either side's priorities, where the benchmark objective function represents their 'true' preferences, are discussed by Hughes Hallett (1987c). These results – reproduced in table 13.A2 – leave two important questions open: to what extent can an *agreed* ideal exchange rate path substitute for full co-operation across all variables; and, if that extent is large enough, could co-operation on picking that ideal path also provide a substantial increase in robustness to model errors or disagreement (in the same way that co-operation increased the robustness to external shocks)?[10] In fact until now both countries have been given the same objectives for the exchange rate: some decline for 1985–7, paralleling actual events, and unchanged thereafter. The exchange rate ambitions are therefore compatible between countries and this might be seen as a form of tacit co-operation. We need to investigate the effects of different disagreements or agreements on alternative ideal paths.

Tables 13.11 and 13.12 show the results, in terms of objective function values, of different disagreements about the best path for the US dollar over 1985–90. In each case the path marked A is no change; the path marked B specifies a 10 per cent depreciation in 1985 and again in 1986, 5 per cent in 1987, and none thereafter (a total of 25 per cent); the path marked C specifies a 30 per cent depreciation in 1985, 20 per cent in 1986, 10 per cent in 1987 and none thereafter (a total of 60 per cent). In order to keep the problem manageable, these alternative paths are tried out on just two models: the MCM model (the best for co-operation under a minimax risk criterion) and the LINK model (the best for non-co-operative policies). The results are presented in payoff matrix form where, within each maintained model–'truth' combination, the nine possible combinations of ideal path choices are represented.

A shared target can in fact lead to any one of four situations. In the non-co-operative case (table 13.11), countries can either select their ideal values independently or choose a compromise set of values which both countries

Table 13.11 Objective function values resulting from conflicting and compromise aims for the shared exchange rate target under non-co-operative policies

ROECD path		US path — MCM maintained			Compromise between		LINK maintained			Compromise between	
		A	B	C			A	B	C		
MCM reality											
A	w_{US}	231.9	279.9	567.1	A/B	436.8	860.7	556.2	506.6	A/B	553.4
	w_{RO}	421.8	1443.2	7802.0		1142.5	1067.8	767.4	647.3		942.8
B	w_{US}	658.5	678.5	921.9	A/C	597.5	632.7	484.8	675.8	A/C	521.6
	w_{RO}	680.7	1345.6	7144.7		1218.7	904.7	707.1	724.7		676.2
C	w_{US}	3443.1	3411.9	3562.1	B/C	1141.5	539.5	632.9	1217.7	B/C	661.3
	w_{RO}	1740.9	1821.2	6652.4		2242.9	998.6	945.3	1198.8		817.4
LINK reality											
A	w_{US}	1792.8	1390.7	7737.3	A/B	1443.2	96.5	487.0	3641.6	A/B	532.9
	w_{RO}	1881.5	2114.1	11757.7		2450.7	288.7	574.7	1750.0		732.1
B	w_{US}	1100.7	5579.9	18387.0	A/C	2404.2	433.2	551.4	3243.0	A/C	777.6
	w_{RO}	1793.7	8403.7	26533.2		5130.8	593.5	750.6	1746.7		976.8
C	w_{US}	9651.8	125614	164188	B/C	17640.5	1985.1	5467.2	5254.2	B/C	1067.1
	w_{RO}	14506.8	208795	243684		15062.9	3250.6	18267.0	18829.1		1281.7

Path A, no change; path B, −10%, −10%, −5%, 0%, 0%, 0% (25 per cent dollar depreciation 1985–90); path C, −30%, −20%, −10%, 0%, 0%, 0% (60 per cent dollar depreciation); path A/B, simple mean of paths A and B applied by both countries; etc.

Table 13.12 Objective function values with agreement and disagreement over the desired path for the exchange target in co-operative policy-making

		US path											
		MCM maintained						LINK maintained					
		Agree			Disagree			Agree			Disagree		
ROECD path		A	B	C	A	B	C	A	B	C	A	B	C
MCM reality													
A	w_{US}	85.9	112.1	564.9	85.9	527.1	3494.9	1719.3	1037.9	2313.7	1719.3	1452.9	5243.7
	w_{RO}	204.4	249.9	683.1	204.4	664.9	3613.1	1739.9	1126.7	2670.1	1739.9	1541.7	5600.1
B	w_{US}	112.1	323.6	1071.6	527.1	323.6	2146.6	1037.9	16087.6	4988.2	1452.9	16087.6	6063.2
	w_{RO}	249.9	450.6	1131.0	664.9	450.6	2204.6	1126.7	9741.5	5420.9	1541.7	9741.5	6495.9
C	w_{US}	564.9	1071.6	2325.3	3494.9	2146.6	2325.3	2313.7	4988.2	11105.5	5243.7	6063.2	11105.5
	w_{RO}	683.1	1131.0	2241.9	3613.1	2206.0	2241.9	2670.1	5420.9	12081.7	5600.1	6495.9	12081.7
LINK reality													
A	w_{US}	916.5	809.9	695.6	916.5	1224.9	3625.6	47.3	117.5	633.8	47.3	532.5	3563.8
	w_{RO}	998.1	962.8	981.5	998.1	1377.8	3911.5	182.3	235.4	752.2	182.3	650.4	3682.2
B	w_{US}	809.9	619.7	650.4	1224.9	619.7	1725.4	117.5	366.3	1168.0	523.5	360.3	2243.0
	w_{RO}	962.8	958.3	1004.9	1377.8	958.3	2079.9	235.4	470.4	1284.4	650.4	470.4	2359.4
C	w_{US}	695.6	650.4	626.0	3625.6	1725.4	626.0	633.8	1168.0	2465.1	3563.8	2243.0	2465.1
	w_{RO}	981.5	1004.9	1151.3	3911.5	2079.9	1151.3	752.2	1284.4	2622.1	3682.2	2359.4	2622.1

Paths A, B, C are defined below table 13.11; disagreement and agreement are constructed according to (13.8) in the text.

adopt in order to gain from reduced conflicts over the shared target without having to select their policies co-operatively. The value of such compromises is shown by comparing the results of using the average of paths A and B (say) with the results when one country adopts path A and the other path B (or vice versa).[11] In the co-operative exercises (table 13.12), policy-makers may either agree to co-operate on policy choice but make no commitment to unify their (private) ideal exchange rate paths or agree to co-operate on selecting both the ideal paths (to reduce wasted effort) and the policy selections. Thus, where there is no co-operation, policy-makers can insert either their private ideals or some compromise values into the appropriate decision rule. In the co-operative case, the shared target components in (13.5) are, say,

$$\alpha w_1 \tilde{e}_{1t}^2 + (1 - \alpha) w_2 \tilde{e}_{2t}^2 \qquad t = 1, \ldots, T \tag{13.7}$$

where $\tilde{e}_{it} = e_t - e_{it}^d$, $i = 1, 2$, for the shared target e_t with private priorities w_1 and w_2. Now if $e_{1t}^d \neq e_{2t}^d$ (disagreement), then (13.7) becomes

$$[\alpha w_1 + (1 - \alpha) w_2](e_t - d_t)^2 + k_t$$

with

$$d_t = \frac{\alpha w_1 e_{1t}^d + (1 - \alpha) w_2 e_{2t}^d}{\alpha w_1 + (1 - \alpha) w_2} \tag{13.8}$$

and

$$k_t = \alpha w_1 (e_{1t}^d)^2 + (1 - \alpha) w_2 (e_{2t}^d)^2 - [\alpha w_1 + (1 - \alpha) w_2]^2 d_t^2.$$

The international priority is the same as always, but a compromise ideal path d_t has been generated together with the extra fixed cost k_t. This contrasts with the case where both countries agree to use compromise values d_t in (13.8), in which case $k_t = 0$ in (13.8).

13.6.3 Divergent aims in a non-co-operative regime

The results in table 13.11 show that the MCM model continues to carry the greater risks with co-operative policies, and these risks are significantly increased by divergent aims (or unfavourable choices) for the shared target. The outcomes of MCM-based policies, when MCM turns out to be true, are improved compared with the results in earlier sections if neither country aims to cause the dollar to depreciate; and broadly speaking they are also improved as long as at least one country aims for no dollar depreciation. In fact the USA does best if it aims to depreciate the dollar but the ROECD does not, while the ROECD does best if it aims to let the dollar depreciate when the USA does not. But the ROECD is always more sensitive to the choice of ideal values than is the USA.

    If, however, we maintain MCM policies when LINK turns out to be true, the outcomes would look very much worse. This is where the main risks appear, and they increase rapidly with disagreement over the ideal exchange rate and with any attempt to generate a large dollar depreciation. And it is the ROECD which carries most of the risk here. However, it is now possible to constrain these risks to be *less* than those in the fixed policy rule regime (the minimax solution, or indeed the MCM solution, of table 13.10) and also to be significantly less than the risks implied by table 13.5. Moreover it is clear that it is the choice of the ideal path which is doing the work here, rather than agreement *per se*. Agreement certainly can help reduce conflicts between countries, but it is more important that the chosen ideal path should be compatible with the model's projections and the requirements of the other targets.

But even if agreement on its own is not sufficient to produce very good results, it can do quite a lot to reduce risks. Given the result that the best performance comes from not forcing a dollar depreciation, it is not surprising to find that the simple compromises solutions (all of which force some kind of depreciation) cannot reach the best outcomes in table 13.11. But the compromise solutions always do better for at least one country than either of the corresponding disagreement solutions, and by quite a large margin in the worst cases of disagreement or for poor choices of ideal values. Thus compromises of this kind are rather effective at cutting down the risks caused by model error; the downside risks are substantially eliminated, even if the potential upside gains are lost.

Most of these observations also apply when LINK-based policies are chosen. Although the LINK model still carries lower risks overall, and would therefore continue to be the best choice for a risk-sensitive policy-maker, these risks increase much more rapidly with divergent aims for the exchange rate, and especially with unfavourable choices for the ideal values. The risks are still carried disproportionately by the ROECD, but this time the USA (rather implausibly) comes off worse if it tries to force a large dollar depreciation and the ROECD is damaged even more when it tries to force that depreciation. Moreover the worst outcomes are associated with the LINK policies which force a large dollar depreciation when LINK is also 'true'. If MCM turns out to be true, the outcomes are fairly stable with a best position where both countries select path B (or possibly where the USA tries to depreciate and the ROECD maintains the status quo – roughly paralleling actual events in 1984–5). Nevertheless the compromises do play some role in reducing the risks introduced by model error, although not nearly as dramatically as in the high risk MCM case. Consequently compromises are more useful for cutting the potential costs of divergent (or poorly chosen) exchange rate aims than for reducing risk.

The conclusions at this stage are that the values chosen for the ideal path of a shared target matter more than the mere fact of securing agreement on them. However, agreement can play an important role in reducing risks from model errors and/or from unfavourable choices of ideal path relative to the model, other targets and realizations of the non-controllable variables. Choice of the ideal path (rather than agreement *per se*) also reduces risk, but an appropriate model selection is more powerful in this respect. However, it is clear that it is extremely important to pick exchange rate parities carefully: major losses may be avoided by co-ordinating the choice internationally, but since what is better for the USA is worse for the ROECD the best compromise may be rather hard to find.

13.6.4 Divergent aims in co-operative policies

Table 13.12 reports the corresponding set of results for the co-operative ($\alpha = \frac{1}{2}$) policies. Once again MCM is the higher risk model from the policy-maker's point of view, but the losses in question are all much smaller than their counterparts in table 13.11. In fact whether policy-makers agree or disagree over their aims for the exchange rate, all the large losses of table 13.11 have been eliminated here; there is a gain to co-operation in every cell, and the larger losses risked have all been removed with factors ranging between 5 and 15. Hence a co-operative policy regime with sensibly chosen ideal values for the exchange rate does more to reduce risk than a careful choice of model, although the latter is also important and suggests the use of MCM.

These results contrast with tables 13.6 and 13.9 in that it now seems that co-operative policies can be more robust to model errors than non-co-operative policies – but this impression is partly due to the fact that not all models have been included as possible realities. However, changing the desired exchange rate parities does show that such a result can be obtained with a careful choice of those parities since the major downside risks of table 13.11 have been removed. Moreover the downside risks of the co-operative policies in table 13.6 can also be avoided. Hence, in as far as these results are representative, choosing exchange rate parities can be vital for generating co-ordination gains and for reducing policy risks. In addition, co-operative policies have the potential for greater robustness – but only when those parities are chosen appropriately. As in table 13.11, an appropriate choice means one or both countries aiming for no dollar depreciation (and preferably an agreement between them on that).

Disagreement here has its costs and those costs clearly increase with the seriousness of divergence. But disagreement is less of a problem than in a non-co-operative environment and the payoffs from avoiding divergent aims are correspondingly smaller. Hence both the choice of the desired parities *and* agreement on them are important for yielding co-operative gains and reduced risks. Indeed, the fact that co-operation no longer contains the risks apparent in table 13.6 and that a choice of the MCM model plus co-operative policies now looks superior to LINK and no co-operation[12] are the most significant results to emerge from this exercise.

13.7 CONCLUSION

In this paper the risks involved in non-co-operative and co-operative policy-making have been compared when there is uncertainty about which model is 'true', when there is a chance of disagreement about the model, and when there is uncertainty about what are the 'correct' values for the objective function parameters. The results answer a number of questions raised by the two earlier studies of model uncertainty, and consider the possibility of using fixed policy rules or simple exchange rate targets as a way of reducing the risks which policy-makers face. The new results are as follows.

1   The risks imposed by model errors were larger than those from other sources (e.g. objective function mis-specifications or prediction errors) except for the risks introduced by mis-specifying the priorities on a *shared* target. In this context, co-operative policies are not safer: they imply larger downside risks, as well as larger upside gains.

2   Model disagreement exaggerates the risks caused by model errors, especially under non-co-operative policies. Rather little can be done to control these risks. Information exchanges, to remove the chance of model disagreement, cut the risks down dramatically without any need for explicit co-operation.

3   Co-operative policies are less disturbed by model disagreement and co-operation is less risky than non-co-operation (in contrast with point (1)).

4   The most powerful way of reducing risks is to pick the model carefully, i.e. to bargain on the model as well as on the policies. Fixed rules provide *neither* a better performance *nor* greater risk protection than that. The security–ambition trade-off is therefore between co-operation or non-co-operation rather than between optimal and fixed rules.

5   Divergent aims for the exchange rate increase risks from model or information errors, while sensible choices for the desired parities give very good risk protection. Compromise parities have the same effect but are less powerful in this respect. But none of these options is as powerful as agreement on a suitable choice of model. In fact the risk reductions obtained by information exchanges (to give an agreed model), plus a suitable exchange rate parity, are larger under co-operative than under non-co-operative policies.

6   The key to successful co-ordination appears to be a procedure for choosing the appropriate model and appropriate exchange rate target. The importance attached to steering the shared exchange rate target shows

that further research is needed to establish the conditions under which improvements can be obtained by manipulating the target parity, what proportion of the full co-operative gains could be secured that way, and how to select the best exchange rate target path.

Appendix

Table 13A.1 Objective function specification

(a) The ideal policy values

	GNP	$\dot{P}$	E/R	TB	G	$\dot{M}$
US variables						
1985	4	1	−10	−100	20	5
1986	4	1	−10	−100	19	5
1987	4	1	−5	−100	18	5
1988	4	1	0	−100	17	5
1989	4	1	0	−100	16	5
1990	4	1	0	−100	15	5
ROECD variables						
1985	5.5	1	−10	+100	22	6
1986	5.5	1	−10	+100	22	6
1987	5.5	1	−5	+100	22	6
1988	5.5	1	0	+100	22	6
1989	5.5	1	0	+100	22	6
1990	5.5	1	0	+100	22	6

(b) Relative priorities (weights on quadratic deviations from ideal values)

	GNP	$\dot{P}$	E/R	TB	G	$\dot{M}$
US variables						
1985	6.5	1.0	10.0	0.02	0.10	1.0
1986	6.0	1.25	6.0	0.02	0.12	1.0
1987	7.0	1.8	2.4	0.02	0.14	1.0
1988	5.0	2.6	1.4	0.02	0.16	1.0
1989	4.0	3.5	0.6	0.02	1.0	1.0
1990	5.1	4.2	0.04	0.02	4.0	1.0
ROECD variables						
1985	6.5	1.0	10.0	0.02	0.1	1.0
1986	6.0	1.25	6.0	0.02	0.1	1.0
1987	7.0	1.8	2.4	0.02	0.1	1.0
1988	5.0	2.6	1.4	0.02	0.1	1.0
1989	4.0	3.5	0.6	0.02	1.0	1.0
1990	5.1	4.2	0.04	0.02	4.0	1.0

Table 13A.1 *cont'd*

(c) Standardized baseline

	GNP	$\dot{P}$	E/R	TB	G	$\dot{M}$
US variables						
1985	2.94	3.90	0.0	−76.18	19.52	4.00
1986	2.83	3.59	−2.49	−88.50	19.66	5.02
1987	3.14	3.69	−2.12	−94.04	19.77	5.28
1988	3.11	3.71	−1.34	−98.25	19.90	5.89
1989	3.12	3.69	−1.42	−98.93	19.95	6.06
1990	3.07	3.83	−1.59	−98.68	20.02	6.09
ROECD variables						
1985	3.30	4.48	0.0	37.32	22.3	4.11
1986	3.52	4.08	−2.49	44.73	22.2	5.87
1987	3.10	3.19	−2.12	50.82	22.0	5.66
1988	3.57	3.80	−1.34	57.17	21.9	5.69
1989	3.49	3.59	−1.42	63.41	21.7	5.70
1990	3.55	3.57	−1.59	73.43	21.6	5.63

GNP, percentage rate of GNP growth per year; $\dot{P}$, annual rate of increase in consumer prices; E/R, US dollar divided by a weighted average of other OECD currencies; TB, net real trade balance in $bn; G, government expenditures as percentage of real baseline GNP; $\dot{M}$, rate of growth of money supply (M1).

Table 13.A2 Sensitivity of the benchmark objective functions to variations in the preference parameters

(a) Non-co-operative policies with the priority on exchange rate stability

Priority set by	Multiplicative factor	w^*_{US}	w^*_{RO}	Priority set by	Multiplicative factor	w^*_{US}	w^*_{RO}
US	0.01	4407.3	2044.8	ROECD	0.01	482.4	3579.6
	0.1	1153.8	850.6		0.1	257.7	2863.7
	1	678.5	1345.6		1	678.5	1345.6
	10	5265.8	1503.6		10	885.8	6801.0
	100	51278.5	1533.7		100	929.3	62026.0

(b) Co-operative ($\alpha = \frac{1}{2}$) policies with the priority on exchange rate stability

Priority	Multiplicative factor	w^*_{US}	w^*_{RO}
Shared	0.01	688.7	808.9
by US	0.1	635.5	760.7
and	1	323.6	450.6
ROECD	10	722.8	360.2
	100	1875.6	901.6

(c) Non-co-operative policies with the priority on GNP growth

Priority On	Multiplicative factors	w^*_{US}	w^*_{RO}	Priority on	Multiplicative factors	w^*_{US}	w^*_{RO}
GNP_{US}	0.01	1082.5	1642.3	GNP_{RO}	0.01	851.0	1724.3
	0.01	935.2	1547.3		0.1	819.6	1629.4
	1	678.5	1345.6		1	678.5	1345.6
	10	656.4	1314.2		10	716.3	2182.5
	100	664.1	1325.4		100	805.9	2739.9

(d) Co-operative ($\alpha = \frac{1}{2}$) policies with the priority on GNP growth

Priority on	Multiplicative factor	w^*_{US}	w^*_{RO}	Priority on	Multiplicative factor	w^*_{US}	w^*_{RO}
GNP_{US}	0.01	2746.1	316.0	GNP_{RO}	0.01	270.0	1933.5
	0.1	792.7	354.7		0.1	283.1	697.0
	1	323.6	450.6		1	323.6	450.6
	10	308.5	508.5		10	419.3	448.7
	100	308.4	527.0		100	626.6	686.1

These tables show the results of multiplying the benchmark priority parameter of the variable indicated, in the objective function of the country indicated, by the specified factor.

Notes

* This paper builds on earlier work on model uncertainty done with Gerry Hottham.

1   See Oudiz and Sachs (1984) for estimates relating to the USA, Germany and Japan; Hughes Hallett (1986a, 1987a) for the USA, EEC and Japan; and Canzoneri and Minford (1986) for nine major OECD countries.
2   This proportion is rather variable for the conventional models but remarkably steady in the rational expectations models. The OECD model shows that non-exchange-rate variables are worse (on balance) for the USA under co-operation than under non-co-operation but dominate the exchange rate for the ROECD. But this is the only 'outlier': the other models all support this observation. Previous studies of the gains to co-ordination have all ignored the exchange rate as a target.

340   A. J. Hughes Hallett

3   See Holtham and Hughes Hallett (1987, table 7).
4   This is the Oudiz and Sachs (1984) method for calibrating the gains from co-ordination.
5   In order to evaluate the risks involved in interdependent policy-making, we need to draw out the worst possible outcomes. Risk management can then be considered in terms of minimax decisions. However, this is a highly risk-averse attitude, and in practice policy-makers may prefer to optimize their expected outcomes with suitable prior probabilities placed on each model's being true. This yields the probability approach studied in detail by Holtham and Hughes Hallett (1987).
6   These losses come from taking tables 13.5 (on the subset of four models) and 13.8 together.
7   This argument appears in several places. Friedman (1953) recommended fixed rules for counteracting uncertainty in model parameters; Fischer and Cooper (1973), Lucas (1976) and Kydland and Prescott (1977) consider fixed rules for counteracting uncertainty in the dynamics, policy responses and expectations. Burmeister et al. (1977) find that fixed rules perform badly in the face of uncertainty over the planning priorities.
8   Notice that disagreement about expectations for future exogenous variables has the same effect as making a prediction error for that variable.
9   In this exercise the USA's effective exchange rate is defined solely in relation to other OECD exchange rates – both countries are targeting the same variable, unlike the trade balances where incompatible aims can (if necessary) be resolved by creating an imbalance in the rest of the world.
10 There are several reasons for supposing that this will normally be the case.

1   In a co-operative regime $\partial w^*/\partial s = \partial w^*/\partial y^d = \mu^{*\prime}$ for small changes around the optimal solution, where μ is a vector of Lagrange multipliers. Hence the sensitivity of the outcomes to external shocks and to changes in the ideal paths y^d will be equal under explicit co-operation. Similarly, for changes around the optimum which are small enough for each country to assume that the other will not respond, $\partial w^{A*}/\partial s^A = \partial w^{A*}/\partial y^{Ad} = \mu^{A*\prime}$, and likewise for country B. Thus, to a first approximation, the sensitivities to shocks and changes in ideal paths will have the same characteristics.
2   If model error sensitivities are positively related to these ideal path sensitivities, then picking ideal values in such a way as to reduce the latter sensitivities will automatically reduce the risks posed by model uncertainty or disagreement at the same time. In a co-operative regime $dw = (\mu^* \otimes x^{*\prime})$ d vec(R) where $x' = (x^{A\prime}, x^{B\prime})$ and R contains the model's multiplier matrices. Similarly, in a non-co-operative world, $dw^A = (\mu^{A*\prime} \otimes x^{A*\prime})$ d vec(R_{AA}, R_{AB}) for small changes around the optimum and no responses by the other country. Since $\partial w^*/\partial y^d = \mu^{*\prime}$ and $dw^{A*}/\partial y^{Ad} = \mu^{*\prime}$, this positive relation exists.
3   The dificulty here is that, in the co-operative case, $w^* = \alpha w^{A*} + (1-\alpha)w^{B*}$ so that to say that the sensitivity of w^* is reduced does not automatically imply that the same is true for both w^A and w^B, although it must be true for one of them. In the non-co-operative case the reductions in sensitivities may

only hold good for a small neighbourhood around the optimum – and may be increased elsewhere because other countries do in fact respond. Finally these results are of interest only in conditions where new ideal paths can be found which reduce the $\partial w/\partial y^d$ sensitivities. There is no proof that such conditions always exist, although they may be widely available. It is not clear, therefore, whether these conjectures will be much use in practice. That is something which can only be tested numerically.

11   Table 13.11 also contains agreed paths when both countries adopt path A or path B etc. These could also be compromise solutions, but not compromises between the disagreement cases considered in table 13.11. The disagreement which would lead both countries to adopt path C, for example, is too extreme to be included, although path C on its own is quite reasonable in that it reflects fairly accurately the actual path of the dollar against the yen and the mark.

12   This result might not survive a comparison across all models, however.

References

Adler, M. and B. Lehmann (1983) Deviations from purchasing power parity in the long run. *Journal of Finance*, 38 (5), 1471–87.

Ahtiala, P. (1984) A synthesis of the macroeconomic approaches to exchange rate determination. *European Economic Review*, 24 (2) March, 117–36.

Akaike, H. (1973) Information theory and an extension of the maximum likelihood principle. In B. N. Petrov and F. Csaki (eds) *Second International Symposium on Information Theory*. Budapest: Akademiai Kiado.

Akhtar, M. A. and R. S. Hilton (1984) Exchange rate uncertainty and international trade: some conceptual issues and new estimates for Germany and the United States. *Research Paper No. 8403 Federal Reserve Bank of New York*, May.

Aliber, R. Z. (1974) Attributes of national monies and the independence of national monetary policies'. In R. Z. Aliber (ed.) *National Monetary Policies and the International System*. Chicago: University of Chicago Press.

Aliber, R. Z. (1984) International banking: a survey and discussion. *Journal of Money Credit and Banking*, 16, 665–712.

Argy, V. and J. Salop (1979) Price and output effects of monetary and fiscal policy under flexible exchange rates. *IMF Staff Papers*, June, 224–56.

Artis, M. J. and D. A. Currie (1983) Monetary targets and the exchange rate. A case for conditional targets. In W. A. Eltis and P. J. N. Sinclair (eds) *The Money Supply and The Exchange Rate*, 176–200. Oxford: Oxford University Press.

Artis, M. J. and M. K. Lewis (1981) *Monetary Control in the United Kingdom*. Oxford: Philip Allan.

Artis, M. J. and M. P. Taylor (1988) Exchange rates, interest rates, capital controls and the EMS: assessing the track record. In F. Giavazzi, S. Micossi and M. Miller (eds) *The European Monetary System*. Cambridge: Cambridge University Press.

Artus, J. (1976) Exchange rate stability and managed floating: the experience of the Federal Republic of Germany. *IMF Staff Papers*, 23, 312–33.

Backus, D. (1984) Empirical models of the exchange rate: separating the wheat from the chaff. *Canadian Journal of Economics*, 17 (4), 824–46.

Baillie, R. T., R. W. Bailey and P. C. McMahon (1983a) Interpreting econometric evidence on efficiency in the foreign exchange market. *Oxford Economic Papers*, 35, 1–19.

Baillie, R. T., R. E. Lippens and P. C. McMahon (1983b) Testing rational expectations and efficiency in the foreign exchange market. *Econometrica*, 51, 553–63.

Banerjee, A., J. J. Dolado, D. F. Hendry and G. W. Smith (1986) Exploring equilibrium relationships in econometrics through static models: some Monte Carlo evidence. *Oxford Bulletin of Economics and Statistics*, 48, 253–77.

Bank of England (1984) The variability of exchange rates; measurement and effects. *Bank of England Quarterly Bulletin*, 24, 346–9.

Bhargava, A. (1986) On the theory of testing for unit roots in observed time series. *Review of Economic Studies*, 53, 369–84.

Barr, D. G. (1983a) Exchange rate overshooting and macro economic policy in an open economy portfolio balance model. *Working Paper No. 473*, Centre for Labour Economics, London School of Economics.

Barr, D. G. (1983b) Identification in dynamic linear rational expectations models. *Working Paper No. 532*, Centre for Labour Economics, London School of Economics.

Barr, D. G. (1984) Empirical investigation of exchange rate determinants: a survey. *Discussion Paper No. 588*, Centre for Labour Economics, London School of Economics.

Barro, R. J. (1977) Unanticipated money growth and unemployment in the United States. *American Economic Review*, 67, 101–15.

Barro, R. J. (1978) Unanticipated money, output and the price level in the United States. *Journal of Political Economy*, 86, 549–80.

Bean, C. R. (1981) Essays in unemployment and economic activity. Unpublished Ph.D. thesis, Massachusetts Institute of Technology.

Bean, C. R. (1986) The estimation of 'surprise' models and the 'surprise' consumption function. *Review of Economic Studies*, 53, 496–516.

Becker, R. G., B. Dwolatsky, E. Karakitsos and B. Rustem (1986) Simultaneous use of rival models in policy optimisation. *Economic Journal*, 46, 425–48.

Begg, D. K. H. (1982) *The Rational Expectations Revolution in Macroeconomics: Theories and Evidence*. Oxford: Philip Allan.

Bhattacharyya, D. (1979) On the validity of the quadratic utility function in mean–variance portfolio analysis: an empirical test. *De Economist*, 127, 422–45.

Bilson, J. F. O. (1978a) Rational expectations and the exchange rate. In Frenkel and Johnson (1978).

Bilson, J. F. O. (1978b) Recent developments in monetary models of exchange rate determination. *IMF Staff Papers*, 201–23.

Bilson, J. F. O. (1981) The speculative efficiency hypothesis. *Journal of Business*, 54, 435–51.

Bilson, J. F. O. (1985) Macro-economic stability and flexible exchange rates. *American Economic Review, Papers and Proceedings*, 75, 62–7.

Bisignano, J. and K. Hoover (1983) Some suggested improvements to a simple portfolio balance model of exchange rate determination with special reference to the US dollar/Canadian dollar rate. *Weltwirtschaftliches Archiv*, 119, 19–37.

Bladen Hovell, R. C. and C. J. Green (1982) Crowding-out and pulling-in of fiscal policy under fixed and flexible exchange rates. *Discussion Paper No. 28*, Department of Economics, University of Manchester, September.

Blanchard, O. J. (1981a) Output, the stock market, and interest rates. *American Economic Review*, 71, 132–43.

Blanchard, O. J. (1981b) Speculative bubbles, crashes and rational expectations. *Economic letters*, 4, 387–9.

Blanchard, O. J. and C. M. Kahn (1980) The solution of linear difference models under rational expectations. *Econometrica*, 48, 1305–11.

Blanchard, O. J. and M. Watson (1982) Bubbles, rational expectations and financial markets. In P. Wachtel (ed.) *Crises in the Economic and Financial Structure*. Lexington: Lexington Books.

Blanchard, O. J. and C. Wyplosz (1981) An empirical structural model of aggregate demand. *Journal of Monetary Economics*, 7 (1), 1–28.

Bomhoff, E. S. and P. Korteweg (1983) Exchange rate variability and monetary policy under rational expectations: some Euro-American experience 1973–9. *Journal of Monetary Economics*, 11, 169–206.

Boothe, P. and D. Longworth (1986) Foreign exchange market efficiency tests: implications of recent empirical findings. *Journal of International Money and Finance*, 5, 135–52.

Branson, W. H. (1977a) Asset markets and relative prices in exchange rate determination. *Reprint Series No. 98*, Institute for International Economic Studies.

Branson, W. H. (1977b) Asset markets and relative prices in exchange rate determination. *Sozialwissenschaftliche Annalen*, 1, 69–89.

Branson, W. H. (1979) Exchange rate dynamics and monetary policy. In A. Lindbeck (ed.) *Inflation and Unemployment in Open Economies*. Amsterdam: North Holland.

Branson, W. H. (1983) Macroeconomic determinants of real exchange risks. In R. J. Herring (ed.) *Managing Foreign Exchange Risk*. Cambridge: Cambridge University Press.

Branson, W. H. and W. H. Buiter (1983) Monetary and fiscal policy with flexible exchange rates. In J. S. Bhandari and B. H. Puttnam (eds) *Economic Interdependence and Flexible Exchange Rates*. Cambridge, MA: MIT Press 251–85.

Branson, W. H. and H. Halttunen (1979) Asset-market determination of exchange rates: initial empirical and policy results. In J. P. Martin and A. Smith (eds) *Trade and Payments Adjustment Under Flexible Exchange Rates*. London: MacMillan.

Branson, W. H., H. Halttunen and P. Masson (1977) Exchange rates in the short run. *European Economic Review*, 10, 395–402.

Branson, W. H. and D. W. Henderson (1985) The specification and influences of asset markets. In R. W. Jones and P. B. Kenen (eds) *Handbook of International Economics, II*. Amsterdam: North-Holland.

Brown, B. W. and S. Maital (1981) What do economists know? An empirical study of experts' expectations. *Econometrica*, 49, 1129–60.

Bryant, R., D. Henderson, G. Holtham, P. Hooper and S. Symansky (eds) (1988) *Empirical Macroeconomics for Interdependent Economics*. Washington, DC: Brookings Institution.

Buiter, W. H. (1982) Saddlepoint problems in continuous time rational expectations models: a general method and some macroeconomic examples. *Discussion Paper No. 114*, Centre for Labour Economics, London School of Economics.

Buiter, W. H. (1987) Does an improvement in the current account or the trade balance at full employment require a depreciation of the real exchange rate? Yale University and National Bureau of Economic Research, mimeo.

Buiter, W. H. and M. H. Miller (1981) Monetary policy and international competitiveness. *Oxford Economic Papers*, 33 (Supplement), 143–75.

Buiter, W. H. and M. H. Miller (1982a) Real exchange rate over-shooting and the output cost of bringing down inflation. *European Economic Review*, 18 (1–2), 85–123.

Buiter, W. H. and M. H. Miller (1982b) Real exchange rate overshooting and the output cost of bringing down inflation: some further results. *Discussion Paper No. 115*, Centre for Labour Economics, London School of Economics.

Buiter, W. H. and M. H. Miller (1983) Real exchange rate over-shooting and the output cost of bringing down inflation: some further results. In J. Frenkel (ed.) *Exchange Rates and International Macroeconomics*. Chicago: University of Chicago Press.

Burmeister, E., J. Jackson and S. A. Ross (1977) The evaluation of simple and optimal decision rules with misspecified welfare functions. In J. D. Pickford and S. J. Turnovsky (eds) *Applications of Control Theory to Economic Analysis*. Amsterdam: North Holland.

Camen, U. (1987) Analysis of world business cycles. Mimeo, June.

Canzoneri, M. B. (1982) Exchange intervention policy in a multiple country world. *Journal of International Economics*, 13 (3–4).

Canzoneri, M. B. and D. W. Henderson (1987) Is sovereign policy making bad? Carnegie-Rochester Conference Series on Public Policy, forthcoming.

Canzoneri, M. B. and P. Minford (1986) When international policy coordination matters: an empirical analysis. *Applied Economics*, 20, 1137–54.

Caves, D. and E. Feige (1980) Efficient foreign exchange markets and the monetary approach to exchange rate determination. *American Economic Review*, 70, 120–34.

Chow, G. C. (1981) *Econometric Analysis by Control Methods*. New York: Wiley.

Coghlan, R. T. (1978) A transactions demand for money. *Bank of England Quarterly Bulletin*, 18, 1–115.

Copeland, L. S. (1984a) The pound sterling/US dollar exchange rate and the 'news'. *Economics Letters*, 15 (1–2), 109–13.

Copeland, L. S. (1984b) Oil news and the petropound: some tests. *Economics Letters*, 16 (1–2), 123–7.

Copeland, L. S. and R. C. Stapleton (1987) Inflation, interest rate risk, and the variance of common stock prices. University of Manchester Institute of Science and Technology, mimeo.

Corbae, D. and S. Ouliaris (1986) Robust tests for unit roots in the foreign exchange market. *Economics Letters*, 22, 375–86.

Cornell, B. (1982) Money supply announcements, interest rates and foreign exchange. *Journal of International Money and Finance*, 1, 201–8.

Cornell, B. (1983) Money supply announcements and interest-rates: another view. *Journal of Business*, 56, 1–23.

Cumby, R. E. and M. Obstfeld (1980) Exchange rate expectations and nominal interest differentials: a test of the Fisher hypothesis. *Working Paper No. 537*, National Bureau of Economic Research.

Cumby, R. E. and M. Obstfeld (1981) Exchange rate expectations and nominal interest rates: a test of the Fisher hypothesis. *Journal of Finance*, 36, 697–703.

Cumby, R. E. and M. Obstfeld (1984) International interest rate and price level linkages under flexible exchange rates: a review of recent evidence. In J. F. O. Bilson and R. C. Marston (eds) *Exchange Rate Theory and Practice*. Chicago: University of Chicago Press.

Currie, D. and S. G. Hall (1986) The exchange rate and the balance of payments. *National Institute Economic Review*. 115, February.

Cushman, D. O. (1986) Has exchange risk depressed international trade? The impact of third country exchange risk. *Journal of International Money and Finance*, 5, 361–79.

Cuthbertson, K. and M. P. Taylor (1987) *Macroeconomic Systems*. Oxford: Blackwell.

Davidson, J. (1985) Econometric modelling of the sterling effective exchange rate. *Review of Economic Studies*, 21, 231–40.

Diba, B. and H. I. Grossman (1983) Bubbles, rational expectations and financial markets. *Working Paper No. 1059*, National Bureau of Economic Research.

Dickey, D. A. and W. A. Fuller (1979) Distribution of the estimators for auto-regressive time series with a unit root. *Journal of the American Statistical Association*, 74, 427–31.

Dickey, D. A. and W. A. Fuller (1981) The likelihood ratio statistic for auto-regressive time series with a unit root. *Econometrica*, 49, 1057–72.

Dixit, A. K. (1980) A solution technique for rational expectations models with applications to exchange rate and interest rate determination. University of Warwick, mimeo.

Dominguez, K. (1986) Are foreign exchange forecasts rational? New evidence from survey data. *Economics Letters*, 21, 277–81.

Domowitz, I. and C. S. Hakkio (1985) Conditional variance and the risk premium in the foreign exchange market. *Journal of International Economics*, 18, 47–66.

Dornbusch, R. (1976) Expectations and exchange rate dynamics. *Journal of Political Economy*, 84, 1161–76.

Dornbusch, R. (1979) Monetary policy under exchange rate flexibility. In *Managed Exchange Rate Flexibility: The Recent Experience*. Boston: Federal Reserve Bank of Boston.

Dornbusch, R. (1980) Exchange rate economics: where do we stand? *Brookings Papers on Economic Activity*, 1, 143–55.

Dornbusch, R. (1983a) Flexible exchange rates and interdependence. *IMF Staff Papers*, 3–38.

Dornbusch, R. (1983b) Exchange rate risk and the macroeconomics of exchange rate determination. In R. G. Hawkins, R. M. Levich and C. Wihlborg (eds) *The Internationalization of Financial Markets and National Economic Policy*. 3–27. Greenwich: JSAI Press.

Dornbusch, R. and S. Fischer (1980) Exchange rates and the current account. *American Economic Review*, 70, 960–71.

Driskell, R. A. (1981) Exchange rate dynamics: an empirical investigation. *Journal of Political Economy*, 89, 357–71.

Driskell, R. A. and S. M. Sheffrin (1981) On the mark: comment. *American Economic Review*, 71, 1068–74.

Eaton, J. and S. J. Turnovsky (1983) Covered interest parity, uncovered interest parity and exchange rate dynamics. *Economic Journal*, 93, 555–75.

Edwards, S. (1982a) Exchange rate market efficiency and new information. *Economics Letters*, 9, 377–82.

Edwards, S. (1982b) Exchange rates and 'news': a multi-currency approach. *Journal of International Money and Finance*, 1 (1), 211–24.

Edwards, S. (1983) Floating exchange rates, expectations and new information. *Journal of Monetary Economics*, 11, 321–36.

Engel, C. and J. A. Frankel (1984) Why interest rates react to money announcements: an explanation from the foreign exchange market. *Journal of Monetary Economics*, 13, 31–46.

Engle, R. F. (1982) Autoregressive conditional heteroscedasticity with estimates of United Kingdom inflation. *Econometrica*, 50, 987–1007.

Engle, R. and C. W. J. Granger (1987) Cointegration and error correcting: representation, estimation testing. *Econometrica*, 55, 251–76.

Engle, R. F., D. F. Hendry and J. F. Richard (1983) Exogeneity. *Econometrica*, 51, 277–304.

Engle, R. F., D. M. Lilien and R. P. Robins (1987) Estimating time varying risk premia in the term structure: the ARCH-M model. *Econometrica*, 55, 391–407.

European Commission (1982) Documents relating to the European Monetary System. *European Economy* (July).

Evans, G. W. (1986) A test for speculative bubbles and the sterling–dollar exchange rate: 1981–84. *American Economic Review*, 76, 621–36.

Fair, R. C. (1970) The estimation of simultaneous equations models with lagged endogenous variables and first-order serially correlated errors. *Econometrica*, 38, 507–16.

Fama, E. F. (1970) Efficient capital markets: a review of theory and empirical work. *Journal of Finance*, 25, 383–417.

Fama, E. F. (1976) *Foundations of Finance*. Oxford: Blackwell.

Fama, E. F. (1981) Stock returns, real activity, inflation and money. *American Economic Review*, 71, 545–65.

Fama, E. F. (1984) Forward and spot exchange rates. *Journal and Monetary Economics*, 14, 319–28.

Fama, E. F. and A. Farber (1979) Money, banks and foreign exchange. *American Economic Review*, 69, 639–49.

Feige, E. C. and D. K. Pierce (1976) Economically rational expectations: are innovations in the rate of inflation independent of innovations in measures of monetary and fiscal policy? *Journal of Political Economy*, 84, 499–522.

Feldstein, M. (1983) The world economy today. *The Economist*, 1 June.

Finn, M. G. (1986) Forecasting the exchange rate: a monetary or random walk phenomenon? *Journal of International Money and Finance*, 5, 181–94.

Fischer, S. and J. P. Cooper (1973) Stabilisation policy and lags. *Journal of Political Economy*, 81, 847–77.

Fleming, J. M. (1962) Domestic financial policies under fixed and flexible exchange rates. *IMF Staff Papers*, 9, 369–79.

Flood, R. P. and P. M. Garber (1980a) A pitfall in the estimation of models with rational expectations. *Journal of Monetary Economics*, 6, 433–5.

Flood, R. P. and P. M. Garber (1980b) Market fundamentals versus price level bubbles: the first tests. *Journal of Political Economy*, 88, 745–70.

Folkerts-Landau, D. (1985) The changing role of international bank lending in development finance. *IMF Staff Papers*, 32, 317–63.

Forsyth, P. J. and J. A. Kay (1980) The economic implications of North Sea oil revenues. *Fiscal Studies*, 1, 1–28.

Frankel, J. A. (1979a) On the mark: a theory of floating exchange rates based on real interest differentials. *American Economic Review*, 69, 610–22.

Frankel, J. A. (1979b) Tests of rational expectations in the forward exchange market. *Southern Economic Journal*, 46 (4), 1083–101.

Frankel, J. A. (1979c) A test of the existence of the risk premium in the foreign exchange market versus the hypothesis of perfect substitutability. *International Finance Discussion Paper No. 149*, Washington, DC: Board of Governors, Federal Reserve System.

Frankel, J. A. (1982a) The mystery of the multiplying marks: a modification of the monetary model. *Review of Economics and Statistics*, 64, 515–19.

Frankel, J. A. (1982b) In search of the exchange risk premium: a six-currency test assuming mean–variance optimisation. *Journal of International Money and Finance*, 1, 255–74.

Frankel, J. A. (1982c) A test of perfect substitutability in the foreign exchange market. *Southern Economic Journal*, 49, 406–16.

Frankel, J. A. (1983) Monetary and portfolio balance models of exchange rate determination. In Bhandari and Putnam (eds) *Economic Interdependence and Flexible Exchange Rates*. Cambridge, MA: MIT Press.

Frankel, J. A. (1984) Tests of monetary and portfolio balance models of exchange rate determination. In J. F. O. Bilson and R. C. Marston (eds) *Exchange Rate Theory and Practice*. Chicago: University of Chicago Press.

Frankel, J. A. and K. Froot (1986a) Interpreting tests of forward discount bias using survey data on exchange rate expectations. *Working Paper No. 1963*, National Bureau of Economic Research.

Frankel, J. A. and K. Froot (1986b) Short-term and long-term expectations of the yen/dollar exchange rate: evidence from survey data. *International Finance Discussion Papers, No. 292*.

Frankel, J. A. and K. Froot (1987) Using survey data to test some standard propositions regarding exchange rate expectations. *American Economic Review*, 77, 133–53.

Frankel, J. A. and K. Froot (1988) Chartists and fundamentalists in the foreign exchange market. In A. S. Courakis and M. P. Taylor (eds) *Policy Issues for Interdependent Economies*. London: MacMillan.

Frankel, J. A. and K. E. R. Rockett (1988) International macroeconomic policy coordination when the policy makers do not agree on the true model. *American Economic Review*, 78, 318–40.

Frenkel, J. A. (1976) A monetary approach to the exchange rate: doctrinal aspects and empirical evidence. *Scandinavian Journal of Economics*, 78, 200–24.

Frenkel, J. A. (1980) Exchange rates, prices and money, lessons from the 1920s. *American Economic Association, Papers and Proceedings*, 235–42.

Frenkel, J. A. (1981) Flexible exchange rates, prices and the role of 'news': lessons from the 1970s. *Journal of Political Economy*, 89 (4), 655–705.

Frenkel, J. A. (1982) Turbulence in the foreign exchange markets and macroeconomic policies. The Henry Thornton Lecture, City University, London.

Frenkel, J. A., T. Gylfason and J. F. Helliwell (1980) A synthesis of monetary and Keynesian approaches to short-run balance of payments theory. *Economic Journal*, 90 (359), September, 582–92.

Frenkel, J. A. and H. G. Johnson (eds) (1976) *The Monetary Approach to the Balance of Payments*. London: Allen and Unwin.

Frenkel, J. A. and H. G. Johnson (eds) (1978) *The Economics of Exchange Rates*. Reading, MA: Addison-Wesley.

Frenkel, J. A. and A. Razin (1982) Stochastic prices and tests of efficiency of foreign exchange markets. *Economic Letters*, 6, 165–70.

Friedman, M. (1953) The case for flexible exchange rates. In M. Friedman, *Essays in Positive Economics*, 157–203. Chicago: University of Chicago Press.

Fuller, W. A. (1976) *Introduction to Statistical Time Series*. New York: Wiley.

Gallant, A. R. and D. W. Jorgenson (1979) Statistical inference for a system of simultaneous, non-linear, implicit equations in the context of instrumental variable estimation. *Journal of Econometrics*, 11, 275–302.

Gavin, M. K. (1986) The stock market and exchange rate dynamics. *International Finance Discussion Papers, No. 278.*

Genberg, H. (1981) Effects of central bank intervention in the foreign exchange market. *IMF Staff Papers*, 451–76.

Genberg, H., M. Salemi and A. Swoboda (1988) The relative importance of foreign and domestic disturbances for aggregate fluctuations in the open economy: Switzerland 1964–81. *Journal of Monetary Economics*, forthcoming.

Geske, R. and R. Roll (1983) The fiscal and monetary linkage between stock returns and inflation. *Journal of Finance*, 38, 1–34.

Geweke, J. and E. Feige (1978) Some joint tests of efficiency of markets for forward exchange. *Review of Economics and Statistics*, 61, 334–41.

Giddy, I. H. and G. Dufey (1975) The random behaviour of flexible exchange rates. *Journal of International Business Studies*, 6, 1–32.

Girton, L. and D. Roper (1981) Theory and implications of currency substitution. *Journal of Money Credit and Banking*, 13, 12–30.

Godfrey, A. R. and D. W. Jorgenson (1978) Testing against general autoregressive and moving average error models when the regressors include lagged dependent variables. *Econometrica*, 46, 1293–302.

Goldfeld, S. M. (1976) The case of the missing money. *Brookings Papers on Economic Activity*, 3, 683–730.

Goodhart, C. A. E. (1986) Should the UK join the EMS? London School of Economics, mimeo.

Goodhart, C. A. E. and M. P. Taylor (1987) Why don't individuals speculate in the foreign exchange market? *London School of Economics Financial Markets Group Discussion Paper.*

Granger, C. W. J. (1981) Some properties of time series data and their use in econometric model specification. *Journal of Econometrica*, 16, 121–30.

Granger, C. W. J. (1986) Developments in the study of cointegrated economic variables. *Oxford Bulletin of Economics and Statistics*, 48, 3, 213–28.

Granger, C. W. J. and A. Weiss (1983) Time series analysis of error-correcting models. In S. Karlin, T. Amemiya and L. A. Goodman (eds) *Studies in Econometrics, Times Series, and Multivariate Statistics*. London: Academic Press.

de Grauwe, P. (1982) The exchange rate in a portfolio balance model with a banking sector. *Journal of International Money and Finance*, 1, 225–39.

Grauer, F. L. A., R. Litzenberger and R. E. Stehle (1976) Sharing rules and equilibrium in an international capital market under uncertainty. *Journal of Financial Economics*, 3, 233–56.

Grossman, S. J. and R. J. Shiller (1981) The determinants of the variability of stock market prices. *American Economic Review*, 71, 222–37.

Grossman, S. J. and J. E. Stiglitz (1980) On the impossibility of informationally efficient markets. *American Economic Review*, 70, 393–407.

Hacche, G. and J. Townend (1981) Exchange rates and monetary policy: modelling sterling's effective exchange rate. *Oxford Economic Papers (Supplement)*, 33, 201–47.

Hacche, G. and J. Townend (1983) Some problems in exchange rate modelling: the case of sterling. *Zeitschrift fur Natinalo Konomic*, 3, 127–62.

Hakkio, C. S. (1981a) Expectations and the forward exchange rate. *International Economic Review*, 22, 663–78.

Hakkio, C. S. (1981b) The term structure of the forward premium. *Journal of Monetary Economics*, 8, 41–58.

Hakkio, C. S. (1986) Does the exchange rate follow a random walk? A Monte Carlo study of four tests for a random walk. *Journal of International Money and Finance*, 5, 221–30.

Hall, S. G. (1987) A forward looking model of the exchange rate. *Journal of Applied Econometrics*, 2, 47–60.

Hall, S. G., S. G. B. Henry and C. B. Johns (1986) Forecasting with an econometric model. Some recent results using the National Institute model. *Journal of Applied Econometrics*, 1, 163–83.

Hamada, K. (1976) A strategic analysis of monetary interdependence. *Journal of Political Economy*, 84, 77–99.

Hannan, E. J. (1970) *Multiple Time Series*. New York: Wiley.

Hansen, L. P. (1982) Large sample properties of generalised method of moments estimators. *Econometrica*, 50, 1029–54.

Hansen, L. P. and R. J. Hodrick (1980) Forward exchange rates as optimal predictors of future spot rates: an econometric analysis. *Journal of Political Economy*, 88, 829–853.

Hansen, L. P. and R. J. Hodrick (1983) Risk averse speculation in the forward foreign exchange market: an econometric analysis of linear models. In J. A. Frenkel (ed.), *Exchange Rates and International Macroeconomics*. Chicago: University of Chicago Press.

Hansen, L. P. and T. J. Sargent (1982) Instrumental variables procedures for estimating linear rational expectations models. *Journal of Monetary Economics*, 8, 272–96.

Hartley, P. R. (1983) Rational expectations and the foreign exchange market. In J. A. Frenkel (ed.), *Exchange Rates and International Macroeconomics*. Chicago: University of Chicago Press.

Hasza, D. P. and W. A. Fuller (1979) Estimation for autoregressive processes with unit roots. *Annals of Statistics*, 7, 1106-20.

Hausman, J. A. (1978) Specification tests in economics. *Econometrica*, 46, 1251-72.

Haynes, S. E. and J. A. Stone (1981) On the mark: comment. *American Economic Review*, 71, 1060-7.

Hendry, D. F. (1986) Econometric modelling with cointegrated variables: an overview. *Oxford Bulletin of Economics and Statistics*, 48, 3, 201-12.

Hendry, D. F., A. R. Pagan and J. D. Sargan (1984) Dynamic specification. In Z. Griliches and M. D. Intrilligator (eds) *Handbook of Econometrics*. Amsterdam: North Holland.

HM Treasury (1985) Modelling the exchange rate: where do we go from here? Treasury mimeo presented at the Treasury Academic Panel.

Hodrick, R. J. (1978) An empirical analysis of the monetary approach to the determination of the exchange rate. In Frankel and Johnson (1978).

Hodrick, R. J. and S. Srivastava (1984) An investigation of risk and return in forward foreign exchange. *Journal of International Money and Finance*, 3, 5-30.

Hodrick, R. J. and S. Srivastava (1986) The covariation of risk premiums and expected future spot exchange rates. *Journal of International Money and Finance*, 5, (Supplement), S5-22.

Holtham, G. and A. J. Hughes Hallett (1987) International policy coordination and model uncertainty. In R. Bryant and R. Portes (eds) *Global Macroeconomics: Policy Conflict and Cooperation*. London: Macmillan.

Hooper, P. and J. Morton (1982) Fluctuations in the dollar: a model of nominal and real exchange rate determination. *Journal of International Money and Finance*, 1, 39-56.

Huang, R. D. (1981) The monetary approach to exchange rate in an efficient foreign exchange market: tests based on volatility. *Journal of Finance*, 36, 31-41.

Huang, R. (1984) Some alternative tests of forward exchange rates as predictors of future spot rates. *Journal of International Money and Finance*, 3, 157-67.

Hughes Hallett, A. J. (1979) On methods for avoiding the a priori numerical specification of preferences in policy selection. *Economics Letters*, 3, 221-8.

Hughes Hallett, A. J. (1986a) Autonomy and the choice of policy in asymmetrically dependent economies. *Oxford Economic Papers*, 38, 516-44.

Hughes Hallett, A. J. (1986b) International policy design and the sustainability of policy bargains. *Journal of Economic Dynamics and Control*, 10, 467-94.

Hughes Hallett, A. J. (1987a) The impact of interdependence of economic policy design: the case of the US, EEC and Japan. *Economic Modelling*, 4, 377-96.

Hughes Hallett, A. J. (1987b) Robust policy regimes for interdependent economies: a new argument for coordinating economic policies. *Discussion Paper No. 151*, Centre for Economic Policy Research.

Hughes Hallett, A. J. (1987c) How robust are the gains to policy coordination to variations in the model and objectives? *Ricerche Economiche*, 51, 341-72.

Hughes Hallett, A. J. and H. J. B. Rees (1983) *Quantitative Economic Policies and Interactive Planning*. Cambridge: Cambridge University Press.

International Monetary Fund (1983) Exchange rate volatility and world trade. *IMF Occasional Paper No. 28*, July.

Isard, P. (1980) Expected and unexpected changes in exchange rates: the roles of relative price levels, balance of payments factors, interest rates and risk. *International Finance Discussion Papers, No. 156.*

Johnson, H. G. (1958) Towards a general theory of the balance of payments. Reprinted in Frenkel and Johnson (1976).

Kawai, M. (1985) Exchange rates, the current account, and monetary–fiscal policies in the short-run and in the long-run. *Oxford Economic Papers*, 37 (3), November, 391–425.

Kearney, C. and R. MacDonald (1985) Asset markets and the exchange rate: a structural model of the sterling–dollar rate 1972–1982. *Journal of Economic Studies*, 12, 33–60.

Kendrick, D. A. (1981) *Stochastic Control for Economic Models*. New York: McGraw-Hill.

Kleidon, A. W. (1986) Variance bounds tests and stock price valuation models. *Journal of Political Economy*, 94, 5, 953–1001.

Kolhagen, S. (1975) The performance of the foreign exchange markets: 1971–7. *Journal of International Business Studies*, 6.

Korajczyk, R. A. (1985) The pricing of forward contracts of foreign exchange. *Journal of Political Economy*, 93, 346–68.

Kouri, P. J. K. (1976) The exchange rate and the balance of payments in the short run and in the long run: a monetary approach. *Scandinavian Journal of Economics*, 78, 280–304.

Kouri, P. J. K. (1977) International investment and interest rate linkages under flexible exchange rates. In R. Z. Aliber (ed.) *The Political Economy of Monetary Reform*. London: Macmillan.

Krasker, W. S. (1980) The 'peso problem' in testing the efficiency of forward exchange markets. *Journal of Monetary Economics*, 6, 269–76.

Kydland, F. E. and E. C. Prescott (1977) Rules rather than discretion: the inconsistency of optimal plans. *Journal of Political Economy*, 85, 473–90.

Leroy, S. F. (1984) Efficiency and the variability of asset prices. *American Economic Review*, 74, 183–7.

Leroy, S. and R. Porter (1981) The present value relation: tests based on implied variance bounds. *Econometrica*, 49, 555–74.

Levich, R. M. (1979) On the efficiency of markets for foreign exchange. In R. Dornbusch and J. Frenkel (eds) *International Economic Policy Theory and Evidence*, 246–67. Baltimore, MD: Johns Hopkins.

Levine, R. (1987) The pricing of forward exchange rates. *International Finance Discussion Papers, No. 312.*

Levy, E. and A. R. Nobay (1986) The speculative efficiency hypothesis: a bivariate analysis. *Economic Journal*, 96, 109–21.

Levy, E. and A. R. Nobay (1988) Using bivariate autoregressive representations in testing exact expectations relations. *Economics Letters*, 28, 343–9.

Longworth, D. (1981) Testing the efficiency of the Canadian–US exchange market under the assumption of no risk premium. *Journal of Finance*, 36, 43–9.

Loopesko, B. (1984) Relationships among exchange rates, interaction and interest rates: an empirical investigation. *Journal of International Money and Finance*, 3, 257–78.

Lucas, R. E. (1976) Econometric policy evaluation: a critique. In K. Brunner and A. H. Meltzer (eds) *The Phillips Curve and Labour Markets*. Carnegie-Rochester Conference Series on Public Policy, 6, Amsterdam: North Holland.

Lucas, R. E. (1982) Interest rates and currency prices in a two-country world. *Journal of Monetary Economics*, 10, 255–60.

Ludlow, P. (1982) *The Making of the European Monetary System*. London: Butterworths.

Lütkepohl, H. (1985) Comparison of criteria for estimating the order of a vector autoregressive process. *Journal of Time Series Analysis*, 6, 35–52.

MacDonald, R. (1983a) Some test of the rational expectations hypothesis in the foreign exchange markets. *Scottish Journal of Political Economy*, 30, 235–50.

MacDonald, R. (1983b) Tests of efficiency and the impact of news in three foreign exchange markets: the experience of the 1920s. *Bulletin of Economic Research*, 35, 123–44.

MacDonald, R. (1985) 'News' and the 1920s experience with floating exchange rates. *Economics Letters*, 17, 379–83.

MacDonald, R. (1988) *Floating Exchange Rates: Theories and Evidence*. London: Unwin Hyman.

MacDonald, R. and M. P. Taylor (1987a) Testing efficiency in the interwar foreign exchange market: a multiple time series approach. Bank of England, mimeo.

MacDonald, R. and M. P. Taylor (1987b) On unit root tests in exchange rates, spot market efficiency and cointegration: some evidence from the recent float. *Economics Letters*, forthcoming.

MacDonald, R. and M. P. Taylor (1988a) International parity conditions. In A. S. Courakis and M. P. Taylor (eds) *Policy Issues for Interdependent Economies*. London: Macmillan.

MacDonald, R. and M. P. Taylor (1988b) The term structure of forward foreign exchange premia: the interwar experience. *The Manchester School*, forthcoming.

MacDonald, R. and T. S. Torrance (1988a) On risk, rationality and excessive speculation in the Deutschemark–US dollar exchange market: some evidence using survey data. *Oxford Bulletin of Economics and Statistics*, 57, 107–23.

MacDonald, R. and T. S. Torrance (1988b) Exchange rates and the news: some evidence using UK survey data. *The Manchester School*, 56, 69–76.

MacDonald, R. and T. S. Torrance (1988c) Expectations formation and risk in four foreign exchange markets. *Discussion Paper No. 88–01*, Department of Economics, University of Aberdeen.

de Macedo, J. B., J. A. Goldstein and D. M. Meerschwam (1984) International portfolio diversification: short-term financial assets and gold. In J. F. O. Bilson and R. C. Marston (eds) *Exchange Rates: Theory and Practice*. Chicago: University of Chicago Press.

Malliaris and Brock (1982) *Stochastic Methods in Economics and Finance*. Amsterdam: North Holland.

Marsh, T. A. and R. C. Merton (1984) Dividend variability and variance bounds tests for the rationality of stock market prices. *Sloan School of Management Working Paper No. 1584-84*, August.

McCallum, B. T. (1976) Rational expectations and the estimation of econometric models: an alternative procedure. *International Economic Review*, 17, 484-90.

McCallum, B. T. (1983) The role of overlapping-generations models in monetary economics. In K. Brunner and A. H. Meltzer (eds) *Money, Monetary Policy, and Financial Institutions*, Carnegie-Rochester Conference Series on Public Policy, 18. Amsterdam: North Holland.

McCormick, F. (1971) Covered interest arbitrage: unexpected profits?: comment. *Journal of Political Economy*, 87, 171-86.

McCulloch, J. H. (1975) Operational aspects of the Siegel paradox. *Quarterly Journal of Economics*, 89, 170-2.

Meese, R. A. (1986) Testing for bubbles in exchange markets: a case of sparkling rates? *Journal of Political Economy*, 94, 345-73.

Meese, R. A. and K. Rogoff (1983) Empirical exchange rate models of the seventies: do they fit out of sample. *Journal of International Economics*, 14, 3-24.

Meese, R. A. and K. Rogoff (1984) The out of sample failure of empirical exchange rate models: sampling error or misspecification? In J. A. Frankel (ed.) *Exchange Rates and International Macroeconomics*. Chicago: National Bureau of Economic Research.

Meese, R. and K. Rogoff (1985) Was it real? The exchange rate-interest differential relation, 1973-1984. *Working Paper No. 1732*, National Bureau of Economic Research.

Meese, R. A. and K. J. Singleton (1982) On unit roots and the empirical modeling of exchange rates. *Journal of Finance*, 37, 1029-35.

Meese, R. A. and K. J. Singleton (1983) Rational expectations and the volatility of floating exchange rates. *International Economic Review*, 24, 3, 721-33.

Merton, R. C. (1971) Optimum consumption and portfolio rules in a continuous time model. *Journal of Economic Theory*, 3, 373-413.

Minford, P., R. Agenor and E. Nowell (1986) A new classical econometric model of the world economy. *Economic Modelling*, 3 (3), 154-74.

Minford, A. P. L. and D. A. Peel (1983) *Rational Expectations and the New Macroeconomics*. Oxford: Martin Robertson.

Modigliani, F. and M. Miller (1963) Corporate income taxes and the cost of capital: a correction. *American Economic Review*, 53, 433-42.

Mundell, R. A. (1963a) Flexible exchange rates and employment policy. *Canadian Journal of Economics and Political Science*, 27, 509-17.

Mundell, R. A. (1963b) Capital mobility and stabilization policy under fixed and flexible rates. *Canadian Journal of Economics and Political Science*, 29, 475-85.

Mundell, R. (1968) *International Economics*. New York: MacMillan.

Mussa, M. (1976) The exchange rate, the balance of payments, and monetary policy under a regime of controlled floating. *Scandinavian Journal of Economics*, 78, 229-48.

Mussa, M. (1979) Empirical regularities in the behaviour of exchange rates and theories of the foreign exchange market. In K. Brunner and A. H. Meltzer (eds)

Policies for Employment, Prices and Exchange Rates, Carnegie-Rochester Conference series, 11, Amsterdam: North Holland.

Mussa, M. (1981) The role of intervention. *Group of Thirty Occasional Papers*, 6, New York.

Oudiz, G. and J. Sachs (1984) Macroeconomic policy coordination among the industrial economies. *Brookings Papers on Economic Activity*, 1, 1–64.

Oudiz, G. and J. Sachs (1985) International policy coordination in dynamic macro-economic models. In W. H. Buiter and R. C. Marston (eds) *International Economic Policy Coordination*. Cambridge: Cambridge University Press.

Padoa-Schioppa, T. (1983) Evidence to the House of Lords Select Committee.

Pagan, A. R. (1984) Econometric issues in the analysis of regressions with generated regressors. *International Economic Review*, 25 (1), 221–47.

Pagan, A. R. and A. D. Hall (1983) Diagnostic tests as residual analysis. *Econometric Reviews*, 2 (2), 159–218.

Parkin, M. (1978) A comparison of alternative techniques of monetary control under rational expectations. *Manchester School*, September, 252–87.

Paulson, J. (1984) Order determination of multivariate autoregressive time series with unit roots. *Journal of Time Series Analysis*, 5, 115–27.

Pearce, D. K. and V. V. Roley (1985) Stock prices and economic news. *Journal of Business*. 58 (1), 49–67.

Phillips, P. C. B. (1987) Time series regression with a unit root. *Econometrica*, 55, 277–302.

Phillips, P. C. B. and P. Perron (1986) Testing for a unit root in time series regression. *Cowles Foundation Discussion Paper No. 795*.

Polak, J. J. (1957) Monetary analysis of income formation and payments problems. *IMF Staff Papers*, 4, 1–50.

Poole, W. (1970) Optimal choice of monetary policy instruments in a simple stochastic macro model. *Quarterly Journal of Economics*, 84 (2), 197–216.

Putnam, B. H. and J. R. Woodbury (1979) Exchange rate stability and monetary policy. *Review of Business and Economic Research*, 15, 1–10.

Radaelli, G. (1987) EMS stability, capital controls and foreign exchange market intervention. *Chase Manhattan Bank Working Paper in Financial Economics No 2*.

Rasulo, J. and D. Wilford (1980) Estimating monetary models of the balance of payments and exchange rates: a bias. *Southern Economic Journal*, 47, 136–46.

Rogoff, K. (1985) Can exchange rate predictability be achieved without monetary convergence. *European Economic Review*, 28, 93–115.

Roll, R. (1979) Violations of purchasing power parity and their implications for efficient international commodity markets. In M. Sarnat and G. Szego (eds) *International Finance and Trade*, 1, 6. Cambridge, MA: Ballinger.

Salemi, M. K. (1984) Comment. In J. A. Frenkel (ed.) *Exchange Rates and International Macroeconomics*. Chicago: National Bureau of Economic Research.

Samuelson, P. A. (1965) Proof that properly anticipated prices fluctuate randomly. *Industrial Management Review*, 6, 41–9.

Samuelson, P. A. (1947) *Foundations of Economic Analysis*, Cambridge, MA: Harvard University Press.

Sargan, J. D. (1958) The estimation of economic relationships using instrumental variables. *Econometrica*, 36, 393–413.

Sargan, J. D. and A. Bhargava (1983) Testing residuals from least squares regression for being generated by the Gaussian random walk. *Econometrica*, 51, 153–74.

Sargent, T. J. (1976) A classical macroeconomic model for the United States. *Journal of Political Economy*, 84, 207–37.

Sargent, T. J. (1979) A note on maximum likelihood estimation of the rational expectations model of the term structure. *Journal of Monetary Economics*, 5, 133–43.

Saville, I. D. and K. L. Gardiner (1986) Stagflation in the UK since 1970: a model-based explanation. *National Institute Economic Review*, 117.

Shiller, R. J. (1978) Rational expectations and the dynamic structure of macro-economic models. *Journal of Monetary Economics*, 4, 1–44.

Shiller, R. J. (1981) Do stock prices move too much to be justified by subsequent changes in dividends? *American Economic Review*, 71, 421–36.

Siegel J. J. (1972) Risk, interest rates and the forward exchange. *Quarterly Journal of Economics*, 89, 173–5.

Siegel, J. J. (1975) Reply-risk, interest rates and the forward exchange. *Quarterly Journal of Economics*, 86, 303–9.

Sims, C. (1980) Macroeconomics and reality. *Econometrica*, 48, 1–48.

Smith, J. R. and C. A. E. Goodhart (1985) The relationship between exchange rate movements and monetary surprises: results for the UK and USA compared and contrasted. *The Manchester School*, 53 (1), 2–22.

Smith, P. N. (1985) Current account movements, wealth effects and the determination of the real exchange rate. *London Business School Centre for Economic Forecasting Discussion Paper No. 149*, May.

Smith, P. N. and M. R. Wickens (1987) A stylised econometric model of an open economy: UK 1973–1981. *London Business School Centre for Economic Forecasting Discussion Paper No. 13.87*.

Smith, P. N. and M. R. Wickens (1988) Assessing monetary shocks and exchange rate variability with a stylised econometric model of the UK. In A. S. Courakis and M. P. Taylor (eds) *Policy Issues for Interdependent Economies*. London: Macmillan.

Solnik, B. (1987) Using financial prices to test exchange rate models: a note. *Journal of Finance*, 42 (1), 141–9.

Stockman, A. C. (1978) Risk Information and Forward Exchange Rates. In Frenkel and Johnson (1978).

Stockman, A. C. and L. E. O. Svensson (1987) Capital flows, investment and exchange rates. *Journal of Monetary Economics*, 19, 171–201.

Sundararajan, V. (1985) Debt equity ratios and interest rate policy: macroeconomics effects of high leverage in developing countries. *IMF Staff Papers*, 32, 430–75.

Swoboda, A. (1983) Exchange rate regimes and US–European policy interdependence. *IMF Staff Papers*, 30, 1, 75–102.

Taylor, J. B. (1977) Conditions for unique solutions in stochastic macroeconomic models with rational expectations. *Econometrica*, 45, 1377–85.

Taylor, J. B. (1986) An econometric evaluation of international monetary policy rules: fixed versus flexible exchange rates. Mimeo, October.

Taylor, M. P. (1986) On unit roots and real exchange rates: empirical evidence and Monte Carlo analysis. Bank of England, mimeo.

Taylor, M. P. (1987a) Covered interest parity: a high-frequency, high-quality data study. *Economica*, 54, 429–38.

Taylor, M. P. (1987b) Testing *ex ante* purchasing power parity using vector auto-regressions in the time domain. Bank of England, mimeo.

Taylor, M. P. (1987c) Risk premia and foreign exchange: a multiple time series approach to testing uncovered interest parity *Weltwirtschaftliches Archiv*, 123, 579–90.

Taylor, M. P. (1988a) A DYMIMIC model of forward foreign exchange risk, with estimates for three major exchange rates. *The Manchester School*, 56, 55–68.

Taylor, M. P. (1988b) Expectations, risk and uncertainty in the foreign exchange market: some results based on survey data. *Bank of England Discussion Paper*. *The Manchester School*, forthcoming.

Taylor, M. P. (1988c) Exchange rates, random walks and news: some robust tests on high-frequency data. Bank of England, mimeo.

Taylor, M. P. (1988d) An empirical examination of long-run purchasing power parity using cointegration techniques. *Applied Economics*, 20, 1369–82.

Taylor, M. P. and P. C. McMahon (1988) Long-run purchasing power parity in the 1920s. *European Economic Review*, 32, 179–97.

Thomas, S. H. and M. R. Wickens (1987) Vehicle currencies, bank debt and the asset market approach to exchange rates determination: the US dollar, 1980–1985. *Discussion Paper, No. 180*, Centre for Economic Policy Research.

Tobin, J. (1969) A general equilibrium approach to monetary theory. *Journal of Money, Credit and Banking*.

Tobin, J. (1979) Deficit spending and crowding-out in shorter and longer runs. In H. L. Greenfield et al. (eds) *Theory for Economic Efficiency: Essays in Honour of A P Lerner*. Cambridge, MA: MIT Press.

Turnovsky, S. J. (1977) *Macroeconomic Analysis and Stabilization Policy*. Cambridge: Cambridge University Press.

Uctum, M. (1986) The stock market and capital accumulation in an open economy with flexible exchange rates. *Queen's University Discussion Paper, No. 632*.

Uctum, M. (1987) Financial flows and physical capital accumulation in an open economy. University of Laval, Quebec, mimeo.

Ungerer, H., O. Evans, T. Mayer and P. Young (1987) The European Monetary System: recent developments. International Monetary Fund, mimeo.

Ungerer, H., O. Evans and P. Nyberg (1983) The European Monetary System: the experience 1979–1982. *IMF Occasional Paper No. 19*, May.

Urich, T. J. (1982) The information content of weekly money supply announcements. *Journal of Monetary Economics*, 10, 73–88.

Urich, T. J. and P. Wachtel (1981) Market response to weekly money supply announcements in the 1970s. *Journal of Finance*, 36, 1063–72.

Vaubel, R. (1980) International shifts in the demand for money, their effects on exchange rates and price levels and their implications for the pre-announcement of monetary expansion. *Weltwirtschaftliches Archiv*, 116, 1–44.

Wadhwani, S. B. (1984) Are exchange rates 'excessively' volatile? *Discussion Paper No. 198*, Centre for Labour Economics, London School of Economics.

Wallace, M. S. (1979) The monetary approach to flexible exchange rates in the short run: an empirical test. *Review of Business and Economic Research*, 98–102.

Wickens, M. R. (1982) The efficient estimation of econometric models with rational expectations. *Review of Economic Studies*, 49, 55–67.

Wickens, M. R. (1986) The estimation of linear models with future rational expectations by efficient and instrumental variable methods. *Centre for Economic Policy Research Discussion Paper*.

Williamson, J. (1985) *The Exchange Rate System*, rev. edn. *Policy Analyses in International Economics, 5*. Washington, DC: Institute for International Economics, June.

Wolff, C. C. P. (1986) Exchange rate models and innovations: a derivation. *Economics Letters*, 20, 373–6.

Wolff, C. C. P. (1987) Forward foreign exchange rates, expected spot rates and premia: a signal extraction approach. *Journal of Finance*, 42, 395–406.

Woo, W. T. (1985) The monetary approach to exchange rate determination under rational expectations. *Journal of International Economics*, 18, 1–16.

Zeiro, J. (1987) Risk and capital accumulation in a small open economy. *The Quarterly Journal of Economics*, 101, 265–79.

Author Index

Subject Index